LIFE AND DEATH IN POMPEII AND HERCULANEUM

LIFE AND DEATH
IN POMPEII AND
HERCULANEUM

PAUL ROBERTS

THE BRITISH MUSEUM PRESS

937.7
ROB

This book is published to accompany the exhibition at the British Museum
from 28 March to 29 September 2013

Sponsored by

In collaboration with

Goldman
Sachs

Soprintendenza Speciale
per i Beni Archeologici
di Napoli e Pompei

First published in 2013 by The British Museum Press
A division of The British Museum Company Ltd
38 Russell Square, London WC1B 3QQ
britishmuseum.org/publishing

A catalogue record for this book is available from the British Library

ISBN 978 0 7141 2276 2 (hardback)
ISBN 978 0 7141 2282 3 (paperback)

Designed by Raymonde Watkins
Printed in Italy by Graphicom srl

The papers used by The British Museum Press are recyclable
products and the manufacturing processes are expected to conform
to the environmental regulations of the country of orgin.

Half-title page: Mosaic of a guard dog. House of Orpheus, Pompeii. See fig. 80.
Frontispiece: Fresco showing a woman's face. From Herculaneum. See fig. 243.
pp. 4–5 background: Cut marble panel with geometric pattern in marble and glass.
House of the Ephebe, Pompeii. See fig. 226.

FSC
www.fsc.org
MIX
Paper from
responsible sources
FSC® C013123

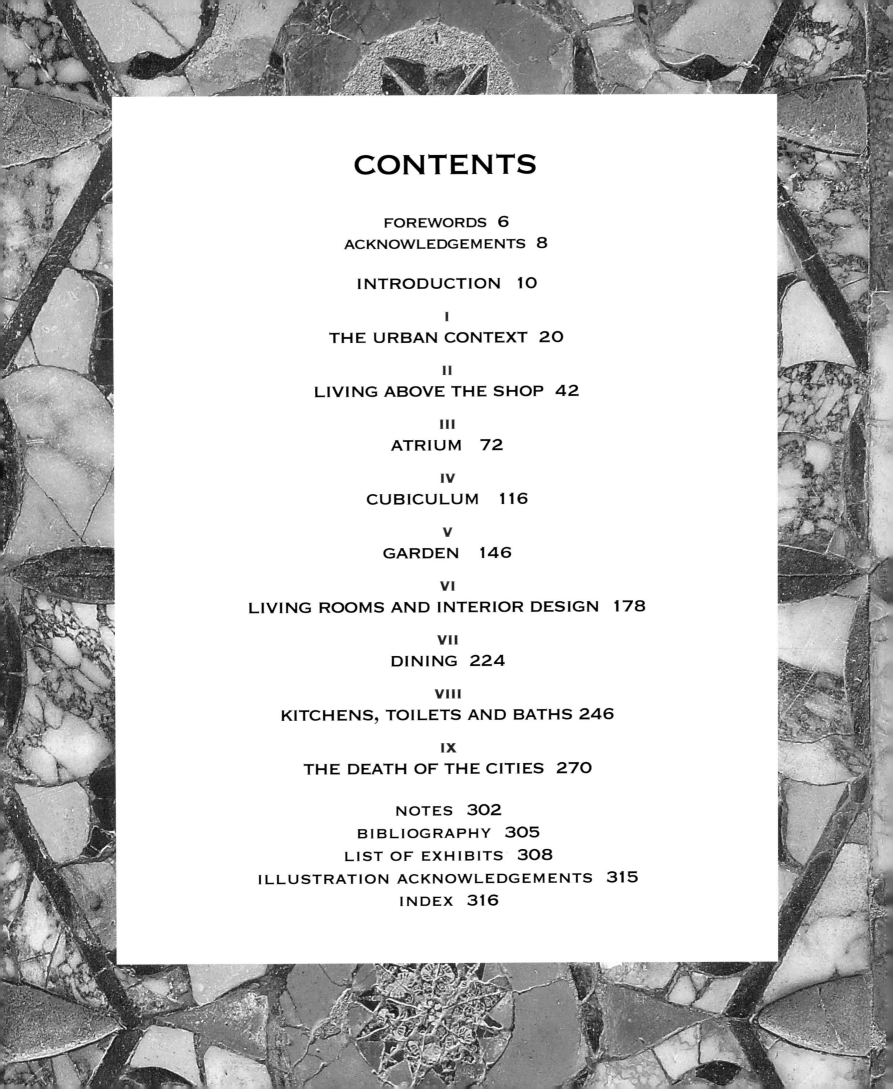

CONTENTS

FOREWORDS 6
ACKNOWLEDGEMENTS 8

INTRODUCTION 10

I
THE URBAN CONTEXT 20

II
LIVING ABOVE THE SHOP 42

III
ATRIUM 72

IV
CUBICULUM 116

V
GARDEN 146

VI
LIVING ROOMS AND INTERIOR DESIGN 178

VII
DINING 224

VIII
KITCHENS, TOILETS AND BATHS 246

IX
THE DEATH OF THE CITIES 270

NOTES 302
BIBLIOGRAPHY 305
LIST OF EXHIBITS 308
ILLUSTRATION ACKNOWLEDGEMENTS 315
INDEX 316

SPONSOR'S FOREWORD

GOLDMAN SACHS is delighted to sponsor the exhibition *Life and death in Pompeii and Herculaneum*, which continues our support of the British Museum.

London is one of the world's leading financial and cultural centres. We believe that exhibitions like this encourage and inspire the exchange of ideas and perspectives across generations, enriching the lives of many.

Pompeii and Herculaneum is an extraordinary exhibition. Including spectacular new discoveries and iconic artefacts, it is unique in its focus on the everyday lives of Romans in the first century AD. We are extremely grateful to the British Museum and the Soprintendenza Speciale per i Beni Archeologici di Napoli e Pompei. Without their effort, dedication and vision this exhibition would not have been possible.

We hope you enjoy this rare opportunity to view the life of the Romans.

Michael S. Sherwood
Richard J. Gnodde
Co-Chief Executive Officers, Goldman Sachs International

DIRECTOR'S FOREWORD

POMPEII AND HERCULANEUM were ordinary Roman cities, destroyed in extraordinary circumstances in AD 79 by a catastrophic eruption of the volcano Mount Vesuvius. Their rediscovery has provided us with a unique opportunity to see daily life in Roman times. Many cities of the former Roman Empire preserve great public buildings such as theatres, baths and gladiatorial arenas. But Pompeii and Herculaneum, in addition to all of this, can offer ordinary streets lined with shops, bars and houses.

This book and the exhibition it accompanies focus on the ordinary people of Pompeii and Herculaneum, looking at their lives in that most universal of contexts, the home. Passing through the rooms of an imagined house, we see a variety of objects, from beautiful statues of bronze and marble, stunning frescoes and mosaics, to wooden furniture and cooking pots. All had a purpose, and by placing these objects in the various spaces of the home, we begin to see the different activities that happened there, and through these activities the inhabitants themselves. Such homes embraced not only the owner's own family but also slaves, ex-slaves (freedmen), dependants and distant relatives. The house is thus a perfect vehicle to explore themes of wider Roman society such as the status and importance of women, the role of slaves and the rising numbers and growing wealth of freedmen.

This exhibition can take place only thanks to the exceptional generosity of our sponsor Goldman Sachs and an extraordinary partnership with the Soprintendenza Speciale per i Beni Archeologici di Napoli e Pompei. As a result of this special collaboration, by kind permission of the Soprintendenza, and the Directors of Pompeii, Herculaneum and the National Archaeological Museum of Naples, over 250 objects are coming to London, many for the first time, to help us on our journey through the home. From the wider, urban context comes a marble statue of Eumachia, a woman who used her own money to build the largest building on the Forum at Pompeii; moving into the home itself a mosaic dog guards the entrance; in the atrium, the main reception area, a bronze bust of a rich banker, who was also an ex-slave, reveals the changing society of the period; also in the atrium, in one of the most famous pieces of Roman art, a well-dressed *nouveau riche* young man and his wife look proudly out at us from a fresco; in the bedroom a wooden cot preserved by the exceptional conditions at Herculaneum, awaits its little occupant; a sumptuous room painted with birds, plants and trees looks over a garden, while in the same garden graffiti on the walls give us the real voice of the Romans, slaves and masters alike. In the kitchen cooking pots, colanders and even a jar for fattening dormice are all used by the slaves as they prepare meals for the household.

When death came to the cities late in AD 79, not only these household effects but many of the people themselves were buried. Their rediscovery, as skeletons on the beach at Herculaneum or the eerie body casts unique to Pompeii, provide the most moving and immediate reminder that these were living, breathing people. This exhibition and book will bring these real people closer.

Neil MacGregor
Director, The British Museum

ACKNOWLEDGEMENTS

THIS BOOK accompanies the exhibition *Life and Death in Pompeii and Herculaneum*. Like the exhibition, it looks at the daily lives of ordinary Romans, but in a way that is different to the other books and exhibitions on the subject. The focus is on the home, its inhabitants and their daily activities, explored through objects placed, as far as we can be sure, in their appropriate domestic context. Very importantly, the book and the exhibition showcase Herculaneum on a par with Pompeii.

I should like to thank the many people who helped make the project a reality. For inspiration, Amanda Claridge for her exhibition *Pompeii AD79* in 1976–7, the first on the subject in Britain; and Rosa Maria Letts, curator of *Rediscovering Pompeii* in 1992. Rosa Maria helped further my plans for a new exhibition, which were honed in discussions with polymath Sam Moorhead at the British Museum. In 2008 Pietro Giovanni Guzzo, then Superintendent of Pompeii, enthused over the exhibition concept in a meeting facilitated by the late Maria Emma Pirozzi, a true catalyst. To these people I owe a very special *grazie*.

From 2009 I began assembling the exhibition through the Soprintendenza Archeologica Speciale di Napoli e Pompei, currently under Soprintendente Teresa Elena Cinquantaquattro, to whom I am extremely grateful.

At Naples, the Director of the Museo Nazionale Archeologico di Napoli, Valeria Sampaolo, provided masterpieces from her Museum's galleries, such as the stunning fresco of the baker Terentius Neo and his wife. This is a considerable sacrifice for Naples Museum and her very great generosity is much appreciated. Warm thanks go to the conservation team, led by Luigia Melillo. *Grazie* also to Paola Rubino, Alessandra Villone and Teresa Giove. Giovanna, Giovanna, Sergio and many others facilitated access.

At Pompeii, the Director Grete Stefani and Antonio Varone beforehand, kindly lent many treasures from the reserve collections at Pompeii and Boscoreale, including the beautiful 'Garden Room' frescoes. Grete was also responsible for the Italian side of the exhibition organization. For all her support, good humour and sound advice I am professionally and personally enormously grateful. Thank you also to Michele Borgongino, Annamaria Ciarallo and Ernesto de Carolis. Giuseppe di Martino and Mattia Buondonno were excellent guides.

I am immensely grateful to Maria Paola Guidobaldi, the Director of the site of Herculaneum, the equal partner to Pompeii. One of the project's earliest and most stalwart supporters, along with her head of Conservation Giuseppe Zolfo, she permitted the presentation of new discoveries and other incredible finds, in particular the assemblage of carbonized wooden furniture – the largest collection ever seen outside Italy. Sig. Sirano kindly opened the reserves.

Thanks also to the Herculaneum Conservation Project, comprising the Soprintendenza, the British school at Rome directed by Christopher Smith, and the Packard Humanities Institute and its founder David Packard. My thanks to Sarah Court, Christian Biggi, Domenico Camardo, Jane Thompson, Domenico Esposito, Mario Notomista, Stefania Siano, Alessandra De Vita, and to Mark Robinson and Erica Rowan.

This book benefited enormously from the efforts of several people who gave so generously of their time. My heartfelt thanks go to Lesley Fitton and Susan Woodford, who with infinite patience helped the book mature from early drafts. Mary Beard and Amanda Claridge made detailed comments, saving me from many errors, while Andrew Wallace-Hadrill and Susan Walker were also very helpful. To Mary and Andrew, a special thank you for curating parts of the exhibition events programme. Others to thank for comments and suggestions include Judith Swaddling, Richard Abdy, Ralph Jackson and Richard Hobbs; Philip Kenrick, Barry Hobson, Jennifer and Arthur Stephens, Peter Baxter; and members of my family, in particular Sheila Roberts, Ken Roberts, Gloria Childs, Sylvia Roberts, Anne Holmes and Martin Roberts.

The images are the work of the British Museum's photographers. I am hugely grateful to the manager of photography Ivor Kerslake for his unfailing, good-humoured support. He, his chief photographer John Williams and the rest of the team, Kevin lovelock, Saul Peckham, Steve Dodd and Dudley Hubbard, tirelessly 'shot' Naples Museum, Pompeii and Herculaneum. The wonderful Kate Morton created the maps, plans and drawings.

Huge thanks to the exhibition core team, headed by Project Manager Rachel Brown (née Dagnall). Stuart Frost, David Francis and in particular Anna Bright handled interpretation; Pippa Pearce co-ordinated conservation, and Philip Kevin and Denise Ling worked at Herculaneum. Alex Truscott, Darrel Day and teams handled installation. The designers were Peter Higgins and Simon Milthorp. Matt Bigg masterminded 2D; Jan Lower and Penny Walker the introductory film. Many thanks to Carolyn Marsden-Smith, Caroline Ingham and Sarah Jameson; Joanna Mackle, Hannah Boulton, Olivia Rickman and Kat Havelock; Christopher Power and Steve Aucott; Jill Maggs and Julia Howard; Nick Lee, Karen Birkhoelzer and others in Conservation; Jennifer Suggitt, Clare MacDowell and Clare Tomlinson; Clare Coveney; David Saunders; Patricia Wheatley and Sian Toogood; Xerxes Mazda, Dan Ferguson, Susan Raikes, Richard Woff, Hilary Williams and Harvinder Bahra; Rosemary Bradley, Mel Morris, Kate Oliver, Kate Hilsen and Ray Watkins; Matthew Cock and the web team.

Others to thank include: in Naples, the Regione Campania and Loredana Conti, the Caivano family at Bellini 67, Pina Bifulco and family, Massimo Perna, Bruno Lazzaro; and in Rome, Carlo Presenti and my friends Helen Patterson and Filippo Coarelli; in the United States, Ken Lapatin and Carol Mattusch; In England, teachers Nancy Rees, A. L. Sockett, David Jenkins and Peter Dennis Jones and the late and much missed John Lloyd. My thanks also to supportive friends, especially Carlo Tono, Andrew Ludington, Anne Desmet, Roger and Cath Llewellyn and Richard Tilbrook.

A warm thank you to volunteers and interns, especially Nicoletta Norman and Amelia Tubelli, for their tireless enthusiasm in everything, from databases to sweeping Pompeian floors, and to Rachel Greenberg and Vanessa Baldwin, funded by the Society for the Promotion of Roman Studies through Fiona Haarer.

Vanessa Baldwin became assistant curator for the exhibition. Her organizational skills, tireless enthusiasm and good humour became valuable to the project. Vanessa helped greatly with this book (edited by my wonderful editor Coralie Hepburn, assisted by Carolyn Jones), and co-authored the gift book (edited by Alice White).

My greatest thanks are for my late Mum Mrs Winifred Roberts, who in 1976 first brought me to Naples, Pompeii and Herculaneum. With love and gratitude, this book is dedicated to her.

Paul Roberts

INTRODUCTION

I N AD 79 the beautiful Bay of Naples in southern Italy, famous in Roman times
for its fertile soil, welcoming climate and luxurious living, was convulsed by a
catastrophic eruption of the volcano Mount Vesuvius. In just one day, two cities,
Pompeii and Herculaneum, were completely buried, along with smaller settlements
such as Oplontis and Stabiae and countless farms, villas, estates and villages.

Vesuvius had been dormant for hundreds of years and so the eruption was
particularly violent, producing not lava but something more deadly, a gigantic volcanic
cloud of ash some 30 km (19 miles) high. Pompeii was directly in its path and
throughout the eruption was gradually submerged under a rain of heavy ash from the
cloud, which made structures collapse under its weight. Herculaneum was shaken by
earthquakes but because of the wind direction no ash fell in the early phase of the
eruption.

But both cities were destroyed and buried as the volcanic cloud finally
collapsed, sending several deadly 'pyroclastic surges' – avalanches of superheated ash
and gas – down the slopes of Vesuvius. About 4–5 m (13–16 ft) of debris buried
Pompeii while Herculaneum was submerged to a depth of as much as 23 m (75 ft).

No-one who was still in the cities at that point could have survived; the
extreme temperatures of the surges killed them instantly. At Pompeii, ash formed
a hard coating around their corpses, preserving the forms of their bodies, and
sometimes even their clothes. The higher temperature of the surges that hit the
people of Herculaneum severely burnt them, sometimes down to the bone. But this
high temperature at Herculaneum preserved articles of wood and even foodstuffs,
which do not normally survive at Pompeii.

A decade or two later the poet Statius lamented, 'In the future, when crops
grow again and this devastated wilderness blooms once more, will people believe that
towns, people and estates are all buried beneath the soil?'[1] In fact, the cities were never
forgotten by local people. Herculaneum, though deeply buried, was explored several
times in the Middle Ages. Marble was taken from monuments for local churches[2] and
a piazza in a nearby village was decorated with statues from the city.[3]

PREVIOUS PAGES **Fig. 1 Mount Vesuvius seen
from Pompeii.**

RIGHT **Fig. 2 Ancient Herculaneum from the south
with modern Ercolano and Vesuvius rising above.**

The area of ancient Pompeii became known as 'La Città' ('the city') and the relatively shallow burial of the city would have ensured regular and frequent finds of material. In the 1590s engineers building a water channel for an aqueduct tunnelled under the city, encountering quantities of ruins and artefacts. About a century later an inscription was found confirming the city was not ancient Stabiae, as once thought, but was in fact Pompeii. Then the two cities burst back into life.

Herculaneum was first. In 1710 a well-digger came down onto the theatre and discovered its coloured marble paving. A local aristocrat bought up the land and began an exploration of the city. The depth of the ash meant the only feasible way to proceed was by tunnelling, and in the next three to four decades a warren of tunnels was driven through the site.

Spectacular discoveries followed, including the theatre and other public buildings, filled with bronze and marble statues, and numerous private buildings. The Villa of the Papyri, explored in 1750, produced the largest haul of ancient statues ever discovered in one place. It also contained a library of papyrus scrolls filled with Greek philosophical texts. One of the most remarkable features of Herculaneum was the way in which organic materials (once-living materials such as papyrus and wood) were preserved. They were carbonized through the extreme heat of the eruption, preserved by the speed with which they were buried and sealed by the ash.

Doors, window frames, ceiling beams and even food were found, and wooden stairways led to preserved upper storeys – very rare survivals from the Roman world. Beautiful wall paintings filled room after room, in some cases as bright and as fresh as the day they were painted. The site proved a magnet for visitors. By torchlight they explored the tunnels, amazed at the preservation of the buildings and their contents.

Publications of the site's wall paintings and statues made Herculaneum the talking point of cultured society.

But then things changed. The tunnellers encountered noxious gases and other dangers, the spectacular discoveries petered out, and the tunnels were gradually filled in, leaving just the theatre able to be visited. The site became an embarrassment to its owners, the Bourbon kings of Naples (who had filled the palace at nearby Portici with its treasures) and they effectively closed the site down.[4] Besides, they had a new source of interest and treasure: Pompeii.

In 1748 excavations were started at Pompeii by the Bourbon kings. During the eighteenth century some fine houses and villas were discovered. The greatest finds were the public buildings, in particular the Gladiators' Barracks, where suits of armour were discovered, and the Temple of Isis, famously visited by the composer Mozart and his inspiration when writing parts of his opera the *Magic Flute*. In addition, the Bourbons were persuaded to keep the excavated areas open. By the early 1800s, in contrast to the gloomy tunnels of Herculaneum, visitors to Pompeii could walk along Roman streets and visit houses and public buildings in the light and air.

Further discoveries included the Forum, the amphitheatre and the theatres. In the nineteenth century came spectacular houses such as the House of the Faun and the House of the Tragic Poet. The city also produced fascinating evidence about the people of Pompeii who had died in the eruption. Skeletons, singly or in couples or groups, were discovered (and occasionally rediscovered for the entertainment of dignitaries). This very human element caught the imagination of visitors such as the British writer Sir Edward Bulwer-Lytton. His novel *The Last Days of Pompeii* (1834) and plays based on it brought the city firmly into the public domain, where it has remained ever since.[5] Herculaneum began to emerge into daylight in this period, though compared with Pompeii excavations were extremely small-scale.

In the 1860s at Pompeii the archaeologist Giuseppe Fiorelli pioneered the technique of creating plaster casts of the victims from the voids left in the ash by their bodies. Not only could visitors see beautiful houses, they could also gaze on the likenesses of the people who had once lived in them. The momentum of Pompeii was unstoppable.

However, the cities as they appear today are not at all how they were first seen

Fig. 4 Archaeologists excavate the mummified bodies of two adults and three children at Pompeii, 1 May 1961.

by the archaeologists. Many buildings had been severely damaged by earthquakes and surges during the eruption. From the later nineteenth century, alongside excavation, there was an ever-increasing amount of reconstruction.[6] Columns were re-erected, walls and upper storeys reconstructed, floors consolidated and roofs rebuilt. The results, if not entirely authentic, certainly helped give the flavour of the cities as they might have been.

From the 1920s to the early 1960s work at both sites was directed by Amedeo Maiuri, who relaunched excavations on a massive scale. At Pompeii the whole south-east quarter of the city was exposed. At Herculaneum most of the area currently visible was uncovered in this period. Here a wide range of public and private buildings was left exposed and astonishing discoveries of foodstuffs, wooden furniture and writing tablets changed our perception of life in the cities. The period was one of great progress, with the notable exception of the shocking Allied bombing of Pompeii in 1943, which caused extensive and irreparable damage to the site and its Museum. The last large-scale excavations in the cities, at Herculaneum in the 1980s and 1990s, cleared the ancient shore line and made the momentous discovery of the hundreds of bodies huddled in and around the ancient.

Today one-third of Pompeii and two-thirds, perhaps more, of Herculaneum remains to be uncovered. Work continues, but not in order to expose more and more

Houses, Shops and Bars
1 Bakery of Modestus
2 Bar of Asellina
3 Bar of Euxinus
4 Bar of Lucius Vetutius Placidus
5 Caupona of Salvius (Inn)
6 Fullonica of Stephanus
7 House of the Ancient Hunt
8 House of the Apartment
9 House of Apollo
10 House of Aulus Umbricius Scaurus
11 House of Caius Julius Polybius
12 House of the Ceii
13 House of the Centenary
14 House of the Chaste Lovers
15 House of the Citharist
16 House of the Cryptoporticus
17 House of Decimus Octavius Quartio
18 House of the Dioscuri
19 House of the Ephebe
20 House of the Faun
21 House of the Fleet
22 House of the Four Styles
23 House of the Garden of Hercules
24 House of the Gilded Cupids
25 House of the Golden Bracelet
26 House of the Greek Epigrams
27 House of Inachus and Io
28 House of the Lararium of Achilles
29 House of the Lararum of the River Sarno
30 House of Lucius Caecilius Iucundus
31 House of Marcus Epidius Rufus
32 House of Marcus Fabius Rufus
33 House of Marcus Holconius Rufus
34 House of Marcus Lucretius Fronto
35 House of Marcus Obellius Firmus
36 House of the Menander
37 House of the Moralist
38 House of the Orchard
39 House of Orpheus

40 House of the Painters at Work
41 House of Pansa
42 House of the Piglet
43 House of the Prince of Naples
44 House of Publius Casca Longus
45 House of the Ship Europa
46 House of the Silver Treasure
47 House of the Silver Wedding
48 House of the Small Fountain
49 House of Terentius Neo
50 House of the Tragic Poet
51 House of the Triclinium
52 House of the Vettii
53 House of the Wounded Bear
54 Praedia of Julia Felix
55 Villa of Cicero
56 Villa of the Mysteries

Public Buildings
A Amphitheatre
B Basilica
C Building of Eumachia
D Capitol (Temple of Jupiter)
E Central Baths
F Forum
G Forum Baths
H Large Palaestra
I Lupanar (brothel)
J Macellum
K Odeon (Covered Theatre)
L Stabian Baths
M Suburban Baths
N Temple of Apollo
O Temple of Isis
P Temple of Venus
Q Theatre
R Tomb of Aulus Umbricius Scaurus
S Tomb of Eumachia
T Tomb of Gaius Vestorius Priscus

Fig. 5 Plan of Pompeii.

Fig. 6 Plan of Herculaneum.

streets and buildings of the cities of AD 79. Instead, the major emphasis is very much on looking below the levels of the eruption, at the city's early history, and above all on conservation. Both sites have developed long-term strategies to ensure their future preservation. At Herculaneum, even the limited excavations involved in this programme of conservation have produced astonishing discoveries.[7] These special cities still have a great deal to tell.

How special are Pompeii and Herculaneum? The circumstances of their destruction and the extent of their preservation are truly extraordinary, giving us an unparalleled glimpse of daily life in the Roman world. There is a temptation to imagine that the cities were extraordinary in their lives, too. But this is not in fact the case. They were ordinary cities, representative of many other small- to medium-sized urban centres throughout Italy and the Roman Empire, which were much more familiar to most of the populace than, say, Rome. This is what makes them so important.

Pompeii and Herculaneum were also quite different from each other. Pompeii was much larger, at almost 66 hectares (163 acres); Herculaneum was only a quarter to a third of that size. Estimating population numbers is very difficult but it is likely that Pompeii had around 12,000–15,000 people, while Herculaneum's inhabitants numbered around 4,000–5,000. The inhabitants of both enjoyed all the amenities of

N

Houses, Shops and Bar
1 House of the Alcove
2 House of Apollo the Lyre-Player
3 House of the Beautiful Courtyard
4 House of the Bicentenary
5 House of the Black Living Room
6 House of the Fabric
7 House of Galba
8 House of the Great Door
9 House of the Hotel
10 House and Shop of Neptune and Amphitrite
11 House of the Relief of Telephus
12 Samnite House
13 House of the Skeleton
14 House of the Stags
15 House of the Two Atriums
16 House of the Wooden Partition
17 Large Shop/Bar (Grand Taberna)
18 Villa of the Papyri

Public Buildings
A Augusteum
B Basilica Noniana
C Central Baths
D College of the Augustales (Curia)
E Palaestra
F Suburban Baths
G Temple of Venus and Sacred Precinct
H Terrace of Nonius Balbus
I Theatre

Structures mentioned in this volume

Public - excavated

Public - known, still buried

Private - excavated

Private - known, still buried

---------- edge of excavation

0   100m

the cities, from baths and theatres to temples and markets, and lived in a wide variety of homes, from luxurious houses to tenement blocks, small flats above shops and live-in workshops.

The two cities of Pompeii and Herculaneum present an unequalled opportunity to view the Romans in the most fundamental and shared context of all, the home. This book focuses on the people and their homes, set in the context of the cities and streets in which they lived.

Both the book and the exhibition it accompanies are centred on an idealized house, the typical home of a wealthy *familia* – wealthy at least by the standards of a comfortable Campanian town, though probably not in comparison to the opulence of Rome, or even nearby Naples. The house has all the trappings expected of people at this level of Roman society. The owners of our notional house are wealthy, but that does not at all restrict us to considering the wealthy alone: on the contrary. *Familia* means much more than natural family. It was a social and legal unit, the building block of Roman society, encompassing slaves, ex-slaves (freedmen), dependents and both close and distant relatives. People of all levels of society lived in, above and around the house, making this 'rich house' a vehicle for a cross-section of society. Even within the ranks of the owners of houses like these, in the cities at this time there was a surprising degree of social mobility. Indeed, some luxurious houses were owned by women and by people who had been slaves only years before.

Within the house are grand areas for reception and display, as well as more intimate spaces such as the bedroom and working areas such as the kitchen. Some rooms had a definite function or functions, but the use of many others seems to have been quite fluid. Dining could take place formally in one room, but informally in several others. Areas for sleeping could be found in various parts of the house, depending on the season or even the time of day. Elsewhere in the home were spaces for administration, storage, business meetings, birth, illness, death, sex, and all the elements of daily life.

In the ancient sites, the ruins of the houses are atmospheric, but cannot on their own bring the people back. Similarly, statues, wall paintings and other objects from the cities now in museums may be beautiful, but they cannot really give the sense of their original setting or purpose. However, when objects and spaces are brought together they can begin to create the idea of recognizable domestic settings, and encourage a contemporary audience to make connections with people living in Roman times.

In this way they no longer seem distant and grand figures, the 'typical' Romans of popular imagination, such as emperors and gladiators, but real people. In Pompeii we find a pub landlady called Asellina and her barmaids, a baker called Terentius Neo about to launch into politics and a priestess called Eumachia, one of the most respected people in the city. In Herculaneum lived the ex-slave Venidius Ennychus and his wife Livia Acte, who became full citizens, and two neighbours, Marcus Nonius Dama and Julia, who went to the courts to settle their property boundary dispute. Then there are all the other people – mothers, sons, sisters, cousins, young and old, slave and free – who died together in the catastrophic events of AD 79.

Fig. 7 Plan of the House of the Tragic Poet, Pompeii – a house that has many of the spaces typical of the wealthy homes discussed in this book.

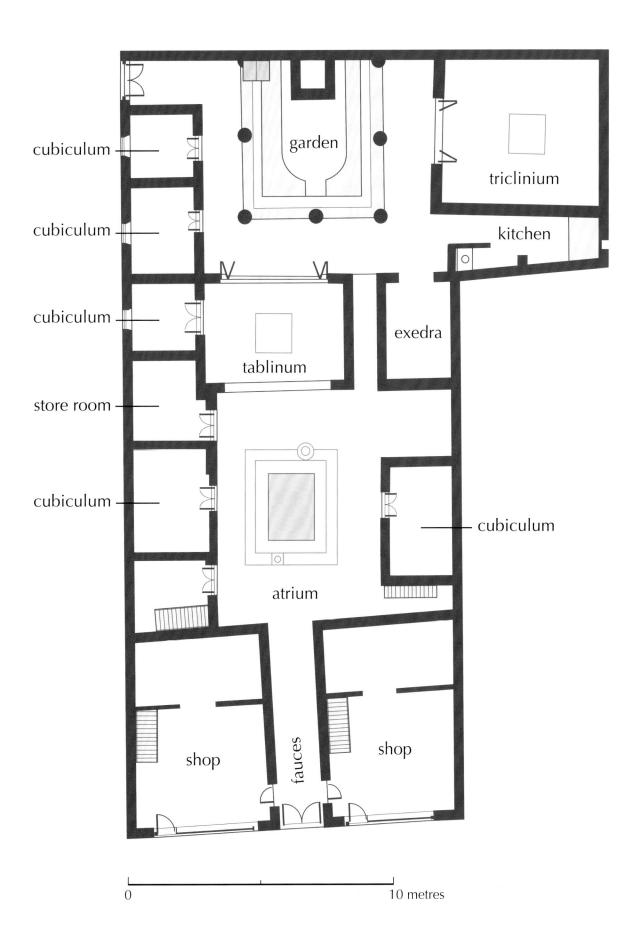

cubiculum

cubiculum

cubiculum

store room

cubiculum

garden

triclinium

kitchen

exedra

tablinum

cubiculum

atrium

shop

fauces

shop

0   10 metres

I

THE URBAN CONTEXT

THE URBAN
CONTEXT

POMPEII and Herculaneum, by modern standards, are not very large. But to Roman eyes they were perfectly formed, self-governing urban centres, and they will be referred to throughout as 'the cities'. They had a long and complex history and at the time of the eruption were part of the broad social and cultural world of the Roman Empire. In order to understand their inhabitants, and the homes in which those people lived, it is important to see how the cities developed and to know something of the history, cultures and individuals that shaped them.

THE PAST – HISTORY AND MYTH

Pompeii and Herculaneum were not originally Roman cities. Most of the major buildings we see now – from the amphitheatre and theatres of Pompeii to the baths and porticoed streets of Herculaneum – are, or seem to be, Roman, but the cities were built on very old foundations that went back many centuries before the eruption of AD 79.

The name 'Pompeii' probably originated from the Italic word *pompe*, meaning 'five'; that is, the city originated as an amalgamation of five towns or groups, which some scholars say can be traced in the archaeological record.[1] Herculaneum's name is clearly based on the name of the demi-god Hercules, by whom, according to legend, it was founded.[2] In myth, Hercules also founded Pompeii, after returning from one of his twelve labours (the taking of the cattle of the three-headed ogre Geryon). The city was named after his *pompa* or triumphal procession.[3]

The geographical historian Strabo,[4] leaving aside the mythological origins of the two cities, links their histories. Both, he says, were built by an Italic people called the Oscans, then the cities were occupied by Etruscans (the powerful, enigmatic people of central Italy whose influence extended to Campania), then Greeks, Samnites (another Italic people from eastern Italy) and finally the Romans.

The archaeological evidence goes some way towards backing up Strabo's account. Nothing at Herculaneum can be dated earlier than the early second century BC,[5] but at Pompeii the first proper town was built around 600 BC.[6] Archaeological data must be treated with caution, because to date only 2 per cent of Pompeii has been excavated below the AD 79 levels.[7] Nevertheless, archaeologists have found evidence for sixth-century BC occupation, such as structures and pottery, extending over much of the site.[8] There are also the first recognizable fixed roads – not with the basalt paving of the Roman cities, but with surfaces of beaten earth. Nevertheless, they were well-defined

PREVIOUS PAGES
Fig. 8 Detail from a fresco showing the riot of AD 59 in the amphitheatre at Pompeii (see fig. 17).

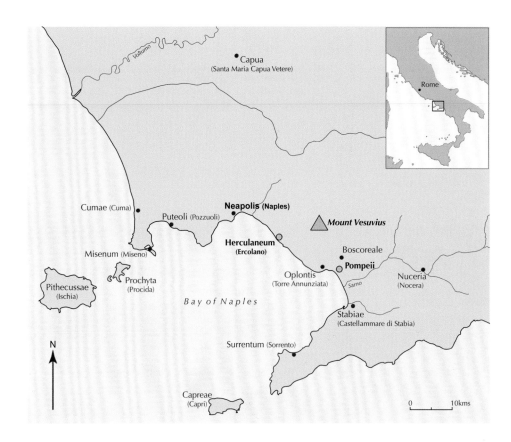

Fig. 9 Map of the Bay of Naples.

streets, some underlying exactly the course of later Roman thoroughfares such as the Via Mercurio in the north-west of the city.[9] Cult buildings such as the Temple of Apollo were first erected in the sixth century BC, as were the city walls. Surprisingly, perhaps, these were on very much the same circuit that existed in AD 79.[10] We do not know who built them: Greeks, Etruscans or the native Oscans, but the mason's marks on the stones are derived from Greek letters.

From about 650 BC Greek cities began to plant colonies nearby on the Bay of Naples, such as Cumae and Partenope (Naples). At the same time Etruscan influence was emanating from towns such as Capua. This influence, for Pompeii, could have involved colonization, political dominance or simply trade.[10] Evidence that both Greeks and Etruscans traded with and perhaps lived in Pompeii comes from Greek and Etruscan finds mixed together in sixth-century BC levels in the city and in graves outside the walls. An example is the typically Etruscan *bucchero* pottery with Etruscan graffiti at the Temple of Apollo, or the *bucchero* pottery found with Attic Greek pottery – one with a Greek graffito – in a house in north-west Pompeii.[12]

Conflict may have been frequent between these uneasy neighbours, and at the naval battle of Cumae in 474 BC the Greeks and Sicilians defeated the Etruscans and their allies,[13] thereby gaining control of much of the Bay of Naples. In the 420s BC the Samnites seized large areas of Campania including Pompeii, and perhaps because of this general political and social instability, the archaeological and historical record between about 450 and 350 BC becomes very silent.[14] Large areas of the city appear empty – in fact it is even possible that the warren of curved streets around the public buildings in the south-west of the city, far from being the original core of the settlement, is in fact a contracted town of the 'dark ages' of the fifth century BC.[15]

In the later fourth and third centuries BC, however, the archaeology and the structural evidence (some still remaining today) show a dramatic improvement in the city's fortunes, amounting almost to a refounding, perhaps by an outside agent, Rome. Through Pompeii's status as a *civitas foederata* ('allied city') of Rome, its citizens gained increased access to Rome's booming trade networks in Italy and beyond.[16] The second century BC was in some senses a 'golden age' for the cities. Public buildings in Pompeii, such as the theatre and some of the main baths, were lavishly built or rebuilt. The urban grid was rebuilt much more densely with new areas reclaimed through substantial levelling and terracing. Private homes, such as the House of the Faun, were renovated and filled with frescoes, mosaics and sculpture. Archaeology shows that Herculaneum, too, was booming in this period, with the building of imposing homes such as the Samnite House and the House of the Wooden Partition.

The early first century BC was, once again, turbulent. In 91– 88 BC the Italian allies of Rome, including Pompeii and Herculaneum, rose up against Rome, demanding full Roman citizenship. The Romans stormed Herculaneum[17] and Pompeii was besieged by the Roman general Lucius Cornelius Sulla Felix.[18] The city walls still bear traces of the impact of stone missiles (FIG. 10), and painted notices in Oscan (the language of the Samnites) may be indicative of troop movements during the siege.[19] Rome was victorious and Pompeii became a Roman *colonia* or colony for veterans from Sulla's legions, along with their families. Pompeii and Herculaneum, once only allies of Rome, were now made very much part of the full Roman system. Shortly afterwards, in 73 BC, the area was convulsed by the rebellion of the gladiator Spartacus, who took refuge from the Roman legions inside the crater of Vesuvius, which was then completely dormant.[20] In later years, a few members of the elite of the cities had nationwide or even empire-wide roles, such as Marcus Nonius Balbus, the major benefactor of Herculaneum, who was governor (*proconsul*) of the island of Crete and Cyrene (Libya). Generally, though, with the exception of wealthy Romans mentioning the area as a retreat (the orator Cicero had a Pompeian villa)[21] or praising its agricultural wealth, influence was one-way from Rome to the Bay of Naples. By and large the subsequent history of the cities is little mentioned by Roman writers, at least until the major earthquake of AD 62/3.

It is difficult to know whether the past history of Pompeii and Herculaneum – the Greeks, Etruscans, Samnites or even Spartacus – meant much to most people in the cities in AD 79, yet there was plenty of evidence for that history in their streets and homes. The following section looks at the buildings of the cities, both public and private. A discussion of all the monuments is outside the scope of this volume, and in any case, extremely useful and comprehensive accounts already exist for both Pompeii[22] and Herculaneum.[23] In this book the focus is on selected public monuments and, most importantly, the people who built them, embellished them or owned them.

Fig. 10 City wall of Pompeii near Porta Ercolano showing holes caused by stone missiles during the Sullan seige in 80 BC.

Fig. 11 Marble inscription written in Oscan.

From the Nola Gate, Pompeii
H. 31 cm, W. 45 cm
The British Museum, 1867,0508.76

Many houses, both in their external appearance and their internal design, had features and decoration centuries old, sometimes intentionally retained so as to remind people of the age and standing of the families who owned them. Public buildings carried statues of emperors, city fathers and magistrates long dead. Walking along the streets, people saw inscriptions painted on the walls or inscribed on stone or bronze, some of them hundreds of years old. No trace has survived of formal Greek or Etruscan inscriptions from the early history, though Greek graffiti of the period before the eruption are not uncommon. There are several places in the cities, however, where the Oscan language of the Samnites could still be seen. Some Oscan survived in graffiti in Herculaneum, in the appropriately named Samnite House.[24] At Pompeii Oscan survives in carved and painted inscriptions on the walls of houses and shops.

One inscription (FIG. 11),[25] dating to about 150 BC, comes from the Nola Gate of Pompeii. It is carved in block capitals on a thin slab of white limestone and was written right to left, using the Oscan alphabet. The inscription states:

Vibius Popidius, the Meddix Tuticus [chief public magistrate], son of Vibius, built this [gate] and certified its completion.

The Meddix Tuticus (literally 'the people's magistrate') was in charge of religion and general civic order in the city during the Samnite period. An early illustration of the gate shows that the inscription was set up prominently next to the keystone.[26] It is uncertain how many, if any, of the people passing through the gate understood what the inscription said, but they knew it was old, providing the pedigree of age that a city needed.

Vibius Popidius was a very important person in Pompeii and about 200 years later members of his clan, the Popidii, were still politically very active in the city,[27] maintaining their family's profile by rebuilding the Temple of Isis after the AD 62/3 earthquake.[28] It is quite likely that these later Popidii were not members of the family related by birth but rather freed slaves (*liberti*) who took part of the name of their former master as their own. The growth in the number of these 'freedmen' and their descendants was one of the most important causes of social change in the cities, and its impact was felt in every area of life.

THE POLITICAL SYSTEM

Pompeii and Herculaneum had a well-developed political system, and through the many inscriptions found there we can be fairly certain of the structure of local government – in particular in Pompeii.[29] In the cities, as elsewhere in the empire, the city Council was called the *Ordo*, and the councillors *Decuriones*.

People generally gained membership of the Council through holding one of the city's four annually elected magistracies. Each year there were elections for two junior magistrates or *aediles,* responsible for practical matters such as maintaining the streets and public buildings and regulating commercial activity, and two senior officials or *duoviri* (singular: *duumvir*) who were former aediles, and were responsible for higher-level administration and the efficient running of the Council. Once elected they retained their place in the Council for life. The highest magistrate was the *quinquennalis.* His responsibilities included regulating the membership of the Council, as part of which he arranged the five-yearly census of the city's wealthy population. This very prestigious post was reserved for members of high-status families.

Fig. 12 The theatre at Pompeii, which was extensively rebuilt by Marcus Holconius Rufus as *quinquennalis.*

One quinquennalis was Marcus Holconius Rufus, who carried out extensive rebuilding of the theatre and was rewarded with a permanent seat, marked by an inscription set into the stone – certainly the best seat in the house (FIG. 13). Interestingly, the architect of the works, Marcus Artosius Primus, a freed slave, is also commemorated in a separate inscription.[30]

ROMAN NAMES

In this and other inscriptions throughout the cities, the name of the person commemorated was always prominent. The people needed to be shown the name of their benefactor. To us, the Roman system of names can seem quite complex, but names can be very informative about a person's background. Marcus Holconius Rufus has the three names (*tria nomina*) that usually identified a male Roman citizen. Marcus is the *praenomen*, chosen by his father, and is the equivalent of a Christian (given) name. Holconius is the *nomen*, the most important element, identifying his clan, or major family group – essentially a family name/surname. Rufus is the *cognomen*, which identified his particular family as a subset of the larger clan (there were several branches of the Holconius clan). In formal situations all three names would be used, but family and close friends would use only the first name, Marcus. A son's name could have exactly the same structures as his father's – a source of endless confusion to people who study inscriptions.

Fig. 13 The inscription marking the theatre seat of Marcus Holconius Rufus.

Women generally only had two names – their father's nomen and cognomen in a feminized form (ending in 'a', instead of the masculine 'us'). For example, Marcus Holconius Rufus' daughter might be called Holconia Rufa. On marriage a woman often took part of her husband's name, so if Holconia Rufa married a man with the cognomen Fabius, she might become Holconia Fabii – Holconia (wife) of Fabius.

Slaves, male and female, generally had only a single name, given by their master. If a male slave was freed he took his master's praenomen and nomen and kept his slave name as a cognomen. So the slave Celer, freed by Marcus Holconius Rufus, became

Marcus Holconius Celer. A woman slave, Martha, kept the feminized clan name (nomen) and her own, becoming Holconia Martha.

From a very different social background to Marcus Holconius Rufus came the young Numerius Popidius Celsinus, admitted to the council of Pompeii by the grateful councillors as a reward for his father's restoration of the Temple of Isis (see below p. 275). His father was almost certainly Numerius Popidius Ampliatus, named in another inscription inside the temple. Both carry the Popidii nomen (clan name) of a well-respected, ancient Pompeian clan, with a centuries-old tradition of public works going back into the Samnite period centuries before (see above p. 25). Numerius Popidius Ampliatus was probably a freedman rather than a member of the family by birth. To his son he had given as a cognomen an element of his wife's name Corelia Celsa, hence 'Celsinus'. The inscription tells us that Numerius Popidius Celsinus was enrolled into the city council without the usual fee in recognition of his father's services to the city. Remarkably he was only six when this happened. His father, the true benefactor, was investing in his and his family's future and status.

ELECTIONS AND ELECTIONEERING

Magistrates were elected by the vote of the body of eligible (male) citizens, and it is important to remember that the 'electorate' of the cities was small, perhaps 1,200 or so in Herculaneum[31] and around 4,000 in Pompeii.[32] There was almost certainly a minimum wealth qualification for Council membership – though this was probably not as high in Pompeii as it was in Rome, where it stood at a colossal 100,000 sesterces – and all candidates had to be freeborn males. It is difficult to say just how free and fair elections to the magistracies were.[33] Some believe that there was in fact very little competition for the posts, especially for the higher post of duumvir.[34] Even so, contests for the aedileships were open, and might have been keenly fought.

Fig. 14 Painted electoral notices on a wall of the Via dell'Abbondanza, Pompeii.

All around Pompeii is evidence of the effort that was expended to make the electorate aware of the candidates and their suitability for office. The white-painted areas of the walls of houses, shops, bars and even tombs outside the city walls were covered with painted signs or 'posters' naming the candidates and their hoped-for posts (FIG. 14). (Though if elections were not so freely contested, perhaps these were elaborate pieces of self-congratulation.) In Herculaneum, however, such political posters are, it seems, absent.[35] This suggests that even in two cities that were so geographically close there could be two different political realities. Pompeii is not necessarily a model for every Roman town.

Political posters were usually painted in clear block capital letters, in red or black paint. Sometimes the notice-painters, very proud of their work, signed the poster. One painter, Aemilius Celer, wrote that he had finished the notice *sing[ulus] ad luna[m]*, 'alone by moonlight'.[36] As time passed, posters were over-painted. On the principle that names appearing most frequently on the notices are likely to be the most recent (presumably names of candidates of AD 79) and that those immediately under them are likely to be from the year before, and so on, some scholars have established a fairly reliable list of candidates for the major posts going back several years before the eruption. Gnaeus Helvius Sabinus was candidate for aedile in AD 79. His posters appear throughout the city[37] and made up 4 per cent of the total number of painted notices.[38] Other magistrates' names can be gleaned from dated inscriptions on statues and monuments and from documents surviving on carbonized wood (see below pp. 109–13).

Painted electoral inscriptions followed a regular format. First came the name of the person seeking election, then an abbreviation of the office he was hoping for, such as *IIVIR* (duumvir) or *AED* (aedile), then sometimes the name of the person or people who were asking for votes on his behalf, usually with *ROG*, an abbreviation of the Latin *rogare* ('to ask') or *O V F* = Latin *o(ro) v(os) f(aciatis)*, 'I beg you to make'.

A typical example from Pompeii (FIG. 15) reads: *Samellium | aed(ilem) o(ro) v(os) f(aciatis) iuvenem p(robum) L(ucium) Albuciu(m) aed(ilem)*, 'I beg you to make Samellius, an upstanding young man, aedile and also to make Lucius Albucius aedile'.[39] Posters mentioning Samellius (= Marcus Samellius Modestus) and Albucius (= Lucius Albucius Celsus), like those of Helvius Sabinus (above) were not painted over, so it seems likely that they were among his rivals for the aedileships in the summer of AD 79. Nearly all the posters naming aedile candidates show paired names, suggesting that two men ran on a joint 'ticket' and pooled resources and supporters. In some cases, aedile and duumvir candidates are named together, suggesting an interest on the part of existing councillors in influencing new entrants.

Sometimes whole families or clans endorsed particular candidates: 'The Poppaei ask for Helvius Sabinus as aedile'.[40] Professional groups, such as the fullers and tanners, also did this: 'The fullers ask for Holconius Priscus as duumvir'.[41] Many groups of tradesmen supported candidates, ranging from fishermen,[42] grape-pickers[43] and mat-makers[44] to barbers[45] and perfume-sellers[46] and even the poultry-sellers.[47] Teachers, too, lent their support,[48] and even an Olympic victor Pyramus Calvos.[49] One curious notice, perhaps fake or mischievous, announces: 'The thieves ask for (Marcus Cerrinus) Vatia as aedile' (*Vatiam aed. Furunculi rog*).[50] But another poster shows that the same Vatia was clearly supported by his neighbours (*vicini*).[51] Some posters tell voters to 'wake up': *suettium…maci vigila*, '[vote for] Suettius…Macius, wake up'.

Over fifty posters show the lobbying power of another, much larger group in the city: women.[52] Although they could not vote or stand for office, women quite freely expressed their opinions to those who could. They supported the chosen candidates from their family, extended clan or neighbourhood, or those to whom they were otherwise linked, financially or socially. Although only 2 per cent of electoral posters feature support from women,[53] they are still important. The wealthy Taedia Secunda stated in her poster that she was the proud grandmother (*avia*) of her grandson, who bid for the aedileship in AD 79.[54] Even the barmaids Zmyrina, Aegle and Maria, who worked in Asellina's bar in the city centre, clearly wanted to make their choices known, though in one case[55] their candidate chose to erase Zmyrina's name!

From the House of the Baker in Pompeii comes possible evidence of another aspect of politics. The fresco (FIG. 16) shows a scene of commercial activity in the

Fig. 15 Painted inscription urging people to vote for Samellius, 'an upstanding young man', as aedile, with his running mate L.Albucius.

Villa of Cicero, Pompeii
H. 70 cm, W. 103 cm
MANN 4714

Fig. 16 Fresco showing the distribution of bread.
House of the Baker, Pompeii (VII,3,30)
H. 69 cm, W. 60 cm
MANN 9071

Forum, in which a baker appears to be selling loaves to two men and a boy from a stall made of wooden planks, all shown in marvellous detail. However, the bread-seller is very well-dressed – in the white toga of a *candidatus* – and so it is probable that he is not selling bread, but giving it away, an example of the very public expressions of generosity which took place before and after the (re-)election of the city's officials and magistrates. He might still be a baker, but the apparent 'shoppers' would be potential voters or existing clients. The scene then becomes a domestic advertisement for the influence and generosity (and hoped-for power) of the politician.[56]

Such distributions of bread may have been quite common. An election poster for Caius Iulius Polybius says: 'he brings good bread' (*panem bonum fert*).[57] This man also featured in a rather unusual painted electoral notice that appears *inside* a home. Just inside the courtyard area is an electoral graffito stating: 'C[aius] I[ulius] P[olibius] was running for the post of AED[ile]'. Was this a piece of publicity intended to make one last impression on guests visiting the house? Or was it a memento – the equivalent of a framed certificate – for an honour won? If the latter, it could suggest that electoral notices – even those on the streets – might not always represent straightforward electioneering.

Office-holders were expected to spend considerable sums of money in their city for the public benefit. They could erect or repair public buildings or they could sponsor the people's favourite events – beast hunts and gladiator fights in the amphitheatre. These were advertised on the same walls as the election posters and slogans.[58] The Latin name for such events was not *ludi*, 'games', but *munera*, 'gifts/rewards', reflecting the almost obligatory nature of such shows. In return for his sponsorship the giver gained the gratitude of the public. A painted notice proclaims: 'Good luck to Gnaeus Alleius Nigidius Maius, the prince of fight sponsors' (...*principi munerarior[um]*).[59]

Gladiatorial games were immensely popular[60] and there are very many posters for gladiatorial games in Pompeii.[61] They state the number of gladiators who will fight, the owner of the gladiators and the date. Interestingly, the games seem to cluster between March and November.[62] One notice advertises the occasion: 'For the well-being of Nero Claudius Caesar Augustus Germanicus [the Emperor Nero] at Pompeii'.[63] It

Fig. 17 Fresco showing the riot of AD 59 in the amphitheatre at Pompeii.

House of Actius Anicetus, Pompeii (I,3,23)
H. 170 cm, W. 185 cm
MANN 112222

then lists the entertainment to come: '...there will be a hunt, athletics and sprinklings (of perfume) (*venatio athletae et sparsiones*)...' and finally the sponsor and the date '...Tiberius Claudius Verus on 25–26 February...'. A more worrying poster proudly announces that at Cumae, to the north-west of the Bay of Naples, there will be 'crucifixions, hunts and awnings' (*...cruciarii ven(atio) et vela*).[64] Two notices from Pompeii tell of gladiatorial combat in Herculaneum, though we do not know where they fought – perhaps in the still-to-be-located Forum.[65] In Herculaneum itself a graffiti in the House of the Corinthian Atrium says that ten pairs of gladiators will fight in the city.[66]

The crowd had their favourites, whom they followed passionately. In an age before mass media or organized sports, the gladiators with their impressive physiques and distinctive armour were the sports stars, film stars and TV celebrities of their day. Their images, names and exploits are recorded in graffiti all over the city, including many private houses (FIG. 18). Large quantities of gladiatorial armour were discovered

Fig. 18 Graffito showing combat between
two gladiators.

From Pompeii (IX,1,12), peristyle
H. 31.4, W. 37.8
MANN 20562

in Pompeii in the eighteenth century in the so-called Gladiators' Barracks behind the theatre and some helmets were found in Herculaneum.[67]

Much could ride on the success of sponsored entertainments – and it could all go horribly wrong. The writer Tacitus, in his *Annals* (14.17) tells how, in AD 59, a disgraced Roman Senator, Livineius Regulus, hoped to impress the locals in Campania by sponsoring gladiator fights in the amphitheatre at Pompeii. The games ended in disaster when spectators from the nearby town of Nuceria came to blows with the Pompeians, resulting in many deaths. The Senate and the Emperor Nero punished the city by banning the games for ten years and outlawing various groups and associations linked to them. A fresco from the garden colonnade of the House of Actius Anicetus shows the event (FIG. 17). It depicts the amphitheatre in great detail – in particular the awnings and the characteristic vaulted double staircases unique to Pompeii's arena – with the fighting spilling out into the area around. Although the ban did not last long, both of Pompeii's duoviri for AD 59 were sacked and Regulus was exiled. Politics, even on the provincial stage, could be a risky business. Why the painting was put into the house (and in such a prominent position) is a mystery. Did the house belong to an official of the city, a reminder of the need to keep order, or to a 'Pompeian nationalist' secretly pleased that Nuceria had been taught a lesson?[68]

PUBLIC VOICES

Painted notices were used for purposes other than elections or games in Pompeii and, to a lesser extent, in Herculaneum. They sometimes advertised property for sale or, more usually, to rent. These notices show that there was a wide range of properties, sometimes arranged together in the same housing block or *insula*.

A notice in the north of the city offered rental property in the Arrius Pollius insula, belonging to Gnaeus Alleius Nigidius Maius (the games sponsor) and comprising 'shops with upper rooms, quality apartments and houses' (...*tabernae cum pergulis suis et cenacula equestria et domus*).[69] Lessees were asked to contact Primus, the owner's slave. Primus was obviously completely trusted with his master's financial affairs and was well-versed in property management. The insula has been identified as the block containing the House of Pansa, with a fine main residence surrounded by at least ten shops, six on the front alone, three small houses and external staircases to the upper floor.[70] Here were more apartments, some of them very well appointed and 'upper class' (*equestria*).

Across the city, occupying a corner block on the Via dell'Abbondanza, was a complex of buildings including a large house, numerous shops with apartments above, an ornamental porticoed garden and leisure and entertainment facilities, such as baths, bars and rooms for dining. A painted notice on the exterior of this building[71] advertised five-year leases on 'elegant baths for respectable people, shops with upper rooms and apartments'.[72] The owner is named as Julia Felix and we know she was not the only woman to own large amounts of property.

There were other, less official, notices that really mirror the humanity of the cities. Someone simply and proudly announces: 'On 19 April I made bread'[73] Outside a shop someone wrote: 'A bronze vase has gone missing from this shop. Whoever brings it back will be given 65 sesterces…'.[74] But there were honest people too: 'If on 25 November anyone lost a mare laden with baskets, apply to Quintus Decius Hilarus, freedman of Quintus…at the Mamii estate on the other side of the Sarno Bridge'.[75] With a hint of foreboding someone scratched by a house door: 'Learn this; while I am alive you, hateful death, are coming'.[76] As if in reply, someone in the Palaestra wrote on a column: *Hic sumus felices*, 'Here we are happy'.[77]

The walls of the cities, in particular Pompeii, were plastered with these notices to such an extent that local wits several times wrote: 'Wall, I'm amazed that you don't topple, under the weight of all that twaddle' (*admiror o paries te non cecidisse ruinis qui tot scriptorum taedia sustineas*).[78]

PUBLIC IMAGES

In the century leading up to the eruption the cities' long-standing and complex web of social, financial and political links was altering. These changes can be seen not only in the inscriptions already discussed, but also in many commemorative bronze and marble statues and busts. These images of people, who in various ways had helped shape their cities and the broader world, stood on plinths in public spaces such as the Forum at Pompeii or the main street in Herculaneum; in public buildings, in particular the theatre and basilica; on arches; and even in some private homes. In a world without mass media this was one of the most effective forms of mass communication – and recognition of benefaction. Roman military and political leaders had exploited the power of portraiture during the first century BC. The first emperor, Augustus, and the imperial family perfected this use of images, and soon those who ruled the cities, and those who wished or believed they should, followed suit.

One of the finest of these public images is an imposing, over-life-size bronze statue of a young man (FIG. 19). An inscription found with the statue tells us his name, Lucius Mammius Maximus. His statue was one of many found in the 1730s in the theatre at Herculaneum, which was systematically investigated and ransacked by agents of the Bourbon Kings of Naples. Driving tunnels around the walls, they located huge quantities of fine marble veneer and large numbers of marble and bronze statues. Many were badly damaged, requiring considerable restoration (over centuries) to bring them to the appearance we see today. Statues included, naturally, deities and members of the imperial family, but also citizens and benefactors of the city, making the theatre a '…portrait gallery in which, if you wanted to be anyone in Herculaneum, you needed to be seen'.[79]

Mammius Maximus had clearly earned his place in this 'gallery' in the traditional way, through generous gifts of buildings or other benefits to the city. In the Roman world whatever the source of your fortune and wherever made, it was ploughed into your home city to beautify it and glorify you. He rebuilt the (as yet undiscovered) *macellum* or market place, and dedicated statues in a major public building, the so-called 'Augusteum' in the north-east of the city.[80] This huge structure, one of the largest so far discovered, with a broad, statue-filled colonnade around a large open-air piazza, has been variously identified as the Augusteum (the centre for the imperial cult), or even as Herculaneum's Forum.[81]

The style of hair and drapery date the statue of Mammius Maximus to the AD 40s.[82] Not surprisingly then, Mammius Maximus dedicated statues to members of the imperial family who were important at just that time: the reigning Emperor Claudius, his wife Agrippina and also Claudius' grandmother Livia – the late widow of Augustus, whom Claudius had recently declared a goddess.[83]

Mammius Maximus is shown wearing a toga. With his right leg slightly back and his right arm raised, he strikes the classic pose of a Roman politician making a speech. The sculpture is of high quality and is very detailed, showing the carefully constructed, heavy folds of his toga, his lighter under-tunic, his footwear or *calcei* (closed boots – sandals were considered unsuitable for formal wear) and even the signet ring on his left hand.

Fig. 19 Bronze statue of Lucius Mammius Maximus.
Theatre, Herculaneum
H. 227 cm, W. 105 cm
MANN 5591

The bronze inscription was set into the plinth of Mammius Maximus' statue and gives other, crucial information about him. This signifies the social change that was occurring at that time, both in the roles that people played in society and in the very make-up of society itself. It reads:

L MAMMIO MAXIMO
AUGUSTALI
MUNICIPES ET INCOLAE
AERE CONLATO

This translates as:

TO LUCIUS MAMMIUS MAXIMUS
AUGUSTALIS [member of the imperial guild]
TOWNSPEOPLE AND RESIDENTS
WITH FUNDS RAISED THROUGH SUBSCRIPTION

Mammius Maximus was a member of the Augustales, a prestigious guild or society, reserved almost exclusively for freedmen (ex-slaves). It was set up by the Emperor Augustus to provide a civic career path for those such as freedmen, who, for legal reasons linked to their status, could not enjoy a full political career through city magistracies. In none of the many inscriptions Mammius set up does he give an abbreviation of his father's name – suggesting he was not freeborn. Mammius Maximus was associated with the great clan of the Mammii, who had played an important role in politics in Herculaneum, and even in Rome.[84] He belonged to them because he (or his ancestors) had been physically owned by the family. Nonetheless, he rose to be a person of considerable wealth and status, perhaps living in one of the largest houses in Herculaneum (see p. 220).[85]

Fig. 20 Bronze inscription for the statue of Lucius Mammius Maximus.
Theatre, Herculaneum
H. 74 cm, W. 50 cm
MANN 3748

FREEDMEN AND SLAVES

Mammius Maximus was not unique. The rise of the freedmen and their crucial role in running the cities was one of the most significant aspects of society. The story of freedmen must, however, begin with slaves.

Slaves were an essential element in Roman life. From agriculture and commerce to the day-to-day running of the house, slaves were everywhere. Slavery seems to have been a feature of Roman society from early in its history. Although there was a resident slave population in Italy and elsewhere, the most common source of new slaves was undoubtedly war and conquest. Slavery in more recent history focuses on the massive traffic in African slaves to the Americas. For the Romans, slaves came from any part of the world that they conquered, irrespective of ethnicity or race. In the second and first centuries BC Rome conquered the Mediterranean from end to end. Many slaves were prisoners of war from Spain and North Africa (modern Libya, Tunisia and Algeria), and in particular from the Greek-influenced kingdoms of the eastern Mediterranean. These included not only modern Greece, but also the Balkans, western and central Turkey, Syria, Egypt and Judaea (modern Israel), where an anti-Roman revolt was put down in

AD 70 with a subsequent wave of new slaves for the empire. The late first century BC and first century AD witnessed an unprecedented rise in the number of slaves and freedmen, as the slaves from Rome's conquests fed through into society.

Slavery in Roman society was in many ways as cruel and oppressive as in any other period or culture. Slaves were the property of their master/mistress, who by law could do with them as he or she wished. But slaves in Roman society had an opportunity not common in other cultures: to leave slavery behind and become a freedman/freedwoman (*libertus/liberta*). These ex-slaves were far higher in status than slaves, and their children would be full Roman citizens with full rights. There were various mechanisms set up by the Roman state to allow regulated membership of this new club: for losing slave status and moving, in many cases, towards full citizenship.

A slave could be freed, at the master's discretion, through manumission,[86] from the Latin for 'with the hand' (*manu*) and 'sent away/let go' (*missus*). There were numerous benefits for the master. Many slaves, especially those attached to wealthier homes, had commercial and financial skills such as banking, shopkeeping and managing, which benefited both the household and the slave himself, who was allowed to keep some of the money he made. An ex-slave remained a close member of the master's clan (taking his name as a constant reminder) and was even obliged to provide business or work services – or give a cash substitute. Freeing slaves helped create a web of dependent contacts in the wider community, increasing the wealth and kudos of the master. Some lucky slaves were even chosen by their masters to be their heirs and successors. It was far better for a family's tradition and standing to continue through its freed slaves than to die out altogether.

Manumission could be done on the owner's death through his will, but it was mostly carried out by a living master in a ceremony in the presence of a magistrate, where the slave was symbolically tapped with a rod (*vindicta*) and declared free. A slave could, in exceptional circumstances, buy his or her freedom. There were certain restrictions on manumission – a master could not free too many slaves in one go and a minimum age was set for both master (twenty) and slave (thirty). Failure to observe these rules resulted in an incomplete manumission, and the creation of a lesser freedman or Junian Latin,[87] who required further processes to become completely free.

In time distinctions blurred and freedmen became masters, who freed their own slaves. Since all members of the family, including freedmen, kept the family nomen (clan name), it is sometimes impossible to tell who had recent origins in slavery and who had been *ingenui* (freeborn) for generations.

Increasingly, in the first century AD, freedmen paid for buildings, statues, public games and feasts. In short, they were beginning to take over responsibility for many things that had once been the preserve of the older aristocratic families.

Herculaneum, in particular, has produced important documents illustrating the rise of these new elements in society. In and around the Basilica Noniana of Herculaneum archaeologists uncovered the remains of inscribed marble panels (FIG. 21), which were once mounted on an inside wall.[88] Six of these panels were originally set up, and parts, sometimes fragmentary, survive of five. On these panels, in neat columns, are inscribed around five hundred names, all of them male. It is estimated that twice this number was originally shown and that these names represent the male citizens of Herculaneum.[89]

These names are listed in groups, or *centuriae*, according to the form of the name, which gives a clue to status and social standing in Roman society.[90] Some have a name which includes the letter 'F' = *filius* ('son of'), and an abbreviation for their voting division or tribe, indicating a full and free citizen of the Roman Empire. Others carry the letter 'L' = *libertus* (freedman, ex-slave). But another group seems to be of uncertain status, perhaps men who were technically freedmen but had not been freed fully, according to law. Some tablets were inscribed in paint rather than carved, showing there was 'work in progress' in the archive.[91]

Another potential indicator of status is the use of Greek names. Almost half of the names are of Greek origin. This is often a sign of slave ancestry, though Greek heritage in this area also produced freeborn people with Greek names, for example Eumachia (see p. 39). Some names on the list match those on preserved wooden tablets from Herculaneum,[92] allowing insight into the individuals' lives and careers. We will return to the remarkable example of the freedman Lucius Venidius Ennychus below (pp. 111–13).

Many elements are missing, including all the senior magistrates. It is also uncertain when they were created, though just before the earthquake of 62/3 seems likely.[93] However, it is very clear that there were numerous freedmen and their families living in the city. This necessarily implies a large number of slaves. Assuming a total of about 5,000 inhabitants for Herculaneum, about 1,500 were probably freedmen with their families, while slaves and their families made up perhaps 2,250 more, with the freeborn population standing at around 1,250.[94] In other words, by the time of the eruption freeborn Romans were in the minority – and had been so for some decades. In his *Annals* (11,24) the historian Tacitus relates how the Emperor Claudius once addressed the Roman Senate, against a backdrop of senatorial unhappiness at the rising influence of newcomers and immigrants. Claudius reminded them that Rome had always relied on new arrivals refreshing society and providing new leaders (including ancestors of many of their own number). What was happening in the cities at the time of the eruption was a large-scale social change, not without precedent, but on a scale not seen before.

THE FABRIC OF SOCIETY

How, if at all, was this change reflected in the populations of the cities? What type of people would a visitor, walking through their streets, have seen? First, it should be said that Pompeii was approximately three to four times the size of Herculaneum and, therefore, much busier. It had amenities of regional importance, such as the theatre and amphitheatre, and administrative and commercial interests that drew people from far afield. In Pompeii the visitor might have seen merchants from abroad – Egypt, North Africa and Greece – following up business affairs from Naples and Pozzuoli; or slaves and servants from overseas – Greece, Judaea (Palestine), Africa and elsewhere in the Mediterranean. Skeletal evidence suggests that people from sub-Saharan Africa may have been present in Pompeii and Herculaneum, though the evidence is not conclusive.[95]

Fig. 21 Fragments of a marble tablet giving the names and status of male citizens.

Basilica Noniana, Herculaneum
H. 41 cm, W. 72 cm
SAP 79062

OPPOSITE **Fig. 22 Bronze statue of Livia, wife of the Emperor Augustus.**

Theatre, Herculaneum
H. 214 cm, W. 100 cm
MANN 5589

Locally born people were ethnically intermixed. The very rich were easy to spot by their fine clothing and, sometimes, their accompanying servants. The very poor were readily identifiable by their appearance and activities. The majority of people, however, were harder to categorize. Shop-owners and managers, business-people and ordinary citizens blended with the (many) freedmen or ex-slaves. Some freedmen were wealthier and better dressed than many of the freeborn citizens – some, indeed, indistinguishable from the 'old' aristocracy they emulated.

Slaves, like the free poor, were sometimes immediately recognizable – particularly if they wore clothing such as simple short tunics, which indicated a menial or manual occupation. But there were no chains or manacles on view. Only two sets of restraining equipment (manacles or stocks) are known from the cities; such items were clearly exceptional. It was a young population. Children were everywhere – evidence from the skeletons on the beach at Herculaneum (to be approached with necessary caution, as assessing age is far from an exact science) suggests that the under-tens made up around 20 per cent of the population.[96] Another feature of the human landscape of the cities was the very visible presence of women. Making their way through the streets, shops and public areas, women mingled freely with men, unthinkable in some other cultures, such as classical Athens. As with freedmen, some freedwomen, who had substantial fortunes through industry, property or marriage, were all but indistinguishable from freeborn women.

COMMEMORATING WOMEN

The high visibility of women in society was also reflected in the relatively high proportion of females represented in statues and busts from the cities.

THE EMPRESS LIVIA

One of the sculptures found with Mammius Maximus in the theatre at Herculaneum – and one of the earliest to be discovered – is a very imposing bronze statue of a woman. She is generally agreed to be Livia,[97] the wife of Augustus, the first emperor of Rome.

The Empress is shown in a dramatic pose with her arms outstretched and hands extended in a Roman gesture of prayer, or public address (though the latter is not likely for a woman). As the senior woman of the imperial household she played a significant role in public life, and after Augustus' death she was appointed High Priestess of the cult which honoured his spirit. The statue almost certainly shows Livia in this capacity. She is formally dressed in a long-sleeved tunic or *stola*, over which she wears a mantle, or *palla*, which envelops her, passing

round the body and over her head before crossing her chest and folding over her left arm. On her feet she wears soft leather shoes. Her formal dress and striking pose underline her seniority and the solemnity of the moment. This statue was one of many portraying the Empress, a member of the imperial family certainly, but nonetheless a woman. The appearance of images of imperial women inspired many women beyond the ruling family.

THE PRIESTESS EUMACHIA

Another striking sculpture (FIG. 23), this time from Pompeii, shows the priestess Eumachia, one of the richest people in the city. She was wealthy in her own right through land and property. Her family's estates included workshops making bricks and tiles[98] and possibly amphorae for the export of their wine. Eumachia was the wife of Marcus Numistrius Fronto, whose family was also very wealthy and prestigious. The marble statue was discovered in a small shrine-like structure to the rear of an enormous building on the Forum known as the 'building of Eumachia'.[99] According to its inscription,[100] the statue was dedicated by the fullers (clothworkers and laundrymen) to Eumachia as Public Priestess or *Sacerdos Publica*. Since women were not able to occupy civic offices, membership of a priesthood, in particular of Venus, the patron deity of Pompeii, was the peak of a woman's civic achievement.

Eumachia, like Livia, is shown wearing the long-sleeved tunic or stola of the Roman matrona (the lady of the household) with a mantle draped around her. The statue still retains traces of its original colour in Eumachia's orange-red hair – most Greek and Roman marble sculpture was at least partly painted.

The building of Eumachia comprised an ornate entrance porch connecting with the Forum colonnade, and a vast open courtyard surrounded by a portico on all sides. The intended use of the building, which seems very similar in structure to the so-called Augusteum at Herculaneum, is unknown, but suggestions have included: a meeting space for the Augustales; an additional market space; perhaps less likely, a meeting space for the fullers who dedicated the statue to Eumachia; or even a slave market.

The main dedicatory inscription of the building has survived, in which Eumachia proudly dedicates the structure to Piety and to Imperial Harmony – 'Concordia Augusta'. She was, perhaps, inspired by the great Portico of Livia, which the Empress had built in Rome. Eumachia may well have been associating herself closely with the imperial family and Rome, giving herself kudos in the provincial society of this part of southern Italy. Clearly Eumachia was not thinking just of herself. She proclaims she built the whole edifice with her own money, in her name and in that of her son – in fact the whole structure may have been a political advertisement for him. If so it worked, because Marcus Numistrius Fronto (possibly Eumachia's husband, but more probably her son) was elected duumvir in AD 2/3.

It is of course possible that Numistrius Fronto was behind it all, extending his

Fig. 23 Marble statue of Eumachia.
Building of Eumachia, Pompeii
H. 194 cm
MANN 6232

own prestige through the high profile of his wife. Nonetheless, on the surface, the building proclaimed Eumachia's own wealth and status to every Pompeian who passed through the Forum. And Eumachia was not alone. At least one other major building in the Forum at Pompeii (the exact location is uncertain) was built from private funds by a priestess called Mamia, who was later honoured by the city Council with a tomb on public property, paid for by the city.[101]

When the priestess Eumachia died she was buried outside the Nuceria Gate in the largest (though not the most ornate) tomb so far discovered at Pompeii. The tomb was built and paid for by Eumachia herself, and is marked with two remarkably simple inscriptions on roughly hewn blocks, translated as, 'Eumachia built this for herself (sibi) and for her people (suis)'. Eumachia's family seems to disappear, at least from the political record, by the AD 30s, but this coincides with the appearance on this same tomb of inscriptions commemorating the Alleii family. One of them was Gnaeus Alleius Nigidius Maius the games sponsor and property magnate (above p. 31), who is known to have had freedman origins. The wealth of Eumachia and her family, no doubt like that of other older families in the cities, was perhaps slowly but surely changing hands, by marriage, adoption and manumission (freeing of slaves).[102]

SOCIAL REALITIES AND SOCIAL MOBILITY

The social experience of women in the upper classes will always have been different from that of other women. They were born into, or married into, wealth and through their family had a ready-made web of connections that opened up opportunities in society. Yet even when we see fine monuments, tombs and statues built by or for women we still cannot gain a full idea of how this translated into real power and influence. It is difficult to say whether women had made substantial social progress in the period leading up to the eruption, because we have no such mass of evidence from any preceding period. There may have been some echoes of the position of Etruscan women, which may have been relatively elevated,[103] but again, we cannot be sure. The fact remains that at the time of the eruption, a freeborn woman could marry and divorce, buy, sell and rent property and bring court cases, provided she was personally involved in the case.[104] However, it would be wrong to imagine that women were equal to men.[105] Women could not vote (though as we have seen this did not stop them trying to influence those who could), nor could they stand for office; but neither could they do so in early twentieth-century Europe, when many, nevertheless, had considerable wealth and influence. There had been certain restrictions on Roman women's freedom of action in relation to the law, requiring the consent of a tutor or official guardian. But by the time of the eruption the tutor's role was much less important.[106] Women were able to play a full role in many areas of society.

The influence of these new powers in society, of women and of freedmen, is not only visible in the grander inscriptions and public monuments. From Herculaneum comes evidence of social realities that must have been present in every street in every town in the empire. A marble plaque found in an ordinary street in Herculaneum gives a glimpse into the ownership of property: not the great blocks of property owned by major landlords, but

two fairly ordinary homes (FIG. 24). It provides a fascinating glimpse of the complex and sometimes difficult relations between neighbours. The marble plaque is inscribed on both sides and was perhaps originally suspended at right angles to the house, as the modern replica is positioned today. On each side is an inscription. One side reads:

> M. NONI.M.L.DAMA
> PARIES.PERPETUUS.PRIVAT[US]

'This is the wall of Marcus Nonius Dama, the freedman (L[ibertus]) of Marcus, private and in perpetuity'.

Fig. 24 A boundary marker for two houses, inscribed on both sides.

From Herculaneum, Cardio IV superiore
H. 15 cm, L. 33 cm, W. 2 cm
SAP 78762

While the other, in a different (and superior) hand reads:

> IVLIAE PARI(es)
> PRIVA[TUS] PERPETUUS

'This is the wall of Julia, private and in perpetuity'.

Most striking here is that the man's inscription explicitly states he is a freedman, M(arci) L(ibertus), while the woman gives only one name, Julia, and no hint of her father's name, suggesting that she, too, is a freed slave. We cannot know the background to the plaque, but it probably marks the settlement of a boundary dispute that was taken to the city magistrates for judgement. Similar disputes are referred to in the archives of wooden tablets that have survived in Herculaneum (below pp. 111–13). They remind us that the daily life of the cities was filled with interactions of all types, including disagreements and conflicts, which had to be resolved in order to keep the urban fabric intact.

The impression given by the sculptures, the inscriptions and the notices is of cities, which, though small, had complex civic and private lives dependent on links and connections, only some of which we are privileged to be able to see through the exceptional circumstances of the burial of Pompeii and Herculaneum. They were also places in which social change was taking place, change that we can also imagine happening in the rest of Italy and large swathes of the empire. Social mobility on a large scale was becoming the norm, and although this certainly marked a major change, it was not, as major social changes can be, a threat to the existing order. On the contrary, the public acclaim achieved through sponsoring public buildings, games and other benefactions, and through acquiring and displaying fine homes, encouraged whole new levels of society, wealthy from business and property, to participate in and to support, not supplant, the existing order.[107]

These new arrivals in society, a direct consequence of Rome's conquests and expansion, became a vital element in the life of the cities, as older families met new money, often ex-slave.[108] In many ways it is the lives of these 'new' people, as well as those of the old families, that can be seen all around. Before entering their homes it is important to look at the streets in which they lived, and the commercial and social links which nourished them and bound them together.

II
LIVING ABOVE
THE SHOP

LIVING ABOVE
THE SHOP

HOUSES opened directly onto the street, with no front gardens or long access paths. Indeed, often the street came into the home in the form of shops and other commercial outlets, which were an integral part of many houses. This section looks at the street and its businesses, the people who owned and ran them, and their close relationship to the home and the household.

We cannot be sure of the Romans' names for their streets or houses. No name plates for homes or streets were fixed to walls. Throughout this book, the names of streets are the modern ones created by archaeologists. For example, the 'Via di Nola' (Nola Street) is so called because it leads to the Nola gate, also a modern name. Ironically, it is the Samnite period, rather than the Roman, that has provided most of our knowledge of street and gate names. The modern Porta Ercolano is almost certainly the 'Veru Sarina' or 'Salt Gate' mentioned in an Oscan inscription of the early first century BC, so called because it led out to the salt pans near the coast. Likewise, an Oscan inscription near the Stabiae gate in the south of the city names three streets: the Jovia, Decuria and Pompeiana. It is likely these names were retained in the Roman period, but sadly we do not know to which streets they belonged.

The principal east–west street of Pompeii, the Via dell'Abbondanza, is named after the personification of abundance (so-named by the archaeologists) which decorates one of the street's fountains. The smaller roads such as Vicolo (alley) dei Vettii are named after important houses situated on them, while others were named after monuments such as the Temple of Isis (Vicolo del Tempio d'Iside), and even the brothel (Vicolo del Lupanare). It is possible that they carried similar names in the Roman period, but we cannot be sure. The archaeological site of Herculaneum uses instead a system of numbered streets going east–west (Decumanii) and north–south (Cardines). Again the original names are not known, unless the Romans, too, simply referred to Decumani and Cardines.

Houses, too, are known by modern names, which come from a variety of sources. Voting recommendations in electoral notices painted on house walls have very often been used to identify the owners of buildings. If these are backed up by other evidence, such as named objects within the home, then identification becomes more

PREVIOUS PAGES
Fig. 25 Detail from a fresco showing people in the Forum at Pompeii buying and selling goods (see fig. 35).

Fig. 26 The Decumanus Maximus (main east–west street) of Herculaneum, looking west.

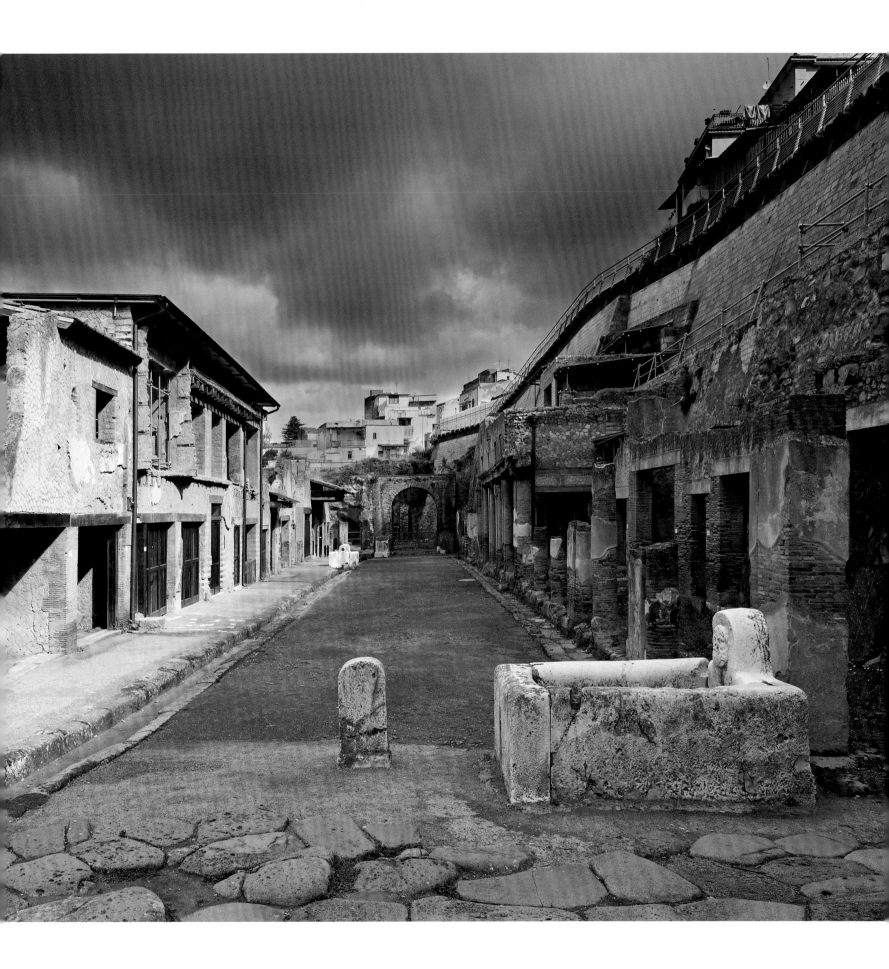

certain; if not, then such notices and graffiti are a useful (but not foolproof) indicator. Other objects which can help in identification include rings with named seal stamps (FIG. 27) and amphorae and other artefacts bearing painted or impressed names. Some houses have, in fact, changed their names on the basis of such evidence. The house once known as that of Loreius Tiburtinus (because of electoral graffiti on the external walls) is now called the House of Decimus Octavius Quartio thanks to a bronze ring seal found in one of the rooms.

To avoid any confusion over location, throughout the book (H) or (P) is used after house names where necessary to signify Herculaneum or Pompeii.

In the absence of any named evidence, houses are often given nicknames from a particular feature or object found there, such as the House of Neptune and Amphitrite (H) after the mosaic in the garden dining area and the House of the Wooden Partition (H) because of its imposing wooden screen. Or a home can be named after a famous visitor such as the House of the Prince of Naples (P), or an event that took place when it was excavated, such as the House of the Silver Wedding (P) (of the King and Queen of Italy).

Fig. 27 Bronze seal ring with, in abbreviated and mirrored form, the name of Marcus Fabius Rufus.
House of Marcus Fabius Rufus, Pompeii (VII,6.17–22)
W. 5.5 cm
SAP 14250

In the mid-nineteenth century the archaeologist and director of the sites, Giuseppe Fiorelli, established a numbering system for the cities, dividing them up into regions, then *insulae* (city blocks; singular *insula*) and finally marking each individual doorway and unit. So, for example, the House of the Tragic Poet has an individual identification of VI,8,3–5. These are not exactly snappy or memorable, but are very useful for mapping the whole city – in particular for identifying the smaller properties which have never had other names. In this book only the 'nicknames' are used, and all the houses discussed can be located on the maps (FIGS 5–6). All of the house, street and gate names are useful labels, essential to help visitors orientate themselves within the cities, but we should remember that they are modern.

THE STREETS

'Streets' could vary enormously, from alleys and back streets, often extremely narrow, dark and unsurfaced, to more primary roads and the broader, brighter main thoroughfares with raised pavements and colonnaded porticoes. These major roads were nearly always paved with large irregularly shaped blocks of local volcanic basalt, often with characteristic wheel ruts worn into their surface (FIG. 28), indicating the frequent passage of carts and wagons. The rarity of these ruts in Herculaneum might suggest a different scale of urban life to that of Pompeii.[1]

Traffic and transport seems to have been very important in Pompeii, and it was carefully managed. Research has suggested that parts of Pompeii had a modern-style, one-way traffic system.[2] Other parts of the cities were pedestrianized zones, to which access by wheeled traffic was blocked by great stone bollards (FIG. 29) or by very steep drops in gradient. Pavements were always elevated from street level, sometimes by half a metre (1½ ft) or more, and a very characteristic feature is the holes in the edge of the pavements (FIG. 30) – almost certainly hitching points used to tether the horses or

Fig. 28 A street in Pompeii with stepping stones and wheel-ruts.

Fig. 29 Pedestrianization, Roman style. Three large stone pillars that blocked traffic using the Via dell'Abbondanza in Pompeii from entering the Forum.

Fig. 30 Pavement edging stone with a hole almost certainly for tethering animals.

(more likely) mules and donkeys that pulled the carts. It is unclear whether the animals stood in the road, thereby partly blocking it but leaving the pavement free for pedestrians, or vice-versa. The Romans understood the importance of traffic flow.

As some scholars have pointed out, this flow would not stop in the evening and night time – on the contrary, some cities (including Rome) probably had laws which stated that carts could enter the city only from late afternoon to early morning.[3] Night will have transformed the cities. Traffic there may have been, but there is no evidence of any organized illumination of the streets and, with the exception of light from some houses, bars and other commercial premises that remained open in the evening, darkness reigned.

At Pompeii, great ovoid stepping-stones of basalt were placed at regular intervals, though for some reason these, like the wheel ruts, are not found in Herculaneum. Perhaps they functioned primarily as stepping-stones, for pedestrians crossing the sunken road from one raised pavement to another. On the other hand, some see their presence at Pompeii as evidence of the sea of 'filth' of all sorts that filled the streets.[4] Very unappealing waste and by-products from shops and businesses such as tanners, butchers and fullers, not to mention waste water from homes, and even the contents of chamber pots, could have formed a very potent brew in the streets, in particular in summer when there was less rainfall to sluice it away. Certainly we can imagine the streets being far from the clean thoroughfares we see today.

Pompeii had no linked-up system of drainage, though drains took water away from the main baths and the Forum and discharged it outside the walls.[5] Herculaneum had storm drains carrying water under the main north–south streets. Ultimately it was the responsibility of the magistrates to keep the city tidy and functioning well. City councillors in Herculaneum painted a notice on the water tower near the main street (Decumanus Maximus)[6] threatening those who dumped refuse in the area with fines (for children) or a beating on the buttocks (for slaves). This is not to say that Herculaneum was necessarily a nicer, less dirty place than Pompeii, but there are at least signs of attempts to keep the streets clean in the smaller city.

A properly organized public supply of clean water was vital to daily life. After the Emperor Augustus brought piped water to the cities through the Aqua Augusta aqueduct, an extensive network of access points to fresh water was established. On many street corners are large rectangular public fountains (FIG. 31), often decorated with images of animals or deities such as Venus, Hercules and Mercury. They were an important part of the streetscape – both as a meeting place for the poor, who had no private water supply, and as a point of reference for everybody.[7] It is estimated that few homes in Pompeii were more than 50 m from a fountain. Blocks and neighbourhoods may even have been referred to (informally) by the names of their fountains.

Fig. 31 A public fountain in front of a water tower, Pompeii.

These fountains are nearly always accompanied by tall masonry structures, so-called water towers (FIG. 31). These were topped by large lead tanks and were used to store water fed down from the large brick-built *castellum acquae*, the 'water fortress', the first deposition area for water within the city walls. These towers served to relieve the pressure of the water which flowed unceasingly from the aqueduct. On some towers are visible the channels that were cut to accommodate the lead pipes which fed the fountain below, or led to private houses in the neighbourhood.

The use of lead pipes for the water supply naturally raises the question of health risks. Exposure to lead will have been reduced by the build-up of limescale on the interior of the pipes; nonetheless, some exposure was inevitable.[8] High quantities of lead in the body are toxic and can cause both mental problems and physical diseases including anaemia, severe stomach upsets and infertility. Recent analysis of the bones of victims of the eruption has shown possible evidence of lead poisoning, resulting not only from the water pipes but also from lead kitchen utensils and lead-based cosmetics, lead water storage and mixing tanks. Inhabitants of Herculaneum may have fared even worse.[9]

Returning to the streetscape, the streets were completely lined with buildings.

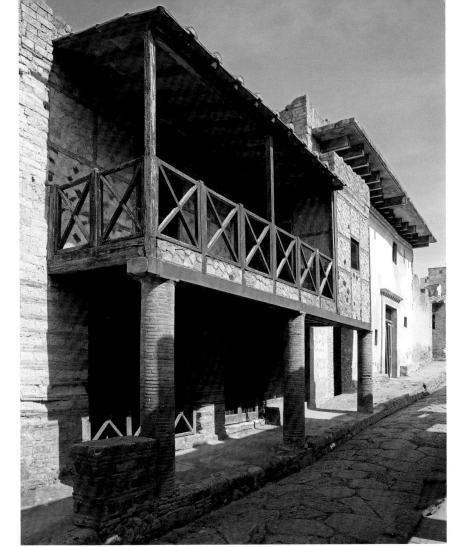

The lower parts of their walls were often painted in characteristic deep 'Pompeian red', with commercial premises and houses rising usually two, and sometimes even three, storeys high. Upper storeys were usually occupied by flats and apartments. Long balconies jutted out from the facades (FIG. 32), both simple, open verandahs and enclosed areas (*maeniana*) which extended the accommodation out over the street. These were often used for storage of foodstuffs and other goods, or as a location for large storage jars (*dolia*), or even toilets. Balconies were usually made of *opus craticium* – a timber frame filled with mortared rubble, forming a light but strong structure that was also used for internal partitions. The balconies provided useful shade and shelter on many streets and there were almost certainly awnings extending out from many shops and bars. Even the wider streets, when lined with balconies on both sides, would have seemed narrower, shaded and more intimate.

In this busy bustling streetscape it was almost possible to lose sight of the houses. Many of the larger older houses, such as the House of the Ceii (P) or the House of the Wooden Partition (H) (FIG. 33) had quite striking, if austere, fronts, sometimes with architectural details such as column capitals or entablatures at the top of the wall, or moulded stucco imitating masonry blocks. Other houses were much plainer and simpler, but all were surrounded by other premises, such as shops and bars. External windows were few, and very small by modern standards. Some external windows were glazed, but the majority had metal grilles (FIG. 34), covered when needed with shutters or sliding panels of wood. The status and prestige of the home was not indicated by large picture windows on the outside, though these certainly existed inside the house. Instead, entrance to and views into the house were strictly by invitation. The door became, in some ways, the only visible external expression of the owner's wealth and pretensions. Great tall doors decorated with bronze bosses and studs spoke of the wealth and sophistication to be found inside. Casts of some doors have survived. Outside many houses, such as the House of the Ceii (P) or the House of the Wooden Partition (H) (FIG. 33), are fixed masonry benches. These were intended partly for the use of clients waiting for the *salutatio* (the morning audience with the head of the household, see below p. 77), but also perhaps for tired passers-by.[10]

COMMERCIAL PREMISES

Commercial properties and the profits and rental income they generated, along with agricultural land and produce, were the basis of wealth for most people who lived in the cities. Shops and other commercial premises, their characteristically wide entrances contrasting with narrower house doors, occupied much of the space in any given street. In fact, so abundant were these premises that the people of the cities could be described, borrowing Napoleon's famous phrase, as 'a nation of shopkeepers'. A wide array of business outlets sold, and indeed often produced, the goods and commodities needed by people on a day-to-day basis, while others such as bars and inns provided food and drink and sometimes a bed. These businesses were very often inextricably linked to the home's financial well-being and physically joined to the home itself.

Retail outlets were everywhere, in the market building (*macellum*), at temporary stalls and in fixed shops; even in the Forum, the heart of political and religious life, the buying and selling of goods was a common sight. A series of frescoes from the leisure

ABOVE **Fig. 34 Metal window grilles.**
House of the Alcove, Herculaneum

BELOW **Fig. 35 Fresco showing people in the Forum at Pompeii buying and selling goods including bronze cooking pots.**
Praedia of Julia Felix, Pompeii
H. 23 cm, W. 66 cm
MANN 9062

and residential complex (*praedia*) of Julia Felix[11] shows the Forum portico alive with a wide range of stalls between the columns, selling shoes, cloth, bread, tools and cooking pots (FIG. 35). Stalls were set up elsewhere on games days and holidays, as seen on the wall painting showing the amphitheatre of Pompeii (FIG. 17) while others, which were permanent, were found in the amphitheatre's external niches, their leases and permits administered by the aediles.[12]

A very high proportion of commercial units, including shops, workshops, bars and inns, were built into houses. Their particular identifying features are fixed masonry counters with the characteristic inset storage jars (dolia) (FIG. 36). Reflecting their mixed business and residential role, they often have stairs leading to living quarters on upper floors, cooking areas and sometimes toilet facilities.

Their open frontages usually have a deep channel carved into the threshold slabs – evidence of their closing device. A detailed cast from the Via dell'Abbondanza, Pompeii (FIG. 37) shows the vertical shuttering panels which were slotted into this groove. This remarkably well-preserved cast shows, in addition to the panels, a separate door which could be used for access when the premises were closed for business. The shop was also a home.

ABOVE **Fig. 36 A large shop/bar in Herculaneum with a characteristic counter with inset storage jars.**

BELOW **Fig. 37 Shop/bar frontage with cast of shuttered panels.**
Via dell'Abbondanza, Pompeii

Commercial units were so often linked to private houses in this way that any obvious 'zoning' or separation of residential and commercial premises would have been impossible.[13] It seems clear that there was little or no stigma attached to the close proximity of the two.[14] Over half of the finest houses in Pompeii, including the House of the Faun and the House of the Menander, have shops or other commercial activity

attached to them.[15] In busy, commercial Pompeii, this might seem unsurprising, but at Herculaneum, too, shops are a regular feature, even of very well-appointed houses such as the House of the Black Living Room and the House of the Bicentenary.

Some scholars, including Amedeo Maiuri, the legendary director of excavations in the cities for most of the mid-twentieth century, thought the proliferation of shops signalled a 'degrading' of the urban fabric. He suggested there was an 'invasion' by shopkeepers and merchants, in particular after the earthquake of AD 62/3. According to Maiuri, houses with any form of commercial activity were considered 'tainted' and inferior.[16] Some businesses were indeed created after the earthquake, but excavations show that very many were established long before, for example the workshop built into the House of the Grand Duke Michael (P) in the later third century BC.[17] Clearly, house owners accommodated retail and manufacturing in or at their homes, where it formed an important part of the household's income. In fact it seems likely that owners, even of the wealthier houses, far from considering such premises an imposition or a 'necessary evil', may have seen it as another visible asset, a further expression of their wealth. Interest in commercial premises went to the very top of Roman society. The statesman Cicero owned shops in the nearby city of Puteoli (Pozzuoli).[18] Clearly he did not run them himself, but his possession of them raised no problem at all.

The presence of counters and storage jars may well indicate premises that were primarily commercial, but in most cases it is not clear what was provided or sold. Attempts to identify and classify them are not helped by uncertainty surrounding the names for retail and hospitality businesses, both in the Roman writers and among modern scholars.[19] The most common Latin word for 'shop' is *taberna* (plural *tabernae*), used in painted signs at Pompeii to describe retail units with lodgings (*pergulae*) on the upper floor. In Latin the term is much broader than 'shop',[20] and can also refer to stalls and workshops, simple lodgings and administrative buildings, and bars or taverns, places for eating and drinking. However, the Roman writers mostly use *taberna* for a retail shop selling everything from books and pottery to wine and shoes.

GOOD FORTUNE IN COMMERCE

Whatever the nature of the business and whoever owned it, its good fortune and that of its customers depended on divine protection. Inside, this could be provided by a shrine to the gods, usually referred to by modern scholars as a *lararium* (FIG. 38), as in the bar of Lucius Vetutius Placidus in Pompeii. This owner's name was suggested through electoral notices (now gone) on the wall and corroborated by inscriptions on amphorae.

In the lararium the *genius*, or personification of the life-force of the owner, and the household gods (*Lares*) are flanked by Mercury, god of commerce and Bacchus, god of wine, very appropriate for a bar. The presence of the lararium, the most visible manifestation of the household gods, reinforced the message that business and home were one: the landlord was also most definitely master of the house. In some businesses, in particular bars, customers were greeted by a hanging bronze wind chime (*tintinnabulum*). Bells were believed to keep evil spirits at bay, but they were often given added potency by association with a symbol of good fortune, the phallus (erect penis). The example shown here (FIG. 41) features a rather grotesque man, seeming to fight his own enormous phallus with his swords (now missing). The figure doubles as a lamp, with the filling hole on his back and the wick, naturally, at the tip of the phallus. Another double-nozzled lamp hangs from the man and the whole is finished off with four bells that dangle from his elbows and phallus.

The Romans saw nothing shocking in this – the protective phallus was everywhere in Roman culture. Intentionally erotic Roman imagery certainly exists, but most 'sexualized' or 'eroticized' images were seen by Romans as symbols of fertility, amulets of good fortune, or just comic. Phallic signs were set into the walls of premises or on street corners (FIG. 39). A shop sign from Pompeii (FIG. 40) showed Mercury, god of commerce, striding on winged feet, preceded by his phallus. Uncertainty over the nature of 'erotic' talismans was expressed in Naples Museum in the nineteenth century, though the objects were eventually consigned to the Gabinetto Segreto.[21]

ABOVE **Fig. 38 Household shrine (*lararium*) showing the *genius*, flanked by household gods (*Lares*) with Mercury (left) and Bacchus (right).**
Bar of Lucius Vetutius Placidus, Pompeii

BELOW **Fig. 39 Phallic plaque set into a street near a crossroads, Pompeii.**

Fig. 40 Painted sign from a shop showing Mercury, god of commerce, with money bag, winged staff, winged heels and a huge phallus.

House of the Chaste Lovers, Pompeii (IX,12,6)
H. 70 cm, W. 70 cm
MANN

RIGHT **Fig. 41 Bronze wind chime (*tintinnabulum*) with hanging lamps showing a man with an enormous phallus. Four bells and a lamp hang from the main figure.**

From Pompeii
H. 21 cm, W. 18 cm
SAP 1260

SHOPS

The shop sited next to the House of Neptune and Amphitrite (H) connected directly with the house and featured an L-shaped counter, with at least three inset storage jars As it appears now, the shop is very much a product of restoration by the archaeologist Amedeo Maiuri. Nonetheless, there are some important original features. In the corner of the shop is a cooking area, suggesting that food or hot drinks were sold, though the absence of seating space suggests it was a 'take-away'. The carbonization of the wooden fixtures has preserved a remarkable wooden partition with a trellis top, above which is a (restored) mezzanine balcony, used to store amphorae, with more amphorae on wooden racks on the short side wall (FIG. 42).

Through the collapsed ceiling there are glimpses of the residential flat above the shop, with its own cooking platform, the base of a small marble table and the bronze leg of a bed. Although not all flats are as identifiable or as well preserved as this example, traces of stairs or ladders, shrine paintings or niches for toilets or beds are all indicators of upstairs lodgings. There is abundant archaeological evidence for habitation in and above tabernae,[22] and writers such as Cicero describe it as a place for work and bed.[23] This type of commercial/residential unit, whether run by a member of the household or rented out, was clearly typical in the cities, and according to one scholar, comprised over a third of the housing stock.[24] Living above the shop is nothing new.

Shops sold a range of fresh and preserved goods.[25] Although it is possible that sacks were used, the majority of finds have come from containers made of pottery or glass. A dolium (large storage jar) set into the ground in a shop in Herculaneum contained walnuts. Amphorae, usually for liquids such as wine or oil, were also used to transport and store dry goods including grain and dried fruit and vegetables. Amphorae discovered in the room above the shop/bar of the House of Neptune and Amphitrite contained

ABOVE **Fig. 43 Two cylindrical storage bottles in light blue glass, with a pottery carrying case.**

From Pompeii
H. 15 cm
MANN 12845

RIGHT **Fig. 44 Large hexagonal storage bottle in mid-blue glass.**

From Pompeii
H. 36 cm, W. 17 cm
MANN 13181

OPPOSITE **Fig. 42 Shop fronting the House of Neptune and Amphitrite, Herculaneum. Amphorae are stored on wooden racks and on the floor beside the shop's cooking range. Above is another cooking range for the upstairs apartment.**

olives and beans, while grain and pulses were found in amphorae above one of the shops in the large tenement block (insula) at Herculaneum (above p. 70). Smaller terracotta jars held goods such as lentils, beans and nuts.

Glass was important for the preservation, presentation and sometimes the sale of goods, and in shops throughout the cities, glass containers were everywhere. Storage jars ranged from ordinary bottles, perhaps for oil, to elegant vessels such as a hexagonal bottle with a wide mouth suited to larger commodities (FIG. 44). Beautiful miniature amphorae, designed for marketing and display, contained dried goods such as raisins, figs and shelled hazelnuts.

WEIGHTS AND MEASURES

The commerce that brought these goods to the cities was largely regulated by imperial edicts and local by-laws. In the Forum at Pompeii there is a marble 'weights and measures table' (*mensa ponderaria*) which gives a set of measures for dry and liquid goods. Originally set up in the Samnite period, the table has an inscription naming the two duoviri who had, in the late first century BC, 'regulated the measures' at the request of the city Council. A similar table has yet to be found in Herculaneum,[26] but another find from that city reminds us of the Council's desire to control retail operations. This is a cylindrical bronze vessel, a *modius* or grain measure (FIG. 48). Grain was poured in, then the three-spoked element at the top served as a leveller to ensure that the measure was properly full. On the exterior is punched the inscription *D.D.P.P HERC*, perhaps an abbreviation of *Decurionum Decreto Praefecti ponderibus Herculanensium* ('By decree of the City Council the property of the prefect of weight and measures, Herculaneum'). Balances and scales (FIG. 45) were similarly controlled. Devices such as funnels (FIG. 46) were used to transfer both liquids and grain or dry goods into containers such as amphorae.

In addition to predominantly local goods, the markets and shops of the cities contained merchandise from all over the empire, ranging from luxury items, such as silk, perfumes and spices, to wine, oil and vessels of pottery and glass. These goods arrived via marketing networks such as the periodic markets (*nundinae*) listed in a graffito from Pompeii.[27] This graffito lists the days of the week with the names of the cities where markets were held on that day. It links Pompeii (Herculaneum is not mentioned) and a group of other Campanian centres including Nuceria and Nola with the major city of Neapolis (Naples), the deep water port of Puteoli (Pozzuoli) and even Rome itself. Pompeii's market day, by this evidence, was Saturday, and for the more ambitious merchant, Rome's was Wednesday.

The Romans, like us, used a seven-day week. The days were named after gods and planets: Sol (Sun), Luna (Moon), Mars (god of war), Mercury (god of commerce), Jupiter (king of the gods), Venus (goddess of love) and Saturn (a very ancient god of agriculture, and perhaps the father of Jupiter). The days were referred to as *dies Solis* (day of the sun), *dies Lunae* (day of the moon) and so on. The English language still preserves three 'Roman' day names: Saturday, Sunday and Monday.

In terms of longer distance networks, it should be remembered that the cities on the Bay, including Pompeii, already enjoyed easy access to the important port of Pozzuoli, with its links to Egypt and the east. A collection of wooden tablets found at Murecine (Moregine), near Pompeii,[28] suggests links between the two cities, as merchants, bankers and tradesmen moved between them, and perhaps travelled much further afield. One of the markers of this trade can be seen in the tableware that was being used in the cities in AD 79.

The refuse found in the drain under the street named Cardo V in Herculaneum (see pp. 265–9) contained a wide range of glass and pottery tableware. The most characteristic table pottery throughout the Roman Empire was Red Slip Ware,[29] named after the slip or coating that gave the pottery its attractive coloured shine. Originating in the eastern Mediterranean in the second century BC, Red Slip Ware was produced in Italy by the 40s BC. Within a century production centres had sprung up all over the empire, from France to Egypt. Red Slip Ware was usually made in workshops, using moulds that permitted mass production and uniformity. As a result, vessels made in very different parts of the empire can look remarkably similar. Stamps on the vessel often give the

ABOVE **Fig. 45 Bronze weighing scales with ornately decorated scale pans.**

H. 40 cm, W. 48 cm
MANN 74157

FAR LEFT **Fig. 46 Large bronze funnel, possibly for dry goods.**

H. 33 cm, D. 32 cm
MANN 73839

CENTRE **Fig. 47 Carbonized figs.**

From a shop north-east of the Decumanus Maximus, Herculaneum
SAP 77615

LEFT **Fig. 48 Bronze measure for dry goods (*modius*) inscribed D.D.P.P HERC.**

From Herculaneum
H. 18 cm, D. 20 cm
MANN 6331

RIGHT **Fig. 49 Double-handled table amphora in Red Slip Ware, made in Tunisia.**

From Pompeii
H. 22 cm, D. 13 cm
MANN 110388

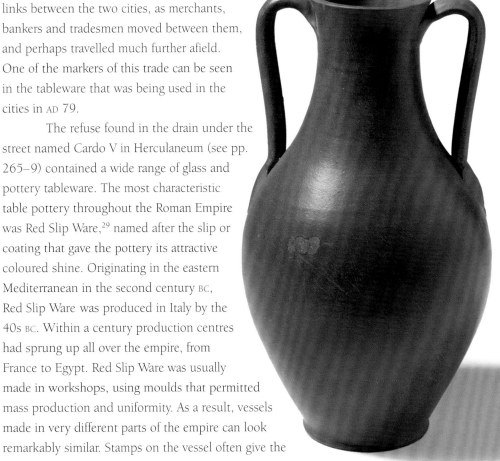

name of the potter or the owner of the workshop (FIG. 51), and many vessels also have the owner's name scratched on the underside of the base.

The three cups illustrated here (FIG. 50) look remarkably similar, but analysis of their clay and finish shows they come from southern France, Italy and western Turkey. The two-handled table amphora that could have filled them with wine came from Tunisia (FIG. 49). Yet all of them could, in theory, have been bought from the same shop or stall. In October 1881 excavations in House VIII, 5, 9, Pompeii, uncovered the remains of a wooden crate containing ninety large Red Slip drinking bowls from southern France (FIG. 52), many showing traces of scorching from the fire that consumed the crate. With the bowls were around forty terracotta oil lamps, many from workshops in the north of Italy. This sizeable cargo was not for normal domestic consumption, but for three shops that fronted the house.

TOP **Fig. 50 (l–r) Wine cup in 'marbled' Red Slip Ware, made in southern France.**

From Pompeii
H. 5.5 cm, D. 12 cm
MANN 109640

Wine cup in Red Slip Ware, made in Italy.

Vesuvian area
H. 7 cm, D. 13 cm
MANN 16482

Wine cup in Red Slip Ware, made in Turkey.

Vesuvian area
H. 6 cm, D. 11 cm
MANN 211957

ABOVE **Fig. 51 Stamp on a bowl of Italian Red Slip Ware giving the letters 'SMF', an abbreviation of Sextus Murrius Festus, working in Pisa from AD 60.**

H. 7 cm, D. 13 cm
MANN 16482

LEFT **Fig. 52 Large drinking cup in Red Slip Ware, made in southern France.**

From Pompeii (VIII,5,9)
H. 8.5 cm, D. 17.5 cm
MANN 112926

EATING AND DRINKING ESTABLISHMENTS

Outlets selling food and drink made up the largest number of businesses. Over 150 such buildings, characterized by painted street signs, counters, cooking platforms and dining rooms, have been found in Pompeii [30] and over a dozen in Herculaneum. The outlets cluster in areas of high traffic – in Pompeii along the Via Consolare and the Via dell'Abbondanza, and in Herculaneum along Cardo V and the Decumanus Maximus.

OWNERS AND WORKERS

Just as today, the commercial premises of the cities were run in a variety of ways by a wide range of people. Since so many were linked physically to houses it is likely that many businesses belonged to the home, and were run by slaves or freed members of the household or by people renting in their own right, as implied in the painted notice regarding property in the Praedia of Julia Felix. Depending on the type of shop and the trade involved, some shopkeepers may have been freeborn, but many would have been freedmen or slaves.

It is sometimes possible to get an idea of the individuals who owned or ran shops, bars and other businesses at the time of the eruption. Just as with houses, electoral notices painted on the shop walls are a potential clue to the identity of the owner or manager. Graffiti, even if sometimes scurrilous, can point towards an owner or at least a worker in the establishment. Painted 'address' inscriptions on transport amphorae and seal rings with the owner's name stamp set in bronze can also give valuable clues.

Fig. 53 Painted bar sign showing a phoenix.

Bar of Euxinus, Pompeii
H. 123 cm, W. 124 cm
SAP 41671

Near the amphitheatre was an inn with its own small vineyard and storage jars for wine fermentation. [31] Painted inscriptions on amphorae *Pompeiis ad amphiteatr(um) Euxino coponi* ('At Pompeii, near the amphitheatre, to Euxinus the landlord') give the addressee as Euxinus and call him *coponi* (landlord). The bar might best have been recognized by the 'pub' sign painted on its outside wall at the entrance to the bar (FIG. 53), a characteristic feature of such establishments. The sign shows a phoenix, the mythological bird that symbolizes hope and renewal, with peacocks and the motto *Phoenix felix et tu* ('The phoenix is lucky, may you be too'). [32]

Further west along the Via dell'Abbondanza is another bar which, when it was excavated at the beginning of the twentieth century, still had all its amphorae stacked throughout the bar, with dozens of vessels in glass, pottery and bronze still on and around the marble-topped counter. There they remained until the Allied bombing of 1943 destroyed many of them. [33] The owner/manager of this bar, mentioned in electoral notices, may have been a woman called Asellina. [34] We also know the names of other women who worked with her, the barmaids Zmyrina, Aegle and Maria. [35]

The Roman name for a bar with food, and sometimes lodgings, was a *caupona*.[36] Lodgings could also be found in a guest house, called a *hospitium* (from which comes the word 'hospice'), or a *stabulum*, the ancestor of the English word for stable, which provided accommodation for travellers and their animals.[37] Some of these gave access to quite refined facilities: 'Guest House. Dining room with three couches and furnishings' (*hospitivm hic locatur triclinivm cvm tribvs lectis et comm[odis]*).[38] A dining room of such a refined nature was found at the House of the Chaste Lovers on the Via dell'Abbondanza. The dining room's size and decorative scheme suggests that it may have been made available to the public. The decoration comprises scenes of post-banquet drinking, with some guests the worse for wear and others looking as if they are about to prove that the house was full of not-so-chaste lovers.[39] The guest house could sometimes have a bad reputation, however; its accommodation was often sub-standard and the clientele, both short- and long-term, were not always respectable.[40]

As for bars and pubs, the word *thermopolium* has been extensively used by modern writers for a place serving hot and cold drinks. Yet among Roman writers that term is rarely used, and then only by the comedian Plautus, writing over 250 years before the eruption.[41] Two terms used more often by the Romans are *caupona* (as mentioned above) or *copo*, applied mainly to a bar with seating, sometimes with

Fig. 54 Bar area with small storage jars set into the counter for the sale of dry goods and liquids. The household shrine (lararium) is at the end of the bar.

Bar of Lucius Vetutius Placidus, Pompeii

accommodation implied; and *popina* for a no-nonsense pub offering food and drink – and sometimes more. Looking at the physical remains of bars it is very difficult to distinguish a perfectly respectable caupona from an all-night, less than reputable, popina – though some have tried.[42] Archaeology cannot always provide evidence for distinctions that the Romans certainly made themselves.

However, the archaeology does preserve evidence of food preparation in some of these establishments. Some shops/bars/restaurants have a cooking area on a corner of the counter or elsewhere.[43] These are sometimes not particularly large,[44] but must have been adequate for their trade. Interestingly, there is a series of references to Roman emperors from Tiberius[45] to Nero[46] regulating and even banning the sale of hot food from the roadside shops and bars. This edict may have been aimed primarily at the establishments in densely built-up Rome, in order to limit the risk of fires and to prevent unruly, and potentially subversive, gatherings.[47] Either way, unless the cooking areas of the establishments in Pompeii and Herculaneum were all redundant, there were a lot of places selling food and hot drinks at the time of the eruption.

A good example of a bar, again on Via dell'Abbondanza, is the caupona of Lucius Vetutius Placidus (FIG. 54). At the front of the bar, overseen by the shrine of the household gods, was a large, U-shaped, marble-topped counter, with eleven inset storage jars or dolia. Such dolia are a distinctive feature of these commercial units, but no-one can agree what they were for. Some say they held, among other things, hot food, dried food, hot and cold drinks.[48] Others argue that they were used only for dried goods such as beans and dried fruit, pointing out that they were too porous for liquids and (a lesser concern for the Romans, perhaps) difficult to keep clean.[49]

Dolia in and around the cities have indeed yielded foodstuffs, from olives and grain to walnuts and flour, but those dolia were set into the floor. No foodstuffs have come from any that were set into counters – not even from Herculaneum, where organic material is much better preserved.[50] As for the possibility that these counter-top dolia held liquids, no trace of waterproofing has been found on the interiors of examples set into counters. But neither does it survive in most of the dolia that were evidently used for wine storage in the estates around the cities. On balance it seems likely that those in bar/shop counters were used for both wet and dried goods.

In the caupona of Lucius Vetutius Placidus, behind the bar and to the left was a large room for eating and drinking. Customers may have reclined here on couches, but the room was more likely equipped with tables and chairs or benches. (These could co-exist, as seen in the praedia of Julia Felix where a fixed *biclinium*, or two-couch eating space, lies opposite masonry tables and benches clearly designed for sitting not reclining.) The more refined dining took place at the rear of the premises. In the garden was a fixed masonry dining area (*triclinium*) (FIG. 55), protected from the sun by a pergola supported on two columns. From here diners looked over the small garden, with its fountain and herm of Bacchus.

Fig. 55 A fixed dining/drinking area (*triclinium*) set in a garden.

Bar of Lucius Vetutius Placidus, Pompeii

An indoor drinking/dining area with an elongated recess designed to take a couch.

Bar of Lucius Vetutius Placidus, Pompeii

Behind the bar area, on the right, was the owners' accommodation, including a small living space, an entrance area (*atrium*) with a small pool inset with coloured marbles, a bedroom and a small garden, colonnaded on one side. Facing out onto the garden and the fixed masonry dining area was a large room, decorated with fine wall paintings. The right-hand wall has a centrepiece showing the Greek mythological scene of Europa riding on the bull. This wall also has a low, angular recess, designed to take the long side of a dining couch (*kline*) (see p. 226). The opposite wall has a narrow niche for the short end of a similar couch. This, too, was definitely a dining room, perhaps for winter use. If these dining areas were for use only by the owners, then clearly they surrounded themselves with a little of the good life. Given the nature of the business, though, customers probably also had access to these areas. The discovery of dozens of amphorae and other pottery and bronze vessels suggests the owner viewed his home as very much part of his business.

It seems that this caupona was popular and busy just before the eruption, because a hoard of coins, probably representing the last few days' takings, was

ABOVE **Fig. 57 Detail of a fresco showing life in a bar.** Two customers squabble over a glass of wine held out by the barmaid.

Caupona of Salvius, Pompeii
H. 50 cm, W. 205 cm
MANN 111482

BELOW **Fig. 58 Two men playing *duodecim scripta* (backgammon) argue over the throw of the dice.**

Caupona of Salvius, Pompeii
H. 50 cm, W. 205 cm
MANN 111482

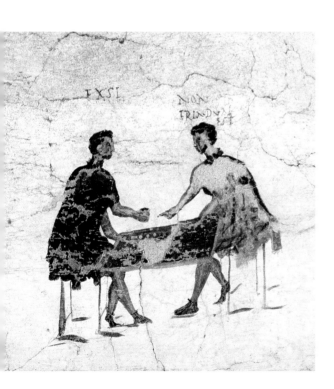

discovered in one of the dolia set into the counter.[51] The coins, over 1,600 in all, were mostly low (bronze) denominations, but together had a value of about 700 sesterces,[52] enough to buy a mule and a dozen new tunics. Many of the coins bore traces of cloth, suggesting they were in different 'cashing-up' bags. The coins date from as early as 285 BC, and came from as far away as Egypt and Turkey.[53] The people who used the bar had over three centuries of history in their hands.

As for the less reputable *popinae*,[54] Horace calls them greasy (*unctae*)[55] and filthy (*immundae*)[56] while Cicero thoroughly disapproves of them and those who frequent them.[57] Four scenes originally painted onto a wall of the bar of Salvius, Pompeii, have been put together into a type of strip cartoon[58] and give us some insight into the day-to-day life of some of these bars. The first shows a man kissing a woman, saying, 'I don't want to... (?) ...with Murtale'; the second shows two customers sitting down in true pub style, eagerly awaiting their drinks (FIG. 57). 'Over here!' calls one while the other cries, 'No, that's mine!' The waitress, carrying a jug and a glass, has seen it all before and says, 'Whoever wants it, come and get it,' then says to Oceanus (perhaps neither of the two men shown here), 'Come and drink.' The third scene shows two men apparently engrossed in a board game, perhaps *duodecim scripta*, a version of backgammon, very popular in the Roman Empire. 'I've got it,' yells one, while the other protests, 'That's not a three, it's a two' (FIG. 58).

The final scene, sadly damaged, shows two men, possibly the players seen before, brawling. Perhaps the dispute over the dice throw got out of hand. As one calls the other a c**ksucker (*fellator*) the landlord drags them out, saying, 'Right you two, outside if you want to fight.' This is perhaps not our typical picture of Roman behaviour, but many bars, even perhaps the caupona of Lucius Vetutius Placidus, must have witnessed such scenes. It is interesting to ponder how many of the customers could have read the 'speech bubbles' that accompanied the cartoons.

Just as the popina was looked down on by certain Romans, so some modern authors also attack it, placing it on the wrong side of the tracks in the 'moral geography' of the cities.[59] An almost logical outcome of looking down on the institution is to look down on those who worked in it, querying, in particular, their sexual morality. The fresco from the bar of Salvius perhaps shows intimacy between a customer and a member of staff, and some graffiti record specifically sexual encounters, for example, from the bar of Athictus in Pompeii: 'I screwed the barmaid'.[60] Elsewhere, graffiti explicitly state that girls could be bought for remarkably small amounts of money. Acria sold herself for 4 asses[61] (the price of a glass of decent wine), while Prima Domina (literally 'First Lady'), contrary to her name, could only demand 1½ *asses*.[62] Some of the sexual liaisons scrawled on the walls clearly took place, but possibly not all, and perhaps not in the way described.[63] Graffiti are not always true.

BAKERIES AND BREAD

Closely linked to ideas of hospitality is the production and sale of essential foodstuffs and drink. Three 'industries' of food and drink – bread, wine and fish sauce – were important to the economies of the cities and were closely linked to houses and their households.

According to the famous saying of Juvenal in his *Satires* (10.77–81) '…*panem et circenses*…', bread and spectacular entertainments were the two main concerns of the urban populace. They were also a priority for state and local government: the bakeries had to produce enough bread. There were around thirty bakeries in Pompeii at the time of the eruption,[64] with apparent concentrations on some roads, such as the Via Stabiana and the Via degli Augustali.[65] In addition, 'private' ovens in some of the larger houses may have had a wider local use – for the whole insula, perhaps. Herculaneum has so far produced evidence for only two bakeries, both situated in the block of properties in front of the recreation area (*palaestra*).[66]

A bakery (*pistrinum*) was divided into distinct areas for five different processes:[67] bringing in and storing the flour; 'kneading' (mixing) the dough; letting the bread rise; baking; and finally sale through connected shops. There is no evidence for independent millers, so the bakery (*pistor*) ground itself grain into flour using large mills made of lavastone (FIG. 61). Usually set on concreted rubble bases, these mills were made of two separate millstones. The lower stone (*meta*) was a hemisphere onto which slotted the upper stone (*catillus*), in the shape of an hourglass, which contained a concave surface in each half, one below for grinding over the meta and the other above for holding the corn to be ground. Holes in the side of the catillus were linked to a wooden and metal frame which lifted it up, creating the essential grinding space between the stones, and connecting them to the 'engine' of the mill: a donkey or mule. Corn was poured into the open part of the rotating catillus and was ground against the surface of the meta. Milled flour fell out onto the base, which was often covered in a sheet of lead

ABOVE **Fig. 59 Oven in the bakery of the House of the Chaste Lovers, Pompeii.**

BELOW **Fig. 60 Terracotta sign from above a baker's oven *HIC HABITAT FELICITAS* ('Good fortune lives here').**
From Pompeii (VI,6,18)
MANN 27741

ABOVE **Fig. 61 Lava millstone – the plinth
(*meta*) is obscured by the upper element
(*catillus*). The area is sheathed in lead
to facilitate collection of the milled flour.**

House of the Chaste Lovers, Pompeii

to facilitate gathering the flour. Research has shown that the millstones in these individual bakeries nearly all came from the area of Orvieto in central Italy.[68] This fine-grained stone allowed the grain to be ground much more finely.

The flour was then made into dough and mixed, sometimes by hand on troughs and tables, or in a kneading machine – a cylindrical vessel with internal paddles, turned by a slave or a mule.[69] Then the bread was left to rise before being baked in large ovens, which look very much like the modern pizza ovens of Naples.

A process as important as baking could not be left to chance, and so the help of the gods and spirits was invoked. Vesta, goddess of the hearth, was a very appropriate deity to guard the bakers and their bread, but to be sure they also used good luck symbols, especially the phallus. One example (FIG. 60) found above the opening of an oven in Pompeii proudly proclaims *HIC HABITAT FELICITAS* ('Good fortune lives here').

The classic loaf at the time of the eruption was round and marked into eight segments by radial lines cut into the bread before baking. A graffito suggests Pompeian bread had a good reputation: 'Traveller, eat bread at Pompeii but drink at Nuceria' (*Viator, Pompeis panem gustas, Nuceriae bibes*).[70] Pompeian bread may have tasted good, but analysis of the teeth of the victims has shown that minute fragments of grit, almost certainly from the lava millstones, gradually wore down teeth, sometimes right down to the root, causing serious health problems.[71]

In 1862 an oven in the bakery of Modestus in Pompeii was opened and found to contain eighty standard loaves, perfectly preserved, though carbonized, plus one much larger than usual with fourteen divisions.[72] A carbonized loaf from the House of the Stags (H) (FIG. 62) carries a name stamp, almost certainly made by a seal ring (below p. 107) reading *CELERIS Q. GRANI VERI SER(vus)* ('Property of Celer, the slave of Quintus Granius Verus'). Sometimes loaves were made at home and taken to bakeries for baking, a practice found until quite recently in much of Europe, so Celer could have belonged either to the baker or to the owner of the house. But his status as *SER(vus)* (slave) is explicit.

Bakers controlled the supply of a crucial daily staple and were familiar figures to most people, so it is, perhaps, not surprising to see them entering local politics. From Pompeii, the portraits of Terentius Neo (FIG. 112) and of the candidate distributing loaves on or after his election (FIG. 16) illustrate their importance. A prominent local politician, Caius Iulius Polybius, was supported by local bakers in two electoral notices, and may well have been the owner of the neighbouring bakery at the House of the Chaste Lovers.

**Fig. 62 Loaf of bread, marked into eight sections
and stamped with the name of a slave, Celer.**

House of the Stags, Herculaneum
D. 21 cm
MANN 84596

THE BAKERY OF THE HOUSE OF THE CHASTE LOVERS

This bakery was built onto the front of the House of the Chaste Lovers on the Via dell'Abbondanza (P). It was equipped with four lavastone mills driven by donkeys, a large oven, kneading and rising areas and a designated area at the front of the house which, it seems, acted as a bread shop – the tallies of sales are still scratched in the walls. The bakery was not functioning properly at the time of the eruption, and only one complete mill was in position (FIG. 61).

Nonetheless, people were clearly working and living there, since rooms, apparently unconnected with baking, were inhabited at the time of the eruption. Bedrooms, living areas (including a kitchen with a cooking platform, on which were the bones of a bird and a small boar piglet) and a large dining room, decorated with scenes of amorous banquets,[73] were all in use or under active repair. The septic tanks that served the toilets in the main house and the flats above were being emptied and serviced. The animals that turned the mills, delivered the flour and perhaps helped to transport the baked bread[74] had been still in their stable within the house, their skeletons lying where they had died (FIG. 63). They were all aged between four and eight years, an ideal working age. Their last meal of hay, now carbonized, was discovered in the manger. Clearly the bakery had been damaged during earthquakes and rebuilding was ongoing, but business was continuing.

Fig. 63 **Some of the donkeys and mules found in the stables next to the bakery area.**

House of the Chaste Lovers, Pompeii

WINE

Wine was the drink of choice in the cities, just as in the rest of the Roman world. Then, as now, vine-growing was a major activity in the countryside around Pompeii, and in Roman times, even within the city. Roman literature and art reflected the importance of the wine 'industry', often depicting the wine god Bacchus and his followers, the wild male satyrs and ecstatic female maenads.

Most of the wine consumed in the cities was made locally. At least forty local farms and estates had *cellae vinariae* or wineries, some producing on an enormous scale.[75] These estates are characterized by large numbers of dolia, buried up to the rim (*defossa*), in which the wine was stored as it matured. The Villa Regina at Boscoreale had eighteen of these (FIG. 64), while the Villa della Pisanella had eighty-four. Some were for olives and grain, but the vast majority contained wine.[76] Many of the dolia in both villas were still capped with terracotta lids and sealed with mortar, showing they were full when the eruption happened. Some, when opened, had traces of sediments and even the smell of wine.[77]

The wine remained in dolia until the following year, when it was sold or taken to the owner's house in the city (most of these estates were owned by wealthy city dwellers). Transportation of large quantities of wine required considerable effort, as each dolium could hold over twenty amphoras' worth (about 120 gallons or 545 litres). Dolia could not be moved easily, so many producers used a *culeus*, or ox-skin, which held the equivalent volume. A very badly faded fresco showing wine being decanted from an ox-skin into amphorae decorated the interior of a bar (VI,10,1) on the Street of Mercury (P). So central were these containers to day-to-day life that the amphora and the *culeus* became fixed imperial measures of liquids.

The arrival of wine in bulk containers might explain the stacks of empty amphorae in some of the finest houses, such as the House of the Silver Wedding[78] or the House of the Faun.[79] Clearly these were ready to be filled, probably with wine, though amphorae were also used for other liquids and dry goods. Hundreds of amphorae were discovered near the atrium (entrance area) of Villa B at Boscoreale, while in the atrium itself resin was being boiled up, perhaps to coat the interior of amphorae to make them watertight, or to seal their stoppers.[80]

Some wine did not travel very far, as several properties in Pompeii produced their own, including the Villa of the Mysteries, with its wine press and dolium yard.[81] One bar in Pompeii on Via di Nola (V,4,6–8) had a wine press, eight dolia and also a small bakery, so customers could have some bread with their wine.[82] The House of the Ship Europa in Pompeii had a sizeable vineyard, while other open spaces in Pompeii, such as the so-called cattle market near the amphitheatre, were in fact vineyards on a large commercial scale.[83] Some areas in Pompeii have today been replanted as an experiment with vines similar to those known to the Romans.

Fig. 64 Storage jars buried up to the rim (*dolia defossa*) used for storing wine.

Villa Regina, Boscoreale

Amphorae often carried a painted inscription (in Italian, *dipinto*). Some were very basic, like those on the amphorae from Villa della Pisanella marked *RUBR* (*um*) = *rubrum*, the Latin for 'red'.[84] Others served as address labels. A fragment of an amphora (FIG. 67) from Pompeii bears the words, 'For Albucia Tyche at Pompeii', suggesting Albucia was a landlady. Dipinti could also date a vintage. One neck and rim fragment is labelled: *Fal(ernum) Lucr(etianum) j L. Cornuf(icio) co(n)s(ule)* ('Lucretian Falernian wine bottled when L. Cornuficius was Consul [i.e. 35 BC]').[85]

Other labels gave the place of origin, both local ones such as 'Pompeianum', 'Falernian' and 'Horconia' (named after the Holconii, one of the elite families of Pompeii), and others elsewhere in Italy and the rest of the empire, especially the eastern Mediterranean ('Creticum' from Crete and 'Rhodium' from the island of Rhodes).[86] A complete amphora from Rhodes (FIG. 66) was addressed to L.(ucius) Sex(tus).

Just as today, wines were priced according to quality. In Pompeii a landlady called Hedone painted a notice on her bar offering 'good wine for one *as* [a low value Roman coin], better for two asses, and Falernian, the best Roman wine, for four *asses*'.[87] In a similar vein, a painted sign marking a tavern called *AD CUCUMAS* ('At the Pans') on the Decumanus Maximus in Herculaneum shows four wine jugs with prices from 2 to 4½ *asses* below each.[88] Above the jugs stands a draped and wreathed figure, with a painted inscription naming either *SANCUM*, the rather obscure Latin god Semo Sancus – god of oaths and a guarantor of good faith – or *SANC(T)UM*, a deity in general.[89] Over in Pompeii, one landlord diluted his wine and angered his customers. A now-vanished graffito says, 'Curses on you landlord…you sell water and drink the wine yourself'.[90]

FISH SAUCE: GARUM

Bread and wine were joined by what might seem to us a less obvious staple: fish sauce. Of all Roman sauces those most frequently mentioned were made from fish. Of the several types such as *garum*, *allec* and *liquamen*, the most popular was garum, a staple of Roman cuisine.[91] It also had medicinal applications and was supposedly useful against dog bites, dysentery and ear infections.[92] It was made in a range of different qualities, using everything from the finest cuts of fish to those parts of the fish you would not like to eat, fermented and processed. The writer Martial mentions 'Noble garum, made from the blood of a still gasping mackerel'.[93]

According to Pliny, garum was made on an industrial scale in Spain and North Africa and other areas of the Mediterranean, including Pompeii.[94] Bulk quantities travelled in amphorae, but smaller amounts were sold in a type of tall, one-handled, spindle-shaped vase, known in Latin as an *urceus* (plural *urcei*). Many urcei have been found in the cities and as far afield as southern France. Painted inscriptions on the vases describe the contents, nearly all stating that the contents are garum or liquamen. Of the more than two hundred of these distinctive vessels found in the cities, over a third have painted inscriptions bearing the name of a local businessman, Aulus Umbricius Scaurus, his family or agents. Umbricius Scaurus made so much money from the sauce that he saw his son become a magistrate, and bought a huge mansion in the west of Pompeii, decorating its atrium with depictions of sauce bottles bearing his name (below p. 102).

It is likely that processing took place away from the city near the sea and the River Sarnus, which provided the fish, salt and (very smelly) steeping tanks required. Once prepared, the product needed to be marketed. An inscription from Pompeii mentions sauce makers/vendors[96] (*salsamentarii*) and painted 'labels' on many urcei show that Umbricius Scaurus had a network of retail outlets, run by freedmen and family.[97] A label on a bottle from Moregine, near Pompeii (FIG. 69) reads *G(ari) f(los) F(los) scombri Scauri, ex officina Agathopi* ('The flower of the flower of [i.e. the absolute finest] mackerel garum, made by Scaurus, from the shop of Agathopus').

Another bottle (FIG. 68), made in Pompeii and discovered at Pozzuoli at the north of the Bay of Naples, carried a short inscription, GAR CAST, almost certainly an abbreviation of *GAR[um] CAST[imoniarum]*, a form of Kosher garum, made from fish without scales, described by Pliny in his *Natural History* (XXXI, 95). In the 1960s a shop selling garum was discovered in Pompeii.[98] This was a converted private house, with several dolia set into the garden, all containing the characteristic residue of garum – scales and fishbones– and a strong smell of fish when first excavated.[99] There were also amphorae, some containing garum residue and others upside-down, waiting to be filled. Clearly this shop on a very small scale was selling on garum made elsewhere, but sadly there was no mention of Aulus Umbricius Scaurus.

OPPOSITE, FAR LEFT **Fig. 65 Bronze lidded jug.**
Vesuvian area
H. 26 cm
MANN 68927

LEFT **Fig. 66 Terracotta wine amphora made in Rhodes.**
H. 64 cm
SAP 31824

BELOW LEFT **Fig. 67 Fragment of an amphora with an address in Pompeii.**
From Pompeii
H. 18 cm
SAP 13915

ABOVE **Fig. 68 Bottle for fish sauce (*garum*) with inscription suggesting it was perhaps Kosher garum.**
From Pozzuoli
H. 46 cm
The British Museum, 1856,1226.337

RIGHT **Fig. 69 Small terracotta bottle for garum from Moregine, near Pompeii.**
H. 24 cm
SAP 81744

WORKSHOPS

Many goods used in the cities, such as pottery, metalware and textiles, were almost certainly locally made. But there is only occasional evidence for 'light industry'[100] inside the city walls. Graffiti in the atrium of the House of Marcus Terentius Eudoxus (P) (VI. 13) suggest the presence of a weaving 'workshop' with up to eighteen weavers of whom seven were men. A house-cum-workshop at Pompeii (I,20,3) contained a kiln and seventeen plaster moulds used for producing terracotta oil lamps.[101] A two-part mould from the workshop is shown (FIG. 70) with an oil lamp almost certainly made on the premises (FIG. 71) depicting an identical scene. The mould was made of plaster mixed with marble dust to make it more durable.

Fingerprints smudged in the coloured slip that stains the mould remind us of the workers, probably slaves, who sat for hours on end making these lamps. Cheaply mass-produced, these lamps were the normal source of light for most people. The upper side, or *discus*, was usually decorated with scenes of mythology or scenes of daily life, in particular gladiators. Produced in quantity from easily available ingredients and found in the cities in large quantities, lamps are precisely the sort of items it made sense to produce locally, though even they were sometimes imported (above p. 58).

Another house in Pompeii (I,8,10) had a painted scene on the outside showing four potters at their wheels, suggesting a small pottery workshop.[102] Weaving was an activity carried out on a small scale in many homes, but there is very little evidence for large-scale textile manufacture. The large number of fullers' workshops (*fullonicae*) at Pompeii may suggest that cloth-making had a greater importance there, compared with the sole example at Herculaneum,[103] but evidence for production on more than a domestic scale is lacking.

Other tradesmen and craftsmen (and women) are known from inscriptions, graffiti or painted notices (usually giving electoral backing) such as barbers, carpenters, cobblers, engravers, perfume-sellers, scribes, weavers and so on. Most of them probably operated from their homes, but it can be difficult to find evidence of these tradesmen and artisans.

In Herculaneum an interesting group of commercial units was discovered on the ground floor of the large insula which fronted the *palaestra* complex at the top of Cardo V. Recent re-examination of the original excavation notebooks and finds has given us a clear picture of commercial life in this part of an 'ordinary' town.[104] There were over a dozen units in this block, including two bakers, two dyeing workshops (*officinae tinctoriae*) and a wine shop with racks of amphorae still in situ, along with the bed of the manager/owner (identified by amphorae with labels as L.R. Antigonus)[105] at the back and a marble bust of Bacchus, god of wine, presiding. There were also two shops/bars with dolia set into the counters and, very interestingly, a gem-cutter's workshop in which many cut and unfinished gems were found. This workshop may have been the source of several (lost?) gems found in the drain under the street (FIG. 72).[106] A graffito from Pompeii, 'Good luck to the gem-cutter Campanus, from Priscus the engraver',[107] indicates the different hands needed to cut gemstones and then engrave designs.

Fig. 70 Two-part plaster mould used for making pottery oil lamps decorated with a cupid holding baskets.

From Pompeii (1,20,3)
H. 5.5 cm, W. 11.5 cm, L. 16 cm
SAP 12398 A

Fig. 71 Pottery oil lamp with an identical scene, made in the above mould.

From Pompeii (1,20,3)
H. 4.8 cm, W. 4 cm, L. 10.1 cm
SAP 12383 B

Fig. 72 Carnelian seal stone showing two men and a ram.

Drain under Cardo V, Herculaneum
H. 1 cm
HCP 98

Fig. 73 The reception hall (atrium) of the Fullonica of Stephanus, with the shallow pool (*impluvium*) converted into a vat for soaking or washing.

Fullonica of Stephanus, Pompeii

Certain establishments have particular features – vats, furnaces and pools – that suggest they were involved in the processing of wool and the manufacture of cloth.[108] An *officina lanifricaria* was where raw wool was processed. These, like many of the bakeries, clustered in the narrow streets to the east of the Forum in a sort of (pre-industrial) industrial quarter. A *fullonica* was an establishment in which woollen cloth was processed – soaked, bleached, combed, dyed, dried and pressed ready for sale – while a *tinctoria* specialized in dyeing cloth. Both could serve as a commercial laundry.[109]

These establishments were often built into private houses, for example the Fullonica of Stephanus in Pompeii (FIG. 73), which was transformed after the quake of AD 62/3. The reception hall (atrium) and garden were radically altered. The pool in the atrium was enclosed by a high wall, turning it into a vat, while the roof was transformed into a flat terrace for drying textiles and clothing. At the rear of the house, part of the colonnade was taken down and the rooms behind converted to accommodate vats and basins for the laundering process.

In Herculaneum three cloth processing/laundry establishments are known, a fullonica built into a private house[110] and two dyeing works in the large residential/commercial block (*insula*) on Cardo V. Remarkable evidence is found in the huge drain that ran below the street, where the mortar of the wall opposite the waste-disposal chutes leading from the dyeing works was stained red by the waste water from the dyeing processes. Herculaneum has even preserved a wooden, screw-style clothes press, a unique survival from antiquity.

Fulleries may have doubled as laundries, but how often did the Romans wash their clothes and did they always use the fulleries?[111] Larger items, such as couch covers, cloaks and togas, were probably washed infrequently but needed the skills and space of the fullery. Smaller, lighter items could have been washed by slaves at home. Given the lack of known fulleries at Herculaneum, it is difficult to know how people would have coped otherwise.

Washing needed to dry. It is, perhaps, surprising to think of the interiors of Roman homes and even the streets strung with washing, the upper storeys and balconies linked by a network of washing lines, with garments and bedding suspended over balconies. Such homely details may serve as a reminder that Pompeii and Herculaneum were inhabited by people whose everyday activities and domestic concerns would be readily recognizable to us.

The streets served as the essential setting for both businesses and fine houses. The two were inextricably linked, parts of the same social and economic systems. For many inhabitants the business was a crucial element of the generation of wealth, which made ownership of such a beautiful home possible. Now it is time to enter the home and see what this wealth would bring and who, in the broadest sense, benefited from it.

III

ATRIUM

ATRIUM

LEAVING the busy street, and entering the heavy, decorated doors of the house, the visitor progressed through the narrow, intentionally restrictive entrance corridor (*fauces*) and reached the wide-open space of the *atrium*. The atrium was the hub of any Roman house of status, from which family and visitors moved to other areas of the home. It was the reception area for those who wished to meet the homeowners, and also the showcase in which the owners typically displayed the basis of their power: their wealth, their devotion to the gods and their ancestry.

It is unclear exactly when and where the atrium house originated. Some believe it came from Etruscan Italy, to the north of Rome.[1] By the 220s BC this type of house had arrived in Pompeii.[2] The name atrium may derive from the Latin *ater* ('dark'),[3] recalling the early history of the space, when it contained the hearth and kitchen; or it may derive from the Greek αἴθριον, meaning 'open to the sky'. The atrium was at one time the home's literal *focus* (the Latin for 'hearth'), its heart, and all family life went on within it, from weaving and washing to sleeping and dining.

In the centuries before the eruption, the atrium, like other areas of the Roman house, adapted to changing political and social needs and reflected increasing wealth. Houses grew in size, room function changed and specialized, and the atrium lost some of its more traditional uses such as cooking and formal dining.[4] Many houses acquired a separate kitchen, a dining area (*triclinium*) and an internal garden, the new focus for much of daily life. Nevertheless, although the form of the atrium varied from house to house and over time, it always formed the public–private interface between the home and the outside world and remained a hub for many day-to-day activities. At times, the atrium was also a workplace: business affairs were often conducted in the home. Some owners of atrium houses were important figures in city life, with great wealth and influence. They had numerous *clientes* (clients or dependents) bound to them through financial, commercial and social ties and favours.

THE PURPOSE AND IMPORTANCE OF THE ATRIUM

An atrium indicated the owner's participation in the web of patronage which powered the cities and the empire. This space was not just part of a home, it was a visual expression of the power and influence of the household and its head.[5] It followed that only those who participated actively in this system needed an atrium. In his work *On Architecture*, Vitruvius writes that ordinary people don't need such rooms; they go to

PREVIOUS PAGES **Fig. 74 Detail of a fresco showing Bacchus next to Mount Vesuvius (see fig. 106).**

Fig. 75 Atrium of the House of the Menander, Pompeii.

others to ask for favours.[6] In fact, 60 per cent of houses in the cities did not have an atrium.[7] But even those who did not possess a house with an atrium were aware of its importance and significance, because at some time or other they visited and came under the patronage of someone who did.

The formalized relationship between the master of the house (*dominus*) and his clients – in effect political and social dependents – was very important. Clients attended a daily morning audience (*salutatio*) with the dominus, usually held in the atrium, though smaller groups could have met in spaces such as the *tablinum*, the area between the atrium and the garden (see below pp. 103–15). The salutatio was an opportunity for various sections of society to approach their patron for support and favours, ranging from financial backing to political string-pulling. The satirist Juvenal portrays clients bickering over the order in which they are admitted to the home,[8] but clearly the ceremony was taken seriously by clients and patrons alike. It was a very Roman affirmation of status and power. On some occasions the dominus, if of magistrate status, sat on an ornate folding stool or *sella curulis*, of a type used by Senators of Rome itself; even the type of seat conveyed authority. If there were fixed daily routines, then the salutatio in wealthier homes may have been followed by business in the Forum, which was the economic, financial and social hub of the city.

The atrium's importance was reflected in its decoration. Some houses, such as the Samnite House (H) (FIG. 76) and the House of the Faun (P) retained their earlier décor in the atrium and elsewhere, even when other areas of the house were redecorated in new styles.[9] Yet although the atrium was clearly a vehicle for the display of power and influence, not all 'ordinary' life disappeared from it. Finds from numerous houses prove

that the atrium was used for all types of storage, for example in amphorae[10] or in wooden cupboards and chests.[11] This furniture has sometimes been preserved at Herculaneum in carbonized form, or cast in plaster of Paris by archaeologists in Pompeii, as in the House of the Ceii. Many storage units have disappeared or not been recognized, their presence indicated only by a heap of household articles and the tell-tale survival of rounded, bone door hinges.[12] A small carbonized cupboard (FIG. 77) from Herculaneum conveys a sense of ordinariness in the grandeur of the atrium.

In addition, the atrium is a common findspot for artefacts for spinning wool and weaving, including spindles, spindle whorls and loomweights, used to hold threads taut on the loom. Spinning and weaving were fundamental activities. Larger houses may have had designated slaves for the task, but in other houses all the women were involved.[13] The looms were clearly set up in some atria and, given that weaving was largely a woman's job, women must have been inhabitants of the space.[14] Women were an integral part of all areas of the home and were not restricted to particular 'women's rooms' or areas.[15] The biographer Cornelius Nepos writes, 'The lady of the house is at the centre of things' (*Matrona versatur in medio*).[16] The same was true, to a greater or lesser extent, for all women of the household.

It is surely reasonable to imagine that along with the women there were children sitting, playing and sleeping in the atrium.[17] Identifying children's possessions in the archaeological record of the cities is very difficult, but the physical remains of young victims of the eruption show that they were there in considerable numbers.[18] Evidence for children who were bored, or just being children, is seen in graffiti almost certainly scratched by children on the walls, for example in the dining room of the House of the Cryptoporticus (FIGS 79 and 236); or the bedroom of the House of the Chaste Lovers. Like women, children were not limited to any particular part of the home, and most of the activities involving them were centred there, including schooling. There is some evidence for schools in public areas, for example in the large *palaestra* (exercise area) where graffiti on columns included a list of pupils and the fees they paid,[19] and by the depiction of a school (with rather draconian discipline) among the colonnades of the Forum in Pompeii.[20] But most children received their fundamental education in the home, from members of the family, in particular the mother and educated slaves, or from trained educators brought in for the purpose.[21]

The atrium was the main crossroads of the house and was used by all members of the household (*familia*). The Latin word *familia* meant more than 'family'. It was a legally recognized term for one of the main building blocks of Roman society, a group of people linked by ties of blood and marriage.[22] It included not only the dominus, his wife (the *domina*) and their children, but also members of the extended family, as well as slaves, freedmen and sometimes even clients. All of these had a place within the life of the home, whether in the main house itself or in annexed commercial or rental properties. It is very difficult to know in absolute terms how many people an 'average' home contained, but in larger households there was probably a high proportion of slaves and freedmen.[23]

Slaves were absolutely central to most activities of day-to-day life. Even a smaller house would aspire to own at least one or two, while a home of reasonably good means could be expected to have a number of slaves. With few exceptions, most household 'servants' were probably slaves, some of whom were acquired through auctions, such as those administered by Lucius Caecilius Iucundus (below pp. 109–110). Others, called *vernae*, were born to slaves already within the household, and by the time of the eruption these may have been in the majority. Vernae were brought up within the home and would have been very much part of the household; in fact, slaves in most houses in the cities could probably expect a more comfortable life than many of the poorer, freeborn citizens. Some slaves had particular skills, such as cooking, hairdressing, gardening or husbandry, but many worked generally at whatever was required for the household's daily needs.

We can, perhaps, imagine, as one scholar put it, a 'promiscuous crowd' in the atrium.[24] The dominus or domina of the house would be receiving their clients, while slaves and

Fig. 78 Fresco showing a woman spinning wool.
From Pompeii
H. 19, W. 11.8
MANN 9523

Fig. 79 Graffiti on the lower part of a frescoed wall.

House of the Cryptoporticus, Pompeii
H. 205 cm, W. 273 cm
SAP 59469B

servants bustled in and about, tending to the day's necessary duties, and all to the background noise of whoops and cries of excited children. Suddenly the Roman family begins to be more visible and audible.

THE LAYOUT OF THE ATRIUM

As we have seen, entrance to the atrium from the street was through a narrow passageway. This often had mosaic decoration, such as the guard dog (FIG. 80) from the House of Orpheus (P). A similar mosaic at the front entrance of the House of the Tragic Poet (P) shows a fiercer dog on guard, his teeth slightly bared, though he is wearing a rather fetching red leather collar. An inscription advises visitors *CAVE CANEM* ('beware of the dog') (FIG. 81).

The atrium often afforded views designed to impress the visitor, whose gaze was directed towards features such as a fountain, as in the House of the Small Fountain (P), or a household shrine, for example in the House of the Tragic Poet (P). In most atria, at the centre of the floor, there was a rectangular pool called the *impluvium*, from the Latin 'where rain comes in'. Rainwater collected here from the opening in the roof, or *compluvium* ('where rain gathers'), and was fed into the domestic cistern below. The compluvium was fitted with waterspouts, often with lion's or dog's heads. Those smaller houses lacking the impluvium/compluvium set-up, and the decorative and functional elements that went with it, conveyed less social status.[25]

The water from the impluvium could be a vital element of the house's water supply, even for the wealthy who had piped water supplies (see below pp. 153–4). These were very often used for fountains and pools in the garden, though some atria also feature fountains. For household purposes such as cooking, washing and cleaning they needed the supply from the house's cisterns, accessed in the atrium or garden through a well-head or *puteal* of marble or terracotta. Around the impluvium in some houses were statues, sometimes incorporating fountains, and a marble table (see below p. 86) used to display family wealth.

There are several different types of atrium, which may in some cases represent chronological development, but which could equally be contemporary and represent varying degrees of wealth. The atrium house was one of the oldest types of house still visible in the cities at the time of the eruption.[26] Possibly the earliest was the 'Tuscan' (i.e. Etruscan) atrium. It was substantially open, its roof carried on beams which spanned the full width. A good example is found in the House of the Wooden Partition (H) (FIG. 109). This type of atrium afforded space and light for practical, domestic purposes as well as for activities such as the salutatio, and gave an uninterrupted vista through the house. A very simple type of atrium existed alongside the Tuscan. It was completely covered, or 'testudinate',[27] after the Latin *testudo* meaning 'tortoise'. Some examples of this type of house survive in Pompeii, for example the House of the Garden of Hercules.

A more ornate structure was the tetrastyle atrium (from the Greek for 'four columns'), with columns at each corner of the impluvium, for example the House of the Ceii (P) (FIG. 82). The most opulent development was the Corinthian atrium, with multiple columns. Though uncommon, this gives an immediate sense of grandeur, and is also very attractive. The finest surviving Corinthian atrium is in the House of Marcus Epidius Rufus (P), perfectly rebuilt after its near total destruction during the Allied bombardment in 1943 (FIG. 83).[28] Its elegant colonnade of fourteen columns is certainly striking, but loses the visual axiality through the house. The owner concentrated his visitors' attention on the atrium – perhaps because his garden was small. The side rooms to left and right have rare carved column capitals showing satyrs and maenads, the followers of Bacchus. These almost certainly date back to the second century BC and are very rare. Clearly the owner wanted to show his wealth and sophistication, and perhaps also to emphasize the age and high standing of his house. There were many factors, both practical and social, at play in the Roman home.

LEFT **Fig. 80 Mosaic of a guard dog.**

House of Orpheus, Pompeii
H. 80 cm, W. 80 cm
MANN 110666

BELOW **Fig. 81 Mosaic of a guard dog with the message CAVE CANEM ('beware of the dog').**

House of the Tragic Poet, Pompeii

Fig. 82 Tetrastyle atrium (with four columns).

House of the Ceii, Pompeii

Fig. 83 Corinthian atrium (with many columns).

House of Marcus Epidius Rufus, Pompeii

A STATEMENT OF WEALTH, ANCESTRY AND POWER

The public/private atrium became the showcase in which the family displayed the criteria which entitled them to retain the respect and loyalty of their peers and clients. Those criteria – wealth, pedigree and religious observance – were all linked.

WEALTH

Wealth, and by implication status and power, was reflected in the architecture, wall paintings, and so on, but in the atrium there were certain features which, more than others, expressed affluence. One of these was a strongbox, or *arca*, positioned in the atrium of some wealthier homes.[29] This had heavy wooden sides covered with iron sheets, held together with heavy, round-headed nails. A strongbox remains in situ in the atrium of the House of Obellius Firmus (P) (FIG. 84). It stands in full view, watched and protected[30] by the *lararium*, the shrine of the household gods, in the opposite corner of the atrium (see below).

A particularly fine arca was discovered at Villa B in Oplontis near Pompeii (FIG. 85).[31] The front is ornamented with a panel, inlaid with silver and copper, showing a theatrical mask surrounded by stars and a wreath of ivy leaves, flowers and tendrils. Above the panel is a bronze lion's head holding a ring and flanked by bronze cupids. Even the feet of the strongbox are decorated with griffins flanking a chalice. The work is exceptional and, unusually, we know exactly who made it. A rectangular panel below the lion's head has a Greek inscription in inlaid bronze, surrounded by acanthus leaves and tendrils: 'Pythonomus Pytheas and Nikokrates, the workmen of Herecleides made (this)'. Many Roman craftsmen had Greek origins, and had been brought to Italy as slaves, either from mainland Greece or parts of the Eastern Mediterranean, especially Egypt, which Rome had conquered. These artisans were probably all freedmen (ex-slaves) or their descendants. As skilled metalworkers they would be valued, and would enjoy higher status and probably better conditions than many others.

The impressive strongbox lid had a complex locking mechanism,[32] requiring several different procedures to open it. 'Guarding' the opening mechanism were two large hunting dogs – so-called Molossian hounds – their heads resting on their heavy paws. Accompanying each dog was a bird, usually identified as a duck – not the most obvious guardian for wealth. A goose is more likely, as it was the sacred geese of Juno Moneta, queen of the gods and patroness of Rome's mint, that in the city's distant past had saved it from Celtic invaders by raising the alarm with their honking.[33] (Because the geese, not the dogs, alerted the Romans, according to Pliny's *Natural History* (XXIX, 57)

FOLLOWING PAGES **Fig. 85 The strongbox from Villa B and details showing a theatrical mask in silver and copper inlay surrounded by ivy leaves and stars in copper; the plaque inscribed in Greek with the names of the makers; and the lid showing a guard dog and a (guard?) goose.**

Villa B, Oplontis
H. 102 cm, W. 140 cm
SAP 85179

Fig. 84 Atrium showing a strong box (*arca*) in situ with a shrine of the household gods (*lararium*) in the distance.

House of Obellius Firmus, Pompeii

LEFT **Fig. 86 Display table (*cartibulum*).**
House of the Prince of Naples, Pompeii

BELOW **Fig. 87 Cartibulum with a single support (*monopodium*) in the form of a panther.**
From Pompeii
H. 89 cm
SAP 54947

OPPOSITE **Fig. 88 Fresco showing a cartibulum with a silver drinking set.**
Tomb of Gaius Vestorius Priscus, Pompeii

every year in Rome a dog was punished by crucifixion.) Perhaps the 'decorative' geese and dogs are a reference to this legendary guarding role. At the centre of the lid is a bronze disc, showing a beautiful young woman or goddess, her hair flowing over her shoulder.

A more conspicuous show of wealth was found on the display table (*cartibulum*) often located at the head of the pool. Here, families displayed part of their family's silver or bronze, as the Roman writer Varro recalls.[34] A famous depiction of a cartibulum with its spread of silver is found on the wall of the tomb of Gaius Vestorius Priscus outside the Vesuvius gate, Pompeii (FIG. 88; below p. 238). Roman society and the home were based on the Roman preoccupation with status, defined by relative wealth – and what better way to show your status than by a display of beautifully crafted and hugely valuable silver?

Three main types of cartibulum are found in the cities.[35] The largest and most ornate was rectangular, with two substantial supports, usually carved with griffins or lion's heads, as in the House of the Prince of Naples (P) (FIG. 86). A less common type had four separate, straight legs, while the most common had a single stand, hence its Latin name *monopodium* – from the Greek for 'one foot'. The podium sometimes featured a face or bust, often Bacchus or a satyr, and occasionally was a complete sculpture, such as a panther, Bacchus' favourite animal (FIG. 87). Livy said the first monopodium was brought to Rome from the Greek kingdom of Asia (Western Turkey) in 187 BC as booty, along with ornate couches and precious covers.[36] This versatile one-footed table was also found in smaller rooms and gardens.[37]

On the cartibulum visitors could see part of the family's dining silverware, the *ministerium escarium*, or their drinking silverware, the *ministerium potorium*. The latter might include such items as drinking cups, and ladles.

Some families were immensely wealthy and the cities have produced major treasures of silverware. The most spectacular of these was found in 1895 in the Villa of the Silver Treasure at Boscoreale, near Pompeii.[38] This consisted of 106 pieces of silverware and large quantities of gold and silver coins and jewellery. Another, larger, treasure was found in 1930 hidden in the cellar below the baths of the House of the Menander (P).[39] This comprised 118 pieces of silverware, from cups, dishes and jugs to spoons, pepper pots, mirrors and even egg cups. There was also a large quantity of jewellery, including eleven rings and three pairs of earrings.

The beds discovered in the same cellar may well have been for slaves guarding this major family treasure. The most recent discovery came in 1999 during excavations at Moregine near Pompeii.[40] Here, twenty vessels of silver, including cups and dishes in groups of three or four, were discovered packed tightly into a wicker basket.

Many other houses would have had silver dinner services and other valuables equal to, or even greater than, the treasures mentioned above, but a great deal of silverware, like sculptures and prized furniture, was almost certainly taken away before the eruption, or salvaged afterwards (below p. 301). On the other hand some families, such as those living in the House of the Silver Treasure (P)[41] or the House of the Theatrical Paintings,[42] seem to have had only a few silver vessels – fewer than a dozen pieces were found in each. Many houses possessed no silver at all.

ANCESTORS AND NOTABLES

Power did not depend solely on current wealth and status. For the Romans, visibly displaying a family's pedigree through portraits and other images was very important.[43] One type of household portrait found in the atrium was a herm, a marble pillar topped by a portrait bust and sometimes given genitals in the case of males. An example found in the atrium of the House of Lucius Caecilius Iucundus (FIG. 90) was inscribed:

GENIO L[UCII] NOSTRI
FELIX L[IBERTUS]

'To the Genius of our Lucius.
I, Felix his freed slave (dedicated this herm)'

The face is almost excessively realistic, creased and furrowed and with a huge wart-like growth (or polyp) on his left cheek. It is truly a 'warts and all' portrait, but the slight smile evokes his personality in a very immediate way. This same house produced a collection of writing tablets (below p. 109) recording the banking and business affairs

Fig. 89 (l–r)

Silver cup on three feet in the form of lion heads.

From Herculaneum
H. 7 cm, D. 10.3 cm
MANN 25601

Silver one-handled cup (*calathus*).

House of the Silver Treasure,
Pompeii (VI,7,20–22)
H. 9.5 cm, D. 13 cm
MANN 25368

Silver ladle (*simpulum*).

From Herculaneum
H. 10.2 cm, D. 6.5 cm
MANN 25707

Silver ladle (*simpulum*).

House of Inachus and Io, Pompeii (VI,7,19)
H. 10.5 cm
MANN 25714

of a man called Lucius Caecilius Iucundus. The portrait may be of him, or perhaps of a predecessor with the same name. It is very significant that this herm was set up not by the person portrayed, but as a gift from one of the family's freedmen. Banking, like many other professions, was run largely by slaves and ex-The freedman Felix, who set up the herm, was clearly a senior figure in the household. By erecting a herm in the centre of the home showing the 'Genius' or life force of Lucius, Felix was recreating in a domestic environment the honours paid in public places to magistrates and other notables for their generosity to the public. Felix may have been thanking his patron for his freedom. One possibility is that Felix is the Lucius Caecilius Felix [44] mentioned on the earliest writing tablet. He set up the herm to his (ex-) master Lucius Caecilius Iucundus, and it was the son (or freedman) of Felix who was the (second) Lucius Caecilius Iucundus named in the tablets.[45] The last record in his archive dates to AD 62, possibly the year of the massive earthquake that shook the area[46] – a precursor of the eruption. This date may be coincidence, but it could indicate a cessation of activities by Lucius Caecilius Iucundus, if not his death. The lararium of the house featured reliefs showing recognizable monuments in the city, such as the Capitoline temple in the Forum, being violently shaken by an earthquake (FIG. 357).

Another realistic bronze head (FIG. 93) was also once part of a herm, the body this time made of wood, not marble.[47] The lined face with its rather startled expression, emphasized by inset marble and glass eyes, seems very modern. For the Romans the lifelike nature of portraits such as these was important as they looked over (and after) the *familia*. We do not know whether these people were alive or dead when commemorated. The portraits resemble Roman funerary portraits, but living people could have been shown, especially a freedman responsible for the rise in wealth and status of his household. Certainly herms were expensive and were an appropriate alternative to the larger statues found only in more aristocratic homes. More importantly, herms gave freedmen an equivalent to the 'ancestor' busts their slave history did not allow them, indicating, as one specialist has nicely pointed out, 'a limited past but a limitless future.'[48] There were also many portraits of women, revealing the respected social status of some of them in this period (above p. 40). From Pompeii comes a beautiful portrait of a woman in mosaic (FIG. 92). Although the mosaic was reused in a decorative panel on the floor in the AD 50s, it was originally probably set into a wall some fifty years earlier.[49] It shows a woman who was clearly a very important member of the household at the time of its commission.

Fig. 90 (left) and Fig. 91 (overleaf) Marble and bronze herm of Lucius Caecilius Iucundus.

House of Lucius Caecilius Iucundus, Pompeii
H. 173 cm, W. 35 cm
MANN 110663

FOLLOWING PAGES
Fig. 92 Mosaic portrait of a woman.

From Pompeii (VI,15,14)
H. 34 cm, W. 29 cm
MANN 124666

Fig. 93 Bronze head of a herm with inset marble and glass eyes.

House of the Citharist, Pompeii
H. 37.5 cm, W. 23.5 cm
MANN 4989

Fig. 94 Marble head of a *materfamilias*, the female head of the household.

From Herculaneum
H. 50 cm, W. 19.5 cm
MANN 6247

From a statue set up in a public building in Herculaneum comes the head of a Roman lady almost certainly named Terentia. In order to be awarded a statue of this sort she must have been a wealthy benefactress, and perhaps also a priestess like Eumachia (above p. 39). She is almost certainly a *materfamilias*, the female head of the household (FIG. 94), looking rather world-weary, but immaculately coiffured. She has done her duty, brought up the children and taken care of the household, but given what we know about Roman society, she could also have operated a very successful real estate business or owned brick and tile factories.

PIETY TO THE GODS

Domestic religion was an important part of daily life. The most visible manifestation of piety to the gods was the presence in many atria of a domestic shrine, called by modern scholars a lararium (plural *lararia*), after the Lares, guardian spirits who protected the home.[50] A common form of shrine was an *aedicula*, from the Latin for 'little temple', a permanent masonry structure with an upper, columned part, as in the House of the Menander (P) (FIG. 95). This form of aedicula is astonishingly similar to the *nicchie* or wall-mounted shrines to the Virgin Mary in modern Naples. In fact, *nicchie* containing Her image, or those of saints, with lights, flowers, and other offerings, give a good idea of the appearance of Roman lararia.

The lararium of the House of Marcus Epidius Rufus (P) was dedicated to the Lares and the Genius or life force of the head of the household (FIG. 96) by his freedman. A marble plaque set into the front reads:

GENIO M(ARCI) N(OSTRI) ET
LARIBUS
DUO DIADUMENI
LIBERTI

'To the Genius (life force) of our Marcus and to the Lares, the two Diadumenus brothers, freed slaves [dedicated this]'

This may be the Marcus Epidius Rufus mentioned on a ring seal from the house. The Diadumeni were freedmen, probably freed by Marcus, so they had good reason to set up the inscription. For them the home was their world and refuge, so it was natural to associate the Lares with their benefactor. Gifts such as these were a concrete manifestation of the social relations within the home and in wider society.

The lararium, great or small, was a main focus for domestic religion.[51] Small statuettes representing the Lares (FIG. 97) and other deities important to the house were placed inside, along with lamps and miniature altars for making sacrifices of incense, nuts and fruit. These altars ranged from fine marble (FIG. 100) to simple terracotta.[52] One of these, from Pompeii, still preserves the ash from its last use (FIG. 99).

At Herculaneum wooden shrines have been discovered.[53] A spectacular example which gave its name to the House of the Wooden Shrine is an aedicula with wooden columns supporting the architrave, framing double doors. Behind the doors were found

LEFT **Fig. 95 Lararium from the House of the Menander, Pompeii.**

BELOW **Fig. 96 Inscription from the lararium in the House of Marcus Epidius Rufus, Pompeii.**

TOP **Fig. 97 Bronze statuettes of household gods (lares).**
House of the Red Walls, Pompeii
H. 21.5 cm, W. 10.5 cm
MANN 113261-2

RIGHT **Fig. 98 Bronze statuette of Jupiter, king of the gods.**
House of King Joseph II, Pompeii (VIII,2,39)
H. 12.5 cm, W. 7 cm
MANN 5050

Fig. 99 Terracotta incense burner with ash from its last use.

From Pompeii (II,8,5)
H. 13.5 cm, D. 25 cm
SAP 10697

Fig. 100 Marble miniature altar with bronze attachments.

From Pompeii (I,7,1)
H. 20 cm, W. 20 cm
SAP 3217

statuettes of the gods, so it almost certainly had a religious function; but below is a cupboard for the storage of more mundane objects such as jugs and cups.[54]

Around these lararia the head of the household, the pater (or occasionally the mater) familias, led the household in daily prayer and probably also on special occasions such as birthdays, or new year, or a child's naming day.[55]

We do not know the details of worship, but it involved fixed rituals, probably culminating in a sacrifice of specific foods for the gods. In Terzigno a real altar was built in front of the painted one, so that genuine sacrifices appeared to be approached by painted sacred serpents. Recent excavations in the garden of the House of the Greek Epigrams (P) uncovered pits containing carbonized remains of possible domestic sacrifices, including chicken and pig bones, pine cones and figs. Pits in the garden of the House of Amarantus contained charred cakes, walnuts, eggs, grain and cockerels' heads, confirming elements of ancient descriptions of sacrifices[56] and corresponding to illustrations of the components of such sacrifices, for example on painted lararia. Carbonized figs, walnuts and pine cones were also found at Herculaneum in the Cardo V drain that served the insula block. Apartment dwellers sacrificed to the gods like anyone else, but in the absence of gardens to take the waste, they may well have put the remains of their sacrifices down the toilet.[57]

ABOVE **Fig. 101 Wooden statuette, possibly representing a female ancestor.**

House of the Wattlework, Herculaneum (III,13-15)
H. 30.4 cm, D. 12.5 cm
SAP 75598

LEFT **Fig. 102 Painted lararium.**

Servants quarters, House of Julius Polybius, Pompeii

Some shrines were painted in niches built into the wall, or painted onto the wall itself – sometimes on a large scale, as in the House of Julius Polybius (FIG. 102). Although the atrium was the usual place to find a lararium, many were situated elsewhere, in the garden peristyle (colonnaded court), toilet or kitchen. In fact the kitchen was the most common place to find a painted shrine, probably through its close association with the hearth.

Alongside the Lares on the shrines were statuettes or paintings of other deities who the family especially honoured.[58] There were the Olympian gods such as Jupiter (king of the gods), Venus (patroness of Pompeii) and Mercury, the god of commerce,and sometimes gods other than the Olympians. In the peristyle of the House of the Gilded Cupids there were apparently two cult areas. The first was an aedicula built against one wall, while the other was painted on adjoining walls in a corner of the peristyle. The paintings show sacred serpents (*agathodaimones*) at an altar, with four Egyptian deities: the goddess Isis, her consort Serapis, their son Harpocrates and the jackal-headed god Anubis. On the other wall were symbols connected with Isis, such as a sistrum (rattle), and a cobra to complete the Egyptian flavour.

The possible existence of a Jewish community in the cities[59] is implied by graffiti mentioning Jewish names, such as Martha, in the House of the Centenary or the Jewish names of vendors of an apartment near the Forum Baths,[60] and a reference to the cities of Sodom and Gomorrah[61] from the Old Testament of the Bible.[58] Also showing familiarity with the Old Testament is a depiction of the Judgement of Solomon from the garden of the House of the Doctor (P).[62] Then there is the manufacture, almost certainly in Pompeii, of garum for the kosher market (above p. 69). Regarding Christianity, however, there is no irrefutable proof. The famous (but sadly no longer extant) 'cross imprint' above a small cupboard on the upper floor of the House of the Bicentenary (H) is more likely to be the trace of a shelf bracket than a cross.[63]

Much rarer than painted images and statuettes are images made as part of domestic worship out of wood or wax. very few have survived, but in the House of the Menander (P), which possesses a formal aedicula-style shrine in the atrium, archaeologists obtained plaster casts of five small herms and portraits (probably intended to represent humans rather than gods) in a separate shrine in a niche in the peristyle (FIG. 103).[64] There was also an altar for sacrifices and a small podium for a lamp. Clearly they had importance for the family. These images may have been present in many houses, but have not survived or been detected.

At Herculaneum several crude wooden images, perhaps portraits, were discovered in the 1960s, including a male herm (FIG. 104) and a female head (FIG. 101). These are very sketchily made, and it is possible that either such naïve carving was intentional, or that the pieces were a local phenomenon, or that they were deliberately old-fashioned (the most sacred statue of Rome was said to be the ancient wooden statue of Athena, the *Palladion* in the temple of Vesta). It is also possible that the busts not only appeared old but really

were old. Some have seen them as portraits of current family members,[65] but it is very possible that these images were part of domestic religion in the form of a cult of ancestor worship,[66] as mentioned by Pliny.[67]

In the House of the Centenary (P) a corner of the service area was transformed into a large domestic shrine, complete with a precinct wall. One wall had an aedicula flanked by painted household gods with birds and garlands above (now mostly destroyed). The other wall bore an image of Bacchus (FIG. 106), his body a mass of grapes, standing by what could be a stylized view of Mount Vesuvius, its lower slopes covered in vine trellises. Bacchus was strongly linked to Vesuvius and was one of the deities most celebrated in the cities.[68] The prominence of Bacchus in the lararium might, perhaps, indicate that the household had commercial links with the wine trade.

Commerce was very important for Pompeii, as we have seen, and the River Sarnus played a crucial role in transport, echoed in a very unusual lararium from Pompeii (FIG.105). The arched, masonry lararium is painted red, with the niche showing the Genius of the household making offerings at an altar. Inside archaeologists discovered two statuettes of the Lares, a bronze bowl and a bronze lamp.[69] On the exterior is a painted scene of daily life in Pompeii's port on the Sarnus, with a barge of goods being pulled by mules and goods being unloaded. All of this is presided over by the reclining figure of the River Sarnus.

OLD MONEY, NEW MONEY

Many of the well-appointed houses in Pompeii and Herculaneum belonged to the established aristocracy, but there is plenty of evidence that newcomers were joining them in buying and embellishing beautiful homes. Some, as we have seen from citizen lists in Herculaneum or dedications and statues (above p. 88), were freedmen (ex-slaves). But not all. Freeborn entrepreneurs were also making fortunes in the cities, and a very good example is the sauce magnate Aulus Umbricius Scaurus, whom we met in the previous chapter.[70]

Scaurus' name has the *tria nomina* (three names) usually indicating Roman citizenship. This Scaurus made his considerable fortune not through ancestral lands or banking, but from a very day-to-day product – fish sauce. The Roman conquest of the Greek kingdoms had transformed Roman art and society and even cuisine.[71] Apicius' cookery books (below p. 231) show the extent to which Roman food had changed, through the increased use of sauces, spices and pickles.

Umbricius Scaurus became wealthy, and he and his family were important figures in the community. Outside the 'Herculaneum gate' at Pompeii was the tomb of Umbricius Scaurus' son – also called Aulus Umbricius Scaurus – who predeceased his father. The inscription records that the Council gave money for his tomb, provided the land and, most extraordinary of all, erected a statue in the Forum showing Umbricius Scaurus Junior on horseback, an honour normally reserved for the highest notables. Umbricius Scaurus Junior had held the duumvirate, a very important magistracy in the city, but even so, in honouring him, the city fathers were really angling for the continued patronage of his father. New money was power in the cities, and the doors of Pompeian society were firmly open for the 'Ketchup king of Campania', as one scholar called him.[72]

We can identify Umbricius Scaurus' home with certainty since his name was written on it in stone – three times. The house[73] is situated on the high slopes at the western edge of Pompeii, set over three levels, with three atria, a colonnaded garden and its own baths. In one atrium, there were four mosaic panels around the pool, each showing an *urceus* (sauce bottle) with an inscription (FIG. 107). Two mention garum, and two the other major fish sauce, *liquamen*, and three give Umbricius Scaurus' name. Some of the inscriptions – identical to those on urcei – describe the contents as the 'flower' of garum or liquamen. Some have drawn parallels between this Umbricius Scaurus and the Scaurus known to Trimalchio, the fictitious freed slave whose vulgarly ostentatious lifestyle is satirized by the writer Petronius in his *Satyricon*.[74] It is certainly likely that some of the 'old money' in the cities considered both the fictional Trimalchio and the real Scaurus vulgar newcomers, but it is unlikely that Umbricius Scaurus, courted by the city fathers and proud of his origins and his trade, would have cared. The future of Roman society was increasingly in the hands of people like him.

For Umbricius Scaurus, and other upwardly mobile members of society, an area of the house off the atrium called the *tablinum* played an essential part in confirming his role in Roman society. It encompassed record-keeping (from business receipts to certificates of citizenship) and archives (and, by extension, literacy and literature), all against a backdrop of the Greek culture that was so important in affirming the status of '*nouveaux riches*' and old wealth alike.

Fig. 107 Panel of a mosaic floor, showing a container of fish sauce bearing the inscription G.F SCOM[bri] SCAURI EX OFFI[ci]NA SCAURI ('the flower of Scaurus' mackerel garum from the factory of Scaurus').

House of Aulus Umbricius Scaurus, Pompeii
H. 74 cm, W. 31 cm
MANN 15190

THE TABLINUM

In many atrium houses the tablinum occupied a space between the atrium and the colonnaded garden or peristyle. Although its positioning is fairly standard, its form can vary, from a distinct room to an enlarged corridor. Even as a room, it is sometimes only minimally separated from the atrium, by a small step or ridge of marble.[75]

In the early history of the Roman house, the tablinum had (allegedly) been the place for the marital bed.[76] As the home developed it was increasingly used as a reception space. Vitruvius includes the tablinum among those spaces considered 'public' and integral to the workings of the atrium house, and unnecessary for the common man.[77] It designated a certain status, [78] and may have been a place to which the owner could retire from the atrium with special guests.Pliny, expanding on the idea of the tablinum as a place of privileged status, describes it as a form of archive or office[79] '…filled with books and records of important events in a political career' (*tabulina codicibus implebantur et monimentis rerum in magistratu gestarum*).[80]

The tablinum could be separated off in many houses. The great wooden partition in a house in Herculaneum (FIG. 109) could effectively seal off the tablinum area, and there is evidence that elsewhere curtains and heavy hangings were also used, held back when required by holders (FIG. 108). In some tablina there is archaeological evidence for couches,[81] used, perhaps, for private meetings with the owner(s), for relaxing or, on some occasions, for dining.[82] The owner wanted an area of beauty for himself, guests and family, so the decoration of the tablinum is often of higher quality

ABOVE **Fig. 108 Bronze curtain holder in the form of a ship's prow.**

House of Apollo the Lyre-Player, Herculaneum
H. 15.5 cm, W. 14.9 cm
SAP 77231

RIGHT **Fig. 109 Wooden partition (central part now missing) used in some houses to screen off the tablinum area from the atrium.**

House of the Wooden Partition, Herculaneum

Fig. 110 Looking across the atrium into the tablinum.

House of Lucretius Fronto, Pompeii

than that of the atrium to which it was attached. A good example is the very finely decorated tablinum in the House of Lucretius Fronto (P) (FIG. 110).

The two side walls of this tablinum (FIG. 241) – it was open on the other sides to the atrium and the garden – feature large expanses of colour framed by elongated architectural details and borders filled with small, detailed motifs of objects from daily life and real and mythical creatures. The side panels feature small but very finely detailed images of seaside villas, while the central panels show two famous mythological couples, Venus and Mars and Bacchus and Ariadne.

In some houses there were libraries (*bibliothecae*). In 1752 at the Villa of the Papyri, Herculaneum[83] (see also below p. 109) hundreds of scrolls were found in and around two rooms, one of which may have been a tablinum.[84] Archaeological evidence for archival use of the tablinum is also provided by wall paintings, which often show writing materials or people reading and writing. The link between writing materials and money is also clearly shown in many frescoes from the cities (FIGS 111–13, 116), implying that writing and accounting often went on in the same area – the tablinum.

There is also evidence, as in the atrium and the areas around the garden, for storage cupboards and chests that contained the pottery, bronze and glass vessels often associated with dining[85] and the general odds and ends of everyday life. Like the atrium, the tablinum had a workaday aspect to its use.

What these storage units in the tablinum did not contain were the remains of documents. In fact no tablets have ever been found in a tablinum; instead they have been discovered in simple rooms and storage areas on the upper floors.[86] Perhaps the role of the tablinum was changing. These collections of tablets preserve different aspects of the complex 'paperwork' of the Roman bureaucracy, but they can only tell part of the story of the houses and their inhabitants. They were assembled over time (the earliest tablet discovered so far, from the House of the Alcove (H), dates to 8 BC)[87] and are only partial, through selection or because of destruction processes during and after the eruption. The original owners could have moved house, or even died, by AD 79.

These records, though incomplete, paint the most detailed picture we have of the complex lives of people in the cities. About a dozen collections have survived (four from Pompeii and eight from Herculaneum), with subject matter ranging from the dealings of the Pompeian auctioneer and entrepreneur Lucius Caecilius Iucundus to

Fig. 111 'Sappho': fresco of a lady holding a stylus to her lips, with a writing tablet in her left hand.

From Pompeii
H. 37 cm, W. 38 cm
MANN 9084

OPPOSITE **Fig. 112 Fresco portrait of the baker Terentius Neo and his wife.**

House of Terentius Neo, Pompeii
H. 60 cm, W. 70 cm
MANN 9058

archives from Herculaneum recording Cominius Primus' property disputes, Calatoria Themis' claim to the young girl Petronia Iusta and the application for citizenship by the freedman Venidius Ennychus and his wife. Through these documents we can glimpse a whole group of real people, residents of the cities.

In the period of the eruption there were two main methods of writing down and storing domestic documents. Literature and personal correspondence was written on lengths of papyrus, a form of ancient paper made from bonded strips of the papyrus reed,[88] originally from Egypt. Papyrus was written on with a split reed (*calamus*), quill or metal pen, using black ink (*atramentum*), made from carbon mixed with gum and water. It was then rolled up into cylinders called scrolls – the most convenient way to deal with lengths of up to 9 m (about 30 ft). Papyrus letters and other documents were sealed with wax impressed with the gemstone of the owner's signet ring.

Other business and legal documents were written on wooden tablets faced with wax. A famous fresco from Pompeii (FIG. 111) shows a beautiful young woman, known widely as 'Sappho' (the Greek poetess), holding tablets and a stylus. Tablets were usually square or rectangular and, although now blackened by the heat of the eruption, were originally made of pale wood: pine for more important documents, boxwood for others. They had recessed surfaces filled with wax, onto which writing was inscribed with a pointed metal 'pen' called a stylus, and were bound together in groups of two (diptychs) or three (triptychs) to form a document folder, or *codex*, the last page of which bore the list of witnesses and the impressions of their ring seals. The whole document was then closed and formally sealed. There was often a summary in black ink on the smooth, outer face of the last page, giving a useful description of the contents.[89] A codex could be reused, but most were used only once, then archived. These documents were so important that the Emperor Nero passed a law insisting on a design that was difficult to forge.[90]

The importance of tablets and scrolls is strikingly shown in one of the best-known images from the cities (FIG. 112). This painting of a man and his wife came from the House of Terentius Neo (P), the owner tentatively identified, like so many others, from the information in painted electoral notices. It was painted in a prominent place on the far wall of the tablinum. The room was decorated in the Fourth Pompeian wall-painting style (see p. 210), and was probably remodelled after the earthquake of AD 62/3. Like the owner of the House of the Chaste Lovers (P), Terentius Neo almost certainly made a living from the bakery set up in his house at some stage after the earthquake. In fact, the painting was positioned in such a way that family, bakery staff and visitors would all see it when they came out of the long corridor linking the bakery and the home.[91] Perhaps the fresco was a reminder that the owners were watching, or an encouragement to 'work hard and maybe you'll get to where we are'. Or perhaps, like busts and dedications in the atrium, it was a gift from the couple's freedmen or clients? A painting of Cupid and Psyche in a passionate embrace (FIG. 133) painted on the wall above the couple[92] reveals that they are husband and wife, partners of the heart as well as the reckoning tablet.

The wife, with a certain air of refinement, wears a red tunic and a mantle over her shoulders and has centrally parted hair, bound by a headband and falling in a series

Fig. 113 Fresco showing writing materials: a wooden writing tablet, scroll and ink pot.

House of Marcus Lucretius, Pompeii
H. 20 cm, W. 31.4 cm
MANN 9818

of thin ringlets on her brow – a hairstyle popular in the AD 50s–60s.[93] Her only jewellery is a pair of heavy pearl earrings, suspended from an emerald at the lobe. Terentius Neo, shown with a rather patchy beard and moustache, wears a white toga. This could well be the specially bleached *toga candida*, identifying him as a *candidatus* – a contender for political office.

In her left hand the woman holds a triptych (three-tablet document), identical to carbonized examples from the cities (above p. 107). In her right, she holds a stylus or writing implement, brought to her lips in a gesture of contemplation. Neo looks out at us, his right hand grasping a papyrus scroll. Sadly its small, red *syllabus* (identification label) is blank. The message of the painting is clear. Would-be successful businessmen or women and politicians chose to be pictured with scrolls and tablets because they suggested learning, influence and power. An interesting point is that the woman stands in the foreground and is the only one of the two shown writing. Was she perhaps scribing for her husband? The painting, executed only some fifteen years before the eruption, is unique among all surviving frescoes from the cities for its realism and is surely intended to be a true portrait of the young couple. Some have commented on the peasant 'Samnite traits' of Terentius Neo's face.[94] But the painter has shown the couple as literate, even learned, and – very importantly – as equal stakeholders both in their business and in their life, both in the household and Roman society.

The connection between documents and status can also be seen in a wall painting from the House of Marcus Lucretius (P) (FIG. 113), a still life with *instrumentum scriptorium* ('writing materials').[95] In the centre is a wooden tablet shown with writing, made by the stylus on the left. At the top is a sealed papyrus letter, addressed: *M. Lucretio flam(ini) Martis, decurioni Pompei(s)* ('To Marcus Lucretius, Priest of Mars and Decurion [City Councillor] at Pompeii'). The Lucretii were an old, established Pompeian family, though the Temple of Mars has not yet been identified. The dark wedge-shaped object below is a label, while at bottom right is an inkwell with a pen inside it. Numerous frescoes (often in the tablinum) show writing materials or people reading and writing. Large numbers of the raw materials for literacy have been discovered in the cities, such as inkwells (for writing on papyri) and styli (for writing on tablets).

The extreme heat and the conditions of the eruption have preserved both papyri and wooden tablets. Some papyri have been found at Pompeii[96] but are now lost. The finest collection of papyri in the cities are those found at Herculaneum in the 1750s in the Villa of the Papyri, an enormous villa to the east of the city, explored by tunnelling through as much as 24 m (80 ft) of volcanic debris.[97] The villa was carefully mapped by the overseer of the works Karl Weber, so it is possible to see exactly where the many finds from the villa were discovered. Mosaics, frescoes and dozens of marble and bronze statues and busts were found, including the 'dancers' (FIG. 180), the piglet (FIG. 182) and Pan and the Goat (FIG. 195). The villa's probable owner was Lucius Calpurnius Piso Pontifex (FIG. 114), a relative of Julius Caesar. The find that gave the villa its name consisted of the carbonized remains of some 1,100 scrolls. Some were heaped on the floor, but others were in special scroll boxes (*capsae*) or still in book presses and shelves. The scrolls were so badly carbonized they were thought to be logs – some were even used as fuel. But within a few years of their discovery a monk from the Vatican library, Antonio Piaggio, succeeded in creating a machine which could (slowly and painstakingly) unravel the scrolls so they could be read.[98] The first publication of these papyri was in 1793.[99] Since then the scrolls have been slowly unrolled and read, a process still continuing today.

There are some fragmentary Latin papyri but most are written in Greek, and many contain the writings of a philosopher of the first century BC, Philodemus of Gadara (in modern north-west Jordan). Lucius Calpurnius Piso Pontifex is known to have been his patron and clearly the owner of the villa knew him and admired his works enough to 'collect the set' and install them in his villa.

THE RECORDS OF POMPEII

Equally remarkable is the preservation in the cities of collections of wooden writing tablets. The first and largest was found in July 1875, during excavations in the House of Lucius Caecilius Iucundus (P).[100] Caecilius Iucundus was a banker, auctioneer and all-round businessman. One hundred and fifty four wooden tablets were discovered in a wooden box, which had been stored in an upper storey room and had collapsed into the peristyle (FIG. 115). The earliest document dates to AD 15 and mentions Lucius Caecilius Felix – perhaps Caecilius Iucundus' father or patron. Caecilius Felix was almost certainly a freed slave, so Caecilius Iucundus' roots were ultimately servile, like those of so many of the cities' entrepreneurs. Slaves and freedmen were needed to run businesses and handle financial transactions, because for those of a higher social rank it was considered demeaning to deal directly with commerce. Caecilius Iucundus and those like him were highly skilled. They probably had a good grasp of business, and probably of many aspects of law as well. In short, they were very experienced staff who could be trusted to look after the business.

Fig. 114 Bronze bust showing Lucius Calpurnius Piso Pontifex, probable owner of the Villa of the Papyri.

Villa of the Papyri, Herculaneum
H. 46 cm
MANN 5601

Caecilius' other tablets range in date from AD 27 to 62, with a concentration in the AD 50s. They are only a selection; many records – for example, those detailing annual (so necessarily recurrent) payments – are missing. Some documents may have been destroyed during, or spirited away after, the earthquake of AD 62/3, which is so explicitly shown in the lararium reliefs of Caecilius Iucundus' home (FIG. 357). Perhaps he was injured or died, or his commercial interests were badly affected.

The documents are receipts for payments he made to lease city property,[101] such as a *fullonica* (cloth processing plant or laundry), and for collecting taxes on the city's behalf – for example tablet 151, dated January AD 62 (the latest to survive), certifying payment of rent on a market stall. The other documents are receipts from those whose goods and property he sold through his auctions – less his commission of about 2 per cent. Auctions were an important element of retail. They could have been held in the *macellum* (market hall), probably on market days – Saturdays in Pompeii[102] – and perhaps in other public areas such as the basilica, the building of Eumachia or even in private homes. These auction receipts mention various goods, including a mule (tablet 1); a partial house clearance for a woman called Umbricia Antiochis (tablet 23); and later a slave belonging to the same woman (tablet 24). This is a useful reminder that slaves were possessions to be disposed of as the owner saw fit. At some point, without much warning, a slave could be uprooted from his/her family (and for many their master's home was all they had known) and sold. Most of the documents relate to relatively small sums arising from the disposal of surplus goods and produce in the local area.[103] But a very large amount of money (40,000 sesterces, enough to buy about eight slaves) was recorded on one tablet (FIG. 115). There are some hints at links with the wider world, for example the linen cloth sold on behalf of Tolomaeus, a merchant from Alexandria in Egypt (tablet 100), and at least one occasion when Caecilius ventured beyond Pompeii; on this occasion to a military camp near Nuceria, to auction property belonging to soldiers there (tablet 45).

Caecilius also extended credit, and several tablets document money owed and repayment dates,[104] though Iucundus himself sometimes fell into arrears (tablet 141). Receipts were signed by witnesses, usually in order of status: magistrates first, citizens next and freedmen last of all. Women very rarely signed documents, as laws insisted they went through male agents. But they could realize the value of their assets and use the money as they wished. Caecilius' archive is the only major example thus far from Pompeii, but there must have been many more.

Fig. 115 Wooden writing tablet recording an auction for Marcus Lucretius Lerus. The sum raised was nearly 40,000 sesterces – enough to buy eight slaves or pay forty soldiers for a year.

House of Lucius Caecilius Iucundus, Pompeii
H. 13.5 cm, W. 12 cm
MANN 155868. CIL IV 3440, X

THE DOCUMENTS OF HERCULANEUM

The burial process at Herculaneum preserved wood extremely well and eight collections of wooden tablets have been found. One, from the House of the Bicentenary, contained about 150 tablets, found in a wooden chest in a small upstairs room.[105] Many of the tablets chronicle a dispute between a young woman Petronia Iusta, either a freed slave (*liberta*) or freeborn (*ingenua*), and her would-be owner and adoptive mother, Calatoria Themis. Claims and counterclaims of family links and servile bonds dragged on for much of the AD 70s and became so acrimonious that the case was taken to Rome and was still unresolved in AD 79. Witnesses were key players in the dispute, with groups lining up behind their preferred lady.

In the House of the Wooden Shrine,[106] up to 200 tablets were found in a cupboard in a room on the upper floor, together with a stack of papyri, though these could not be saved. Another box of tablets was found stashed under a bed – the eternal storage place in the home. A further collection of tablets was discovered in the House of Two Atria[107] in a wooden box, together with bronze vases, a bell, two bags of coins and a small box containing silver coins and spoons, glass perfume bottles and 80 g (3 oz) of pepper. The presence of pepper in the box underlines its status as a precious commodity.

Fig. 116 Fresco from a tablinum showing shelves with writing materials below and bags of money above.

Praedia of Julia Felix, Pompeii
H. 298 cm, W. 447 cm
MANN 8958

The largest archive in Herculaneum came from an apartment above shops overlooking the Decumanus Maximus.[108] It contained over 200 tablets from a wall-mounted cupboard and three boxes, recounting the dealings of one Lucius Cominius Primus, a very wealthy landowner, and almost certainly a freed slave. A recurrent theme is strife with neighbours, both in the city (he complains that his door was pelted with stones by a neighbour's slaves) and in the countryside, where he quarrels with at least three neighbours (though not his 'special' neighbour Ulpia M.f Plotina, aunt of the future emperor Trajan …).

Excavations in the House of the Black Living Room produced a large archive, shelved on an upper-storey corridor over the colonnaded garden. The archive recorded a fascinating series of events in the life of Lucius Venidius Ennychus,[109] by far the most important being the request – and eventual grant – of Roman citizenship. Three documents are especially important. The first, dating to 24 July AD 60,[110] written on the exterior of a tablet in ink, declares that his wife, Livia Acte, had given birth to a daughter. This seems an uncontroversial certificate of birth to a citizen family – Lucius Venidius Ennychus has the three-part name of a full Roman citizen. But other documents show that, in fact, Lucius Venidius Ennychus fell into the category of Junian Latins, ex-slaves who had not been freed in full accordance with the law,[111] and he wanted full status and citizenship for himself and his family.

A second tablet[112] takes us forward a year, when their daughter marked her first birthday, and talks of a meeting of the city Council in Herculaneum's Basilica Noniana, though details are lost:

Fig. 117 Wooden tablet, with ink writing, recording the birth of a daughter to Lucius Venidius Ennychus and his wife Livia Acte.

House of the Black Living Room, Herculaneum
H.6 cm, W. 11.5 cm
MANN no inv. / T.Herc. 5

C. Vel(l)eio Paterculo M. Manlio Vopisco [cos]

VIIII k(alendas) Augustas

L.Venidius Ennychus testatus est

sibi filiam natam esse ex Livia

Acte uxore sua

Ac[tum Herculani]

'During the Consulship of C. Velleius Paterculus and M. Manlius Vopiscus (AD 60)
on the VIIII day before the Kalends of August [24 July],
Lucius Venidius Ennychus is witnessed
to have had a little girl by Livia
Acte his wife.
Certified at Herculaneum'

All becomes clear in the third document of 22 March AD 62.[113] Written by a *praetor* (senior magistrate) in Rome, it confirms that the Council of Herculaneum has supported Lucius Venidius Ennychus' request, in accordance with a law (*anniculi probatis* – literally

Fig. 118 Bronze vessel for mixing wine (crater), decorated with mythological figures.

House of Julius Polybius, Pompeii
H. 60 cm, W. 35 cm

'the proof of a little one-year-old') which granted citizenship to a Junian Latin, such as Venidius Ennychus, through proof of his child reaching its first birthday.[114] Their little girl turning one year old ensured the petition was successful and, once the praetor had legalized everything, their names were set up on bronze tablets in the Forum of Augustus in the heart of Rome. Venidius Ennychus and Livia Acte were now full citizens of Herculaneum and of the empire.

The story of Venidius Ennychus continues in the marble tablets discovered in and around the Basilica Noniana of Herculaneum (above pp. 35–6). Among the five hundred names of male citizens of Herculaneum, one fragment happily preserves the name of Lucius Venidius Ennychus himself.

LITERATURE, CULTURE AND THE GREEKS

The social changes reflected in the tablets, in particular the rising numbers and status of freedmen and women, were part of the fundamental transformation of Roman culture and society caused by Rome's conquest and absorption of the Greek Mediterranean during the previous three centuries BC. Apart from a huge influx of agricultural, industrial and domestic slaves (echoes of whose servile origins can be heard in their Greek names), craftsmen, ranging from sculptors, architects, and painters to writers and even cooks, were brought to Italy. Many of these had Greek as a first language, and many teachers, merchants and other traders needed at least some Greek for their daily life and work. In many different ways Roman culture was effectively Hellenizing, or becoming Greek.

In literature, Romans such as the poet Horace acknowledged their debt to Greece: *Graecia capta ferum victorem cepit et artes intulit agresti Latio* ('Captured Greece took her savage captor [Rome] captive and brought culture to rustic Latium [Italy]').[115] Romans of good social standing, or who wanted to be perceived as such, had to show familiarity with the Greek element of Rome's culture. Greek works of poetry, tragedy, comedy and philosophy were widely read and inspired many works of art in the cities, as elsewhere in the empire. A panel from a Fourth Style wall shows the scene from Homer's *Iliad* in which the wooden horse is brought into Troy (FIG. 245).

Greek writers also inspired many works of Roman literature. Vergil, the greatest of all Latin poets, wrote works in the first century BC such as the *Aeneid*, with its epic journeys and the founding of states inspired directly by Homer, the early Greek epic poet, and the *Eclogues*, a collection of short poems set in an idyllic rural setting, based on the work of the Greek poet Theocritus, who lived in the third century BC.

Around fifty graffiti quoting Vergil have been found in Pompeii,[116] though nearly half report the first line of one or other of the books of the *Aeneid* – memories of school exercises perhaps? Or possibly a statement of pride in a 'national' poem?[117] Strangely, Herculaneum, which is sometimes considered to have been, in material and cultural terms, somewhat superior to Pompeii, has not so far yielded a single graffito quoting Vergil or any of the major Roman poets.[118]

One graffito from Pompeii, from the House of the Ship Europa, quotes *Eclogues* Book 2, 21 and is addressed to 'Severus'. It reads: *Mille meae Siculis errant in montibus ag[nae]* ('a thousand of my sheep graze on the hills of Sicily'). This is a strange quotation in isolation, but we do not know the context. In the original poem these words are spoken by a spurned lover, whose beloved is not moved, even by all his woolly wealth. Was the writer here in Pompeii trying to influence a lover – or making a learned declaration that his efforts were useless?

This is a major problem with interpreting quotations; we recognize them, but cannot know exactly what they meant to the people who wrote or read them. The *Eclogues* quotation was probably not as famous as Shakespeare's 'To be or not to be…', and of course not everyone who quotes that line could quote much more – or give the context.[119] But in the cities people were quoting poetry and, at least in Pompeii, writing it down. The fact of the message is as important as its meaning. Greek and Roman literature was an important part of 'cultured' life for the Romans and knowledge of it, however superficial, percolated into many layers of society.

Similarly, statues and busts of Greek writers, philosophers and historical figures were common sights in the cities.[120] A large group of busts was found in the Villa of the Papyri (H) including one (FIG. 120) showing Pyrrhus, a king of Epirus in north-west Greece, who invaded Italy in the mid-third century BC. He famously won the war, but suffered appalling losses, giving us the phrase a 'Pyrrhic victory'.

A statuette from Pompeii (FIG. 119) shows a man in Greek military armour, holding a sword in his right hand, a spear (now missing) in his left, and wearing the protective *aegis* or cape of Athena over his right shoulder. The figure is finely made and the *cuirass*, or body armour, is decorated with silver inlay showing

Fig. 119 Bronze and silver inlay statuette of Alexander the Great.

From Pompeii (VI,10)
H. 65 cm, W. 35 cm
MANN 5014

Fig. 120 Marble bust of the Greek king Pyrrhus, who invaded Italy in the 270s BC.

Villa of the Papyri, Herculaneum
H. 46 cm
MANN 6150

Fig. 121 Fresco showing a young man holding a scroll labelled 'Homer'.

House of the Apartment, Pompeii
H. 44.4 cm, W. 44.8 cm
MANN 120620a

Fig. 122 Fresco showing a young man holding a scroll labelled 'Plato'.

House of the Apartment, Pompeii
H. 44.8 cm, W. 44.7 cm
MANN 120620b

a four-horse chariot – perhaps that of the god Apollo. It almost certainly represents Alexander the Great, shown most spectacularly in the magnificent 'Alexander' mosaic (FIG. 225) from the House of the Faun (P) and further demonstrating the impact of Greek history and culture on Roman society.

A fusion of Greek and Roman culture can perhaps be seen in two roundels from the tablinum of the House of the Apartment (P) (FIGS 121–2). These show two boys holding scrolls and wearing wreaths. The label on a scroll held by the boy in white reads *Homerus* (that is, Homer, the Greek epic poet), while the label of the other scroll reads *Plato* (the Greek philosopher). The wreaths suggest the boys took part in and won a literary contest. They perhaps learned some works by heart: some people certainly did, since at least one graffito in Pompeii reproduces a line of Homer's poetry.[121] Literary contests might have taken place in public buildings, such as the Odeon in Pompeii, or even in private homes, perhaps in the tablinum. The boys' faces suggest that these could be real Pompeians, perhaps members of the family, proudly commemorated in their home – or perhaps that of their tutor.

The atrium is the portal to the Roman home, and introduces themes that will be encountered again and again throughout the house: the need to show visitors the wealth and sophisticated tastes of the owners and their family, alongside the basic requirements for everyday life, and the essential 'service' functions that kept the house running. The success of the Roman home depended on marrying these different strands together in a way that allowed each to function in harmony with the others. Proceeding further into the home it will become clear how well the Romans succeeded in achieving this.

IV
CUBICULUM

CUBICULUM

L EADING off the atrium and garden of many houses were small to medium-sized rooms, often known to us by their Latin name of *cubicula*. *Cubiculum* is most usually translated as 'bedroom' but, as this chapter shows, a whole range of activities could have taken place there. These included washing, dressing, grooming and adorning the body, but also some rather more unexpected activities such as eating small meals and holding business meetings. Sometimes the cubiculum even served as a toilet. Not all homes had recognizable cubicula, but even when they did, sleeping arrangements could have been more flexible than today. Where it did exist the cubiculum, like other spaces in the home, was versatile.

Roman writers often refer to the cubiculum as a place for sleeping, rest and convalescence.[1] The number of such spaces in some houses suggests that people often moved between them, perhaps according to the season.[2] Writers such as Varro[3] and Pliny the Elder[4] say that such rooms, when located around the atrium, were used for different purposes, even including one fitted with shelves to make a library. A cubiculum could also serve as a dining area or as a meeting room – Latin authors speak of special guests being allowed into the bedchamber for important discussions.[5] On many occasions they make it clear that the cubiculum was the venue for a lot of sexual activity, but also for intrigue, adultery and even murder.[6]

There is archaeological evidence for sleeping and resting in these spaces, such as the remains of beds or couches, and the structure of the rooms themselves can sometimes give clues. In grander houses there are rooms with alcoves, vaulted ceilings and patterning on the floor indicating the intended positions of couches or beds. Some have recesses set into the lower part of the wall (FIG. 125) to take a bed end, while others feature higher rectangular recesses, in effect cupboards or wardrobes for clothes (FIG. 124).

All members of the household, including the slaves, had to sleep. Some larger houses had designated areas for slaves, including rooms for sleeping. Many other slaves, in all probability, slept wherever they could – in or above the shops that fronted the home, in the kitchen area, in areas around the garden in summer months, outside their master's door or even at the foot of his bed – wherever space allowed.

PREVIOUS PAGES
Fig. 123 Detail of a fresco showing two lovers on a bed (see fig. 131).

Fig. 124 Cubiculum with designated spaces for beds and a built-in alcove/cupboard where clothes were once stored.
Villa of the Mysteries, Pompeii

LIGHTING AND FURNITURE

Cubicula were generally darker than the adjoining atrium and garden, so artificial lighting was necessary. Oil lamps of terracotta and bronze were frequently used.[7] A pottery oil lamp, perhaps made in Pompeii, shows a satyr with an enormous phallus (FIG. 127). Perhaps it served as a bedroom lamp, illuminating and protecting those inside. Martial alludes to different preferences over light during sex: *Tu tenebris gaudes: me ludere teste lucerna…* ('You like it in the dark, I like it with a lamp as our witness').[8] Martial even gives a voice to such a lamp from a cubiculum: 'I'm the nice lamp who knows all about what goes on in your bed – do what you fancy – I won't say a word.'[9] Lamps were placed on shelves or in niches, and sometimes on tall bronze lampstands. These often had elaborate feet, and the shaft might be decorated with fluting or a knobbed finish, imitating a wooden stem or branch. A lampstand from Herculaneum (FIG. 126) has a shaft that can be disassembled, enabling the stand to be stored away in a small space.

The evidence of whole or fragmentary beds and couches confirms the use of this space for sleeping, but how does this evidence fit with the literary sources and the representations in wall paintings? The Roman writer Varro[10] identifies three types of bed (*lectus*), which he calls *lectus tricliniaris* (bed for dining), *lectus cubicularius* (bed for resting and sleeping) and *lectus grabatus* (plain bed).

Several types of bed or couch are known from the excavations.[11] Herculaneum in particular, where wood was often preserved, gives a good idea of how the beds appeared. We can also get an idea of the size of Roman beds; many are (to our eyes) 'single' beds, but there are very respectable 'doubles' or

ABOVE **Fig. 125 Cubiculum with niche for a bed end.**
House of the Centenary, Pompeii

BELOW **Fig. 126 Elements of a bronze lampstand which could be assembled when needed.**
House of Neptune and Amphitrite,
Herculaneum (V,6-7)
H.136.3 cm
SAP 76214

even 'kings' with lengths of around 2–2.2 m (about 7 ft) and widths between 1.1 and 1.8 m (3½–5 ft).[12] Some very small beds have been found, presumably for children, while a unique find from Herculaneum is a baby's cradle (FIG. 128). Many others probably have not survived. Its form is immediately recognizable, with two curved stands that can still act as rocking supports. There seems to be no evidence in the cities, or in the empire as a whole, for the existence of nurseries, or of spaces set aside specifically for children. Young ones probably slept in various rooms according to the time of day or the season, like the adults. Indeed, many infants and younger children probably slept with the family members or slaves who looked after them.

Even where the bed does not survive there are clues to its former presence – for example, the impressions left by the end of a bed in solidified ash in the House of the Lararium of Achilles (P) . Sometimes fittings of bronze, iron or wood survive from a particular type of bed. This is important because some scholars have tentatively used the frequency of beds, especially at Herculaneum, to assess population density and even absolute numbers of house inhabitants.[13]

The most common type of bed is the *kline*, or 'couch' in Greek. This is Varro's bed for dining (*lectus tricliniaris*). In Latin literature the ornate versions of these couches, decorated with bronze, ivory and mother-of-pearl, are described as being an import to Rome in the wake of Rome's victory over the kingdom of Asia (in western Turkey) in 187 BC.[14] It had a body of wood or metal and wooden or bronze-covered legs. The most distinctive feature of the kline was the presence at one or both ends of a curved bed-end called a *fulcrum* (FIG. 129), usually decorated with heads and busts of people or animals linked to Bacchus (very appropriate for couches used for dining, drinking and after-dinner love-making).

Another kind of bed preserved in several examples from Herculaneum had no fulcrum but was surrounded on one or more sides by vertical panels, and so was more suited for rest and sleeping; perhaps this is Varro's *lectus cubicularius*. It may also have been used for sitting, like a modern sofa. The high back and sides were often decorated, this example having rich decoration of inlaid wood (FIG. 130). Unlike the kline, the high-backed bed's decoration could be seen only from one point of view – affecting its positioning and use.

The third type, much plainer, possibly Varro's *lectus grabatus*, is the one most commonly seen on 'erotic' paintings in Pompeii. Assuming these are not scenes of 'commercial' lovemaking, then sleeping in the bed may have followed the sexual activity.

No trace has survived of mattresses and covers, though wall paintings give an idea of their appearance. Mattresses in wealthier homes were probably filled with wool or down, while poorer families probably used straw or even went without a mattress altogether.

Fig. 127 Pottery oil lamp in the shape of a satyr with an enormous phallus.

H. 22.3 cm, W. 11.5 cm
MANN 116661

OPPOSITE **Fig. 128 Carbonized wooden cradle.**

House of Marcus Pilius Primigenius
Granianus, Herculaneum (OI,1a)
H. 49 cm, L. 81 cm, W. 50 cm
SAP 78444

RIGHT **Fig. 129 Ornate metal couch end (*fulcrum*)
from the end of a dining/resting couch (*kline*).**

Said to be from Campania
H. 17 cm, L. 25 cm
The British Museum, 1784,0131.4

BELOW **Fig. 130 Wooden high-backed bed
decorated with geometric wooden inlay.**

From Herculaneum (OII,10)
H. 55.3 cm (not including legs),
L. 195 cm, W. 106 cm
SAP 81597

SEX AND SEXUAL IMAGERY

The bedroom is an appropriate place to consider Roman attitudes towards love and sex. In general the Roman world was more comfortable with some aspects of sexuality, such as nakedness and sexual imagery, than many other cultures, and Roman art was filled with depictions of the body and human intimacy. The quantity and diversity of sexually related images discovered during excavation of the cities prompted a re-evaluation of attitudes to the sexual mores of the Romans – and roused very mixed feelings in contemporary scholars (see below p. 169).

Trying to understand how the Romans viewed such images is a challenge. Some imagery is intentionally erotic, such as the frescoes showing couples making love (FIG. 131), though this does not mean, as some have argued, that wherever such paintings appeared there was 'debauchery' or even commercialized sexuality. In fact, the fresco shown here came from the garden area of the very respectable house of the banker Lucius Caecilius Iucundus (above pp. 88–9). One building – the so called 'Lupanar' at Pompeii – was most certainly a selling place for sex and some scholars have suggested that there could be more brothels, ranging in number from nine to thirty-five.[15] But could not erotic imagery be used in the home without the implication of sex for sale? A room in the House of the Centenary has erotic paintings on three walls, but differentiated flooring suggests space for two couches or beds. The erotic art in this bedroom was almost certainly for the benefit of the owners of the house, rather than for any commercial purpose.

An interesting aspect of depictions of lovemaking is the frequent presence of slaves and servants.[16] In the fresco from the House of Lucius Caecilius Iucundus (FIG. 131) a female slave wearing a light blue tunic can be seen behind the bed. Slaves would certainly be in attendance in the cubiculum to help with all the different activities that took place there. Some larger homes even had designated bedroom slaves (cubicularii). Assuming the frescoes reflect reality, then some slaves could be present at even the most intimate moments. In effect they were thought of as invisible,[17] just a part of the fixtures and fittings for their masters' pleasure, to provide drinks, towels or whatever was necessary. Some slaves were also, on occasion, participants rather than spectators. Roman writers cite numerous examples of slaves satisfying (willingly or unwillingly) the sexual desires of their masters.[18] One graffito from the basilica in Pompeii sums up the attitude, sadly probably quite widespread: 'Seize your slave girl whenever you want; it's your right'.[19]

Most painted scenes of human lovemaking are set indoors, usually in a bed, with luxuriant bedding. Sex outdoors – for example on a boat – or as part of an outdoor scene, usually involving dining, was considered un-Roman, and this was emphasized by the inclusion of characters considered grotesque, such as dwarves or pygmies, often in a 'decadent' Egyptian setting. Some depictions of 'indoor' lovemaking are very tender, while others focus on the sexual act. The vast majority of representations are of heterosexual couples, with one or two examples of homosexual behaviour. There are also images involving hermaphrodites, people of dual gender. At Pompeii there are also numerous graffiti describing candidly people's love and sex-lives, showing a reality of

Fig. 131 Fresco showing two lovers on a bed, attended by a slave.

House of Lucius Caecilius Iucundus,
Pompeii (V,1,26)
H. 51.7 cm, W. 44 cm
MANN 110569

multiple sexualities, more varied than is shown in the art.[20] Some were intended as a joke, a slur, or just wishful thinking, but they show us what the people of the cities were thinking, and possibly doing, in their private lives.

THE GODS OF DESIRE

In addition to these explicit depictions of human sex and love, there were countless representations of the gods and other supernatural beings, who (many believed) influenced the love lives of mortals.

Venus (Greek Aphrodite), goddess of love and beauty and patroness of Pompeii, ruled the hearts of gods and men, and unsurprisingly many graffiti mention her. 'If there's anyone who doesn't believe in Venus, let them look at my girl,' writes one happy lover.[21] Another graffito carved onto a panel featuring a sacred serpent from a house in Pompeii (FIG. 132) reveals the other side of the goddess.[22] It contains a warning from a girl called Ario to her man to beware of Venus, 'the weaver of webs...' (*plagiaria*) who is out to get him. The choice of the snake perhaps strengthened Ario's plea. Another writer railed against the goddess: 'I want to break Venus' ribs with sticks, and smash her thighs with sticks. If she can pierce my gentle heart, why can't I smash her head...'.[23]

Venus's mischievous, malicious son Cupid (Greek Eros) was frequently depicted, always with wings to represent flighty love, and sometimes a torch to inflame

desire, and/or a bow and arrow to pierce hearts. In one fresco (FIG. 133) he is shown in a mellow moment with his own lover Psyche – the Greek word for soul. They are shown in a passionate embrace with Cupid literally sweeping her off her feet. The shawl-like objects at the back of her neck are in fact her delicate wings, since Psyche was also the Greek word for butterfly.

The most popular figure in the art of the cities was Bacchus or Liber Pater, god of wine and fertility, and an important patron of the cities through his control over wine; he represented wilder, frenzied love. He was accompanied by satyrs, men/animal hybrids, with tails and pointed ears, and female maenads, human by nature

ABOVE **Fig. 132 Fresco with a graffito warning a lover about the snares of wild Venus.**

Pompeii (VI,7,6)
H. 54.7 cm, W. 41.1 cm
MANN 4694/CIL IV 1410

LEFT **Fig. 133 Fresco showing Cupid and his lover Psyche in a passionate embrace.**

House of Terentius Neo, Pompeii
H. 57 cm, W. 40 cm
MANN 9195

OPPOSITE **Fig. 134 Fresco showing a satyr and maenad in an intimate embrace.**

House of Caecilius Iucundus, Pompeii (V,1,26), tablinum
H. 51 cm, W. 52.7 cm
MANN 110590

but superhuman in fervour and sexual desire. A fresco from Pompeii (FIG. 134) shows a maenad and a typically lust-filled satyr.

Human fertility, pregnancy and childbirth were in the hands of Diana (Greek Artemis) and Juno (Greek Hera). It is possible that the terracotta figurine showing a nursing mother (FIG. 355) found in the Cardo V drain in Herculaneum may have been in a new mother's home as a good luck charm. Ultimately, if people did not want to leave everything in the hands of the gods, there were some man-made solutions.[24] These included oral contraceptives containing, for example, ivy,[25] and even a potion of myrrh, rue and lupin for women who had decided on termination.[26]

TOILETS

After waking, members of the household, alone or with the help of slaves or servants, began to get ready for the rigours of the day. Going to the toilet was naturally one of the first considerations. Given the nature of many fixed domestic latrines (discussed below in the context of the 'working' areas of the home, pp. 261–5), many opted to have a chamber pot, or 'potty', brought by a slave to the cubiculum.[27] In the Roman literature the potty is called *matella*, *lasanum* or *scaphium*, the last two Greek-sounding names betraying supposed Greek origins. These objects appear in satires on the lives of the better-off,[28] most famously in the *Satyricon*, in which the *nouveau riche* Trimalchio urinates into a solid silver potty.[29] But there were more modest versions available for the not-so-rich. A graffito from a cubiculum in House VII.7.6 at Pompeii, a boarding house or inn, proclaims: *Minximus in lecto fateor, peccavimus hospes, Si dicis quare: nulla matella fuit* ('Landlord, we've done something terrible, we've pissed in your bed.' 'Why!?' you may ask ...' 'There was no pot.')[30]

Ordinary vessels, such as jugs and amphorae, could certainly have been pressed into use.[31] Near-complete vessels found in latrine contexts, for example in the Cardo V drain at Herculaneum, could be improvised chamber pots or vessels used for sluicing and washing, lost after an over-enthusiastic flush.

Recent research has attempted to match the literary descriptions with archaeological finds on other sites.[32] In Pompeii several vessels, surely purpose-made chamber pots, have been discovered, all quite large and basin-shaped, but with ovoid mouths. One type has a tall tapering body, with two handles on the exterior of the wall, and two small horizontal

ABOVE **Fig. 135 Bronze oval basin (chamber pot).**
Vesuvian area
H. 15.6 cm
The British Museum, 1814,0704.1576A/B

LEFT **Fig. 136 Pottery chamber pot.**
Vesuvian area
H. 19 cm
SAP 31699

projections on the interior. This vessel, with high capacity and deep form, may be the matella. A second type (FIG. 136) is more rounded and squat, again with an oval mouth, and longer, wider projections. This could perhaps be an example of a scaphium used, perhaps, more by women. A third, rare, type is similar in concept to a modern bedpan. It is squat, slipper-shaped, with a projection around the inside of the rim that becomes a raised area at the front (or back?). This could, perhaps, be the lasanum, used primarily for solids. Its low, protected form might also be more suitable for children. An example in Pompeii still has yellowish white calcitic coating over much of the interior – traces, perhaps, of its contents.

In the store-rooms of Pompeii only seven of these distinctive pottery vessels were found. There ought to be more. The answer may lie in vessels of bronze, which, with its water-resistant qualities, was an obvious choice. In his *Satires*, Juvenal (10.64) says chamber pots (*matellae*) were cast from melted-down bronze statues of the once-feared imperial official Sejanus. Investigation of the store-rooms at Pompeii and at Herculaneum has revealed numerous examples of shallow bronze vessels with curiously ovoid mouths. In the British Museum are two examples, one still fitted with a lid (FIG. 135) – a useful feature for a vessel of this kind.

WASHING

Don't let your armpits stink like a goat…don't be lazy and let your teeth get black… clean your mouth every morning.
Ovid *Ars Amandi* III, 193–9

One obvious question regarding daily life is, how and where did people wash? There were the public baths, though some may have been out of action in AD 79 through disruption of the water supply. Bathing is always considered to be an important element of Roman life and most people would attend the baths. But how often? Seneca says in his *Epistles* (86.12) that most people probably bathed only once or twice a week. The average person, if he or she washed regularly at all, may have settled for a quick wash down using a basin first thing in the morning. There was no running water in the cubiculum, even in the most luxurious homes. Instead, water from the well was heated, if necessary, in the kitchen and brought to where it was needed, then poured into basins.

ABOVE **Fig. 137 Bronze shell-shaped scoop used for washing and rinsing.**
From Pompeii
H. 8.9 cm, W. 22.8 cm
The British Museum, 1856,12-26.928

RIGHT **Fig. 138 Bronze basin, used for washing.**
From Pompeii
H. 11.7 cm, D. 41 cm
SAP 12097

These basins are abundant and readily identifiable (FIG. 138) – broad, hemispherical vessels with large handles. The medallion in the centre of the vessel was often decorated with scenes from mythology – classical Greek culture had fused with Roman culture everywhere in Roman art, in the home, even in the washbasins. Shell-shaped vessels called *forme di pasticcera* (literally 'baker's moulds')[35] were often found with these bowls (FIG. 137). Very similar silver vessels from dining sets show they were, in fact, vessels for washing. Silver vessels were probably finger bowls, but bronze examples in the cubiculum were probably scoops or pourers for washing skin and hair.

BEAUTY ROUTINES

With washing completed, Seneca suggests that a woman should attend to hair first, then make-up, jewellery and finally clothes. However, it is important to remember that what the (exclusively male) writers on this subject said women should do, and what they did, may have been very different. Precisely because of this uncertainty, the repeated discovery of particular artefacts in cubicula can help us gain an idea of what happened there.

It is certain that beauty routines varied considerably, depending on a whole range of factors including personal preferences, wealth and available time. The poet Ovid advised: 'There is more than one type of look; every woman should choose her own, having taken the advice of her mirror.'[36]

Silver-backed glass mirrors were unknown at the time of the eruption. Full-length mirrors had been invented, but were prohibitively expensive.[37] Everyday mirrors, usually round or square, were made of polished bronze or silver, often with a handle (FIG. 140). A fresco from Stabiae shows a woman seated on a stool, dressing her hair, while looking into her silver mirror. A wooden stool from Herculaneum (FIG. 141), decorated with inlaid wood, may once have been used in a cubiculum. Some houses, such as the House of the Gilded Cupids or the House of the Workman, had mirrors of polished obsidian, a naturally occurring volcanic glass, set into the walls, usually in the garden peristyle (colonnaded court).

Teeth could be cleaned with toothpicks (FIG. 287), fingers or sticks (there were no toothbrushes), using abrasive powders made of soda, ground horn or shell, or even pumice,[38] and breath could be freshened with pastilles.[39] For initial washing and cleansing of the skin, sponges, cloth and abrasives such as crushed or solid pumice were used. A pumice stone from Pompeii (FIG. 142) still preserves its bronze holder. Unwanted hair was removed with tweezers (*volsellae*) or by other means. Ovid in his *Ars*

Amandi or Art of Loving (III, 194) advised ladies '… don't let your legs be rough with wiry hair'. *Dropax* was a depilatory ointment for legs, head and private parts made of resins and pitch.[40] Pliny describes other depilatories, including the generic *psilothrum*, with ingredients such as the blood of wild she-goats and seaweed.[41]

There was no lathering soap, though olive oil was recognized (then as now) for its cleaning properties. There was also a bewildering range of unguents, salves and lotions to cleanse and soften the skin and improve its appearance.[42] For a deep cleanse, some women used a face pack, similar to a beauty mask, but sometimes wrongly translated as 'soap', called *lomentum*.[43] This fine cream, made from broad beans, was renowned.[44] From Pompeii have come at least two vessels bearing painted labels stating that the contents were lomentum.[45]

Ovid describes another cream of broad beans, lupins and wine that made the skin 'smoother than a mirror',[46] while a more alarming mix of lentils, barley, iris bulbs, honey and powdered deer antler whitened and softened the complexion.[47] Ovid also extols the virtues of poppies in soothing the skin.[48] Ovid was neither a woman nor a make-up manufacturer, but even in his intentionally humorous poetry he may be shedding some light on real Roman cosmetics. A whole range of plants and minerals were pressed into the service of the ladies of the cities: onions mixed with chicken fat were an ideal remedy for spots and pimples, while swan fat alone was very good for the complexion.[49] Poppaea, the second wife of Nero, kept her skin in good condition by bathing in asses' milk. Pliny even mentions a special cosmetic for ex-slaves – a mixture of pigeon dung and vinegar, which was used to remove 'stigmata' (branding marks).[50]

After cleansing and depilation came artifice. Ovid suggests a woman can create the rosy look of health.[51] She can enhance her eyebrows with a pencil, '…and there's no shame in bringing out your eyes with a pencil or crocus flower'. A foundation of

(TOP ROW L–R)

Fig. 142 Pumice stone and bronze holder.

From Pompeii
H. 4.5 cm, D. 5.7 cm
SAP 7150

Bronze toiletry casket with residues of cosmetics.

Praedia of Julia Felix, Pompeii
L. 11.2 cm, W. 6.5 cm
SAP 9042

(BOTTOM ROW L–R)

Bronze tweezers.

From Pompeii
L. 7.5 cm
SAP 12938A

Bone lidded vessel (*pyxis*) with pink pigment (cosmetics?).

From Pompeii
H. 2.3 cm, D. 2.8 cm
SAP 12412C

Folding razor with a bone handle.

From Pompeii
H. 9.3 cm, W. 11.5 cm
SAP 11148

white lead carbonate (*cerussa*) was then sometimes applied to the face, neck and arms.[52] Sold in tablets and mixed with honey or oils, it reproduced the fashionable youthful pallor of a lady who had never had to work outdoors. Eyeshadow was derived from crocus, or powdered minerals such as azurite and malachite. Lips could be reddened with expensive concoctions that included cinnabar (red lead) and the purple dye from the shellfish *murex*. Finally the whole face could sparkle with a dusting of finely crushed golden mica.[53]

PERFUMES AND COSMETIC CONTAINERS

Perfumes and scents were among the many luxuries introduced to Romans (who embraced them wholeheartedly) after the conquest of the eastern Mediterranean in the second and first centuries BC.[54] Perfume was condemned as wasteful by Roman males. Pliny criticized perfume as the most absurd of all luxuries; at least jewellery and other deluxe items could be passed to your heirs. [5] To this the satirist Martial replied, in effect, 'Don't leave it to them – use it all yourself.'[56]

Roman perfumes were derived from flowers such as violets and roses, lavender or jasmine, bark such as cinnamon, fruits such as lemon and bergamot, or seeds such as aniseed.[57] Many modern perfumes are fixed with alcohol, but the Romans marinated ingredients in oil.[58] Olive oil was originally used, but the Romans increasingly made use of *omphacium*, a refined and less oily product of unripe grapes or immature olives.[59] Among other advantages, it was odourless and less likely to stain the wearer's clothes.[60]

The enormous demand for scents was originally met by imports from Egypt and the Near East. Egypt is the first recorded major source of perfume,[61] but Campania came a close second.[62] Many of the raw materials were abundant in and around the Bay of Naples. Capua produced a perfumed oil called *seplasium* from its famous roses.[63] Paestum, too, was renowned for its rose industry, while Naples produced oil of lavender and roses.[64] Fragrances could also be produced in powdered form: *diapasmata*[65] was a fine powder of rose flakes used as a deodorant or for freshening laundry.[66]

There is no firm evidence for any large-scale production of perfumes in the cities, but some small workshops probably operated – one, perhaps, based in the House of the Gardens of Hercules, Pompeii. *Unguentarii* or perfume-sellers, perhaps also producers, are certainly recorded in painted electoral notices.[67] Local materials, combined with some imported essences and ingredients, could have produced some of the most famous Roman perfumes, such as Rhodinum,[68] made of rose, fennel or myrrh, and Melinon, made from marjoram, bitter almonds, quinces and vine leaves.[69]

All these creams, lotions, perfumes and powders (and ingredients to make them), had to be transported and stored safely and

ABOVE **Fig. 143 Alabaster perfume bottle (*alabastron*).**

From Pompeii
H. 13.5 cm, D. 6 cm
SAP 12043

RIGHT **Fig. 144 Bronze *pyxis* with chased 'scale' decoration.**

Decumanus Maximus, Bottega 4, Herculaneum
H. 10 cm, D. 8.5 cm
SAP 78274

conveniently.[70] Bulk transport was done in amphorae, similar to those used for wine and olive oil. In shops the product was decanted into smaller containers of stone, metal, pottery and glass, of all shapes and sizes. Martial in his *Epigrams* (IX, 37) quipped that one Roman lady used so many bottles and jars, her face didn't sleep with her, but rested on a shelf overnight.

One of the oldest such containers was the *alabastron*, made from soft alabaster stone, imported principally from Egypt. This characteristic vessel, with its elongated form and slightly rounded base, was considered by Pliny[71] to be the best for storing perfume and was still popular in the cities at the time of the eruption (FIG. 143).

In the second and first centuries BC, with the vastly expanded market for luxury goods, pottery containers for perfumes and unguents became very popular. A pottery vessel, called an *unguentarium* by modern scholars, had a spindle or tear-shaped body. With the discovery of glass-blowing in the mid-first century BC, glass became much more available – and its lack of odour and resistance to absorption made it ideal for oily perfume. Glass unguentaria with characteristically elongated bodies are very common finds in the cities (FIG. 146).

Another popular toiletry item was a lidded vessel called a *pyxis*. Made usually of bronze or shaped bone, but sometimes of glass or pottery, the pyxis held more solid creams and unguents. A bronze example from Herculaneum (FIG. 144) has fine incised scale decoration, while a bone pyxis from Pompeii (FIG. 142) contains traces of a pink pigment, part of a Pompeian lady's make-up regime in the last days before the eruption. Creams and ointments could be removed from these vessels with the fingers or with bronze or bone spoons and spatulas.

ABOVE **Fig. 145 Scallop shell used as a cosmetics container, containing reddish-orange pigment.**

Cardo V drain, Herculaneum
W. 8.5 cm
HCP 105

BELOW **Fig. 146 Glass perfume bottles (*unguentaria*) and a glass spatuala or mixer.**

Cardo V drain, Herculaneum
H. 7.7–13 cm
L–R: HCP 70, 69, 68, 66, 85, 31

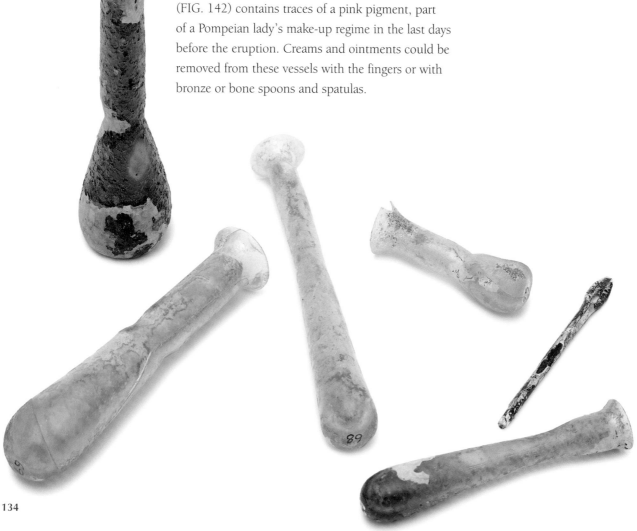

Some women had bronze toiletry boxes with separate compartments for their cosmetics – an example from Pompeii still retains some coloured lumps of pigment. Others used a traditional scallop shell, such as an example (still containing make-up), found in the Cardo V drain in Herculaneum (FIG. 145).

WOMEN'S HAIR

Fig. 147 Bronze furniture ornament featuring the head of a lady wearing a gold hairband.

Decumanus Maximus, Herculaneum
H. 14 cm, W. 6.5 cm
SAP 77838

Attention to hair was very important and there were many different styles. Ovid in his *Ars Amandi* (III, 133ff) says, '...in the same way you can't count the acorns on an oak tree, so you'll never be able to count the different ways of doing women's hair … many women look great with a bedraggled careless look. You'd think it was yesterday's hairdo (but she's only just done it…). Contrived styles must look casual.'

From the time of the emperor Augustus (27 BC–AD 14) to the time of the eruption, the hairstyles of women, in particular wealthy women, were changing. Early in the first century AD some women still wore the *nodus* style, popularized by Augustus' wife Livia, comprising a large roll of hair at the forehead with the hair behind centrally parted and pulled back. Gradually this style disappeared, and instead women wore some variation of a central parting with greater or lesser waves, and the hair gathered at the back into a bun or knot (as seen in a mosaic portrait from Pompeii, above p. 92). In some cases there were ringlets on the fringe or down the sides of the cheek (as worn by the wife of Terentius Neo, FIG. 112).

Some women had an *ornatrix*, a slave who specialized in dressing and caring for the hair. Dyeing the hair was popular both for women and, to endless disapproval from authors such as Martial (see below), for men. For maintaining dark brown or black hair, there were various recipes, including long-dead leeches rotted into red wine.[72] For those who wanted red or blond hair, there were blond wigs made with the hair of women from Britain or Germany, or a French import called *sapo*, made from beechwood ash and goat suet, which was supposed to turn hair red.[73] Nero's wife Poppaea was reputedly responsible for introducing a rich amber hair dye.[74]

Straight hair could be tended with combs (*pectines*) of bone or tortoiseshell. For those who wanted curls there was a kind of heated roller – a bronze tong called a *calamistrum*, around which the hair was wound. Too much use of dye or rollers, however, could weaken the hair and make it fall out. Ovid humorously warned one lady, 'now Germany will send you the hair from slaves…'.[75] One remedy for hair loss included ashes of rabbit mixed with myrtle oil.[76] There were other risks in hair care. The poet Martial imagines a slave called Lalage being beaten because of her mistress's misplaced curl.[77]

Pins of bone, bronze and even silver and gold and bands and ribbons were commonly used to keep the hair in place (FIG. 148). These allowed more complex styles, and also kept the oils and perfumes on the hair from staining clothing.[78] Some women wore hair-bags, or hairnets,[79] as can be seen on the young woman in the private dinner party fresco (FIG. 159) or on the famous so-called 'Sappho' in a fresco now in the National Museum, Naples (FIG. 111). However, these nets and bags have left very few traces in the archaeological record. A furniture ornament from Herculaneum shows a good example of a headband (FIG. 147), and what may be a headband made of woven gold thread was discovered on the beach at Herculaneum.[80]

MEN'S GROOMING

Some Roman men clearly paid attention to their appearance – too much, in the eyes of critical writers. The satirist Martial mocks Laetinus, who dyed his hair, suddenly changing from a white swan to a dark crow.[81] The owner of the House of the Menander in Pompeii is described in an electoral graffito as *fulbunguis*, 'red-nailed'.[82] This could be a nickname, or an intriguing indication that men sometimes coloured their fingernails.

Some of a man's 'beauty' regime took place in the public baths, where an army of slaves provided services such as depilation, shaving and hair cutting. Seneca, who lived over a bathing establishment in Rome, complains about the noise of the '...flat smacks and cupped blows...'[83] of a (cheap) masseur and the screams of someone having the hairs torn out of his armpits, not to mention the grunts of bodybuilders and the shouts of vendors and hawkers. Some households had their own private bathing suites (below pp. 258–61), and at least one – the villa of Agrippa Postumus near Pompeii – had its own masseur (*unctor*) called Xanthus.[84]

We know the names of several barbers (*tonsores*) in Pompeii at the time of the eruption. Graffiti and painted inscriptions suggest that barbers were concentrated around the large exercise area, or *palaestra*, near the amphitheatre and, in common with other tradesmen, they were happy to lend their electoral support to particular candidates.[85]

Fashion dictated that Roman men, for most of the first centuries BC and AD, wore their hair short. Instead of scissors the Romans used one-piece shears, like those still used for sheep-shearing in some parts of the world. The results were not always successful. 'People are laughing at me...because the barber cut my hair unevenly,' laments Horace.[86]

SHAVING

Shaving could be performed by professional barbers, but often took place in the home, particularly for the wealthy.[87] At this period men were mostly clean-shaven, the only exceptions for many being the sparse facial hair of adolescence and beards grown in times of mourning.[88] When a male came into adulthood he shaved off his juvenile facial hair and dedicated it to the gods of the household in a ceremony known as *depositio barbae*.[89] Full beards were sometimes an indication of foreign and/or slave status, though it is possible that men living outside the cities, or even those in the cities who did not participate in the niceties of civic life, may not have shaved regularly.

Most men in civic society would shave (or be shaved) using a distinctive folding razor called a *novacula*, with a heavy, four-sided iron blade and a broad bone or ivory handle (FIG. 147). On the one occasion that shaving is described in detail by a Roman

Fig. 148 Bone hairpin decorated with a woman's head.

From Pompeii
L. 11 cm
SAP 12244

writer,[90] there is no mention of cream or lotion being applied to the face before, during or after shaving, only plain water – though this does not mean it never happened. There is no suggestion that the water was heated, and cuts must have happened, however sharp the blade or skilful the barber. Luckily a remedy was at hand. The best treatment for shaving cuts, according to Pliny, was a spider's web soaked in vinegar and oil.[91]

JEWELLERY

The cities provide an unprecedented opportunity to see the jewellery that people actually wore. Items of jewellery discovered by archaeologists in graves were deliberately chosen for funerary purposes and may not reflect the whole assemblage the person possessed. The jewellery found with the victims of Vesuvius – on their bodies, in purses, bags and boxes – varying as it does in quantity and quality, gives a good idea of the range of jewellery present in provincial towns. Importantly, because some jewellery was found in domestic contexts, it provides the opportunity to compare finds with their surroundings. It also permits a statistical overview. If we assume a figure of around 1,100 bodies in Pompeii and 400 in Herculaneum, then approximately 10 per cent of the individuals found so far have associated jewellery.[92]

The Roman love of jewellery, like that of perfumes and other luxury items, arose mainly from contact with the Greek world,[93] and was just as heavily criticized by Roman writers. Tacitus spoke of Rome's wealth being transferred to foreigners and our enemies to pay for jewels,[94] while Pliny raged at India, China and Arabia, which 'each year snatch hundreds of thousands of sesterces from our empire. That is what women and luxury cost us...'[95]

The cities have not produced jewellery ensembles as opulent as those of the ladies of the imperial court.[96] Pliny describes Lollia Paolina, wife of the emperor Caligula, appearing 'covered with emeralds and pearls...with jewellery gleaming on her head, hair, neck, ears, and fingers...'[97] Nonetheless, for their jewellery, the people of Pompeii and Herculaneum wanted gold. Far fewer pieces were found in silver or iron,[98] though bronze, in particular, may tell a fascinating story (see below). To gold, the Romans added pearls from the Red Sea and the Persian Gulf, gems such as emeralds and amethysts from Egypt, opals from the eastern Mediterranean, rock crystal from the Alps and carnelians from the Eastern Mediterranean and India.

In the cities four main types of jewellery were found: finger rings, earrings, necklaces and armlets/bracelets. Finger rings were worn by both sexes. Some rings were functional, for example signet rings for impressing seals on documents and other artefacts, while others were simply decorative. There was no widespread use of wedding rings, though some evidence exists for a ring marking engagement.[99] Pliny adds that the ring was made of iron.[100] Signet rings usually had a decorated bezel – either engraved directly onto the ring or added on a

Fig. 149 Gold ring with a carnelian seal stone showing a bird eating cherries.

Herculaneum, ancient shoreline, vault VII, skeleton 8
D. 2 cm
SAP 78959

gemstone set into it. These seal stones are among the most common jewellery finds in the cities, which indicates their practical function and underlines the importance in this society of writing, witnessing and signing documents.

We cannot always be sure where the jewellery from the cities was made, because styles were universal across the empire, but there is definite evidence for the manufacture of engraved carnelian gemstones at Herculaneum. Reddish-orange carnelian is the stone most frequently set into rings used as seals, maybe because it was cheaper than the other gems or, as Pliny suggests, because wax does not easily stick to it.[101] In a graffito from the House of Fabius Rufus (P) a lover wishes he could be the gemstone on his beloved's signet ring, so every time she moistened it with her lips (to stop it sticking to the wax) he would kiss her.[102]

Earrings are the most common type of jewellery found in the cities.[103] Many took the form of a large gold hemisphere, sometimes with a smaller sphere below (FIG. 151), attached to the ear by a long S-shaped hoop. This type of earring was popular throughout the empire at this period and appears frequently on the mummy portraits of women from Roman Egypt.[104] Other earrings included threaded hemispheres or hoops, such as a pair now in the British Museum, densely threaded with emeralds (FIG. 150). Pearls were a favourite element in earrings and other jewellery and grew ever larger. Pliny says pearls were very much a Roman passion in jewellery and came in many varieties.[105] Long dangling pearls used in earrings were called *crotalia* (literally 'castanets') by Pliny,[106] presumably because they clashed together as the wearer moved her head. Juvenal adds that a woman thinks she can get away with anything when her lobes stretch under the weight of big pearl earrings.[107] Trimalchio, the *nouveau riche* hero of Petronius' *Satyricon*, said if he had a daughter he'd cut her ears off to avoid huge future expense.[108]

The cities have produced many examples of necklaces.[109] Two major types have been found. *Monilia* were short necklaces, necklets or chokers, often with simple link or woven chains. Some had a crescent pendant (FIG. 152) – a symbol that brought good fortune to the owner – while others had a pendant featuring a gem such as a pearl or an emerald. Pliny explains the popularity of emeralds, which were almost certainly imported from Egypt:[110] 'There is no colour more pleasing than green…and there is

ABOVE LEFT **Fig. 150 Pair of gold ball earrings.**
Oplontis, Villa B, skeleton 27
D. 2.4 cm
MANN 73408

ABOVE RIGHT **Fig. 151 Pair of gold earrings decorated with numerous small, irregular, emeralds.**
From Vesuvian area
D. 2.2 cm
The British Museum,1856,1226.1405

OPPOSITE **Fig. 152 Gold necklace of linked circles. Found with the ring, fig. 149.**
Herculaneum beach, vault VII, skeleton 8
L. 33 cm
SAP 78958

nothing more intensely green than emeralds. The eye never tires of them.'[111] A less common type of necklace was the long, chain-style necklace called by the Romans *catena* or chain. This was worn crossed over the shoulders, in effect as a body chain rather than a necklace, and often carried the representation of a wheel, a symbol of renewed life and good fortune.

A major class of jewellery was the *armilla*, an armlet or bracelet, which derived its name from the Latin *armus* (arm). Like rings, this was a unisex item of jewellery, though the most famous examples from the cities have been associated with women. A flexing spiral snake armlet was inscribed: 'To my slave girl from her master'. We can only guess at the relationship between the two, but the nature of the armlet suggests she was highly esteemed. Another snake bracelet of solid gold has a distinctive wavy tail, as if curling its way around the wrist of the wearer. Its head and tail are covered in very fine chasing imitating scales. There is further floral ornament on the plain gold body. Another type of armlet popular at the time of the eruption was formed of a double row of hollow gold hemispheres (FIG. 153). This fashion was clearly well known and desirable, as it inspired imitations in base metal (see below FIG. 155).

JEWELLERY FOR THE LESS AFFLUENT

Not all jewellery was made of gold and gems. Examples have been found made of more affordable materials such as iron, bronze or glass paste. Such jewellery might be thought to be simply for the poor. Certainly emperors such as Tiberius are reported to have restricted the use of gold rings to people of long-established free ancestry, though it seems inconceivable that all the gold rings found in the cities necessarily belonged to people of such high social rank. Perhaps restrictions were loosening up. Likewise, although iron was certainly the cheapest material, there are several references by Roman writers to people of elevated social rank, such as the equestrians (knights) choosing to wear iron rings.[112] For others, such a ring may have been thought to have protective properties. One of the rings carried by the girl who died outside the Porta Nola, Pompeii (see p. 300), had a hoop made of iron (FIG. 396).

Bronze jewellery has also been found. In the House of Gratus (P) a skeleton was discovered together with fifty-nine silver coins, one silver and one gold ring, some bronze mirrors and statuettes of the Lares and the god Mercury. The person also carried several bracelets/armlets made of bronze. One (FIG. 154) was made of a beaten and folded sheet of bronze and was decorated with a crude, though very recognizable, image of Venus rising from the sea and wringing out her hair. It is very similar to the gold armlet found with skeleton 27 at Oplontis (FIG. 379). With the House of Gratus group were five bracelets, made of bronze wires twisted together in 'rope' style. These all had traces of gilding and would have looked like gold. Another armlet from the group (FIG. 155) is formed of linked bronze hemispheres with large oval settings containing 'gems' of green glass paste. This armlet/bracelet was originally completely gilded and when new must have looked similar to the gold hemisphere armlets which were so popular in the cities.

Other cheaper jewellery includes a bronze armlet (FIG. 156) with a thin beaten silver medallion featuring the sun-god Sol, his head surrounded with the sun's rays.

ABOVE **Fig. 153 Gold armlet/bracelet formed of a double band of joined hemispheres.**
From Pompeii
L. 9.5 cm
The British Museum, 1946,0702.1

OPPOSITE **Gold bracelet in the form of a snake.**
From Pompeii
D. 7.6 cm
The British Museum,1946,0702.2

This armlet imitates more expensive versions in gold, such as the piece found in the House of the Golden Bracelet (FIG. 388).

Jewellery of all types was, of course, passed on down the generations. One possible hand-me-down is the gold and emerald ring found in the bar of Salvius (FIG. 157), which has been pinched at the back of the hoop, almost certainly to allow it to be worn by a new owner – perhaps a younger adult or even a child.

CLOTHING

The cubiculum was also the space where dressing and undressing took place. Clothing was folded and stored on shelves or in wooden cupboards such as those discovered (and now recreated) in the peristyle corridor of the House of Caius Julius Polybius (P). They were sometimes set into purpose-built recesses, as in the cubicula in the Villa of the Mysteries (P) (above FIG. 124). Alternatively clothes could be placed in linen chests. One such chest has survived at Herculaneum, though records exist of a dozen or so more in Herculaneum and others at Pompeii (FIG. 158). It was made of maple wood and, when it was accidentally broken open during excavation, it was found to contain carbonized textiles.[113] Cato recommends rubbing boiled olive oil on linen chests to keep away moths.[114]

Some people may have owned very few items of clothing, but some clearly had an extensive wardrobe:

> Just like Mount Ibla in Sicily is tinged with different colours when spring flowers give
> their nectar to the bees, so your wardrobes are ablaze with piles of clothing, your linen
> chests sparkle with countless robes and your white tunics made from the flocks of
> Puglia could clothe an army…
>
> Martial, Epigrams 2, 46

So which pieces of clothing did the Romans take from the cupboards and chests on a daily basis? At Herculaneum, in particular, remains of textiles have been found preserved. A large quantity of fabric (*stoffa* in Italian) discovered in one of the houses gave the house its name: 'la Casa della stoffa'. These discoveries are quite fragmentary. For a better idea of the clothing regularly worn at the time of the eruption we can turn to statues, paintings, descriptions in the classical authors, and archaeological finds elsewhere, in particular those preserved by the dry conditions of Egypt.

Most clothing in the cities was made of local wool or of linen (imported from Egypt, but also produced locally or, to a lesser extent, cotton from the Eastern Mediterranean and India. The most luxurious fabric was silk, called *sericum* from the Latin name for its main country of origin, Seres (China).[115] Imported via Afghanistan and Syria or the Indian Ocean, silk was used to make light, smooth, diaphanous dresses and wraps that became very popular among Roman women – sometimes those of a low reputation.[116] The woman having a private drink with her male companion in a fresco from Herculaneum (FIG. 159) seems to be naked from the waist up, but in fact wears an almost invisible garment of silk.

The types of clothing used by the Romans did not vary hugely from person to person, or even from male to female, but the quality of the cloth and colours used made all the difference.[117] Clothes were dyed with similar pigments to those used in wall paintings – reds, yellows and blues – though some dyes were very expensive, such as the purple dye from Lebanon obtained from the murex shell.

Fig. 158 Wooden clothes chest.

Decumanus Maximus, Herculaneum
H. 45 cm, L. 103 cm, W. 63 cm
SAP 77619

Men would wear a loincloth (*subligar*), which representations on mosaics and frescoes suggest looked rather like a streamlined baby's nappy, and then a wool or linen short-sleeved tunic, which came to the knees. Men of higher status gathered it at the waist with a belt. A distinctive feature of the time on tunics of some (not all) adults and children was the presence of *clavi* – vertical stripes that fell from each shoulder. Servants or slaves, and often citizens too, would also wear the tunic, though for poorer people and slaves it was open at one side and fastened at the shoulder by a bronze or bone brooch or pin. A cloak (sometimes hooded) was worn in colder weather. Men wore strapped sandals informally and in the house, but for any formal occasion wealthy men would put on closed shoes (*calcei*), the finish and colour of which were also indicators of social position. The most important element of the male citizen's formal wear was the toga, a big, heavy, voluminous outer garment formed of a large extended semicircle of woollen cloth. Although the satirist Juvenal joked that most people only wore the toga to their own funerals,[118] the toga remained the norm when attending to civic, religious and judicial business in the Forum and for other formal occasions in public – and perhaps even on some occasions within the home, for example at the morning audience (*salutatio*).

The toga was very possibly derived from the *tebenna*, the heavy over-garment of the Etruscans.[119] In fact, the conservatism and formality of Roman clothing in general is probably owed to them.[120] The toga was difficult to put on correctly – fortunate wearers had the help of a slave skilled in toga management (*vestiplicius*). Once on, the toga required the wearer to remain vigilant. The raising of the left arm above a certain height risked an embarrassing unravelling. Togas, too, were made in different types. The *toga praetexta*, with its purple striped edge, was used by young men under the age of seventeen and magistrates, while the pure white *toga candida*, whitened by bleaching, was worn by contestants for political office, giving us the English word 'candidate'.

Women would also put on a *subligar*, and often a bra-like band of material called a *strophium*. Women, like men, also wore a tunic, though women's tunics might have long sleeves (*tunica manicata*) and usually reached down to the ankle (*tunica talaris*). Over the tunic a matron (the dutiful female head of the household) wore a heavy,

ABOVE **Fig. 159 Detail of a fresco showing a man and woman drinking together in a bedroom, attended by a slave.**

From Herculaneum
H. 66 cm, W. 66 cm
MANN 9024

LEFT **Fig. 160 Terracotta statuette of a man wearing a toga with a purple stripe, the *toga praetexta*, indicating that he is a magistrate.**

Moregine, Building B
H. 25 cm
SAP 85201

apron-like shift with straps at the shoulders called the *stola*. This garment was the sign of a respectable lady. Over everything went the *palla*, a sort of female version of the toga, but less voluminous and made of lighter material. Shoes for women were similar to those for men. In general, sandals were worn informally around the house, while closed shoes were necessary for formal occasions.

THE UNSEEN PRESENCE

Some activities of the cubiculum could, of course, have happened out in the more open spaces. Hair could easily have been dressed in the spaces around the garden – or in the atrium itself. Yet it is likely that certain activities would necessarily have taken place in the privacy of the cubicula. 'Privacy' in the modern sense, however, may have meant very little to the Romans, and the cubiculum, just like other parts of the house, was always busy with slaves. The Roman playwright Plautus, in his comedy the *Poenulus*, features a conversation between two women who are attending to their daily toilette.[121] They compare themselves to boats, with a never-ending need for washing, painting and general maintenance. They remark that they have two maids (*ancillae*) each and two male servants who have 'nearly died' carrying all the water that was needed. Plautus casts the two women as (unwilling) prostitutes, but the daily routine of many privileged Roman women may have been similar.

The slaves were the engine, the mechanism of the house, though there remain few physical traces of these vital cogs themselves. It is important to bear in mind that so many of the artefacts and spaces belonging to and used by the owners of the house necessarily imply the presence and assistance of slaves. A perfume pot, a chamber pot, a comb, a razor: all were the preserve of slaves and servants. To most people today this seems a very alien idea, but we should remember that it would have seemed normal to some elements of society well into the twentieth century.

The members of the household were now ready for the day ahead. For some there was the formal greeting of visitors, a visit to the Forum, or activity elsewhere in the city; for others there was relaxation in their own homes, in living rooms or in the green tranquillity of the garden.

V
GARDEN

GARDEN

FOR CENTURIES before the eruption of Vesuvius many houses in the cities had a garden (*hortus*). At first these were mainly functional spaces, planted with useful trees and plants for food or medicine.[1] By AD 79 the garden, though never quite losing its functional role, had been transformed into a place for relaxation and sometimes luxury (FIG. 163): often a beautiful, colonnaded space with plants, fountains and statues. This section traces the development of the garden and describes its different forms and features, the various activities, both work and pleasure, that took place in it and its beautiful (and sometimes surprising) decoration.

About a third of houses in the cities had a garden of some sort,[2] some of which remained primarily functional, working spaces. In the House of Caius Julius Polybius (P) archaeologists found evidence of five large trees in the garden including olive, fig and cherry or pear, as well as the imprint of an 8-m (26-ft) tall ladder, probably used to gather the fruit from the top branches.[3] Gardens sometimes reveal large-scale production of foodstuffs, for example at the House of the Gardens of Hercules (P), where excavators discovered planting patterns in the soil and planting pots indicating possible semi-industrial production, notably of plants and flowers – perhaps for medicine or cosmetics[4] – but also, perhaps, of young trees.[5] The large 'market' garden of the House of the Ship Europa was planted with vines, fruit and nut trees and vegetables.[6] It has been estimated that almost one-fifth of the excavated area of Pompeii was under gardens, vineyards and other cultivation.[7]

THE TRANSFORMATION OF THE GARDEN

The domestic garden was transformed, like other areas of the Roman house, by the blending of Roman and Greek ideas and concepts. The Greeks introduced the colonnaded courtyard or *peristyle* (from the Greek words *peri* 'all around' and *styloi* 'columns') to their public buildings and houses. The Romans later introduced the peristyle into their public architecture in the great forums and temple precincts of Rome, and from the second century BC it began to appear in houses.

The great innovation of the Romans was that they, completely unlike the Greeks, used the peristyle as a setting for ornamental gardens. This green space at the centre of the home was, for some Romans, a link with their agrarian roots and simpler (and more moral) times, but for others it was a demonstration that the countryside had been tamed.[8]

PREVIOUS PAGES

Fig. 161 Fresco from a room (north wall) showing garden scenes.

House of the Golden Bracelet, Pompeii
H. 200 cm
SAP 40690

Fig. 162 Fresco of Flora, goddess of flowers and spring. The rural idyll comes into the house.

Villa of Ariadne, Stabiae
H. 39.5 cm, W. 32.5 cm
MANN 8834

Fig. 163 The classic image of a Roman garden.

Reconstructed garden of the House of the Vettii, Pompeii

This internalized 'outside' space of flowerbeds and tended shrubs, along with sculpture and fountains, was also a refuge from the hustle and bustle of city life. The garden was for many not a functional growing space but a place for relaxation and contemplation. It spoke of *luxus*, the good life, and *otium*, relaxation – the exact opposite of *negotium*, work or business.

Gardens were not confined to the houses of the rich, however. Many smaller, poorer houses had a very small inner garden with a few plants and herbs,[9] as did many bars and restaurants. Even apartment-dwellers could grow plants on terraces and balconies.[10]

The peaceful rural idyll evoked by many domestic gardens is embodied in a painting of extraordinary delicacy and beauty from the Villa Arianna at Stabiae (FIG. 162). Shown against a green background is Flora, goddess of fertility and abundance and the embodiment of spring. Wearing a golden yellow tunic and a white mantle, which falls from her shoulders, she walks away from us, plucking a flower to put with the others in the *cornucopia* (horn of plenty). The countryside had been brought into the home and was an integral part of it.

ABOVE **Fig. 164 Two-sided peristyle.**
House of the Small Fountain, Pompeii

RIGHT **Fig. 165 Open courtyard with outdoor dining area and ornate fountain (*nymphaeum*).**
House of Neptune and Amphitrite, Herculaneum

A colonnaded peristyle in a house was a status symbol, indicating wealth and culture. Some of the finest homes had more than one peristyle, such as the House of the Dioscuri (P). In the garden, as in the atrium, columns (the more the better) transported family and guests to a '... world of luxury and monumentality'.[11] But not every house had a peristyle, and even where it did, the house layout did not always allow a full, four-sided one. So some had three colonnades, as in the House of Caius Julius Polybius (P), where a false fourth colonnade was added in stucco against the garden wall; or two, as in the House of the Small Fountain, Pompeii (FIG. 164).

Such a garden with a restricted peristyle, or no colonnade at all, is often referred to by modern scholars as a *viridarium*, literally a 'greenery' though it is likely the Romans called it by a different name, perhaps a *hortulus* ('little garden').[12] The external openings of these spaces could pose a risk to the security of the home. Sometimes a metal grid was fitted to deter unwelcome visitors, as in the House of the Skeleton (H). A viridarium often made up for in decoration what it lacked in space, with ornamental fountains and bright frescoes. Some of these frescoes showed plants or garden ornaments such as statues and fountains. Others were murals on a very large scale, showing subjects which might, perhaps, strike us as strange in a garden space. At the House of the Ceii in Pompeii, the viridarium (in this case a small paved area, in fact) was decorated in the final decades before AD 79. The side walls show peaceful

scenes on the banks of the River Nile in Egypt, a popular subject in the first centuries BC and AD. But the main wall is completely taken up with a very different scene (FIG. 166).

Against a wild background of a lake, rocks and scrub is a chaos of wild animals. A lion chases a bull, while on the other side of the lake, deer scatter as hounds attack boars and a panther leaps at fleeing rams. The frame of this scene is strange. The lower, barrier wall is flanked by painted fountains and covered with greenery. The sides are also decorated with illusionistic painting of statues, sculpted panels, and ornamental shields. In fact, the whole frame looks like a theatrical curtain opening to reveal the scene, or perhaps the awnings of a tent or marquee.

When the parapet wall of the arena at Pompeii was first discovered, it was covered with life-size frescoes (all destroyed by one night of frost) of wild animals, hunters and musicians. Similar scenes in houses may depict events in the arena. It is possible that some owners had these scenes painted to remind themselves of entertainments they had provided (or wished they had provided) for the public. Or perhaps they were expressing the power of the owner in bringing together these animals (albeit virtually) under his roof.[13] Such scenes are almost certainly intended to represent a *paradeisos* – a form of wildlife park first created by eastern Mediterranean kings and then adopted by very wealthy Romans. Such parks were used for private hunts and probably provided some inspiration for settings of animal hunts in the amphitheatre.

In the House of Lucretius Fronto (P) an entire portico was decorated with seven large-scale animal hunts involving random collections of animals. As in the House of the Ceii, we look over a low wall to the wild landscapes beyond. If the garden represented a desire to bring a wilder outside into the home, then these animal scenes are its ultimate, though curiously safe, expression. They may show real events or they may be a fantasy. Perhaps the scenes are simply meant to be a series of pictures, turning the portico into a large pinacotheca (picture gallery), a style popular from the AD 30s.[14]

ABOVE **Fig. 166 Scene of a landscape with wild beasts in a courtyard garden (*viridarium*).**

House of the Ceii, Pompeii

BELOW **Fig. 167 Terracotta puteal with moulded decoration of columns and Bacchic figures.**

From Pompeii
H. 55 cm, D. 45 cm
SAP 44908

ABOVE **Fig. 168 Marble puteal with vertical grooves showing extensive use over time.**
House of the Dioscouri, Pompeii

BELOW **Fig. 169 Carbonized wooden windlass (water winching device).**
House of the Two Atria, Herculaneum
H. 60 cm, W. 70 cm
SAP 77283

WATER SUPPLY

However relaxing and luxurious the garden might be, it was also a place for work, and many everyday activities were carried out there. Water was vital for every household and its supply was often centred in and around the garden. In the cities water had traditionally been obtained from wells. This was relatively easy at Herculaneum, where the water table was only some 8 m (26 ft) below ground, but more difficult at Pompeii, where it lay at a depth of 30 m (98 ft).[15] The collection and storage of rainwater in cisterns was, therefore, very important.

Private cisterns became common in the third and second centuries BC with the invention of *signinum*, a waterproof surface also used for floors (below p. 183). Even after the introduction of piped water, most households still depended on cisterns for much of their water supply. In most atrium houses the shallow pool or *impluvium* (above p. 79) fed down into a cistern below the house. Gardens provided more rainwater, collected either from the channel around the garden or from the roof via downpipes. Pliny (*Natural History*, XXXI, 21)[16] refused to drink cistern water because it was bad for the throat and bowels, slimy and full of revolting creatures. Most people, even those with cisterns, depended on public fountains for clean drinking water.

Water from the cistern was drawn from a shaft in the garden or (more rarely) in the atrium itself. These shafts were fitted with flat covers or cylindrical heads called *puteals*, made of marble or terracotta. One terracotta example (FIG. 167) is decorated with applied motifs. The main field is divided by columns into three scenes, each showing a maenad, with tambourine and castanets (*crotalia*), with seated figures, perhaps Bacchus, and satyrs playing the twin pipes (*auloi*).

Puteals, plain or decorated, were functional. They were the point of access to the primary water supply and used frequently every day. Many marble puteals have deep grooves on the inside of the rim, caused by ropes holding buckets being lowered into them over decades and even centuries (FIG. 168). In some cases a windlass was used, a wooden device positioned above the puteal, which consisted of two rounded end-panels, joined by several bars, around which the rope was wound or unwound with less friction and effort than was involved in lowering buckets over the side.[17] A single windlass in carbonized wood survives from Herculaneum (FIG. 169), but traces of others have been found, for example in a cistern in the House of the Four Styles (P).[18]

THE ARRIVAL OF PIPED WATER AND FOUNTAINS

The garden was further modified by the introduction of a pressurized, piped water supply. In the late first century BC the emperor Augustus built an aqueduct (the Aqua Augusta) to bring fresh water from Serino in the mountains 30 km (18 miles) east of Vesuvius to the military base at Misenum and the other settlements around the Bay of Naples. This water transformed many aspects of urban life (above p. 48). The great baths were restructured on an even grander scale and public fountains sprang up on street corners, augmenting or replacing the supply from cisterns and wells. For the first time, private houses in the cities could also tap into their own supply of piped water.

Water from the aqueduct was forced under pressure through lead pipes to the

houses. Surprisingly, this private water supply was not directed to kitchens or toilets but was largely reserved for the atrium, domestic bath suites and, in particular, gardens. This caused a revolution in garden design; piped water allowed the development of fountains, which became a major feature of the new gardens. The ornamental use of water – the ultimate control of nature – became a vital part of the conspicuous display of wealth and status. When most ordinary citizens still used wells and cisterns, the ability to maintain fountains was a badge of pride. The first emperor had brought this piped water to the cities, so fountains, pools and watercourses also showed the benefits of, and dependence on, the new imperial order.

The piped water was under constant pressure and there were no recycling pumps, so waste water flowed, together with rainwater from the roof, into cisterns or, as an overflow, through channels to the area outside the house. These overflows are often visible, in some cases emerging from right under the main threshold of the home. Sometimes they were simply cut through external walls, as at the Caupona of Vetutius Placidus (FIG. 170).

In an odd way, even this waste water was a sign of sophistication and wealth. Here was piped water, one of the most valued of commodities, running though the streets (and admittedly helping to clean them) but effectively simply going to waste.

In some houses taps (FIG. 173), stopcocks and valves (FIG. 172) allowed water to be switched from one function to another. The House of Decimus Octavius Quartio (P) (FIG. 171) had an extensive water system, with pools and channels providing a cooling backdrop for the outdoor dining area, and then an extensive watercourse running the length of the (very large) garden. In the House of the Vettii (P) (FIG. 163), no fewer than ten fountains spouted from marble and bronze statues into marble basins.

Ornamental fountains and spouts made of marble and bronze came in many shapes and sizes, from elegant basins with fluted and scalloped decoration (FIG. 174) to statues of everyday objects, humans, animals and mythological creatures. Water sprayed from the multiple holes of an elegant pine cone (FIG. 177), poured from the mouth of a rabbit (FIG. 179) – an import from its native Spain[19] – or spouted from the beak of a peacock with its ostentatious plumage (FIG. 178).

Not all fountain spouts were of bronze or stone. In the House of the Silver Wedding, Pompeii, several spouts were made in a bluish glazed pottery-like material known as faience, including a crocodile (FIG. 176) and a large frog (FIG. 175). These had been made not in Naples or Rome, but in Egypt. About twenty exist, a small, though important, indicator of the thriving trading circles in which the cities were involved. Aside from any prestige attached to these novelties, they added a touch of fantasy and humour to the garden, which was, after all, partly an area for rest and play. The garden transported the viewer to Egypt, or the domain of Bacchus on the slopes of Vesuvius, or far beyond.

ABOVE LEFT **Fig. 170 Sometimes the drainage system for waste water from a garden simply cut through the external walls.**
Caupona of Lucius Vetutius Placidus, Pompeii

ABOVE **Fig. 171 Part of a garden watercourse.**
House of Decimus Octavius Quartio, Pompeii

BELOW **Fig. 174 Fountain basin with fluted bowl and podium.**

From Pompeii
H. 77 cm
MANN 126203

LEFT **Fig. 172 Lead tank with valves for the hydraulic system in a garden.**

From Pompeii
H. 17 cm, L. 48 cm
MANN 56309

LEFT **Fig. 173 Bronze tap.**

From the Vesuvian area
L. 15 cm
The British Museum, 1856,1226.864

BELOW **Fig. 175 Faience statuette of a frog.**

House of the Silver Wedding, Pompeii
H. 17.5 cm, W. 23 cm
MANN 121322

Fig. 176 Faience statuette of a crocodile.

House of the Silver Wedding, Pompeii
H. 9 cm, L. 39 cm, W. 13 cm
MANN 121324

RIGHT **Fig. 177 Bronze fountain spout in the form of a pine cone.**

From Pompeii
H. 53.5 cm
The British Museum, 1856,1226.1007

Fig. 178 Bronze fountain spout in the form of a peacock.

House of Camillus, Pompeii (VII,12,22-24)
H. 30cm, W. 11.5 cm
MANN 69784

Fig. 179 Bronze fountain spout in the form of a rabbit.

H. 13 cm, W. 12 cm
MANN 124912

GARDEN SCULPTURE AND FURNISHINGS

Gardens usually featured many practical and beautiful objects in addition to fountains, including bronze and marble sculptures. The finest collection of sculptures found in the cities comes from the Villa of the Papyri (H). This villa, clearly the residence of immensely wealthy people, possessed three peristyle gardens, filled with dozens of bronze and marble statues of gods, poets, philosophers and historical figures, nearly all from the Greek world.

Between the columns of the large peristyle were five life-size bronze statues of women, sometimes known by their Italian name as *le danzatrici* or 'the dancers'. It is more likely they are striking poses, or 'attitudes', emphasizing their grace and beauty. Their clothing is Greek, not Roman, with a long tunic, or *chiton*, under an upper robe, or *peplos*, held together on the shoulders by large bronze brooches. Their severe expressions and their hairstyles were inspired by a period of Greek art centuries before the eruption of Vesuvius, which greatly appealed to some Romans. Their faces may be somewhat formal and cold, but their eyes, of inset stone and ivory, give the sculptures great presence and power. Each statue has a different pose and attributes: one carried a tall bronze vessel (now missing) on her head, while another has ornate patterns of copper inlay on her headband and on the hem of her upper robe. A third, with tight corkscrew curls, fastens (or unfastens) her robe with a pin or brooch decorated with a rosette (FIGS 180–1).

Alongside these fine examples of Greek-style sculptures stood others which were less grand, but no less accomplished, such as two life-size bronze statues of deer, or a bronze piglet balancing on its back trotters as it leaps heroically into eternity (FIG. 182). The Romans loved novelties and observations of everyday life – simply capturing a moment, perhaps a humorous one.

Sculptures in and around gardens were often arranged in pairs, such as a group of four marble statues from the garden of the House of the Stags (H) (FIGS 183–4). The exact original positioning of the sculptures is uncertain, but they were probably set in pairs in a room facing onto the garden. They comprise a pair of stags (after which the house was named) attacked by hunting dogs, a statue of a satyr pouring wine from a wineskin and another showing the hero Hercules, in a far from heroic pose. His wreath

OPPOSITE AND ABOVE **Figs 180–1**
Bronze statue of a woman fastening her dress.

Villa of the Papyri, Herculaneum
H. *c*.150 cm
MANN 5619

RIGHT **Fig. 182 Bronze statue of a piglet.**

Villa of the Papyri, Herculaneum
H. 96 cm
MANN 4893

FOLLOWING PAGES, LEFT **Fig. 183**
Marble statue of a stag and hounds.

House of the Stags, Herculaneum (IV,21)
H. 63.7 cm, W. 62.7 cm
SAP 75796

FOLLOWING PAGES, RIGHT **Fig. 184**
Marble statue of the drunken Hercules.

House of the Stags, Herculaneum (IV,21)
H. 55.4 cm, W. 31.5 cm
SAP 75802

shows he has come from a banquet and he is clearly the worse for drink, barely able to stand and urinating drunkenly. Hercules has succumbed to the power of Bacchus, god of wine.

Some gardens also had a shrine (*lararium*) in addition to, or instead of, the shrine in the atrium. As well as a practical place for diners in the garden to offer food sacrifices to the gods, these could be a focal point for visitors looking through the house, as in the House of the Tragic Poet (P).

Set around the garden and peristyle were other fixtures and fittings. In Roman society there were established times for carrying out certain civic and domestic labours. Sundials appear in several gardens in the cities, for ornament as well as for practical time-keeping. One example (FIG. 185) from the House of Caius Julius Polybius (P) still preserves the bronze gnomon (hour indicator) and the red paint delineating the hour zones. The Roman day had twelve hours of day and twelve of night, rigidly set by sunrise and sunset. So as the seasons changed, the twelve hours had to expand and contract accordingly. In other words, a day hour in the summer would necessarily be longer than a day hour in the winter. For night hours the reverse would be true.

People gazed at the beauty of the garden sitting on wooden benches (FIG. 186), like one example from Herculaneum recently reconstructed for use in the House of Caius Julius Polybius (P). Traces of a garden bench like this were found *in situ* in the peristyle of the House of the Painters at Work (P).[20] Above the birdsong and the sound of the fountain, garden visitors might hear the tinkling of bells coming from a *tintinnabulum*, suspended from one of the trees. One spectacular example from Pompeii (FIG. 187) has a winged phallus (with its own phallus and a phallus tail) with five bells hanging from it. Its feet and tail are modelled on those of a lion, adding feral strength to the phallus' protective powers.

More sculpture decorated the spaces between the columns, where round marble or terracotta discs (each one called an *oscillum*, from the Latin *oscillare*, 'to spin') could be suspended from the architrave along the top of the columns, or perhaps from the garlands which hung between them. Oscilla were decorated with mythical creatures such as griffins (FIG. 188) or with characters linked to the worship of Bacchus, such as the god Pan, or satyrs and maenads.

ABOVE **Fig. 185 Marble sundial.**
House of Caius Julius Polybius, Pompeii (IX,13,1-3)
H. 26 cm, W. 25.5 cm
SAP 24544

BELOW **Fig. 186 Carbonized wooden bench.**
Decumanus Maximus, Herculaneum
H. 40 cm, L. 104 cm, W. 41 cm,
SAP 78450

OPPOSITE **Fig. 187 Bronze wind-chime in the form of a phallus with hanging bells.**
From Pompeii
H. 13.6 cm
The British Museum, 1856,1226.1086

Fig. 188 Marble decorative disc showing a griffin.
From Pompeii
D. 30.5 cm
The British Museum, 1856,1226.1671

WHAT GREW IN THE GARDEN?

The occupants of fine houses wanted to look out over attractive scenery as they relaxed, so trees and plants were just as important as fountains and sculpture. Which plants did they use and what did Roman gardens look like?

Literary sources can suggest when species were first introduced, but do not give much detail of their appearance. More helpful are detailed 'garden' paintings, such as the superb 'garden room' from the House of the Golden Bracelet discussed below (pp. 171–6), but it is difficult to know how realistic such depictions are. Recent work has revealed a great deal about the nature of gardens, the way that things were planted and, in some cases, positive identification of the types of plants used.[21]

Some gardens were divided up into different beds bounded by trellis fences. Excavations at the House of the Painters at Work revealed clear demarcations in the soil and lines of small, angled holes indicating trellis fences. The sides of the paths through the garden contained large numbers of clamshells, perhaps the remains of ornamental borders, or perhaps of snacks dropped by people as they walked, contemplated and chatted.[22] The evidence was detailed enough to enable a reconstruction of the beds and fences, which can be seen *in situ* at the site. In this particular case, roses and cypresses filled the borders, with ferns along the gutters of the colonnades.[23]

Just as today, Roman gardeners often raised plants elsewhere and then planted them out. The gardens in the cities have produced huge quantities of pottery vessels used for planting out small trees and shrubs. Sometimes these were reused cooking pots and jars,[24] but usually they were specially made vessels called *ollae perforatae* or *pertusae* ('pierced pots'),[25] with 'breathing' holes in the base and sides (FIGS 189–90). In literature these are first mentioned by the writer Pliny.[26] They have been found in the gardens of at least twenty houses in Pompeii and three in Herculaneum,[27] and they were also discovered in public contexts, such as the garden around the Temple of Venus (P).[28]

The garden of the House of the Greek Epigrams (P) provided some surprising evidence for an alternative method of transplanting. Careful excavation revealed grid points of areas of lighter soil against the darker matrix of the garden, and even marks in the soil where it had been worked with a hoe (FIG. 191).[29] The lighter soil was alluvial, of a type found near the River Sarnus, suggesting that trays or boxes of plants may have been brought into the city from that area and then planted out. Were these transferred from the owner's suburban estate to his town house, or purchased from commercial nurseries, a Pompeian garden centre perhaps?

In smaller homes the garden might well have been tended by the owners, but larger homes had slaves for planting, weeding and watering, and specialist gardeners. The grandest homes may even have had *topiarii* who tended and shaped plants.[30] So what were these gardeners planting or transplanting? For the borders there were evergreen plants such as box – still used today as an edging plant – as well as ferns and irises, both of which are frequently depicted on the painted dadoes of gardens and in other rooms.[31] Some scholars have pictured a largely evergreen garden, adding plants such as myrtle, acanthus, ivy and oleander.[32] Oleander provided welcome colour, and there were other flowering plants such as roses, violets and poppies. Flowers *per se* were

ABOVE **Fig. 189 Pottery planting pot with drainage hole.**

House of the Ship Europa, Pompeii
(I,15,2–3,4,6)
H. 16.5 cm, D. 15 cm
SAP 14583

BELOW **Fig. 190 Pottery planting pot with drainage hole.**

House of the Ship Europa, Pompeii
(I,15,2–3,4,6)
H. 13 cm, D. 11.5 cm
SAP 14574

not as necessary to Roman gardens as they are today;[33] in fact Pliny the Elder[34] talks about flowers only in the context of making garlands for religious ceremonies or banquets. There was, however, a thriving local trade in flowers for perfume-making and it is possible that some gardens in Pompeii grew flowers commercially. Carbonized flowers, perhaps the remains of garlands, have been found in garden pits containing residues from household sacrifices.[35]

Many Roman gardens featured trees, from attractive fruit trees including hazelnut, fig, cherry and olive, to those for ornament and shade, such as plane trees, umbrella pines and cypress. Perfectly preserved roots and lower trunks of many cypress trees were discovered in the 1990s near Pompeii,[36] and umbrella pines probably shaded the road leading to the Villa Regina at Boscoreale.[37] In some cases it has been possible to gain a visual idea of the impact of tree planting by taking casts of tree roots. Casts sometimes allow tentative identifications of the trees.[38] They can also give an idea of the age of the tree, and some were well over a century old at the time of the eruption. It is possible to imagine the centres of some houses as an oasis of calm, with greenery, from tall trees to shrubs and flowers, interspersed with sculpture and fountains.

ABOVE **Fig. 191 Iron hoe.**

From Pompeii
H. 5.5 cm
SAP 40372

BELOW RIGHT **Fig. 192 Glass window pane.**

From Herculaneum
H. 54 cm, W. 31 cm
The British Museum, 1772,0317.21

LIVING AROUND THE GARDEN

This transformed garden became a focal point for the family's activities. Rooms for dining, sleeping and relaxing were often sited round it or even situated within it. The garden was a natural place in which to eat, relax and sleep, especially during the oppressive heat of the Mediterranean summer.

Some rooms had glazed windows, allowing the garden to be enjoyed in comfort even in the depths of winter.[39] Panes of glass, formed by pouring molten glass into flat rectangular moulds, were set into mortar surrounds or into wooden window frames and provided a degree of comfort and light not possible with wooden shutters and sliding flaps. An alternative to glass panes was to use sheets of a transparent, yellowish white

ABOVE **Fig. 193 Fresco on the wall of a garden showing the goddess Venus.**

House of Venus in the Shell, Pompeii

BELOW **Fig. 194 Fixed masonry couches in a garden overlooked by paintings of Narcissus (left) and Pyramus and Thisbe (right).**

House of Decimus Octavius Quartio, Pompeii

stone, muscovite mica, called by the Romans *lapis specularis* (literally 'seeing stone'). Pliny[40] relates that panes of glass[41] or mica could also be used to make cloches to protect plants. Some houses, such as the House of the Mosaic Atrium (H) or the House of Marcus Fabius Rufus (P) have evidence for the closure of spaces between columns with glazed wooden frameworks, allowing the area to be enjoyed all year round.[42]

Perhaps the most pleasant way to pass time in the garden was in dining and drinking and even making love, as seen in the frescoes in the House of the Chaste Lovers (P). External dining facilities are found in properties ranging from rich houses to taverns. The House of the Gardens of Hercules (P) has a fixed masonry *triclinium* in the garden with shade provided by a bower of vines supported by the corner columns, as reconstructed today (FIG. 262). In the garden of the House of Decimus Octavius Quartio is a *biclinium* of two fixed couches (FIG. 194). It was built at the end of a long vista with a central elongated pool, originally lined with small sculptures, and frescoes of a beast hunt down the portico wall. Flanking the central niche of the biclinium, which once contained a statue of Hercules, are two paintings, one showing Narcissus gazing lovingly at his own reflection, and the other showing Pyramus and Thisbe. They were star-crossed lovers who committed suicide, each believing the other had died – the Romeo and Juliet of classical mythology.

These fixed masonry couches were usually faced with smooth plaster, often painted red or pink, on which mattresses would be placed for the diners. Occasionally the sides of the couches were decorated with scenes, as in the House of the Ephebe (P). The paintings that line the interior

and ends of this triclinium show scenes from the Nile. Some are scenes of religious devotion, while others are more colourful, showing a couple of pygmies making love in the open air – comical and very un-Roman. In another a group of diners is about to be interrupted by a hungry crocodile.

GODS, EXOTICA AND EROTICA IN THE GARDEN

It seems strange, and indeed offensive, to us to have pictures of pygmies or any 'different' people displayed as figures of fun. But the Romans saw nothing wrong with this. Just as the exotic animals killed in the arena showed mastery over nature, so the portrayal of pygmies from Egypt showed superiority over foreign lands and people. Nonetheless, the Romans were fascinated by these distant countries – in particular Egypt. As can be seen above, the representations of what the Romans (jokingly) considered to be Egyptian life were intentionally mocking, but the fascination was always there. Frescoes showing scenes of life by the Nile have already been mentioned, and there are many representations of the Egyptian goddess Isis, for example the painted shrine in the House of the Gilded Cupids.[43]

Some gods had particular links with the garden. Venus, according to Pliny,[44] was the patroness of gardens and features in sculpture or wall painting in many of them, most famously in the House of Venus in the Shell. Occupying the rear wall of a large garden is a mural of the goddess (FIG. 193) reclining sensually on a large shell, wearing only her jewellery and an enigmatic smile. The illusionistic statue of Mars on one side and fountain on the other aim to give a sense of perspective – of Venus floating in the background. The owner's guests could either see Venus or imagine the presence of Venus herself, the protectress of the garden and the voluptuous goddess of love. Frescoes had many interpretations.

The deity most commonly associated with the garden was Bacchus. His mastery of the countryside and its produce (in particular wine) and his connection with rural life made it inevitable that when the countryside was brought into the home, he came with it. He and his followers, satyrs and maenads, and animals such as fauns and goats, are popular subjects of wall painting and sculpture in the garden. One of the best examples of a 'Bacchic' garden is the House of Marcus Lucretius Fronto, once filled with over a dozen small, brightly painted Bacchic sculptures.[45]

With Bacchus and his followers another god came into the garden, the goat-legged god Pan. A startling representation of this god made an unexpected appearance at Herculaneum in the mid-eighteenth century. It immediately forced people to re-examine what they believed about the meaning of Roman 'erotic' art and ever since it has been the subject of intense interest and debate.

On 1 March 1752, during 'excavations' of the Villa of the Papyri, the tunnellers unearthed a statue of the god Pan intently making love, not, as usual, to a nymph, a satyr or even a male/female hermaphrodite, but to a nanny goat. Nothing like it had been seen before, and even by the standards of the sexually 'liberated' art emerging from the cities, it was extremely surprising.

Pan had always been an ambivalent god. He was, after all, half man and half goat, as his shaggy legs, cloven hooves and horns confirmed. He was, as goats were always believed to be, endowed with endless sexual energy. (When the emperor Tiberius retired to his island palace at Capri his gardens were known as the 'goat's place' because of the sexual excesses that happened there.)[46] Yet people mostly linked Pan to the world of men, as a slightly capricious companion for country people. Here,

Fig. 195 Marble statue showing the god Pan making love to a she-goat.

Villa of the Papyri, Herculaneum
H. 44 cm, base 49 cm x 47 cm
MANN 27709

Fig. 196 Terracotta statuete of Pan and the Goat, possibly made by Joseph Nollekens.

H. 16 cm
The British Museum, M.550

his goat side is dominant and he wants another goat. Naturally enough, perhaps – not only was he part goat anyway, but he was in his element, the countryside, or at least that part of the countryside encompassed in the garden.

Pan is penetrating the goat, but the whole composition is remarkably calm. This is no surprise attack – in fact Pan and his love have settled into a position of relative comfort. The pose is very ungoatlike, with the nanny goat flat on her back – certainly unusual for an animal – while Pan gently grasps her beard. Is he going to bring her face towards his? It might well have been seen by the Romans as a humorous, even (dare it be said) tender, coupling.

Unsurprisingly, this was not the reaction in the middle of the eighteenth century. The sculpture was not put on public view, unlike the other treasures from Herculaneum displayed in the King of Naples' collections, though (contrary to those who want to see complete royal censorship in operation) the piece could be viewed with the king's permission. Some people certainly viewed it, including many Englishmen on the cultural 'grand tour' of Europe, so popular in the mid- to later eighteenth century. Among them was an English sculptor Joseph Nollekens, and either he or another English visitor sculpted a small-scale terracotta, now in the collection of the British Museum, inspired by the marble group in Naples (FIG. 196). The terracotta had a paper label which reads, 'copy from memory of ye marble group in [Portici Museum]'. Clearly it was made after the artist had viewed the original (implying that sketching *in situ* was not permitted). By the early 1820s the Royal Museum at Naples, transferred from its old seat at Portici near Herculaneum, had formally created a *gabinetto degli oggetti riservati* ('room of reserved objects'). However, 'remote access' was in effect assured as a catalogue of the material was already circulating.[47]

The *oggetti riservati* in their Gabinetto Segreto (secret room, or rather rooms as there was more than one) of Naples had a complex history with varying degrees of access, sometimes depending on political circumstances.[48] The *oggetti* were only revealed in their entirety to the public in 2000, while the Nollekens statuette followed a parallel course into the Museum Secretum of the British Museum. The reactions to the statue of Pan and the Goat when it is in its permanent home in Naples Museum range from amusement to embarrassment (or a mixture of both) and, occasionally, horror.[49] The piece is confusing and disorientating and does not correspond to any other, more conventionally 'naughty' Roman art. Is it raw eroticism, is it affectionate, or is it simply meant to raise a smile?

GRAFFITI

The garden, like the atrium, was a major hub for the household. Everyone from master to slaves passed through, and there must have been times when they paused to rest or sit under the colonnades for a moment. As they did so, they scribbled and scratched on the walls and columns. Some graffiti may have been made when houses were being rebuilt, but the majority seem to be genuine echoes of the inhabitants of the house.

An example, still on the curved section of a column (FIG. 197), talks about quantities of garden stakes, some sharpened, others not, for use in a vineyard or as fence posts. These may well have been of chestnut, very durable and still used by vintners today.[50] A graffito *in situ* in the garden of the House of the Painters at Work (P) tells us (in slightly incorrect Latin) *balneus* [sic] *lavatur* ('the bath is cleaned'), while another (FIG. 198) from the next column proclaims: *Severus verna val(e)* ('Severus, slave born in this household, farewell'). Both make the presence of slaves abundantly clear. On the wall of the peristyle of another house, someone drew two gladiators, a reminder of the world outside the home (FIG. 18).

One graffito (FIG. 199) was scratched onto a peristyle wall near a domestic shrine. It records only a date and year – perhaps commemorating an important family event.[51] The year is given in the traditional Roman way by the names of the Consuls for that year, Caius Laelius Balbus and Caius Autistius Veteris = 6 BC. But the day date is given through the complex calendar system. By the time of the eruption the Romans had a year of twelve months with names very recognizable to us, such as Aprilius, Augustus and December. Within each month were three important, sacred days: Kalends, Nones and Ides. Kalends were always the first of the month, but Nones and Ides varied according to the length of the month. In long months (for the Romans March, May, July and October) the Nones fell on the seventh and the Ides on the fifteenth day – so Julius Caesar's assassination took place on 15 (Ides) March. For all the other months the Nones were the fifth and the Ides the thirteenth. To calculate a date it is necessary to count back from one of these fixed points, including the starting day. For example, *III Id Martis* would be the third day before the Ides of March. Including the 15th, going back three days arrives at 13 March. In our inscription the date is written *AD XIIII K NOVEMBR* = *Ante diem XIIII Kalendas Novembres*. This gives a date of fourteen days before 1 November (counting the 1st as well), that is 19 October.

TOP **Fig. 197 Graffito discussing quantities of garden posts.**

Villa of Agrippa Postumus, Boscoreale
H. 17 cm, W. 23 cm
SAP 20518

ABOVE **Fig. 198 Graffito saying 'Severus slave born in this house farewell'.**

House of the Painters at Work, Pompeii

BELOW LEFT **Fig. 199 Graffito from the wall of a peristyle giving the date of 19 October 6 BC.**

House of Amarantus, Pompeii
H. 16 cm, W. 42 cm
SAP 20514

BELOW RIGHT **Fig. 200 Graffito with numerous inscriptions.**

House of Marcus Fabius Rufus, Pompeii
H. 20 cm, W. 63 cm
SAP 20564

A piece of wall plaster (FIG. 200) from the House of Marcus Fabius Rufus (P),[52] has at least eleven graffiti in more than four different hands mentioning aspects of life and love. A slave wrote: *Epaphroditus cum Thalia hac* ('Epaphroditus and Thalia were here'). A would-be poet asks (in Latin rhyme): 'Who is spending the night in happy slumber here with you? If it were me I'd be so much happier' (*Felicem somnum qui tecum nocte quiescet/hoc ego si facere, multo felicior esse*). Someone else wrote *Suabe mare magno* ... ('How sweet [it is] on the mighty sea...'), from the beginning of a book by the Roman writer Lucretius. It uses an alternative spelling (*suabe* instead of *suave*), a reminder that Latin, like all languages, was not monolithic. Someone in the garden of the House of Marcus Holconius Rufus (P) clearly had far too much time on their hands: 'If you want to waste time, scatter millet seeds...then pick them up again'.[53]

THE GARDEN ROOM

The Romans had brought the garden and much wilder spaces into the centre of the home, and now the garden was also brought into individual rooms. Across the cities several examples survive of 'garden rooms'. These were usually larger rooms, primarily used for dining, but also including smaller spaces such as the two cubicula in the House of the Orchard (P) (FIG. 201). Garden rooms occur even in homes with abundant access to real gardens so they are not a substitute. They seem instead to express a desire to bring the garden inside whatever the size of the home.[54]

A very fine example of garden painting was discovered in the 1960s in the House of the Golden Bracelet at the western edge of Pompeii. The house extended over three levels, on the lowest of which were two adjacent rooms. Under the nearby staircase archaeologists discovered the remains of a family: mother, father and two children, who had died sheltering there (see p. 298). The rooms looked out over a small garden terrace with pools and fountains and stunning views of the sea beyond. The larger room, open to the garden, was a permanent triclinium or dining area, with fixed masonry couches, partly sheathed in white marble. The walls featured a garden scene, including sphinxes which gave it an Egyptian feel, but this decoration paled compared to the decoration of the smaller adjacent room, which completely immerses the viewer in the greenery of a garden.[55] The original use of the room is uncertain. It is next to a summer triclinium, yet although the decoration of this smaller room would have reminded diners of a summer garden – and plump birds and lush greenery might have

Fig. 201 Cubiculum painted with a garden scene.
House of the Orchard, Pompeii

Fig 202 Fresco from a room (south wall) showing garden scenes.

House of the Golden Bracelet, Pompeii (VI,17,42)
SAP 40692

stoked the appetite – there are no definite indications that it, too, was a dining room. The patterning of the floor delimits space for only one movable couch, so perhaps this room was a study for the owner,[56] a hideaway for relaxation and contemplation.

Each wall was divided into three horizontal sections, the upper and lower zones serving as a theatrical frame for the central scene (FIG. 202). The lowest section shows a black garden wall with plants, including irises, in front, and a trellis fence with openings, revealing lush greenery. The upper section shows architectural details against a black background, with garlands, discs and *pinakes* (decorative panels; singular *pinax*) with faces and a leaping lion. The room had a vaulted ceiling, so there were semicircular panels or lunettes at the top of the shorter end walls. On the back (east) wall are doves perched on and around a bronze or gold bowl filled with water (FIG. 203), perhaps echoing a famous mosaic showing doves drinking that was described by Pliny.[57] However, the central area of the walls was the intended focus.

Looking at the complete north wall (FIG. 161) we see a wild garden, with a wealth of plants and birds. There are some man-made elements: at the centre is a fountain with a scalloped basin, and on either side is a herm supporting a marble pinax (FIG. 161). The female herm on the left holds a picture of Ariadne, the lover of the god Dionysus/Bacchus. The male herm, with a satyr's wild face, holds a panel showing a maenad. Bacchic images were very common features in a garden, a reminder that we are looking into the wild.

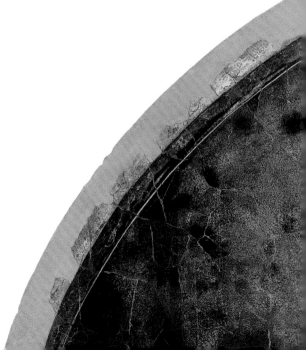

This wilder landscape invades and envelopes the man-made, and the fountain base is almost hidden among ivy and marigolds. The ground is a disorderly carpet of flowers and small plants, such as lilies, roses, poppies and ivy, while above are larger bushes of oleander and arbutus, plane and palm trees. The walls are alive with birds; wood pigeons, jays (FIG. 206), swallows, magpies, golden orioles (FIG. 207) and blackbirds perch on bushes and take to the skies. On the east wall a swamp hen (FIG. 208) creeps through the undergrowth, while at the top is a beautiful black-headed dove, its wings outstretched as it soars heavenwards. The south wall is badly damaged but has a charming detail of a nightingale perching on a beautifully detailed rosebush; even the tie holding the bush to its stake is depicted (FIG. 209).

In reality these birds and plants would never normally be seen together at the same time of year.[58] The paintings are idealized and fantastic. It is possible that certain plants or birds had symbolic significance, just as the tapestries and paintings of mediaeval Europe could be 'read' for religious meanings; but perhaps the owner and painters just wanted to create a beautiful fantasy.

Some suggest that particular frescoes – garden room and beast hunt – represent the rather vulgar taste of upwardly mobile freedmen. It seems more likely that they reveal a shared tradition cutting across social strata.[59]

Gardens, whether real or painted, encouraged relaxation. In wealthier homes this relaxation was enhanced by beautiful fountains, pools, sculptures, frescoes and other ornaments, and was set against a natural background of plants and trees. The countryside, and all that came with it, had been brought into the home. The garden was a lovely place in which to sit, but it was also beautiful to look at and, as the next chapter shows, the garden was the backdrop to some of the finest rooms in the house.

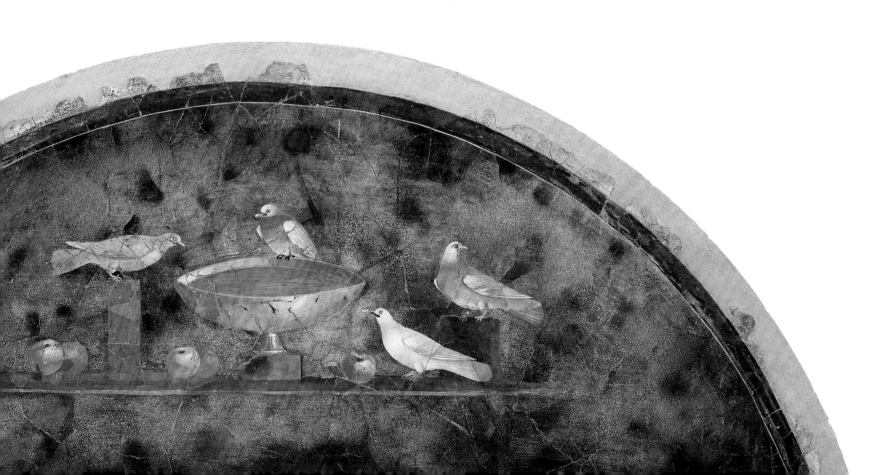

VI
LIVING ROOMS
AND
INTERIOR DESIGN

LIVING ROOMS
AND INTERIOR DESIGN

THE GARDEN, like the atrium, became an important focus of family life. Around these areas, in many houses in Pompeii and Herculaneum, are rooms which, judging from their size, proportions, and superior decoration, clearly had great importance (FIGS 211 and 212).[1] If the majority of activities involving *negotium* (business) took place within the atrium or tablinum, then these other rooms were for *otium* – for relaxation, leisure, entertaining and dining. This chapter looks at these rooms and their decoration, and tries to give an idea of who commissioned and created them and how and by whom they were used.

We cannot be certain exactly what these rooms were called by the Romans. It is likely that rooms with such an array of functions may have had a range of labels. In some larger, wealthier houses certain types of 'living rooms' had particular names. Vitruvius[2] and Pliny[3] use the names *oecus*, from the Greek word for 'house', and *exedra*, a Greek word for 'a place to sit outside'.[4] They suggest both rooms are finely decorated and spacious, with the exedra perhaps more open,[5] wider than deep, with an open front wall giving onto a garden or peristyle, and the oecus deeper than wide. A possible exedra in the House of Obellius Firmus (P) (FIG. 211) looked out onto the colonnaded garden, and preserves casts of the folding wooden shutters that could close off the room. Modern scholars sometimes use the word exedra, which can also have the

PREVIOUS PAGES **Fig. 210 Detail of a fresco showing a music lesson (see fig. 213).**

OPPOSITE **Fig. 211 Casts of multiple shutters in an *exedra* overlooking a garden.**
House of Obellius Firmus, Pompeii

ABOVE **Fig. 212 The *oecus* or Mysteries Room.**
Villa of the Mysteries, Pompeii

meaning of an outdoor semi-circular seat or bench, to describe grand apsidal rooms, such as the example in the House of the Skeleton (H). It is possible that in Roman times only the very wealthy used these Greek names.

Examples of rooms that, because of their form, scale and décor, have been given the label *oecus* by modern archaeologists can be seen in the House of the Stags (H), the House of the Menander (P) and the House of the Black Living Room (H). These feel like assembly rooms and, given the implied wealth and importance of the owners, they may occasionally have served as such.

In these finely decorated rooms, with views out to a beautiful garden, the owners and their family could unwind and live their lives. We can imagine the whole family sitting, reading, entertaining themselves with games and board games, making and listening to music and, very importantly, dining and drinking. Of course, similar family activities took place in the smaller, less well-appointed houses, and in apartments.

Games such as backgammon (*mensae*), shown in a fresco on a bar wall (above p. 63), were also played at home. Counters and dice are frequent finds in the cities, for example in the Cardo V drain (FIG. 214), showing they were used across the social spectrum. Music in Roman towns was not restricted to public venues such as the amphitheatre, the Odeon or temples. It played an important role in many wealthier houses, as an accompaniment to domestic religion but also as entertainment, together with recitals of poetry, singing or dancing.[6] Instruments that appear in the domestic archaeological record are the flute (*tibia*), cymbals, lyre, tambourine and the Egyptian-style rattle (*sistrum*). The lyre was very popular, but is less likely to survive, being largely made of wood. A fresco (FIG. 213) shows a lyre lesson in progress, though music is not top of the young couple's minds.

Whatever the exact range of activities that took place in them, these living areas were some of the best-appointed rooms in a Roman house, and were filled with the finest mosaics, wall paintings and sculpture. It is important to remember that no decorative styles were pioneered in the cities and that wealthier cities, such as Naples or Pozzuoli, will have had a much higher quality and quantity of frescoes, mosaics and other décor. However, the cities preserve by far the greatest surviving concentration of Roman interior design, so they provide an ideal opportunity to look at the different types of decoration used in Italy and the empire. In the cities we have a horizon of AD 79, but by no means does everything in the houses date to that year or just before. The houses of the cities, just like our own, were never in a fixed state. New owners, natural disasters (such as earthquakes), changing circumstances and even changing fashions all had an effect on the interiors. There is no one set type of design in the cities – and it is this chronological and stylistic range and diversity that makes the cities so important.

ABOVE **Fig. 213 Fresco showing a music lesson.**
From Pompeii
H. 58 cm, W. 80 cm
The British Museum, 1867,0508.1353

BELOW **Fig. 214 A selection of counters and a dice.**
Cardo V drain, Herculaneum

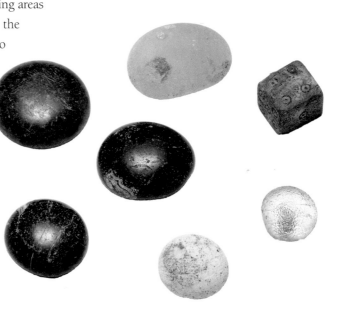

FLOOR DECORATION

The most common flooring in the cities was a form of plain concrete called *signinum*,[7] sometimes known by its Italian name of *cocciopesto*, literally 'crushed pot'. It was made of crushed brick and tile in mortar, often coated with a thin layer of red or black plaster. In the cities a version called *lavapesta*, using crushed lava instead of tile, was very popular. Signinum was hardwearing and waterproof, and from about 200 BC was enlivened with designs of stones. The floor in the oecus in the Samnite House (H) (FIG. 215) has a circle with geometric patterns inside an intricate meander border, all made of white *tesserae* (small cubed pieces of stone, from the Greek word for 'four-sided'). A corridor around the garden of the House of the Gilded Cupids (P) also added cut shapes in coloured stone or marble, a technique known as *crustae*. Signinum floors, especially decorated examples, remained in many houses, sometimes in quite fine rooms, even when the walls around them were updated.

Perhaps most of us, asked to imagine a Roman house, would picture it with a mosaic floor. Mosaics, decorative surface coverings made entirely of tesserae, appear in about 250 BC[8] in Greek cities in Sicily and elsewhere, such as Alexandria in Egypt and Pergamon in Asia Minor (modern Turkey). The Romans acquired a taste for tesserae mosaics when they conquered the Greek cities of the eastern Mediterranean, using them in public buildings, such as baths (FIG. 216), but also in private houses.

Figurative mosaics composed of brightly coloured tesserae were usually found only in grand properties, in particular atrium houses.[9] In many houses thresholds were decorated with a motif, for example a guard dog (FIGS 80 and 81). Mosaics linked spaces,[10] just like modern carpeting or tiles, as in the atrium and tablinum of the House of the Wounded Bear (P), or the courtyard of the House of the Bel Cortile (H). Such geometric 'carpet' patterns, in particular in black and white tesserae, were a trademark of Italian mosaicists. Some first-century BC stone floors were made out of cut marble shapes (*crustae*), like those used in some signinum floors (FIG. 215).

Fig. 215 Crushed tile and mortar (*opus signinum*) floor with patterns in white *tesserae*.

Samnite House, Herculaneum

OPPOSITE **Fig. 216 Mosaic of black and white tesserae showing a Triton surrounded by sea creatures.**

Women's Baths, Herculaneum

ABOVE **Fig. 217 Geometric mosaic with central panel (*emblema*).**

Cubiculum of the House of Marcus Fabius Rufus, Pompeii

ABOVE RIGHT **Fig. 218 Small mosaic emblema showing a theatrical mask.**

Vesuvian area
H. 15 cm, W. 15 cm
The British Museum, 1856,1226.1643

FOLLLOWING PAGES **Fig. 219 Detail of mosaic emblema showing sea creatures.**

From Pompeii (VIII,2,16)
H. 103 cm, W. 103 cm
MANN 120177

This perhaps served to make expensive marble go further, or used up off-cuts from other marble decoration.

Mosaics could also be used in smaller spaces, such as the cubiculum in the House of Marcus Fabius Rufus (FIG. 217), or *caldarium* (hot room) of the baths of the House of the Menander, which has a gloriously polychrome mosaic (FIG. 322).

Sometimes the patterns and zoning of the mosaic can give clues as to the positioning of types of furniture, and so to the room's use.[11] Rooms sometimes had a central motif, suggesting that the space around was occupied by couches on three sides or at one end. The use of mosaics certainly indicated wealth, but an *emblema* (plural *emblemata*), a highly detailed mosaic panel, placed as a focal point at the centre of a plainer floor, was an indicator of even greater refinement.[12] Some were made of tesserae (FIG. 219), others of *opus sectile* (cut marble; FIG. 221).

Emblemata could be small, as in the theatrical mask illustrated above (FIG. 218), which is similar to the example in the cubiculum of the House of Marcus Fabius Rufus (FIG. 217). However, the finest were usually 60 cm (2 Roman feet) square, made of extremely fine tesserae, called *opus vermiculatum* (literally 'worm work'), showing scenes of daily life, still life and mythology. One (FIG. 219) shows sea creatures centred around an octopus in combat with a lobster. Another (FIG. 220) has a beautifully depicted cat snatching a bird from a shelf of birds, seafood and fish, all destined for the table. There were also scenes from the theatre or of exotic life on the River Nile, symbols and allegories.

Emblema panels in *vermiculatum* were produced by skilled craftsmen from specialist workshops. Working on- or offsite they set the emblema panels in trays of terracotta or marble, ready to be slotted into the floor (and subsequently relocated if

required). Some trays are made of local clay, implying that they were made close by; if not in the cities themselves, then in nearby Naples or Pozzuoli. Parallel scenes or motifs across the cities indicate there were multiple copies of well-known originals. One possible explanation for this is that mosaicists (and clients) were able to consult drawings of existing or planned mosaics – in effect, catalogues – or that the mosaicists were very mobile.[13] No trace of such catalogues has been found, but the similarity of some mosaics seems too great to be coincidence.

MOSAIC ARTISTS AND SUBJECTS

Mosaicists are largely anonymous and were probably not of very high status.[14] Only occasionally are the names of the artists recorded. Two emblema panels, found in the so-called Villa of Cicero at Pompeii in the 1760s, each has an inscription in Greek (FIG. 244) saying: 'Dioskourides of Samos made (this)' (ΔΙΟΣΚΟΥΡΙΔΗΔΗΣ ΣΑΜΙΟΣ ΕΠΟΙΗΣΕ). This artist was a Greek-speaker, originally, we are told, from the island of Samos in the eastern Aegean, but he could have been working in Naples or Rome. One mosaic shows a group of women sitting around a table (FIG. 222), while the other (FIG. 223) shows musicians, men playing a tambourine and cymbals and a woman playing the double flute. Almost all the characters are wearing masks – they are actors. The mosaics are fascinating works of art in their own right, but what, if anything, did these scenes mean?

The mystery was only solved 200 years later, thanks to a discovery on the Greek island of Lesbos.[15] Archaeologists working at the town of Mytilene in the 1960s discovered the remains of a fine Roman house dating to the fourth century AD. In it they found several mosaics, including one very similar to the 'seated ladies'. Remarkably, the Mytilene mosaic had a title. This identified the panel as a scene from the *Synaristosai*,

'The Breakfasters', a play by the Greek comic poet Menander, which is now totally lost, save for a few scraps on papyri from Egypt. The panel even had the characters' names spelt out above their heads. Another mosaic in the Mytilene house paralleled closely the Pompeii 'musicians mosaic': this is labelled as the *Theophoroumene*, 'The Possessed Girl', another mostly lost play by Menander. By chance, another depiction of the lady 'Breakfasters', labelled with the name of the play, recently emerged in Zeugma in eastern Turkey – again from a late Roman house.[16]

The Pompeian mosaics were made in about 100 BC, so by the time of the eruption they were almost 200 years old. Very much of what has survived from the cities was old, sometimes very old, by the time of the eruption. Heirlooms and antiques are not modern inventions. The musicians mosaic finds another close parallel in a wall painting from Stabiae, which dates to about AD 50, over 150 years later than the Pompeii mosaics (FIG. 224), showing that past works were admired and copied and that mosaicists, perhaps, worked closely with painters and other artists.[17]

This does not necessarily mean that these antique plays of Menander were still being performed at the time of the eruption[18] – we cannot prove whether they were or not. Either way, it does show that the scenes and images of these ancient plays still meant something to the owner of this house, just as they meant something to the owners of the fourth century AD houses in Mytilene and Zeugma. It also underlines the immense importance of the mosaics and wall paintings of the cities to us today. They have often preserved precious echoes of works of art and literature that would otherwise have been lost.

Another antique mosaic was discovered in the House of the Faun in Pompeii in 1831, the most spectacular domestic mosaic found in the cities (FIG. 225). It measures

ABOVE LEFT **Fig. 222 Mosaic by Dioskourides of Samos showing the 'Breakfasting Ladies'.**

Villa of Cicero, Pompeii
H. 42 cm, W. 35 cm
MANN 9987

ABOVE RIGHT **Fig. 223 Mosaic by Dioskourides of Samos showing street musicians.**

Villa of Cicero, Pompeii
H. 43 cm, W. 41 cm
MANN 9985

OPPOSITE **Fig. 224 The same scene of street musicians shown in a much later fresco.**

From Stabiae
H. 29 cm, W. 38 cm
MANN 9034

Fig. 225 **The Alexander Mosaic.**

House of the Faun, Pompeii
H. 317 cm, W. 555 cm
MANN 10020

approximately 6 m by 3 m (19 ft by 10 ft), and shows Alexander the Great defeating King Darius III of Persia in battle, perhaps at the River Issus in south-west Turkey in 333 BC. Details such as Alexander's face and breastplate are so finely shown that they look painted. The mosaic is possibly a copy of a wall painting[19] commissioned by the Macedonian king Cassander from the painter Philoxenus in about 300 BC. The mosaic in the House of the Faun was made in about 150 BC, and so was over 200 years old in AD 79. The quality is extraordinary, as the tesserae, approximately 1.5 million of them, are the size normally used in the smaller emblemata panels. This mosaic would have been almost impossibly difficult to transport as a laid-out unit and must surely have been laid *in situ*.[20]

OPUS SECTILE FLOORS

Another kind of flooring was *opus sectile*, a modern term used to describe the decoration of floors and walls with pieces of marble cut to shape. In houses in the cities it first appears as small emblemata (FIG. 221), often with mosaic surrounds. A spectacular example from the dining area of the House of the Ephebe (P) features a large, rectangular, multi-coloured marble panel, with a very detailed and precious central panel of marble and blue, red, green and even gold glass (FIG. 226). The panel is a masterpiece, unique in the cities, and its owners clearly treated it with due respect. Its beauty was reserved for guests and special occasions, as archaeologists discovered the panel under a sheet of lead, obviously placed to protect it from the day-to-day traffic of family and servants.[21] In the homes of the very wealthy, opus sectile was later spread across whole floors and also the walls (below pp. 216–17). For their sheer quantity and quality, the diversity of marbles used and the complexity of patterns, the best surviving examples are to be found in Herculaneum.[22]

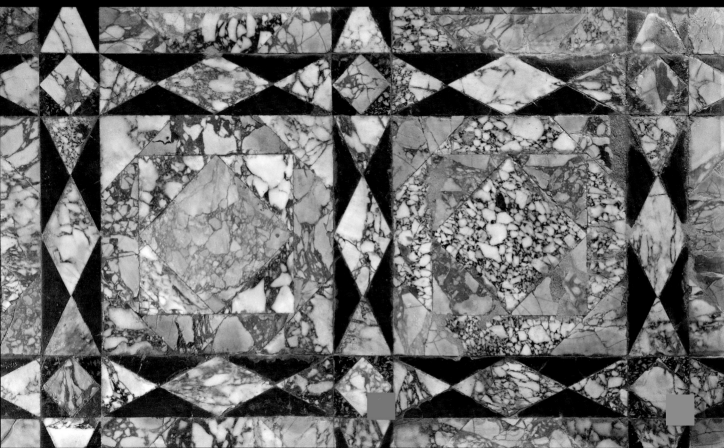

OPPOSITE ABOVE **Fig. 226 Cut marble (*opus sectile*) panel with geometric patterns in marble and glass.**
House of the Ephebe, Pompeii

OPPOSITE BELOW **Fig. 227 Detail of a cut marble (*opus sectile*) floor.**
House of the Relief of Telephus, Herculaneum

RIGHT **Fig. 228 Fresco showing yellow ochre scorched to red by the heat of the eruption.**
House of the Relief of Telephus, Herculaneum (Ins.Or.1)

BELOW **Fig. 229 Pottery bowl containing solid white pigment stamped with the name ATTIORU[m].**
Workshop of the Attii, Pompeii (IX,2,11)
MANN 112228

WALL PAINTINGS

The walls were a main focus for attention. They were usually decorated with wall paintings (frescoes) but also, in the last decades before the eruption, with mosaic, marble veneer and sculpted reliefs.

Wall paintings, often seen now as beautiful but isolated fragments in museums, were once part of vibrant, colourful decorative schemes linking floors, walls and ceilings. They are, perhaps, the single most important indicator of the status of the house owner,[23] as well as a marker for the spreading of the fashion for beautiful interior design.[24] On a practical level, Vitruvius writes about the techniques of creating wall paintings: in *De Architectura* (VII 3, 5–9) he advises applying several different layers of plaster, and painting when the topmost layer is still wet. This technique is called *alfresco* in Italian, giving wall paintings their other name – frescoes. Vitruvius states that when the painting is dry it should be 'set' and given a sheen by polishing.[25] Paints were mixed as needed from balls or cakes of pigment, crushed up and made into liquid paint with water and with other ingredients, such as honey, as a binder.

Among the colours used,[26] Pliny cites vibrant (*floridi*) colours,[27] which he implies could be more expensive, such as indigo, 'red lead', or cinnabar (*minium*), as seen in the paintings of the opulent Villa of the Mysteries (P) (FIGS 237–40); and more ordinary colours (*austeri*) such as red and yellow ochre, and white calcium carbonate. A bowl from Pompeii contains lumps of white pigment (FIG. 229), one stamped *ATTIORU[M]* ('made by the Attii').[28] These colours were remarkably stable even during the eruption, except for yellow ochre which, above 300 degrees Celsius, dehydrates and changes from yellow to red.[29] This effect is seen at Herculaneum and Pompeii in swirling patterns too random to have been designed (FIG. 228). According to Pliny,[30] prices of pigments varied enormously; red and yellow ochre cost the low price of 2 *denarii* per Roman pound, indigo 20 *denarii* and red lead 70 *denarii*. Even within the same house, quality and colour varied according to the room's function and status and the budget of the person who commissioned the decoration. It was the customers, not the painters, who supplied the pigments.[31]

Like other artisans, painters were not high on the social scale.[32] Most were anonymous slaves and freedmen,[33] though a painter's signature, *Lucius pinxit*, 'Lucius painted (this)', was discovered on the biclinium in the House of Decimus Octavius Quartio.[34]

Painters may well have been organized in fairly fixed groups (*officinae*) of artisans,[35] like mosaicists, plasterers and stucco workers.[36] There were two main types of painter: the *parietarius*, from the Latin for wall (*paries*), who painted expanses of colour; and the *imaginarius*, who dealt with more complex figurative pieces and was paid twice as much.[37] Working on wet plaster, the usual technique for wall painting, required close co-operation between painters and plasterers. On larger jobs this was probably organized through a foreman or *institor*,[38] who co-ordinated works and liaised with the client, who himself was represented by an agent 'procurator'. A probable painters' workshop was discovered in the east of Pompeii, which contained over 100 small pots filled with pigments of different colours, including blue, red, green, orange and white.[39] They had not yet been made up into paint. With them were found a mortar and pestle to grind the pigments into fine powder, spatulas to help mix the paints, and compasses and a plumb bob to help with the layout of the decorative scheme.

As soon as the plasterers had finished, the painters plotted out their designs with scored lines or in *sinopia*, a reddish-brown pigment (FIG. 231). A sinopia panel was found in the House of the Painters at Work (P), named after its abundant evidence for painters working at the time of the eruption.[40] The house was undergoing major renovation and redecoration at the time. The oecus or 'living room' of the House of the Painters at Work had a large, impressive emblema (central floor panel) of marble opus sectile, and the walls were being painted in the style most fashionable at the time of the eruption, but were not finished. One wall (FIG. 230) had a central red panel flanked by narrower panels of stylized architectural detail. Because of the fatal interruption, the panel on the right is only drawn in sinopia, the large central mythological painting of the red panel was not even begun and the dado or socle was missing altogether. In a rare survival of evidence for the *a secco* technique (in which colours are applied to dampened, but not fresh, wet plaster), elements and motifs were discovered still proud

of the surface and not in their finished state, after polishing (*expolitio*).[41]

Analysis of 'joins' in the plaster, which represent days of work, has allowed scholars to estimate a total workload of only a month for the completion of the whole house.[42] But work stopped very

ABOVE **Fig. 230** *Oecus* **showing various stages of work suddenly halted.**

House of the Painters at Work, Pompeii

BELOW **Fig. 231 Fresco panel with outline in reddish-brown paint (*sinopia*).**

At the bottom corners of the panel are two holes, probably to support a shelf that held paint and other materials.

House of the Painters at Work, Pompeii

suddenly indeed. At the bottom of the sinopia panel (above, FIG. 231) on another wall are holes to support a shelf for materials, while on the floor were scaffolding nails and about sixty bowls, some still containing pigments, and others gathered up in a basket.[43] The presence of different stages of completion within the same room suggests craftsmen working simultaneously, in close collaboration. This is one of the very few opportunities to see evidence for the working practices of Roman tradesmen.

Similarities in paintings, both in 'filler' motifs and more ornate elements, can be explained perhaps by shared workshop training or by the existence of pattern books (or papyri) from which clients and craftsmen chose the decoration,[44] though the existence or not of these books for frescoes, as for mosaics, is a contentious point with some scholars. Some mythological scenes, for example Theseus and the Minotaur (FIG. 242) or Narcissus (FIG. 194), are so frequent and so similar in their details that there must have been common sources. As we have already seen, motifs frequently cross over media, for example the wandering musicians who appear in paint at Stabiae and in mosaic at Pompeii (above FIGS 223 and 224).

Different houses may well show work of the same group of workers,[45] for example the garden room of the House of the Golden Bracelet and the bedrooms in the House of the Orchard (P). There may not have been many of these groups, or officinae, working in the cities, but many examples of 'work in progress' suddenly arrested show they were all very busy at the time of the eruption. During renovations, images could be salvaged and used again. One Second Style fragment, with theatrical masks, was reused a century later in a Fourth Style wall in the House of Marcus Fabius Rufus (P).[46] Vitruvius mentions paintings cut from walls in Greece and brought to Rome in wooden frames: *picturae ligneis formis inclusae*.[47]

Not all painters worked indoors. Pliny mentions a painter called Serapio who decorated balconies.[49] Artists specializing in the simpler, jollier imagery of the streets, in effect a form of 'folk art', brightened the cities with shop and tavern signs of still lifes, gods and goddesses, animals and many other subjects. The same painters also worked on domestic shrines. Here, too, the work of the same officinae appears again and again.[50] The kitchen shrine of the House of the Piglet (FIG. 301) features a hog's head, sausages and other edibles, which are presented almost identically on the kitchen lararium from a villa near Pompeii (FIG. 302). Kitchen painters had their market, too.

As with mosaic emblemata (above p. 185) and marble reliefs (below pp. 217–20), some painted panels were made offsite and slotted into the wall.[51] An example from Herculaneum (FIG. 232),[52] still in its original wooden frame, shows cupids at the sacred tripod of Apollo at Delphi, playing with objects associated with the god such as his bow and his musical instrument, the lyre.

THE REDISCOVERY OF THE TRIPODS

Tripods like that in FIG. 232 were thought to survive only in art, until a recent discovery. In 2007 archaeologists excavating a luxurious pavilion that belonged to the Villa of the Papyri, on the ancient shoreline of Herculaneum,[52] discovered two large groups of fragments of carbonized wooden furniture. Careful analysis revealed parts of six different pieces of furniture, two tables and no fewer than four ornamental tripods,[53] resembling the piece illustrated in the fresco.

Most of the furniture fragments were veneered with panels of carved ivory. Some carried decorative friezes, while others had scenes relating to the god Bacchus, such as cupids making offerings at rural shrines. Some large-scale figures were of exceptional quality. One shows Bacchus as a baby, on the knee of a satyr who holds up a mask to entertain him. Another (FIG. 233) shows Bacchus, naked except for his cloak and a wreath of ivy, and carrying a *thyrsus* or sacred staff in his left hand. Tripods of a kind previously known only through wall paintings had been rediscovered.

THE FOUR 'POMPEIAN' STYLES OF WALL PAINTING

The cities preserve more frescoes than the rest of the Roman Empire put together, and from the earliest excavations these paintings have inevitably attracted the attention of scholars. A German professor, August Mau, analyzed the frescoes in the 1880s. Combining this analysis with the account of fresco painting given by the Roman architect Vitruvius,[54] Mau outlined what he saw as the 'Four Pompeian Styles' of painting. He defined their basic characteristics and gave the various styles approximate dates,[55] envisaging a relatively straightforward linear progression through time, culminating in the last or Fourth Style. In AD 79 the House of the Painters at Work and many others were being decorated in this Fourth Pompeian Style of wall painting, which Mau decided had originated in the 40s or 50s AD.

Mau knew, of course, that wall painting had not been invented in Pompeii, but he used the city's name because frescoes were found in such numbers there (as well as at Herculaneum, Stabiae and Oplontis). His observations are still a very useful general guide to the broader divisions of wall paintings in the cities, but new research is showing that there are plenty of variations within each style, and that there was no sudden, definitive switch from one style to another.[56] The Third and Fourth Styles, in fact, are sometimes confusingly similar.

Houses often retained elements of more than one style,[57] for example the Samnite House (H). Sometimes they show all four, as in the aptly named House of the Four Styles (P). Supposedly 'grand' styles (the First and Second) are sometimes found in not-very-grand rooms, such as bedrooms. Some paintings in earlier styles were replaced by later styles, and others in the same house were not.[58] Such survivals of 'early' style paintings were surely not always the result of chance or lack of funds,[59] but of conscious decisions. Owners were concerned to enhance their home and status – always with an eye to the homes of their peers and superiors.[60] Mau's categories are still recognized as a useful starting point,[61] but there is endless debate among scholars over the development of the styles and the meaning of painted schemes in general.

THE FIRST POMPEIAN STYLE

The First Style was imported from the Greek parts of southern Italy and the eastern Mediterranean, and first appeared in the cities from about 150 BC, revolutionizing the interiors of wealthy houses. Vitruvius notes that, in olden times, 'people first began to imitate types of marble veneer...'.[62] This style used raised and shaped stucco plaster to imitate marble architectural elements and slabs of wall veneer. The plaster was then brightly painted in imitation of different types of marble.

Recent excavations below the House of the Fleet (P) have revealed one of the earliest examples from the cities from about 150 BC (FIG. 235).[63] The addition of a small bird against the upper band of blocks is a very human touch of humour in this monumental style. First and Second Style schemes are often repaired and restored in the atrium and other reception areas of some of the older houses, where appearances were

very important. In the House of the Faun (P), the First Style was retained to the end. In the Samnite House (H), the First Style scheme includes a false upper storey made of stucco and brightly painted 'veneer' slabs in the entry corridor (FIG. 234). The First Style also appears in some less grand spaces, for example in the cubiculum in the House of the Ship Europa (P). It seems less popular than other styles, but that is only because it has been largely replaced by later ones.

ABOVE **Fig, 234 Detail of entrance way with First Style decoration imitating marble slabs.**

Samnite House, Herculaneum

LEFT **Fig, 235 Fragment of First Style fresco imitating marble**
House of the Fleet, Pompeii
(VI,10,11)
H. 50 cm, W. 53 cm
SAP 87283

In the 90s to 80s BC, painters began to do away with raised stucco, replacing it with adventurous painted representations of domestic and civic or religious architecture in plausible perspective (FIG. 236). Vitruvius remarks that people began 'to imitate the profiles of buildings and the projecting features of columns and pediments...'.[64]

Simpler schemes showed architectural elements such as columns and herms seeming to project inwards into the room, while in more complex pieces the painters suggested views beyond the wall that revealed, often through colonnades or portals, Greek-influenced scenes of temples and cityscapes receding into the distance. The decoration of a dining room of the House of the Cryptoporticus (P), dating to the 30s or 20s BC (FIG. 236), depicts male and female herms projecting from a yellow-ochre coloured wall.[65] Above are paintings (*pinakes*) of still life and mythological scenes behind false folding screens. The pinakes include a beautifully observed still life of a basket filled with food, including a salami sausage, covered with a linen cloth, all observed by a finely drawn cockerel. The lower part of the wall is covered with graffiti, perhaps made by the children of the house, of animals and hunters.

Some Second Style schemes completely cover the wall, with continuous friezes of gods and people. The principal assembly room of the Villa of the Mysteries features a *megalography* (from the Greek meaning 'big painting'), a frieze of over life-size figures in front of a panelled background showing Bacchus and his followers. Many scholars have already written about this frieze,[66] including its many restorations; the beautiful walls are far from 'as discovered'.[67] The walls are divided up into numerous scenes, comprising groups of people and supernatural beings in a series of activities. Many scholars believe these to be related and to tell a particular story.

Fig. 236 Second Style fresco with details in false perspective of herms and *pinakes*.

House of the Cryptoporticus, Pompeii (I,6,2)
H. 205 cm, W. 273 cm
SAP 59469B

The long, north wall (FIG. 237) seems calm enough at the beginning. As a draped woman looks on, a little boy reads from a scroll and a woman carries in a tray (FIG. 239), but transfixes the viewer with her gaze – and what is on the tray? A woman sitting with her back to us is busy preparing something with two servants. Then things take a supernatural turn, with the appearance of Silenus, chief of the satyrs, and two other satyrs, with their distinctive pointed goat ears. A woman dramatically turns so her cloak billows behind her. On the far (east) wall (FIG. 238) another group of satyrs are entertaining themselves with the reflection of a mask in a silver bowl, and finally we see the star of the show, the god Bacchus, reclining against his lover Ariadne. Events reach a crescendo as a woman is poised to unveil an object in a basket (in all probability a metre-high sacred phallus). Then a very striking female figure, a demon with sweeping outstretched wings, poses, brandishing a cane. On the long, south wall we see a half-naked woman. And all this to the sound of cymbals clashed together by another woman more naked than the first (FIG. 240). The action finishes with tranquillity once more, as, in a sadly damaged section, a seated woman arranges her hair with the help of a cupid who holds her mirror.

Some scholars see the paintings as a continuous narrative, suggesting several of the women shown are the same person. The presence of Bacchus and his followers and the unusual nature of some of the scenes suggests the theme is largely religious. Perhaps the paintings show a type of initiation ceremony, or perhaps they show a passage of a different kind – to womanhood or marriage. We may never know the full meaning, but the paintings remain one of the glories of Roman art.

Frescoes from the Villa of the Mysteries, Pompeii showing initiation rites.

ABOVE **Fig. 237 Fresco from the north wall.**

OPPOSITE **Fig. 238 Fresco from the east wall.**

FOLLOWING PAGES
Fig. 239 Detail of a woman carrying a tray from the north wall.

Fig. 240 Detail of women from the south wall.

In the 30s to 20s BC, coinciding with the reign of the first Roman emperor, Augustus, which brought sweeping changes to all aspects of art and culture, taste and fashion in wall paintings also began to change. The illusionistic Second Style seems to have gone out of favour and the viewer's attention was directed once again to the surface of the wall. The First Style had intended to create an impressive façade for the wall, mimicking public architecture, and the Second Style had followed this to its logical conclusion by introducing the illusion of architectural elements and landscapes. The Third Style rejected this and the focus shifted to mythological panels, set against a flat expanse of colour, framed by a theatre-like structure of thin and spindly columns. In effect, this scheme created a mini-gallery in each room. These pictures become more important than vistas, perhaps in imitation of public picture galleries or *pinacothecae*.[68] Such landscapes as there were were restricted to small side panels, along with still life, cupids and so on, sometimes supported by candelabra, almost as easel paintings, adding to the impression of a *pinacotheca*.

The grand illusions of internal and external perspectives dwindled to completely unrealistic sketches in the upper parts of the wall. All around were garlands or other vegetal motifs, often with people or animals springing out from them. Vitruvius deplored this new style – the product, as he put it, of 'bad taste….instead of columns to support the roof there are thin reeds…candelabra hold up images of buildings…and there are disembodied images of the heads of men and animals…'.[69] How on earth, he wails, can a reed really support a roof: *quemadmodum enim potest calamus vere sustinere tectum?*[70] And he had a point.

Fig. 241 South wall of the tablinum.
House of Marcus Lucretius Fronto, Pompeii

Fig. 242 Fresco showing Theseus with the body of the minotaur.

House of Gavius Rufus, Pompeii
H. 97 cm, W. 88 cm
MANN 90043

At the centre of walls in both the Third and Fourth Styles were panels, often of very high quality, showing scenes from Greek mythology. Many of these panels showed gods and goddesses and heroes such as Theseus (FIG. 242), who killed the bull-headed Minotaur. Others might show the three Graces (FIG. 244), or the wistful face of Acte (FIG. 243), one of the Greek spirits of the hours of the day. To us these may seem simply ornamental motifs, but to many residents of the cities they may have had more than decorative significance. Gods and heroes were believed by many Romans to have protective powers and, once painted on the walls, they could have brought this assurance to the home, just as they did to commercial premises.[71]

Pictures of gods could have other meanings. Mars, god of war, and his wife Venus, goddess of love, were important deities in their own right, but to a Roman home

they could be doubly important. Mars, as father of the mythical founders of Rome, Romulus and Remus, was also the father of the Roman race. Venus was the patroness both of Rome and of Pompeii. Putting these deities on the walls of your home could be a declaration of Roman status. This might not have been the primary aim – that was beauty and decoration. Yet some paintings could be seen as a statement, even an assertion, of the owner's 'Roman-ness'.[72]

Any type of painting on the wall was, of course, decorative and a symbol of wealth and status. The First and Second Styles were imposing, but the later Second Style paintings had a visual narrative (for example the Villa of the Mysteries frieze). In the Third and Fourth Styles this narrative, in the form of central panels, became more important. Paintings served as a jumping-off point for telling the story (in Greek, *ekphrasis*) of the particular heroes and scenes depicted.[73]

Some scholars have taken the interpretation of these paintings much further and have constructed very complex relationships within and between paintings in the same room and beyond. There is doubtless a lot to be said for these theories, but it will never be possible to understand fully the processes that came together in the planning of interior decoration. The owner may well have known the myths and his guests were probably enthralled by the stories on his walls, but he was equally interested in the admiration and kudos these beautiful paintings would earn him and his family, as well as (or even instead of?) complex spatial relationship. He may even have been simply copying the images and designs he had seen in another house.

OPPOSITE **Fig. 243 Fresco showing a woman's face.**
From Herculaneum
H. 19.7 cm, W. 15.4 cm
MANN 9094

ABOVE **Fig. 244 Fresco showing the Three Graces, 'Charites', of Greek mythology.**
From Pompeii (IV)
H. 53 cm, W. 47 cm
MANN 9231

RIGHT **Fig. 245 Fresco showing the wooden horse of Troy.**
House of Cipius Pamphilus, Pompeii
H. 40 cm, W. 62 cm
MANN 9010

ABOVE LEFT **Fig. 246 Fresco showing still life of a harbour scene.**

From Boscoreale
H. 32 cm, W. 61 cm
The British Museum,
1899,0215.2

ABOVE RIGHT **Fig. 247 Roundel showing a little boy dressed as the god Mercury.**

House of Lucretius Fronto,
Pompeii

Less ambitious, though generally well-executed, images were centred in the side panels and sometimes even the dado or skirting board, including landscapes with villas, often by the sea, or harbour scenes (FIG. 246). In smaller rooms, panels were often occupied by floating cupids or maenads, or roundels containing portraits. Some of these roundels, too, may have had a meaning. The figure in one roundel, found on the wall of a bedroom, is shown in the guise of Mercury, but is clearly a young boy (FIG. 247). Was this a member of the household, perhaps even the occupant of the bedroom? We cannot be sure, but it is certain that many of the schemes and individual decorative elements have meanings that we may never be able to unravel.

THE FOURTH POMPEIAN STYLE

In August Mau's scheme, by the 50s AD the Third Style had evolved sufficiently to see the emergence of the Fourth Style, the last before the eruption in AD 79.[74] Differences between the Third and Fourth Styles are perhaps the least easy to distinguish and classify since so many factors remained common. In the Fourth Style mythological panels remained the main focus, with side panels, even on grander walls, inhabited by a single, floating figure. There was a return to the architectural vistas of the Second Style, but in a far less realistic way. Columns, candelabra and garlands continued in the Fourth Style, with ever larger numbers of creatures such as griffins, insects, birds, panthers and a surprising number of goats gambolling over every fiddly detail. Fortunately, Vitruvius, who had so despised the Third Style (above p. 206), did not live to see the development of the Fourth.

Fourth Style paintings in Pompeii were infinitely varied, from the finest and most ornate, as in the House of the Prince of Naples (P) (FIG. 248) to simple schemes in apartments and shops. There were also regional variations. In Herculaneum, where surviving First and Second Style paintings are uncommon (above pp. 200–202), the Third and Fourth Styles are abundant, as in the House of the Black Living Room, but they have a distinct identity.[75] There are unusual features, for example the painted wall hangings from the House of the Grand Portal. Also, colours used for main blocks (black, light blue and mid-green) are far less common in Pompeii.[76] Scholars have proposed as few as two Fourth Style officinae (groups of craftsmen) in Pompeii, and only one for Herculaneum.[77] This seems too few, but the principle of self-sufficient workshops with a distinct output seems very likely.

Some attribute the popularity of Third and, in particular, Fourth Style paintings to both painters and customers having access to an infinite choice of backgrounds and motifs. The walls blazed with sheets of colour, or sometimes just expanses of white, and were populated with birds, animals and people. Other scholars point to the effects of earthquake(s) and the major rebuilding programme(s) that followed, which necessarily used the current (Fourth) Style. Also, the AD 40s–60s saw the continued rise of new elements in society, in particular freedmen and their families. They wanted (and needed) to 'buy in' to the trappings of the good life and respectable society, including beautiful interior design.[78] In effect, the Fourth Style was the first to appear in a fairly wide range of homes.[79]

It is worth mentioning here some examples of wall painting of this period

Fig. 248 *Oecus.*

House of the Prince of Naples, Pompeii

which are quite different in style. For example, there is the intricate, flowered 'wallpaper' in the House of the Gilded Cupids (FIG. 250), in effect a ceiling pattern applied to the walls, decorated with the gilded glass discs featuring Cupid which gave the house its name; the Trojan War-themed friezes in the living room of the House of Decimus Octavius Quartio; the Centaur frieze in the House of the Menander (FIG. 249); and the multi-banded frescoes in the lower 'marble room' in the House of the Relief of Telephus, Herculaneum.[80] Evidence from Herculaneum suggests that fabric hangings and curtains decorated the upper parts of some walls,[81] which would explain the appearance of blank upper bands in rooms which seem in every other respect completely finished, such as the garden bedroom of the House of Apollo (P).

ABOVE **Fig. 249 Fresco with frieze of centaurs.**
House of the Menander, Pompeii

BELOW **Fig. 250 'Wallpaper' fresco.**
House of the Gilded Cupids, Pompeii

**Fig. 251 The 'Etruscan Room'
Osterley House, Isleworth,
London, mid-1770s (Robert Adam).**

These later styles proved as popular after the rediscovery of the cities as they had in the last years of the cities' lives, and found eager new audiences among the elite of the eighteenth and nineteenth centuries. Excavations in Herculaneum from 1738, and Pompeii a decade later, were electrifying events for European scholars of the classical world (see the Introduction). The kings of Naples jealously guarded their treasures, admitting by personal royal permit only the selected few. Visitors, including collectors and dilettanti such as Sir William Hamilton, British ambassador to Naples, made paintings and sketches and published the discoveries.[87] Soon, publications of the finds from the cities began to appear.

Nine volumes of *Le antichita' di Ercolano esposte*, filled with illustrations of finds ranging from frescoes to cooking pots, were published (for private circulation) by the Royal Court at Naples between 1757 and 1792, and were hugely influential. Soon architects and interior designers were importing elements of Third and Fourth Pompeian Style frescoes into their designs. The neo-classical 'Painted Room', designed by James 'Athenian' Stuart for Spencer House, central London, drew on Greece, Herculaneum and the Renaissance 'grotesque' paintings in the Vatican, which were derived in turn from Fourth Style paintings from Nero's palace. The influence of 'Herculaneum' had arrived.[83]

The eighteenth-century interior designers and architects Robert and James Adam made full use of Third and Fourth Style motifs. Of course, when the Adams were working, the 'Four Pompeian Styles' had not yet been defined, and the frescoes were

simply recognized as the most popular, characteristic wall paintings of the cities. In the mid-1770s at Osterley Park House in West London, Robert Adam created the 'Etruscan Room' (FIG. 251), a Fourth Style scheme, named after the medallions and panels of illustrations from 'Etruscan' Greek vases, inspired by d'Hancarville's (1766–7) publication of Sir William Hamilton's vase collection.

Other important publications appeared, in particular the fully illustrated colour volumes *Pompeiana* by the archaeologist Sir William Gell and the architect and draughtsman John Peter Gandy.[84] These presented views of excavations, details of frescoes and mosaics and even florid reconstructions. Built soon afterwards, the 'Pompeian Parlour' in Hinxton Hall, South Cambridgeshire, featured large central panels with illusionistic views over gardens, while side panels and the upper walls depicted maenads, birds garlands and animals floating in the best Fourth Style manner.

In 1844 Prince Albert commissioned a Pompeian room as part of the garden pavilion of Buckingham Palace (FIG. 252). Contemporary drawings[85] show brightly coloured panels – green at the centre with mythological panels, and deep red at the sides with floating figures. The upper wall, ceiling, dado and floor were suitably ornate.

Perhaps the most public display of the cities' wall painting was in the great Exhibition Hall of the Crystal Palace. Here, in 1851, a Pompeian house was recreated, part of a series of ancient spaces including Greek, Egyptian and Roman rooms.[86] Modelled largely on the House of the Tragic Poet (P), made famous only a few years earlier by Bulwer-Lytton's *Last Days of Pompeii*, the Pompeian House recreated several rooms including the atrium (in which Queen Victoria and Prince Albert were entertained to dinner), the tablinum and cubicula.

MOSAICS AND OTHER WALL DECORATIONS

With such emphasis on painted wall decoration, it is easy to forget that in the mid-first century AD, when the Fourth Style became so fashionable, there were other major innovations in interior design.

In this period mosaics began to appear on the walls, and the cities have the largest and finest collection of these early Roman wall mosaics.[87] Pliny, writing in the 70s AD, remarks, 'in a new development (*novicium inventum*) mosaics, now made of glass, have been driven from the floor and onto the walls'.[88] This was made possible through the use of very light glass tesserae, which could be mounted vertically on a much thinner bedding. These tesserae, cut from tablets of glass, did not have smooth surfaces like stone tesserae, and their rough edges reflected the light in an attractive way. They were ideal for decorating walls, especially open-air spaces, because, unlike frescoes, they were also waterproof. Mosaic was thus the perfect decoration for fountains – as in the House of the Small Fountain (P) (FIG. 254).

One of the finest surviving wall mosaics comes from the House of Neptune and Amphitrite (H) (FIG. 253). This was set into the wall of a triclinium, visible on the axis from the main door, via the window of the tablinum, so the visitor's gaze fell on it from the moment they entered. The polychrome mosaic shows Neptune, god of the sea, with his lover Amphitrite, framed by columns and floral motifs, shaded by a multi-coloured

awning, and set against a central panel of tesserae backed with gold. The canopy and the floral surrounds of the main panel are very close to motifs in Fourth Style frescoes, suggesting they are contemporary, and confirming Pliny's statement that they were an invention, or innovation, at the time of the eruption.

Visitors had another visual treat in store. On another side of the dining room was the façade of the water tank, turned into an attractive feature covered in mosaics showing hunts, garlands and peacocks,[89] and with niches for small statues.

MARBLE VENEERING

From the 50s to 60s AD opus sectile on the floors was joined by marble veneer on the walls, reflecting trends in Rome.[90] Such rooms once existed in Pompeii, for example in the House of Marcus Fabius Rufus or the House of the Dioscuri, but their decoration has mostly disappeared, either since excavation or, in some cases, through salvage and looting after the eruption (below p. 301).

The most impressive surviving examples are found in Herculaneum,[91] and the two finest come from a single house, the House of the Telephus Relief, named after the marble relief discovered there. In a prominent position overlooking the sea, it had a four-storey, tower-like structure, the upper two levels of which contained rooms encrusted with marble.

The lower room had a floor with an intricate polychrome design of squares and triangles with a band of marble around the lower wall.[92] The floor of the upper room (FIG. 255) is a beautifully chaotic mass of coloured marbles, and zones within the patterning indicate the placement of couches. The wall was veneered with great sheets

TOP **Fig. 253 Glass mosaic showing the sea-god Neptune and his wife, Amphitrite.**

House of Neptune and Amphitrite, Herculaneum

ABOVE **Fig. 254 Mosaic used as decoration for a fountain.**

House of the Small Fountain, Pompeii

Fig. 255 Room decorated with tall veneer panels on the walls and cut marble (*opus sectile*) on the floor.

House of the Telephus Relief, Herculaneum

FOLLOWING PAGES **Fig. 256 Marble relief showing a ceremony in honour of the god Bacchus/Dionysus.**

House of the Dionysiac Reliefs, Herculaneum
H. 56 cm, W. 109.5 cm
SAP 88091

of marble to a height of at least 1.5 m (5 ft), interspersed with tall columns, interrupted only by the huge picture windows that looked over the sea.[93]

MARBLE RELIEFS

Wall mosaics and marble veneer were ostentatious, but another truly conspicuous display of wealth was seen in marble sculpted reliefs. Here, too, Herculaneum has produced some amazing new discoveries.

In 1997 excavators found the remains of the huge House of the Dionysiac Reliefs in Western Insula (city block) I, near the shore.[94] They partly explored a large room, about 10 x 6.5 m (30 x 21 ft), and discovered a sculpted marble panel set into the south wall (FIG. 257). The relief is in a style some scholars call 'neo-Attic' (New Greek) meaning it looks back to the styles of ancient Greece centuries before. It was probably not made in Greece, however, but in the workshops of Naples or Rome at the time of the Emperor Augustus, over fifty years before the eruption. The relief shows a naked, resting satyr and a barely dressed maenad drinking water from a lion-headed fountain spout, while a younger satyr pours wine into a cup.

Ten years later, during careful excavation and recording of the same room, another incredible discovery was made.[95] Archaeologists cleaning the east wall uncovered another relief, also Greek in style. It shows a ceremony in front of a statue of Dionysus/Bacchus (FIG. 256). Two figures, with male features but rather odd clothing,[96] stand in front of the statue. Behind them is an older man, turning towards a maenad, who approaches from the right. Imagery related to Bacchus was very popular in Roman art – in fact some scholars take this further and see a special link between the god and

ABOVE **Fig. 257 Marble relief showing followers of Bacchus/Dionysus resting and drinking.**

House of the Dionysiac Reliefs, Herculaneum.
H. 39.5 cm, W. 97 cm
SAP 79613

OPPOSITE **Fig. 258 Painted marble panel showing women playing knucklebones.**

House of Neptune and Amphitrite, Herculaenum
(V,6–7)
H. 42 cm, W. 49 cm
Naples, MANN 9562

the cities in this fertile area.[97] The second relief had been set into a shallow recess in the wall and secured with metal clamps, and the wall plaster was then smoothed over the edges to make it an integral part of the Fourth Style decoration of the room. The two reliefs, probably with a third on the (now lost) north wall, were clearly the focal points of this Fourth Style scheme.

Interestingly, it may be possible to identify the owner(s) of this large, opulent house. Fragments were discovered of an inscription dedicating a statue to Octavia, one of the daughters of the emperor Claudius. The person responsible was Lucius Mammius Maximus, who had also dedicated all the statues to Claudius' family in the so-called Augusteum (above pp. 33–4). It is possible that the presence of a named imperial portrait in a private house means the home belonged to Mammius Maximus himself.[98]

Sixteen marble reliefs have been found in the houses of the cities.[99] Half of them, and to date, the most accomplished, come from Herculaneum,[100] suggesting the wealth and refinement of some of its citizens. The Romans called such a relief sculpture a *typus*; in his *Letters to Atticus*, written in the 60s BC, Cicero talks about acquiring '...reliefs that I can set into the walls of my hall'.[101] Both the reliefs from the room in the house in Western Insula I showed signs of having been reused, suggesting that the owner, like Cicero, had brought them in from elsewhere or had repositioned them after renovation work.

PAINTED MARBLE PANELS

The rarest wall decorations of all are the painted marble plaques, found almost exclusively in Herculaneum. The paint is applied straight to the marble and seems to lack any form of sealant, so the pigment is extremely vulnerable and fugitive. Where it survives, however, as on the plaque showing girls playing knucklebones (FIG. 258), the quality is superb and its delicacy and detail produce an unparalleled effect far surpassing fresco.[102] The girls are all named (in Greek letters): the girl at the top left is Leto. Just to the left of her head the artist signed the work: *Alexandros Athenaios Egraphen* (Alexander of Athens drew [this]).

CEILINGS

Decoration of rooms did not stop at the floor and walls. Many ceilings were also highly decorated, in particular during the Third and Fourth Styles, when complex decorative schemes are carried on across the ceiling without interruption, as in the House of Caius Julius Polybius (P) (FIG. 259).

Other ceilings were made of wood and were decorated with coffering. Though sometimes reproduced in painted plaster, the originals were virtually unknown until a remarkable discovery at Herculaneum in 2008.[103] During a project to improve drainage of the ancient shore area, archaeologists came across a mass of wooden beams, tiles and other debris. These were the remains of a roof, almost certainly from the upper room of the 'tower' building of the House of the Telephus Relief. The Roman roof, unlike the modern reconstruction in place over the room, used remarkably few nails, relying instead on wooden dowels and careful joinery.

Mixed up in the debris were over a hundred fragments from the coffered ceiling that had once graced the room. One large coffering panel was found with raised geometric patterns (FIG. 260), together with other, smaller panels still set into their

ABOVE **Fig. 259 Painted plaster ceiling.**
House of Julius Polybius, Pompeii

OPPOSITE **Fig. 260 Wooden panel from a ceiling with traces of paint remaining.**
From Herculaneum
H. 71 cm, W. 64 cm

supportive framework. There were also edging panels decorated with raised hexagons. The fragments were waterlogged, not carbonized, so bore traces of their original finish in red, white, black, blue and green paint. On a handful of fragments there were even traces of gilding. This was clearly a very rich ceiling and it may in some way have echoed the zoning and patterning of the intricate marble floor of the room.[104] The ceiling from the House of the Telephus Relief represents the earliest surviving example of this type of structure and is a find of international importance.

The decoration of the houses of Pompeii and Herculaneum, even that of the less well-appointed homes, was usually the result of many different processes over a period of time, reflecting the tastes and budget of the owner(s). Their needs were satisfied by a veritable interior design 'industry' with skilled workers collaborating on various aspects of the work. Against the resulting backdrop of fine decoration, the family went about their normal lives, and a very important part of that daily life was dining.

VII
DINING

DINING

I N THE LARGE and well-appointed rooms discussed in the previous chapter, a wealthier family could relax in luxury, surrounded by beautiful objects, decoration and scenery. Perhaps the most typical leisure activity in the Roman home was dining. The hospitality extended by the master of the house was a defining feature of Roman social interaction, bringing the family and their guests together, and affirming ties of kinship and dependence and the dominant role of the head of the household. Less well-off families might not enjoy such sumptuous surroundings but, irrespective of wealth and status, for most people food and the rituals surrounding its consumption were always pillars of social and political life.

DINING ROOMS

For the rich, at least, Greek influence on dining was strong, from the food to the tableware and luxurious surroundings. Even the name of the dining area, the *triclinium*, came from the Greek for 'three couches'. It was called the room of the *three* couches because the most common eating arrangement seems to have been three couches arranged in a U shape.

Some spaces can be identified as dining areas with absolute certainty. In some rooms and in particular in gardens, the dining space is literally set in stone with three fixed masonry couches (FIG. 262), or in some cases two couches (*biclinium*). Identifying less obvious eating spaces is more difficult. Scale and location can be a useful guide, as can archaeological evidence for couches or their positioning, or the discovery of eating and cooking utensils.

Airy rooms that face onto gardens or courtyards, benefiting from daylight and privileged views, are obvious places for a triclinium – the owner always wanted to impress his guests. Sometimes these rooms hint at the presence of couches. Some have areas of differentiated floor decoration,[1] as in the large 'tower' room in the House of the Relief of Telephus (H) where the ornately patterned floor has plainer sides, as if couches were placed there. A room in the House of the Menander, looking out into the peristyle corridor, has a black and white mosaic floor with a central polychrome *emblema* (panel) showing a Nile scene with pygmies, around which couches were arranged. The emblema was a natural focus of attention and a source of conversation among the guests, just like the frescoes. The 'Mysteries' room of the Villa of the Mysteries (P), very well illuminated and with beautiful views over the garden towards the sea, has a border

PREVIOUS PAGES
Fig. 261 Detail of a fresco showing drinkers at a dinner party (see fig. 293).

Fig. 262 Fixed masonry triclinium.
House of the Gardens of Hercules, Pompeii

of diamond-shaped tiles around the edge of the mosaic where couches may have been placed (above FIG. 212). In some cases the wall has recesses designed to take the ends or sides of couches, as in the rear dining room in the bar of Lucius Vetutius Placidus (above pp. 61–2).

The triclinium was a place for family and their immediate circle. It was not routinely open to visitors, but there were certainly occasions when it hosted invited guests – relatives, business contacts or political associates. They dined with the owner and his or her family, served with abundant food and wine in beautiful silver vessels. In finer houses they reclined on couches with elaborate covers, surrounded by sumptuous decoration, listened to music, and looked out onto the garden with its fountains and sculpture. It was not just a culinary experience, but full immersion in the owner's wealth,

Fig. 263 Fresco showing guests arriving for a dinner party.

House of the Triclinium, Pompeii (V,2,4)
H. 68 cm, W. 66 cm
MANN 120029

power and influence. Evenings like this put the house on show. The satirist Juvenal (*Satires*, XIV, 59) describes the slaves frantically preparing, sweeping the floors, polishing the silver and even scrubbing the columns.

In a formal dining situation, diners seem to have reclined on their sides to eat – a pose seen in wall paintings – but we are not exactly sure how this tradition arose. The Greeks and the Etruscans greatly influenced Roman life, and both cultures reclined to eat and drink in formal situations, though not in the Romans' peculiar position. Frescoes such as FIG. 263 and FIG. 267 imply that more than one person, and as many as three, could lie on each couch. This might have been possible on some of the fixed masonry triclinia, but it does not seem very likely for many of the narrow, individual metal and wooden couches that have survived.[2] As for the occupants of the couches, it seems to have been normal in Roman society for men and women to dine together.[3] Some Roman writers describe children at dinners, sitting (rather than reclining) on the ends of the couches.[4]

One fresco (FIG. 263) offers intriguing insights into the very important social interaction that characterized such evenings.[5] There are three couches, with the number of occupants varying from three to two. All of them, interestingly, are male. On the left two men look deep in conversation; one is more relaxed (and less dressed) than the other. Above them someone has scratched *IO* ('hurrah, look here!'). The middle couch has a young man who is looking at the centrally positioned older man. The young man is wrapped in a green cloak and wears a gold diadem around his head, and he is very close to a small, black child whose status seems unclear. Above the senior man's head another graffito says *VALETIS* ('hello everyone'). The last couch contains a lone drinker, seemingly happy in his own company, with the word *BIBO* ('I'm drinking') scratched above his head. We may never fully understand the social (and almost certainly sexual) connotations of the painting, but it sheds a fascinating light on an aspect of elite Roman life.

ABOVE **Fig. 264 'Restaurant' showing fixed masonry tables and chairs.**
Praedia of Julia Felix, Pompeii

BELOW **Fig. 265 Carbonized wooden table.**
House of the Mosaic Atrium, Herculalneum (IV,1-2)
H. 60 cm
SAP 81601

OPPOSITE **Fig. 266 Fresco showing a private drinking scene.**
From Herculaneum
H. 66 cm, W. 66 cm
MANN 9024

This form of triclinium dining was probably not the everyday norm, however. It is likely that on many occasions even a wealthy family, together or separately, ate less formally, perhaps in other rooms or in the garden. All that was needed, after all, was a couch or chair and a small table, all easily portable. Some less well-off people – probably the majority of the population – did not have a triclinium and probably never ate in one. Evidence from taverns and bars show people using chairs (above FIGS 57–8), and the 'café' in the Praedia of Julia Felix (P) has a series of fixed masonry benches and 'tables' (FIG. 264) next to a fixed masonry triclinium.

In fixed masonry triclinia there is a central round or square 'table' for food and drink. In other triclinia there was no such platform, and round, three-legged tables of wood or metal were placed by the side of the couches. Wooden tables have survived in Herculaneum, their legs often decorated with the heads of people or animals. The table shown in FIG. 265, decorated with lion heads, is almost identical to the example pictured next to a couch or bed in a fresco from Herculaneum (FIG. 266). But the party illustrated here is small and private. To understand the full importance of dining for the household it is necessary to look at a larger, more formal dinner party, inevitably in a fairly well-off home.

DINNER PARTY

Having arrived at the house, the guests settled onto the couches in the triclinium. No trace has survived of the mattresses and expensive coverings that would have been placed on the couches, but wall paintings give some clues. The dining area needed light, and on these occasions the finest candelabra would be used, such as the bronze and silver ornamental stand from Pompeii (FIG. 268). This held four large bronze lamps and would have created a bright glow for dining inside or outside. To add to the atmosphere of luxury and relaxation, slaves put perfumed oils into the bronze and pottery lamps,[6] delighting the diners with wafts of expensive scents. On the beautifully

LEFT **Fig. 267 Fresco showing drinkers at a dinner party with a singing guest.**

House of the Triclinium, Pompeii (V,2,4)
H. 60 cm, W. 64 cm
MANN 120031

BELOW **Fig. 268 Bronze lampstand with four hanging lamps.**

House of Pansa, Pompeii
H. 121 cm, W. 58 cm
MANN 4563

inlaid base of the stand (recalling the drinking that would take place during the dinner party) was a statuette of Bacchus (FIG. 269) riding his animal, the panther, and raising a drinking horn as if to toast the diners.

Entertainments, such as singing and dancing, are also likely to have taken place during banquets. A fresco from the House of the Triclinium (FIG. 267) shows guests at a banquet. It was found in the same room as FIG. 263, but shows a different group of people, with men and women mixing freely on the couches. Slaves attend them on the far right and far left and there is a three-legged table covered with drinking paraphernalia in the centre. One of the women says, 'All get comfy, I'm going to sing'. A man replies, 'Yes, you go for it'. Singing and music at meals was not to everyone's taste. Martial the satirist comments that, 'the best banquets are those without flutes'.[7]

The owner wanted his parties to be a success, but there was a domestic etiquette and code of behaviour. The owner of the House of the Moralist in Pompeii went so far as to paint his 'rules' of dining on the wall of the summer triclinium.[8] It is not clear whether these were serious or humorous, and perhaps it did not matter.

Beginning with the preparation for the meal, with guests arriving, he admonishes:

Let water wash your feet and a slave dry them
Cover the couch with a cloth – take care of our covers.

Then, on the almost inevitable effects of good food and wine (namely wandering eyes):

Take those lustful looks and sweet, flirting eyes from that other man's wife; a modest
expression is more fitting.

Fig. 269 Bronze statuette showing Bacchus riding a panther (detail of fig. 268).

House of Pansa, Pompeii (VI,6,1)
H. 20 cm
MANN 4563

And finally:

*… please put off those boring squabbles,
And if you can't then go home and take
them with you!*

Entertained, comfortable and fully
aware of the rules of the table, the
guests now wondered what they
would be served to eat.

FOOD

Modern perceptions of Roman dining are usually of imperial-style banquets, with vast
quantities of exotic foods, rivers of wine and excesses of all sorts both on and off the
dining couches. Certainly, food and dining customs, at least for the wealthier Romans,
had been transformed – like so many other aspects of their culture – by the conquest
and assimilation of the Greek world in the early second century BC.[9] An indicator of
this change is the sumptuary law, passed by the Roman Senate,[10] which tried (in vain)
to ban dormice as a decadent luxury. Food varied hugely, from the fine meals consumed
in the triclinium of a grand house, to pies wolfed down in a tavern or snacks eaten in
the single room of a small flat. Even within the same house, the diet of owner and slave
differed. What light can archaeological evidence and the Roman writers shed on the
food consumed in the cities?

FOOD: THE WRITTEN SOURCES

Our major source on Roman food is a recipe book called *De Re Coquinaria* ('On the
Art of Cooking') by a gourmet, not necessarily a cook, called Marcus Gavius Apicius,
or simply 'Apicius',[11] who lived in the first century AD, though the text which preserved
his recipes was written down three centuries later. Nevertheless, this is our most

Fig. 270 Three still-life scenes of food.

House of the Stags, Herculaneum
H. 41 cm, W. 129 cm
MANN 8644

complete overview of Roman food, and provides ammunition for those who want to see Roman meals as extravagant and decadent: peacocks, rare spices and flamingoes all had a place at his table. It is, of course, a recipe book for wealthier families. The less wealthy did not write their recipes down, so for their diet it is necessary to look to archaeology (below p. 233).

Returning to the wealthy table, writers such as Suetonius and Martial talk of three main meals. *Ientaculum* (breakfast) was a light meal, perhaps with bread, cheese and olives. *Prandium* (lunch), served at about midday, possibly included some meat, again with bread and vegetables. The main meal was *cena*, usually eaten at about 6 or 7 pm. In poorer households this may well have been similar to prandium – perhaps with the addition of meat or fish or stew – but in some wealthier homes this was a grand occasion.

The evening meal had three elements: *gustatio* (appetizers), *mensae primae* (main course) and *mensae secundae* (dessert). Gustatio could include eggs, snails, fish and seafood, vegetables, cheese, and, of course, dormice. Eggs began the meal – in fact, according to Horace,[12] the Latin phrase for 'from beginning to end' is *Ab ovo usque ad mala* ('from the egg to the apples' – i.e. from appetizer to dessert).

Among his gustatio recipes Apicius serves up the following: sea urchins[13] baked with bayleaf, honey, fish sauce oil and eggs, and sprinkled with pepper; and cabbage,[14] boiled with pepper, fish sauce and coriander, then sprinkled with raisins and pine nuts. If your cabbage becomes dull, Apicius advises that: 'Every vegetable becomes bright green if cooked in soda'.[15] Then came dormice stuffed with pork mince, dormouse [16] meat, pepper, pine nuts and garum and cooked under a *clibanus*, a two-part domed terracotta vessel used for baking and roasting (FIG. 305).

In wealthier homes at least, the main course was a celebration of meat – kid and goat, pig meat of all types, prepared meats, game and poultry. Interestingly, beef is rarely mentioned, corroborating the archaeological record. Cattle bones, by far the most

common animal bone in rubbish pits of the fourth century BC in Naples and Pompeii, plummet to 10 per cent or less of such deposits at the time of the eruption. By contrast, sheep or goat make up 30 per cent and pig bones 60 per cent.[17]

Ham could be prepared á la Wellington: 'Boil with figs and bay leaves. Remove skin and make criss-cross incisions and fill with honey. Make pastry of flour and oil and cover ham. Bake until pastry is cooked'.[18] The womb of a sterile sow made a very convincing haggis: 'Pound pepper, cumin, leeks, rue, garum. Add mincemeat, peppercorns, pine kernels. Press into the well-washed womb. Cook in water, oil, garum, with bouquet of leeks and dill.'[19] For that special meal, a flamingo always went down well, cooked in pepper, caraway, coriander, vinegar mint, rue and dates.[20] Apicius tells us this recipe can also be used for parrot.

The more complicated a meal was, or appeared, the better, and spice-filled sauces were vital not only to add novelty and exotic ingredients, but also to mask the flavour of food sometimes past its best. After concocting a particularly complex dish, Apicius says proudly, 'No-one will even know what he is eating'.[21]

Dessert consisted predominantly of fruit. Dates, damsons, quinces and dried figs are most common in Apicius – these are recipes for cooking with fruit, not eating raw – but apples, peaches, plums, grapes, apricots, melons, cherries and figs were all consumed. There were some hot desserts, for example dates stuffed with nuts, pine nuts and pepper, and cooked in honey.

FOOD: THE ARCHAEOLOGICAL EVIDENCE

This was the literary ideal, but did the people in the cities, even those in the wealthier houses, always (or ever?) eat according to Apicius' recipes? Lists of provisions scratched onto the wall of an atrium in Pompeii suggest they did not.[22] The lists show remarkably uniform purchases made over an eight-day period. Bread, oil, leeks, onions and cheese appear regularly, but fish and sausages on one day only, implying that they were 'special' purchases, treats among the staples. The shopping could be for slaves, since bread specifically for a slave is mentioned on several days. The sample is admittedly small, but compared to Apicius' recipes it seems a very dull diet; yet this could have been the reality for many people in the cities.

A different picture was recently revealed at Herculaneum. Excavation of the large drain under Cardo V in the city produced huge quantities of household and human waste from a range of properties in the *insula* (city block) in front of the exercise area. Preserved by being either burned (carbonization) or part-fossilized by the chemicals present in the sewage of the drain (mineralization), was the largest quantity of food preparation, cooking and dining waste ever recovered from the cities.[23] The waste is necessarily mixed, but it gives a good picture of the food consumed here in the years just before the eruption.

Bread and other soft foods, such as cheese, will not survive in these conditions, but there was a wide range of other foods ranging from vegetables (including celery, cabbage, beans, olives and lentils) to seafood in huge quantities (such as scallops, mussels, cuttlefish and sea urchins). Fish included sardine, eel, anchovy and turbot; and chicken, sheep and pig bones were also found. Evidence of rich sauces and seasonings similar to those of Apicius was provided by seeds of dill, coriander, mint and by black peppercorns – the last imported from India. Finally came fruit and nuts such as fig, date, apple, pear and grape, walnut and hazelnut. It is not possible to try to reconstruct any particular dishes found in Apicius from the evidence preserved here. The ingredients are similar, but we do not know the original presentation. Nonetheless, the diet, in this corner of Herculaneum at least, was a good one.

HOW WAS FOOD SERVED?

As we have seen (above p. 228) the Romans, famous for excessive banquets, ate from relatively small tables. Instead of having everything on the table at once, a Roman diner enjoyed a large number of small courses, one after the other. There is evidence for the practice of inducing vomiting in order to be able to continue eating: *Vomunt ut edant, edant ut voment* ('They vomit in order to eat, they eat in order to vomit').[24] Large surfaces were generally unnecessary because anything bulky, such as suckling pig or other delicacies, was carved up by slaves behind the scenes and brought out in easy-to-eat chunks. This also determined the types of eating implements used. People ate mainly with their hands (the fingertips, never the full hand). Knives could be used at the table, but were not common, and forks were unknown. The main eating tool was the spoon, in particular the *ligula*, resembling a modern dessert spoon, and the *cochlea*, with a small round bowl.[25]

We must imagine, as Pliny the Elder describes, in a larger house, a 'small army of slaves' (*mancipiorum legiones*)[26] bringing out course after course, serving wine and tending to the guests' every need. They also cleaned up spillages of all sorts, brought potties if necessary and finally cleared away and swept up waste and scraps. It is possible that scraps from such a banquet provided a welcome supplement to the more mundane diet of the slaves. An idea of the presence of slaves is given by one of the frescoes (FIG. 263) from the House of the Triclinium (P). A guest on the left has his shoes removed by one slave and is offered a silver cup of wine by another. A third supports a guest who has already had far too much wine and is feeling wobbly. The presence of the young black boy on the far couch is interesting, as it unclear whether he is a slave or a guest at the table.

One piece of sophisticated dinner equipment to assist the slaves in their work was a food heater (FIG. 271). This example was found in the House of the Four Styles (P), stored away in a niche in the servants' quarters, an early example of an integrated appliance. Fuel, almost certainly charcoal, was placed inside the cylinder through the miniature doors while the food to be heated was put into the separate, lidded upper part of the cylinder. This practical device was also attractive. Palmette motifs ringed the vessel, and even the feet were modelled as lion's paws. On top of the vessel is a triton, or lord of the sea, holding an oar in his left hand and a tiny sea creature in his right. The handles of the upper part are made of bronze dolphins, while the lower handles are grasping hands with silver inlaid fingernails.

Another interesting device (FIG. 273) heated liquids in a way similar to a modern samovar. Charcoal in the hollow centre of the vessel heated the water within the double wall, which was drawn off through a small tap. The samovar, too, was finely

Fig. 271 Bronze food heater.
House of the Four Styles, Pompeii (I,8,11)
H. 96 cm, W. 44 cm
MANN 6798

BELOW **Fig. 272 Bronze and silver statuette of a vendor with a huge phallus holding a tray.**
House of the Ephebe, Pompeii (I,7,11)
H. 26 cm
MANN 143761

Fig. 273 Bronze heater for liquids.

From Pompeii
H. 41 cm, D. 27 cm
MANN 111048

decorated. On the shoulder were three suspension terminals for the bronze carrying-chain, which was made up of applied masks of very high quality showing a beautiful woman's face against a large bird. Even the tap was decorated with the head of a foreigner from the East.

SILVERWARE

From the casseroles, frying pans and cooking pots, spits, heaters and samovars, food and drink was transferred into vessels to be placed in front of the diners. In wealthy homes these were of silver, while for others most vessels were of pottery or glass.

Silverware vessels, as mentioned above, were grouped into a *ministerium* or service, the *ministerium escarium* for eating and the *ministerium potorium* for drinking. Discoveries of silver plate from in and around Pompeii, including the treasure from the House of the Menander, the smaller group from the House of Inachus and Io (P) and the treasure from the Villa of the Silver Treasure at Boscoreale just outside Pompeii, give a very good idea of the range of vessels that belonged to very wealthy families.

A dining service had a range of large and small dishes, cups and bowls. Dishes and plates were used for solid foods, and bowls or deep cups (distinct from the range of forms used for drinking – see below) for more liquid foods such as soups, sauces, dips and purées. Eating vessels often came in sets, with four to six of each type in the service; the exceptions were some of the larger dishes and tray-like vessels (FIG. 274), which were presumably for serving or shared dining. It was clear that these services were sold or commissioned with communal eating in mind. Some bowls and cups may have been containers for a special dish, perhaps a dessert. Some suggest that the 'frilled' dish (FIG. 278) shown in wall paintings from Pompeii contained desserts, perhaps even ricotta cheese, as seen in frescoes.[27] Accompanying these were serving

FOLLOWING PAGES

Fig. 274 Silver serving tray with incised scale pattern.

From Pompeii
H. 4.5 cm, W. 20 cm, L. 16 cm
MANN 25362

(L–R) **Fig. 275 Silver bowl with fluted edges.**

House of Inachus and Io, Pompeii (VI,7,19)
H. 5.5 cm, D. 12 cm
MANN 25554

Fig. 276 Small silver bowl.

House of Inachus and Io, Pompeii (VI,7,19)
H. 2.7 cm, D. 10.5 cm
MANN 25321

Fig. 277 Silver plate.

House of Inachus and Io, Pompeii (VI,7,19)
H. 2.5 cm, D. 20.5cm
MANN 25302

Fig. 278 Silver dish/bowl.

House of Inachus and Io, Pompeii (VI,7,19)
H. 3 cm, D. 14.2 cm
MANN 25318

Fig. 279 Silver spoon.

Vesuvian area
L. 18 cm
MANN 25413

vessels such as an elegant spoon (FIG. 279), and even a pepper pot to provide the spices the Romans craved.

The silver on the table was a reminder of wealth and status, but it was also literally the 'family silver', with an intrinsic value as bullion in addition to its symbolic and artistic importance. The service may actually have been put together over some time, possibly generations. On some pieces there are scratched or punched inscriptions recording the weight of the piece in ounces or the name of the owner.

Looking now at the drinking vessels, we can compare the real vessels with the abundant depictions in wall paintings. A painting from the tomb of Vestorius Priscus shows a display table (*cartibulum*) (FIG. 88) set against a draped background, and groaning under the weight of a full display of drinking silver.

In the centre are three larger pieces; an ornate bucket-shaped vessel (*situla*) flanked by drinking or mixing bowls (*craters*). Behind and to the side of each is a tall jug and a drinking horn or *rhyton*, popular at drinking parties (FIG. 281). Drinking

ABOVE LEFT **Fig. 280 Glass drinking horn (*rhyton*).**
From Pompeii (I,16,5)
L. 21.2 cm, D. 5 cm
SAP 12493

ABOVE **Fig. 281 Fresco showing a man with a drinking horn (*rhyton*).**
From Pompeii
H. 14.5 cm, W. 21.5 cm
The British Museum, 1856,1226.1623

Fig. 282 Silver shallow two-handled drinking cup (cantharus).

H. 9 cm, D. 12 cm
MANN 25295

Fig. 283 Silver cantharus.

House of Inachus and Io, Pompeii (VI,7,19)
H. 11 cm, D. 10 cm
MANN 25381

Fig. 284 Silver cantharus decorated in high relief with tendrils, leaves and berries of ivy.

House of the Silver Treasure, Pompeii (VI,7,20-22)
H. 12cm, D. 11 cm
MANN 25379

Fig. 285 Tapered drinking cup (modiolus).

House of Inachus and Io, Pompeii (VI,7,19)
H. 11.3 cm, D. 13.2 cm
MANN 25300

Fig. 286 Three vessels stand on three-legged stands (mensulae).

House of Inachus and Io, Pompeii (VI,7,19)
H. 3.3 cm
(L-R): MANN 25549, 25550, 25551, 25548

horns were also made in pottery and glass (FIG. 280). At the front of the table are three pairs of drinking cups, a tall and a medium *cantharus* and a very elegant shallow vessel similar to a modern champagne bowl. At the very front are four examples of a ladle (*simpulum*), used for mixing honey or spices into the wine.

Drinking cups were handled and admired the most, and so were sometimes beautifully decorated. There were two main types: the two-handled cantharus appeared either as a shallower, undecorated, rounded vessel (FIG. 282) or as a deeper, narrower cup, usually with abundant decoration. The cantharus was the most popular form of drinking cup found in the cities. The *modiolus* was a tapering, mug-shaped vessel, again usually finely decorated. At dinner parties these vessels were often placed on small stands or *mensulae* ('little tables').

The silver found in the cities suggests that cups were usually made and used in pairs. Two canthari from the House of the Silver Treasure (P) show centaurs heading for a banquet, with cupids hitching a ride. The male centaur carries a cantharus in one hand and a *thyrsus* (the sacred staff of Bacchus) in the other, while the female holds a *patera* (libation dish) in one hand and a drinking horn in the other.

Bacchic imagery is abundant on drinking vessels. A superb cantharus (FIG. 284) is decorated in high relief with tendrils and leaves of ivy, the plant closely connected with Bacchus and used for garlands at banquets. These cups were not simply to hold liquid; they stood for the wealth and taste of the owner, and provoked discussions on their workmanship, imagery and decoration. Most of all they were a sheer joy to hold.

Not all drinking or eating services were of silver, of course. Many households had only a handful of silver vessels and most used only vessels of pottery and glass.

Red Slip Ware pottery (above p. 57), was well represented on tables in the cities. From Arezzo in Italy came cups and dishes, often with applied decorative motifs, and a large chalice-like cup, decorated with warriors fighting lions. Vases from southern France included large drinking bowls, some carrying mottos such as *BIBE AMICE DE MEO* ('Drink, my friend, from me') (FIG. 289).

Locally made table pottery included a lot of drinking cups and beakers in many different forms. Some beakers carried crudely modelled faces – a typical Campanian style (FIG. 288). One particular example had a phallus on the left cheek. One small pottery beaker (FIG. 287) was too small to drink from and instead held something very useful for the meal – toothpicks, each individually hand-crafted from bone.

Finds from the Cardo V drain in Herculaneum suggest that at the time of the eruption glass vessels were very numerous. The Romans did not invent glass, but following the invention of glass-blowing in the middle of the first century BC glass workshops sprang up, first in Egypt, Palestine and Lebanon, but then in Italy and elsewhere. Blown glass and mould-made glass in a very wide variety of forms began to be mass-produced. Glass from the Cardo V drain in Herculaneum included small cups and bowls, usually in the normal greenish-blue colour, but occasionally more strongly coloured in cobalt blue or emerald green. More unusual pieces included elegant tall drinking glasses and mould-made vessels, including shallow lidded dishes or *pyxides*.

LEFT **Fig. 287 Pottery cup holding bone toothpicks.**
From Pompeii (I,9,9)
H. 5 cm
SAP 9498a-b

BELOW **Fig. 288 Pottery cup decorated with a face.**
House of the Gem, Herculaneum (oI,1)
H. 9.2 cm, D. 13.5 cm
SAP 76550

Fig. 289 Pottery bowl from southern France with a motto BIBE AMICE DE MEO.
H. 12 cm, D. 26 cm
MANN 203894

LEFT **Fig. 290 Amber glass handled cup (*modiolus*), similar in form to silver vessels.**
House of the Menander, Pompeii (I,10,4)
H. 12 cm, D. 13 cm
SAP 4960

BELOW **Fig. 291 Emerald green glass dish in the form of a boat, possibly for condiments.**
From Pompeii
H. 7.6cm, L. 22.5 cm
The British Museum, 1868,0501.153

DRINKING AT (OR AFTER) DINNER

In most homes food and wine, always the drink of choice, were taken simultaneously throughout the meal.[29] It is possible that in some houses dinner was followed by, or punctuated by, drinking in the tradition of the Greek drinking party, or *symposium*. Interestingly, most of the frescoes described as showing a dinner party in fact, show drinking. None of them shows eating in progress, and nowhere can we see the normal dishes and bowls of food consumption.

A wall painting (FIG. 293) from the triclinium in the House of the Chaste Lovers shows two couples lying on couches while a third man has collapsed, and a third woman – perhaps his partner – is apparently being held up by a servant. In front of their couches are shown two wooden tables, each containing only items relevant to drinking. On the first table is a thin juglet and two drinking cups. Also on the table is a ladle. The second table has two more drinking cups and two more ladles.

Another fresco from the House of the Chaste Lovers shows a crucial element of the dinner party, the preparation of the wine. Our obsession with fine wines, vintages, and wine as an investment is nothing new. The Romans too had their favourite wines – the Emperor Augustus particularly liked Falernian wine from Campania. Wine did not arrive at the table in bottles; it was considered very vulgar to drink wine neat. It was transported from the cellar or store in an amphora, and, as the fresco shows, it was poured by one of the slaves into a larger mixing vessel, such as a crater or a bucket-shaped situla (FIG. 292) and blended with water and other ingredients. These included honey, spices and even *garum* (fish sauce) and helped make the often heavy, resinous contents of the amphora more palatable. Wine was served several times during the dinner party, mixed on the spot to accompany the various courses. A Greek-style bronze crater illustrated here (FIG. 118) is decorated with figures from mythology, perhaps the Argonauts who with the hero Jason sought the Golden Fleece. It was a prized item. When discovered in the 1970s it had been placed in the centre of the room for safekeeping with other valuable bronzes.

To prepare guests for more drinking, snacks such as roasted chickpeas were handed out.[30] The poet Horace suggested that sausages or joints of meat were more suitable to accompany prolonged drinking.[31]

As we can see in the frescoes, guests at drinking parties and banquets very often wore garlands. These were sometimes made of sweet purple violets, attractive and also, according to Pliny the Elder, a precaution against drunkenness.[32] Sometimes the slaves wore them as well, for example the jaunty slave in the mosaic of the baths of the House of the Menander (FIG. 320). He carries in both hands a type of flat, single-handled jug called an *askos* (FIG. 295), used almost exclusively for serving wine. A mosaic, probably once the central emblema of a dining room, shows a skeleton holding an askos in each hand (FIG. 294). Though rather bizarre in our eyes, the message to the Romans was 'seize the day' in the face of the inevitability of death, and this

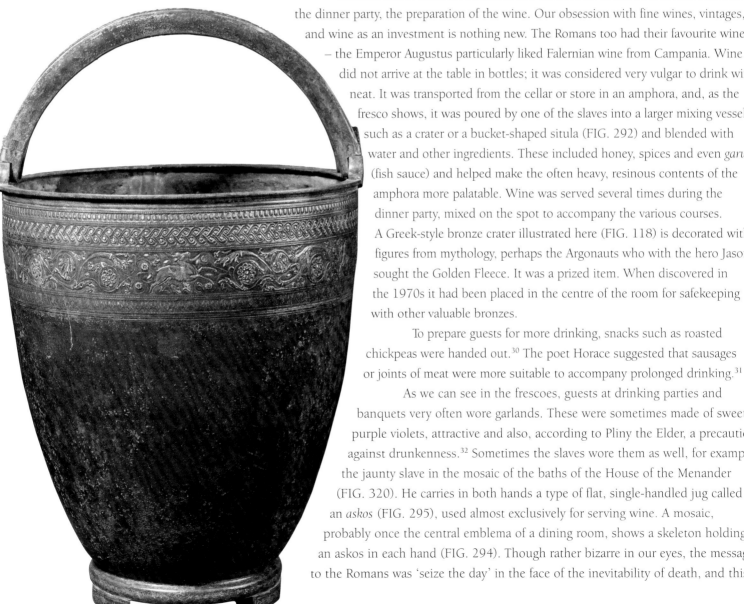

Fig. 292 Bronze vessel (*situla*) for mixing wine with water and other ingredients

H. 41.5 cm, W. 33 cm
MANN 68866

OPPOSITE **Fig. 293 Fresco showing a drinking party (convivium) in progress.**

House of the Chaste Lovers, Pompeii

RIGHT **Fig. 294 Mosaic showing a skeleton holding two wine jugs (askoi).**

From Pompeii (VI, Ins. Occ.,19–26)
H. 91 cm, W. 70 cm
MANN 9978

BELOW **Fig. 295 Bronze wine jug (askos) with a lizard handle.**

House of the Greek Epigrams, Pompeii (V,1,18)
H. 14 cm
MANN 111563

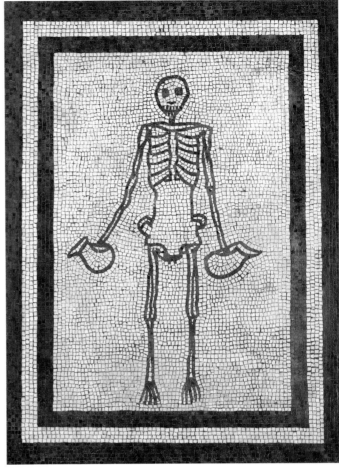

would have been considered perfectly suitable for an area of enjoyment and relaxation.[33]

Among many duties during banquets, slaves carried wine in askoi to and from the table. It is unlikely that the owner or his guests would have ever touched these vessels, since they were used for preparation, storage and all the processes with which the guests were not expected to sully their hands. The most commonly used serving jug, again with its roots in Greek tradition, was the *oinochoe*, literally 'wine pourer', used at table by slaves for pouring wine into individual cups.

THE AULDJO JUG

One particular oinochoe was much more prized – the Auldjo Jug (FIG. 296). The history of this jug involved Pompeii, the British poet Sir Walter Scott, a Prince of Naples and a young English woman named Madeleine Auldjo. The jug was made of cameo glass, like the famous Portland Vase. In this technique there are superimposed layers of glass, with the upper, usually white, carved away to create decorative patterns against the darker background, usually dark blue. Cameo glass is rare, but Pompeii has produced four of the finest surviving pieces: the Auldjo Jug, a table amphora called the 'Blue Vase', similar in form to the Portland Vase,[34] and two rectangular plaques, which decorated the House of Fabius Rufus (FIG. 296). The Auldjo Jug, some sixty to seventy years old in AD 79, was a prized possession rather than an object of day-to-day use. Around the body is an intricate vine in high relief, laden with bunches of grapes, and intertwined with laurel and ivy. On the shoulder are acanthus plants and birds. The jug was probably discovered during excavations at the House of the Faun (P) between 1830 and 1832 and passed into the collections of the British Museum in two separate parts. The base and lower body were bought from a 'Dr Hogg' in 1840, while the neck and the handle was bequeathed to the Museum by the heiress Miss Madeleine Auldjo in 1859. But what happened to the jug in the intervening years?

Dr Hogg had accompanied Sir Walter Scott on his trip to Italy in early 1832, which included a visit to the House of the Faun in Pompeii. Perhaps this illustrious visitor was given a memento by the site guardians – or someone much more senior. A clue to the identity of this 'senior' person is perhaps provided by the fortunes of the piece given by Miss Auldjo. She was the niece of John Auldjo, who in 1832 dedicated a volume entitled *Sketches of Vesuvius*, to Charles, Prince of Capua, brother of the King of Naples. In 1833 Prince Charles took from the storerooms of Pompeii 'the neck of a jug with a handle – blue in colour with white decoration'[35] – the upper part of the jug, perhaps? Four years later a German traveller confirmed '…a lady has an important part (of the jug) given to her by a high up person…'. This lady was perhaps Anna Maria Auldjo – Madeleine's mother – with 'the important person' (Prince Charles), returning John Auldjo's favour with the gift of the jug fragment. It is highly likely, therefore, that the prince was behind both gifts, which were eventually reunited some twenty-five years later.

LEFT **Fig. 296 The cameo glass Auldjo Jug.**
From Pompeii
H. 22.8 cm, D. 14.3 cm
The British Museum, 1859.2-16.1

ABOVE **Fig. 297 Cameo glass plaque showing a maenad, a satyr and Ariadne, the lover of Bacchus, reclining to drink.**
House of Fabius Rufus, Pompeii (VII,16,22)
H. 25.5 cm, L. 39.5 cm
MANN 153651

During all the banquets and drinking parties in the finely decorated rooms, slaves would have been a constant and essential, if unsung, presence: preparing, serving, cleaning up and clearing away. In all the parts of the house and garden that these chapters have visited, through all the everyday domestic routine, the family would have taken for granted the efforts of the servants who kept the household running. It seems appropriate now to turn to the 'service' areas of the house, in particular kitchens, toilets, storerooms and baths, which, more than any other spaces, were the slaves' domain.

VIII

KITCHENS,
TOILETS
AND BATHS

KITCHENS, TOILETS AND BATHS

THE parts of the house that have been considered so far were areas of reception and display and spaces associated with the family. The atrium, the garden, the cubicula and the other rooms had a variety of functions and were filled at various times of the day with different members of the household. But there were parts of the Roman house, behind the scenes, used largely or wholly for 'service' functions and almost exclusively the domain of slaves. These areas were devoted to the storage, preparation and cooking of food and the disposal of human waste and domestic refuse. Domestic storage and water supply were often situated in 'respectable' areas of the home, so it would be wrong to look for a strict division between elegance and utility. Nonetheless, it made sense for the sake of the smooth running of the household to bring certain activities together. As this section will show, there were many different elements to these 'service' areas, but there were certain features that remained constant.

KITCHENS

A large proportion of houses had some form of cooking area,[1] though it is misleading to think of a multi-functional kitchen such as the ones we are used to. Cooking areas are recognizable from finds such as cooking pots and other utensils and storage vessels and from fixed elements, in particular the cooking platform. This was a solid masonry structure about 1 m (3 ft) in height and 1 to 2 m wide, usually built against the wall. It was composed of a raised platform with a plain, solid tile or mortar surface, with a heavy rim designed to keep ash and hot vessels in place. A misleading resemblance to modern cookers is given by the arched space below the surface. This is not an oven or a way of feeding the flames on the platform, but storage space for solid fuel in the form of wood or, more often, charcoal. Slaves cooking with either of these in a poorly ventilated space would have inhaled smoke and harmful gases such as carbon monoxide.

It seems very likely that the Romans called a cooking space a *culina*,[2] though this was not the only place in the Roman home where cooking could take place. Separate cooking areas were built near dining areas outside the main part of the home, for example the summer triclinium in the House of the Gardens of Hercules (P) (FIG. 262). Reheating food and even preparing it could have been done nearer the main living areas, using braziers (FIG. 300) and other devices.

Many culinae were set in an out-of-the-way area, with none of today's

PREVIOUS PAGES
Fig. 298 Still-life fresco.
House of the Stags, Herculaneum
H. 41 cm, L. 129 cm
MANN 8644

ABOVE **Fig. 299 Kitchen.**
House of the Ephebe, Pompeii

OPPOSITE **Fig. 300 Terracotta brazier –
the main cooking facility in poorer
houses and flats – or a 'barbecue' in
the gardens of the wealthy.**
Building B, Moregine
H. 43 cm, D. 46 cm
SAP 85204

preoccupations with light or cleanliness. Most kitchens, even those in wealthy houses such as the House of Obellius Firmus, were dark, even dingy. The windows, if any, were small. Even during daylight hours, more light was needed for food preparation, so this could have taken place outside, in corridors, or in the garden. During late afternoon and early evening, when the evening meal was being prepared, artificial lighting was required, and in addition to the glow from the fuel of the fire there were oil lamps set in niches or on ledges or hooks on the wall.

Sometimes kitchens were set in the courtyard or garden,[3] as in the House of the Piglet or the House of Caius Julius Polybius (P). In the House of the Piglet, kitchen facilities had originally been located elsewhere, but were relocated to the garden, using a corner pillar of the much-reduced colonnade as a structural support. Perhaps this was in order to get rid of what the Roman writer Seneca called '…that stink of smoky kitchens…' (*illum odorem culinarum fumantium*).[4]

Portable braziers in bronze and iron or terracotta (FIG. 300) supplemented fixed cooking facilities in some richer homes, allowing food to be prepared and served anywhere in the house. They may have been the main or only method of cooking in small houses or flats. As with fixed kitchens the use of wood or charcoal in enclosed areas would have created a very unpleasant atmosphere.[5] It is possible that some poorer households had no cooking facilities at all, their occupants relying on the numerous food and drink outlets lining the streets (above pp. 59–63).

Some kitchens, as in the House of Caius Julius Polybius (P), were fitted with a 'chimney' tile in the roof, but even so there would have been lots of smoke and strong smells from the food and waste. In this enclosed and airless space, the heat would have been intense, especially in summer. With little hygienic food storage, not to mention the frequent location of toilets within cooking areas (below pp. 261–2), flies and vermin crawled on and around uncooked and cooked food. The floors of the kitchen area were usually made of waterproof materials, such as *signinum* – with good reason, as liquids from food preparation, cooking and toilets swilled around.

Surprisingly, a piped water supply was almost never found in a kitchen in the cities. Piped water was more likely to be used in the garden, where some food would be prepared. One exception is the kitchen in the House of Marcus Fabius Rufus (P), which boasts two water taps. The higher one may have been for drawing water into vessels, while the lower seems to have been used to sluice an area (*trua*) of the floor delimited by a tall ridge. In this house the trua incorporated the latrine, but in others it was separate and was probably used for the disposal of general kitchen waste and slops.[6]

Kitchens can be an important indicator of the vitality (or not) of the cities in AD 79 (see below p. 277). There is some debate over the extent to which houses were inhabited at the time of the eruption, but it is fairly certain that any house where people were living needed a functioning kitchen area. In fact the presence of *in situ* cooking vessels is – arguably – a major sign of life in the home.[7]

So who worked in this area of the home; who prepared and cooked the food? In contrast to the Greek world, where cooks could be very highly esteemed, and on one rare occasion even honoured with a statue,[8] the status of Roman cooks was generally

LEFT **Fig. 301 Fresco showing food including a pig's head and kebabs, painted above the cooking platform.**
House of the Piglet, Pompeii

OPPOSITE **Fig. 302 Domestic shrine (*lararium*) painted on a kitchen wall.**
Villa 6, Terzigno
H. 223 cm, W. 286.5 cm
SAP 86755

low. With one or two exceptions, they are described as slaves who could cook, rather than culinary specialists. Cicero mentions one slave who doubled as the porter,[9] and elsewhere[10] he puts cooks among the basest professions, along with butchers, fishermen and dancers – anyone, in short, who provided earthly pleasures. Cicero's own personal prejudices may be a major factor here. But Roman cuisine, at least for the upper classes, became ever more elaborate, and for the most expert chefs there developed a hiring market[11] and even training courses for carvers (*carptores*).[12] Most of the named cooks in the Roman writers are male, but there is every reason to believe that equal numbers of women worked in the kitchen. In smaller houses there may have been just one slave who cooked, but in larger households more slaves will have been involved in preparing and cooking, especially if the evening meal was grand.

The importance of the kitchen for those who worked in it can be seen in the sometimes ornate decoration of the servants' *lararium* (shrine). In fact kitchens were one of the most common places to find these shrines, and painted examples are, almost without exception, restricted to the kitchen area.[13] The cooking area formed a very natural context for worship of the gods. It was, after all, the location of the hearth, on which offerings could be made, just as on an altar. From a villa in Terzigno, near Pompeii (FIG. 302), comes a painted lararium which once filled a complete wall of the kitchen. The upper part of the wall on the left shows a sacrifice taking place in a typically rustic setting. In the centre is a man making offerings at an altar. He is formally dressed and *capite velato* (literally 'with his head covered' by his toga), like an emperor at a state sacrifice. Carrying a horn of plenty, he represents prosperity and security and is the *Genius*, the spirit and life force, of the master of the home. To the left (now largely missing) and right are the household gods or Lares, with their garlanded long hair, belted tunics, high laced boots and mantles draped over their arms. They each hold a drinking horn, from which wine pours out. 'Libation' (poured offering) of wine or

honey was an important part of the sacrifice. Below the scene of sacrifice two large *agathodaimones* (snakes of good fortune) approach a painted sacrifice of eggs and a pine cone, which clearly mimics the actual sacrifices that took place on the real altar erected in front of the shrine. Above, to the right, is a large niche, which probably once held lamps and statuettes of deities related to the shrine, rather than practical culinary equipment. Above this are painted foodstuffs: spits holding an eel and pieces of meat, a hog's head and a ham.

In the kitchen of the House of the Piglet (P) (FIG. 301) is another lararium scene extending over the cooking platform. In the centre are two spits of eel and meat and a hog's head, so similar to those on the Terzigno lararium that they must have been painted by the same person. At the top are suspended salami and a bow-like string of songbirds. At the bottom of the picture, shown almost sitting on the platform, is a jar directly placed on the flames, and a tripod waiting for a vessel to be placed on it.

COOKING

In use, the cooking platform had one or more areas of burning charcoal or wood on which to cook directly. This was in effect simply a sophisticated, literally elevated, version of the ancient 'on-hearth' cookery, a feature of Roman cooking from early times. Most platforms were flat-topped, but some had raised blocks that could be used to position cooking pots, grills or spits.

In some houses, usually the larger ones in each block of the cities, there was also a private oven, a sign of prestige. This was either a separate structure, as at the Villa of the Mysteries (P), or built onto the cooking platform, as in the House of the Two Atria (H). Most houses, however, did not have their own fixed ovens, but relied instead on those of the adjacent large house or the cities' bakeries. The latter probably offered a service for baking and roasting when their ovens were not full of bread, a practice not uncommon in fairly recent times. Nevertheless, a large number of houses possessed small mills for grinding grain (FIG. 303), operated by hand with a short pole. These small mills are usually made of local Vesuvian lavastone. This was less fine than the Orvietan lavastone used for the industrial-scale mills, and gave a coarser result, suitable for flatbreads and for porridge-like dishes.[14]

An unusual vessel from Pompeii (FIG. 305) is almost certainly a form of portable oven for use on a hearth or cooking surface. This vessel, known to the Romans as a *clibanus* or a *testum*,[15] had a domed upper body with a broad flanged rim. When positioned over the food to be cooked (usually bread, but also, according to Apicius, dormice), the clibanus was covered with ash.[16] This was kept in place by the flange and the vessel formed a closed baking unit.

Other vessels used on cooking platforms included a cooking pot or *caccabus*, like a modern saucepan or casserole, made of terracotta or bronze (FIGS 307 and 308).

BELOW **Fig. 303 Hand quern in lava stone.**
House of Caius Julius Polybius, Pompeii
H. 43.5 cm, D. 33 cm
SAP 27086

Fig. 304 Cooking platform with a built-in oven.
House of the Two Atria, Herculaneum

BELOW **Fig. 305 Pottery domed cooking vessel (*clibanus*).**

From Herculaneum
H.10 cm, D. 46 cm
MANN

Fig. 306 Bronze cooking jar (*olla*) with lid attached by a chain

H. 20 cm, D. 29 cm
MANN 6478

ABOVE **Fig. 307 Bronze casserole/cooking pot (*caccabus*).**

From Pompeii
H. 27 cm, D. 53 cm
MANN 73120

BELOW **Fig. 308 Pottery cooking pot (*caccabus*) on an iron tripod.**

House of the Tragic Poet, Pompeii (VI,8,3)
H. (with tripod) 41.5 cm, D. across handles 30 cm
MANN 23322

Identical cooking pots, apparently of bronze, can be seen in frescoes, offered for sale by a vendor in the Forum at Pompeii (FIG. 35). Generally, anyone wealthy used the more expensive metal pans, while the poorer used pottery. However, it is worth remembering that Apicius, one of our main sources for Roman cooking in this period, mentions the importance of using vessels of terracotta for particular dishes, irrespective of wealth.

The broad angular body of the caccabus, with a wide rim and gently rounded base, diffused heat across a wide area, making it ideal for heating large quantities of foodstuffs in liquids, such as stews. Examples have been found on stoves throughout the cities, containing foods such as lentils, broad beans, onions and bran, all of which could have been ingredients for stew-like meals that were in preparation when the eruption happened.[17] In the flat above the *lupanare* (brothel) of Pompeii the tenants, perhaps the working girls themselves, were preparing a hearty stew of beans and onions in a metal cooking pot in the kitchen.[18] Onions were a speciality of the area around Pompeii, as were cauliflowers.[19]

Other vessels, this time in pottery, included cooking jars of various forms and baking or frying dishes. Hanging above or near the platform was a host of cooking equipment, ranging from colanders, ladles, hooks and spits to pans, dishes and moulds. A pan with six separate compartments (FIG. 309) may have been used for making cakes or coddling eggs, while another (FIG. 310) was perhaps used for meat, its pouring lip helping to drain the juices. A square dish was almost certainly for baking. Apicius has a recipe called *patina Apiciana*,[20] which has layers of crushed meat between layers of doughcakes – a kind of Roman lasagne, perhaps? Perhaps the most unusual mould is a large bronze example shaped like a hare, probably used for savoury dishes such as paté or meat in aspic. It would have made a very impressive centrepiece for a dinner party (FIG. 311).

ABOVE **Fig. 309 Pan with six circular compartments, perhaps for eggs or cakes.**
L. 35 cm
The British Museum, 1856,1226.699

Fig. 310 Bronze pan with a pouring lip, perhaps a meat dish.
L. 47 cm
The British Museum, 1856,1226.1008

BELOW **Fig. 311 Food mould in the form of a hare.**
Bakery of Donatus, Pompeii (VII,12,1)
L. 65 cm, W. 16 cm
MANN 76355

Before cooking, ingredients had to be prepared. A very common household device was the mortar and pestle, used to grind and blend together ingredients to make the sauces and purées that were so important in Roman cuisine. Lack of refrigeration caused smells and problems for food storage in the kitchens and store rooms, making rich, spice-filled sauces important. Mortars and pestles were usually made in pottery or marble and equipped with a pouring spout. One unusual example from Pompeii has a grotesque face carved on the underside (FIG. 312). This female (?) face, with its straggly long hair and elongated features, could only be seen when the vessel was not in use and was suspended on a wall. We do not know whether the face had any particular significance; it does not seem quite weird enough to be the head of the snake-haired Gorgon Medusa, used often in Roman art to ward off the evil eye.

Another curious vessel, found in some kitchens in the cities, takes us to the heart of 'decadent' Roman cuisine. The vessel comes in two main forms, a rounded globular shape or a squat cylindrical vessel (FIG. 313), but both share the same characteristics. The vessel wall is pierced with numerous holes, and just inside the rim are one or two shallow horizontal cups. The strangest feature is on the interior, where a narrow projection runs from the rim to the base. Various suggestions have been put forward for the use of these jars, including beehives and snail farms. But it is almost certain that this type of vessel was used for rearing dormice. The dormouse is best known now as a pest, but to the Romans it was a delicacy. This vase may be the *glirarium* (dormouse-rearing jar) mentioned by the Roman writer Varro.[21] He describes how the animals lived in these specially built vessels, scampering up the ramp to get acorns and water and then running back down to the bottom where they grew fat in the warm and dark interior.

The culina was the primary space for cooking, but not necessarily the main area for storage of provisions. Long, narrow rooms near the garden and kitchen, fitted with shelving or cupboards, were the most likely food storage areas. In some gardens there were large, bulk containers or *dolia* (globular storage vessels for wine, oil, grain and other commodities), like those found in bars and taverns, but larger, with a capacity of up to 1,000 litres (1,760 pints).

Very common in a domestic context were amphorae, large pottery storage and transport containers. The presence of amphorae could mean simply a well-stocked cellar and larder, but they might indicate that the household was in some way linked to agricultural production. Many wealthy home-owners in the cities also had country estates, and people and goods flowed continuously between them. In several houses in and around Pompeii, empty amphorae were found in the garden and peristyle, often in large quantities, upside down, ready for reuse.

The absence of refrigeration meant much food was bought and consumed on the same day, or was processed by pickling or drying, or preserving in honey. The vast majority of food and liquid storage involved smaller quantities, sufficient for household use, in smaller containers of pottery, glass, metal and organic materials such as straw and wicker. Many vessels normally for cooking or for serving may also have been used for storage.

Glass storage vessels were common, often in thick glass with squared, cylindrical or even hexagonal bodies. The necks of these vessels, usually quite narrow, were stopped with bungs of wood, fibre or cloth, and they contained commodities of all types. One cylindrical bottle (FIG. 314) still retains its organic stopper and the remains of its contents, probably olive oil. Another squared bottle from Pompeii,[22] now on display at the Museum of Boscoreale, still smells strongly of rancid olive oil, more than 1,900 years after the eruption. Smaller, chunkier bottles resemble modern preserve jars and served the same purpose. Foods found in these include onions[23] and olives in their own oil.[24]

There was also a wide variety of pottery vessels for storage and cooking, made of two different types of clay. Cooking-vessel clay is rougher and full of small fragments of minerals, in this area mostly volcanic, thanks to Vesuvius. This clay was sometimes made even coarser by the addition of mineral inclusions. This made the vessel

LEFT **Fig. 314 Cylindrical glass jar with its stopper still intact. The contents were almost certainly olive oil.**

From Pompeii
H. 27.8 cm, D. 10.3 cm
MANN 313337

Figs 315 and 316 Pottery storage jars.

From Herculaneum, Cardo V drain
H. 23 cm; 31 cm
HCP 37, 36

Fig. 317 Remains of eggs in the 'negative' imprint of a pottery vase.

From Pompeii
H. 25 cm
SAP 355

more resistant to thermal shock – the rapid, extreme heating that happens when a vessel comes into contact with direct flames, which can cause the vessel to crack or shatter. Cooking pottery is often a dark reddish orange/brown colour and the surface may appear much darker, even black, because of this direct heat.

Pottery usually intended for storage was made of clay that had been partly cleaned or 'levigated', producing a finer, lighter, less grainy fabric, but one that had little or no resistance to direct heat and was totally unsuited for use in cooking. Storage containers in this fine fabric included flagons for liquids such as oil or honey and wide-mouthed, tapering vessels (FIG. 316) that were found containing hazelnuts, barley and lentils. Cups, bowls and jars contained a whole range of foodstuffs, including barley, beans, olives, dates, figs and lentils.

A remarkable negative 'imprint' of a squat pottery vessel (now missing) from Pompeii (FIG. 317) still contains the remains of hen's eggs. Organic materials, more fugitive in the archaeological record, were also commonly used. Baskets are frequently shown in Roman art – for example the basket of ripe figs from the living room (*oecus*) at Oplontis Villa A. We must imagine that many of the foodstuffs found in the cities may originally have been in organic containers, but that these have only been recognized or salvageable in more recent scientific excavations: for example, the two baskets from Herculaneum (FIGS 318 and 319).

Vessels for storage, cooking and serving, whether of pottery or metal, needed to be cleaned occasionally, though perhaps not as thoroughly or frequently as today. Slaves used water, fine sand as an abrasive, or cloths to wipe vessels clean. In most kitchens there was no fixed 'sink' so washing up would have involved (wooden?) containers in larger kitchens or in spaces around the garden.

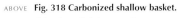

ABOVE **Fig. 318 Carbonized shallow basket.**

House of the Beautiful Courtyard,
Herculaneum (V,8)
H. 4.5 cm, D. 14.5 cm
SAP 77190

Fig. 319 Carbonized basket with lid.

From Herculaneum
H. 6.5 cm, D. 13 cm
SAP 79127

WASHING AND BATHS

The Romans had no concept of domestic bathrooms, that is, specific rooms where washing would take place. There was certainly no modern-style bathroom, with toilet and washing facilities combined. Instead, it is quite likely that most people would wash themselves (probably not every day) using a portable basin and jug, often in the cubiculum, after waking or before going to bed. Even where piped water was available there was no provision of hot running water, except in the public baths and the (rare) private baths. Instead, in most houses water was boiled in kettles and cauldrons in the kitchen, or in special heaters or samovars, and taken to where it was needed. A particular type of lidded bronze vessel with a broad, shallow shape was found in many kitchens in the cities.[25] One particular example (FIG. 321) strongly suggests it and the others were used just for boiling water, since layers of limescale have built up inside it, just as on a modern kettle. It is possible that most washing would have taken place in the comparative privacy of the bedroom, but washing and shaving or the washing of infants or children could have taken place in more communal spaces in and around the garden or even in the kitchen.

Private *thermae*, that is domestic suites of baths that had the standard Roman run of cold, tepid and hot rooms, have now been found in over thirty-five houses in the cities, mostly in Pompeii. The baths in the House of the Menander seems to have been in the course of upgrading and expansion at the time of the eruption, with the *caldarium* (hot room) and *tepidarium* (tepid room) already completed and decorated.

The mosaic floor of the caldarium is remarkably well preserved (FIG. 322). The semicircular apse is decorated with a geometric radiating scale pattern. The main area, surrounded by a fine frame of wave and Greek key motifs, features a very lively scene of sea life, centred on a polychrome roundel filled with luxurious acanthus leaves on which perches a twittering bird. The main scene itself shows marine creatures including dolphins, fish, a crab and an eel. Joining them are two black fishermen. One is shown burning a dolphin with a torch before spearing it with his trident. The other swims among the creatures, with his comically large phallus dangling underneath him.

At the threshold of the room another man greets us, his large genitals hanging below his loincloth (FIG. 320). He carries two wine jugs (*askoi*) and wears a wreath, indicating that he is serving at a dinner banquet – a common activity after bathing. Below his feet are four artistically arranged strigils, curved bronze implements that were used to scrape sweat, dirt and oil off the skin after exercise and bathing. The complex was

Fig. 320 Mosaic from the entrance to a hot room (*caldarium*).

House of the Menander, Pompeii

LEFT **Fig. 321 Bronze lidded vessel used for boiling water.**

H. 20 cm, D. 29 cm
MANN 74806

OPPOSITE **Fig. 322 The hot room (*caldarium*) of a private bath suite.**

House of the Menander, Pompeii

completed with a small peristyle with a pool decorated with coloured marble and bordered by mosaic panels (FIG. 323). The columns of the peristyle were originally discovered lying in a service corridor in another part of the house and were reconstructed in the 1950s. They were thus evidence of the building works taking place in AD 79.

For some houses without a private bath suite, such as the House of the Stags, there were bronze bath tubs that were filled with water when and where needed – similar to the tradition of tin baths in front of the fire that persisted in many working-class homes in Britain until the mid-twentieth century.

TOILETS

The Romans, like everyone else, needed an organized system for the disposal of human waste, but their solutions to this everyday problem, such as siting the toilet in the kitchen, were in some ways quite surprising. The Romans usually referred to this space as the *latrina*, but they also had slang terms such as *secessus* ('privy') – still preserved in the modern Italian *cesso* and *cella* ('chair'). [26]

A 'typical' toilet (FIG. 324) featured a hole leading to a cesspit with a pair of masonry uprights supporting a seat, usually of wood – marble 'keyhole' seats are rare.[27] An arched niche cut into the wall behind the toilet provided increased comfort. In front of the toilet was a tiled surface, sloping toward the cesspit, and sometimes a footrest with a gap underneath so that water used to sluice the tiled area could flow into a pit.[28]

The second, simpler 'squatter' toilet, popular in upper storeys, was built over a downpipe with a small niche, but without a seat or partitions. These needed less water to flush. Flushing, however cursory, was important to keep pipes open (particularly narrow downpipes from upper storeys), to keep the area in a bearable condition, and to speed the breakdown of waste.[29] All latrines needed to be flushed and rinsed regularly, especially in summer, in spite of problems in obtaining the necessary water. Flushing water, drawn from fountains and cisterns, was kept in wooden, pottery and metal storage vessels until needed.[30]

Downpipes sometimes reveal the existence of toilets in upstairs rooms which may not have survived, especially at Pompeii.[31] These could simply be rainwater pipes, but 90 per cent of samples taken from them contained traces of mineralized faeces.[32] Remarkably, almost every home in Pompeii has evidence of at least one latrine somewhere in its structure,[33] and the same high incidence of latrines has been confirmed by recent research in Herculaneum.[34]

There were several typical locations for toilets within the Roman home:[35] near an external door (which made cess removal much easier); in or near the garden, where water supply rendered their use more convenient; under the stairs; or even on a covered balcony (*maenianum*). What surprises and appals us today is that the toilet was most frequently located in the kitchen area, often right next to the cooking platform: for

OPPOSITE **Fig. 323 Peristyle of a private bath suite.**
House of the Menander, Pompeii

BELOW **Fig. 324 A typical toilet.**
House of the Chaste Lovers, Pompeii

example in the House of the Two Atria (FIG. 304) or the House of Marcus Fabius Rufus (P) (FIG. 325). In some cases there was a masonry partition between the toilet and the cooking area. This may have been heightened with wooden panels, now gone,[36] or with screens or curtains. But very often there is no sign of any barrier or partition.

The location of toilets in the middle of the service areas makes it less likely, in all probability, that the owners of the house or their family used them.[37] They might have been tempted to use toilets in 'nicer' areas such as the garden or its colonnaded peristyle, but generally they may have stuck to using their chamber pots, conveniently brought to them as needed and emptied by the slaves (see pp. 128–9).

The vast majority of domestic toilets were single-seaters. Exceptional two-seater toilets include the large separate latrine in the House of the Dioscuri (P) (FIG. 326), quite well-appointed and relatively well-lit.[38]

All the private latrines in the cities, however grand or awful, fed their waste not into mains sewers, but into cesspits. Mains sewerage systems existed in some other towns and cities such as Rome and Ostia, but Pompeii and Herculaneum had no city-wide sewers. Their drains, where they existed, were almost exclusively for excess water from the baths, streets and fountains.[39] Sewerage systems were expensive, needed maintenance, and in any case the porous nature of the rock, at least under Pompeii, made cesspits a practical alternative.

Each house maintained its own cesspit, near the outer boundary of the house or toward the garden area, making emptying easier.[40] Cesspits were emptied at regular intervals, by slaves known as *stercorarii* (from the Latin *stercus* or faeces), who then sold on the contents as fertilizer for fields and even domestic gardens.[41] They are immortalized in a graffito from the House of the Black Living Room in Herculaneum, where one of the workers wrote on a column *Exem(p)ta stercora a(ssibus) XI* ('Shit from this [cesspit] emptied for 11 asses').[42]

DECORATION: INFORMAL AND FORMAL

Graffiti were surprisingly rare in the latrines of the cities, perhaps because they were not places where anyone wanted to linger,[3] and also because it may not have been easy to see, let alone write. There are two notable exceptions. In the well-appointed latrine of the House of the Gem (H), a man recorded his successful use of the toilet: *Apollinaris, medicus Titus Imp. Hic cacavit bene* ('Apollinaris doctor of the Emperor Titus had a good shit here').[44] A graffito in the servants' latrine in the House of the Centenary (P) with idiosyncratic spelling reads *Marthae hoc trichilinium est nam in trichliino cacat* ('This is Martha's triclinium, because in her triclinium she shits').[45] This suggests that only servants used it – and the name Martha may also indicate the presence of a Jewish slave in the household.

On the whole, toilets were not normally decorated. Around sixteen latrines have painted décor in Pompeii, with four more in Herculaneum.[46] There were probably more but they (or the décor) have not survived.[47] Where decoration remains, the most

TOP **Fig. 325 Cooking platform (left) directly next to a toilet (right).**
House of Marcus Fabius Rufus, Pompeii

ABOVE **Fig. 326 Two-seater toilet.**
House of the Dioscouri, Pompeii

OPPOSITE **Fig. 327 Fresco from a corridor leading to a latrine with Isis protecting a man relieving himself and the words** *Cacator cave malu(m)* **('Shitter beware the evil eye').**
From Pompeii (IX,7,22)
H. 68.7 cm, W. 80.3 cm
MANN 112285

LACATOR

CAVE MAIN

common theme is the representation of Fortuna, goddess of Fortune, her identity merged, as often occurs in Roman art of the period, with the Egyptian goddess Isis. The most famous example was discovered in a Pompeian tavern (IX,7,22) in 1880, decorating a small domestic lararium in a corridor that led to the toilet.[48] The painting shows the goddess holding a horn of plenty in one hand and the rudder that steers fortune in the other. She looks at a naked man, crouching to relieve himself, who is approached (though protected and not threatened) by two protective serpents. Painted above the man are the words *CACATOR CAVE MALU(m)* ('Shitter beware [the] evil [Eye]'), a name for the malignant forces that attacked people when vulnerable – for example when going to the toilet.

The phrase *CACATOR CAVE MALU(m)* could be a warning as well as a protection. It was painted in white letters 1 m (3 ft) high on the wall of an alley to the north of the Via dell'Abbondanza, Pompeii,[49] and a little poem painted on a wall near the Vesuvian Gate, Pompeii, says *Cacator sic valeas ut tu hoc locum transeas* ('O Shitter may health smile on your face, as long as you go from this place').[50] Most importantly Fortuna protected against the sheer awfulness of Roman domestic toilets and their danger to health. Many were dark and full of smells.[51] The Romans had no u-bend and the smells of the cesspit, acrid ammonia from urine and stomach-turning smells of faeces must have found their way into the kitchen and home.[52]

HYGIENE

What we understand by 'hygiene' meant little or nothing to the Romans. The Romans, of course, had a concept of health and sickness, and they even had a goddess Hygiea, from whose name come our words hygiene and hygienic – but she was a goddess of health.[53] There was no understanding of infection or germs, but rather a belief that internal forces caused illnesses and disease, and that the environment created unhealthy atmospheres that aggravated them. Gods and spirits were a useful barrier between humans and these forces.

Toilet paper was unknown. Instead, there is some evidence to back up the popularly held idea that sponges were used.[54] The writer Martial talks about tonight's sumptuous dinner being tomorrow's fodder for a '...doomed sponge stick',[55] while Seneca describes a gladiator, about to face the crowd, who chose death – by ramming the toilet sponge down his throat.[56] Other things possibly used for wiping include moss, grass or cloth. Small fragments of mineralized cloth are frequent finds in the Cardo V drain in Herculaneum, but the drain also received domestic refuse, so we cannot be sure this was 'toilet cloth'.

Having cleaned yourself you might wash your hands in a bowl or trough of still water (in which many others had already done so) in order to remove unpleasant residues from your hands, but not with any awareness that such residues were harmful to your health. There was nothing equating to soap, so people with hands covered in faecal matter and bacteria of all sorts walked to and from the toilet, through the kitchen area, touching other people, surfaces, vessels for cooking and serving, raw and cooked food, and spreading germs throughout the whole area. In addition flies, cockroaches, mice, rats and other vermin spread potentially dangerous germs from toilets and

cesspits across the kitchen and dining area. They were regarded as a nuisance, but the real danger they posed to health was never recognized.[57]

The toilet and toilet/kitchen became a breeding ground for disease. It is likely that these conditions, with contamination of water and food, led to serious infections both bacterial (such as typhoid, cholera, diarrhoea, salmonella and Weil's disease) and multicellular (such as amoebic dysentery and worms).[58] Writers such as Celsus clearly recognized the dangers of diseases such as diarrhoea and dysentery, but did not make the connection with dirty conditions.[59]

Downpipes in Pompeii have preserved traces of worms.[60] The writer Celsus warns that worms can take possession of the bowel – recommending a medicine involving garlic, induced vomiting, pomegranate roots and bicarbonate of soda.[61]

THE GREATEST SEPTIC TANK: THE CARDO V DRAIN IN HERCULANEUM

Recent excavations at Herculaneum have revealed the grandest and most extensive septic tank ever discovered.

The major streets of Herculaneum, and some in Pompeii, had solidly built drains of brick and concrete running below them for waste water. But the 'drain' flanking the fifth *Cardo* (north–south street) at Herculaneum was different. At the beginning of the first century AD a building complex known as an *insula*, comprising shops with apartments above, was built along Cardo V. Although insulae are common in cities such as Rome, this is the only known example from the cities. It fronted the *palaestra* complex, a pool and an open area surrounded by a colonnade intended for physical and intellectual education, but also a general centre of social interaction of all types. All the properties in the insula were given disposal systems for domestic and human waste, through chutes that led from the insula down to the drain.

The drain was first investigated in the mid-twentieth century, but few records were kept and no finds were retained. Fortunately, in 2005–6 the Herculaneum Conservation Project, reactivating the drain as part of an ancient solution to Herculaneum's contemporary drainage problems, excavated the remaining part of the fill.[62] The drain, some 3 m (10 ft) high and almost 1 m wide, extended for 86 m (282 ft) under the buildings to the side of the Cardo and still retained some 40 m (130 ft) of its

Figs 330–33 Red Slip Ware from (L–R) South France, Britain, Italy and Turkey.

From Herculaneum, Cardo V drain
(L–R) H. 13.5 cm; 4 cm; 5 cm; 5 cm
(L–R) HCP 6; 13; 16; 11

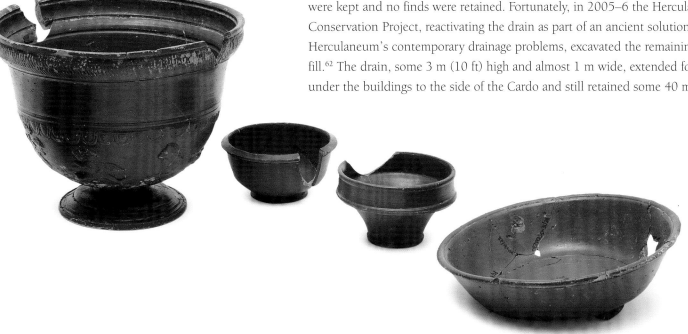

original fill, crammed with material. Fortunately the cesspit emptiers (*stercorarii*) had not visited just beforehand. It soon became clear that this drain, unlike some others in Herculaneum, did not carry waste out to sea. There was a small trickle of water out of the system but not enough for it to function as a true drain. Instead, under Cardo V the Romans (perhaps exploiting an existing cistern or quarry) had constructed an enormous septic tank, designed to take refuse of all types from the insula.

Rubbish is useful because it gives clues about aspects of daily life not often referred to in literature or preserved in the remains of the household. The most important find amongst the 'rubbish' was food waste from the preparation, cooking or excreting of foodstuffs (above pp. 233–4). But there were also countless fragments of pottery vessels, which came together to reconstruct coarse cooking pots, frying pans and storage jars used in the kitchen, and also more refined dishes, bowls and jugs and bottles used for serving, and cups and bowls for drinking. Imported vessels shed light on the trading networks in which the city was involved, while glass vessels are evidence for a taste for finer goods, their variety and quality hinting at the tastes (and spending power) of the people in the insula.

This rubbish is particularly important because, with the exception of levelling deposits from renovation and rebuilding, deposits of household rubbish contemporary with the eruption are surprisingly rare, perhaps the result of 'grubbing' (recycling) or tidy residents sweeping up in front of their respective homes, or simply a failure to record such finds.[63] Exceptions are the recent evidence for 'fly-tipping' outside the walls of Pompeii which give some evidence for the rubbish generated by the residents of the city at the time of the eruption.[64]

ABOVE AND BELOW LEFT **Figs 334–5 Locally made beakers.**
Herculaneum, Cardo V drain
(L–R) H. 10 cm; 10 cm
(L–R) HCP 41; 40

LEFT **Figs 336–7 Thin-walled wares.**
Herculaneum, Cardo V drain
(L–R) H. 9.5 cm; 5 cm
(L–R) HCP 30; 27

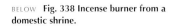

Herculaneum, Cardo V drain
H. 7.5 cm
HCP 43

RIGHT **Figs 339–42 Four mould-made oil lamps.**

Herculaneum, Cardo V drain
(Clockwise) D. 7.5 cm; 8.5 cm; 6.5 cm; 7.5 cm
(Clockwise) HCP 81; 19; 18; 79

BOTTOM **Fig. 343 Mould-made oil lamp in the form of an eagle.**

Herculaneum, Cardo V drain
H. 10.5 cm
HCP 91

In the Cardo V drain, by contrast, excavators encountered a depth of ancient waste around 1.4 m (4½ ft) high, sealed by the volcanic ash, now rock hard, that had originally flowed in through all the different chutes and entry points. Excavations were carried out metre by metre along the drain, taking account of the different layers of deposited refuse, and produced a huge quantity (over 750 sacks) of organic waste, in particular human waste and food debris. The dietary refuse from the drain is by far the most important element recovered. Food waste included processes of preparation, cooking and plate waste. An incredibly rich range of foodstuff remains included fish and meat bones, vegetables and fruit, seeds and pips, spices and herbs and even probable remains of domestic sacrifices. All these food remains were preserved either through being burnt (carbonization) or through part-fossilization caused by the contents of the drain (mineralization) (above p. 233).[65]

There was also a huge quantity of other refuse, from vessels of pottery, bronze and glass to terracotta figurines, coins, bricks and other building material, as well as accidental losses – for example gems, jewellery and complete vessels and lamps.[66] Coins[67] and datable pottery and lamps allowed archaeologists to be fairly certain that, although some material was almost seventy-five years old when the eruption took place, the vast majority had accumulated in the last five to ten years before the eruption of AD 79.

The pottery covered every area of domestic life and came from all over the Roman Empire. It included transport amphorae (FIG. 329); cooking vessels; fine table ware, in particular Red Slip Ware (FIGS 330–3); and local table pottery cups and beakers (FIGS 334–5), often with walls as thin as glass (FIGS 336–7). There were also hundreds of mould-made pottery lamps, most broken and intentionally discarded, but others intact and probably lost accidentally – perhaps dropped down the toilet during a nocturnal visit. Alongside more ordinary lamps (FIGS 339–42) decorated with motifs such as gladiators was a rare example moulded in the form of an eagle (FIG. 343).

In addition there were large quantities of glass, including cups and bowls and many thin, elongated bottles for perfumed oils (*unguentaria*). Given their quantity and good state of preservation, these may have been used as part of personal hygiene around the toilet.

Alongside these pottery and glass discards and losses, from activities in and around the kitchen and table, were other objects, representing other activities elsewhere in the home. These include gaming counters in glass and stone (FIG. 214); small incense burners (FIG. 338) from household shrines, perhaps in the kitchen; a scallop shell (FIG. 145) used in toilette, still containing orange-red make-up; bone pins (FIG. 148); and loomweights.

A gold ring with a gem (FIG. 346), showing a cantharus or drinking cup, must have been an accidental loss. Perhaps the owner might even have contemplated trying to retrieve it – but then thought better of it. Several engraved carnelian gemstones were also found. Showing subjects as diverse as satyrs with a goat (FIG. 348), a cupid riding a ram (FIG. 344) and the god Mercury (FIG. 345), these gems may have come from the workshop of a *gemmarius* (gem-cutter) discovered in the insula in the 1930s (above p. 70).[68] For an artisan to lose such precious pieces seems careless, but given the light levels and probable interior conditions of workshops, it is possible.

Figs 344–8 Group of carnelian gems and a gold ring: gemstone showing satyrs and a goat; fragmentary gemstone showing a satyr; ring with gem stone showing a drinking cup; gemstone showing a cupid riding a goat; gemstone showing the god Mercury.

Herculaneum, Cardo V drain
D. 1 cm; 1.1 cm; 1.8 cm; 1 cm; 1 cm
HCP 97; 96; 95; 102; 98

RIGHT **Figs 349–54 Building materials. Clockwise from left: part of a tile from a bath building; terracotta roof ornament (*antefix*) showing the snake-haired gorgon Medusa; fragments of marble veneer.**

Herculaneum, Cardo V drain
(Clockwise from left) H. 8.5 cm; H. 14 cm;
W. 12.5 cm; W. 8.5 cm; L. 7 cm; L. 8.5 cm
(Clockwise from left) HCP 106; 89; 110;
112; 109; 111

BELOW **Fig. 355 Terracotta statuette showing a mother nursing her baby.**

Herculaneum, Cardo V drain
H. 12.5 cm
HCP 92

Building materials from demolition and rebuilding, perhaps linked to the series of earthquakes between AD 62 and the eruption, also found their way into the drain. As well as bricks and tiles of all shapes and sizes there were also fragments of marble veneer (FIGS 351–4) and a terracotta ornament (*antefix*) from the edge of a roof (FIG. 350), showing a large palmette rising above the head of the Gorgon Medusa. Identical antefixes were found during excavations of buildings near the insula.

Among all the human waste and domestic refuse, archaeologists discovered a very human and very touching artefact, almost perfectly preserved. This terracotta statuette of a very rare type (FIG. 355) shows a woman nursing a small baby, either laying him into or taking him out of a crib. We do not know how this statuette ended up in the drain, nor can we be sure what this, or the numerous other terracottas that survive from Pompeii and Herculaneum, were used for. Some, featuring deities and animals, were certainly used in domestic shrines and have been discovered there by archaeologists. Others, featuring characters from daily life, such as gladiators or portly senators and slaves, may have been simple ornaments or children's toys, souvenirs or New Year gifts. But we can only guess at the function of this piece. Was it simply a nice ornament, or a gift to a young mother to celebrate her new arrival, or was it a purchase by the mother herself to bring good fortune and fend off, like Isis Fortuna, the evil eye? Her calm expression and tender gesture are timeless. It is heartbreaking to think that, in all probability, the owner of this terracotta was about to become caught up in the terrible events that marked the destruction of the cities.

IX
THE DEATH OF
THE CITIES

THE DEATH OF THE CITIES

IN AD 79 Mount Vesuvius broke its centuries-long silence with devastating results for the cities and their inhabitants. Was this eruption totally unexpected? Did the people of the cities have any idea of the forces that were about to be unleashed, and if so, what had been the events which alerted them to their potential danger?

Roman writers were aware that Vesuvius had once been active.[1] Vitruvius stated there had been 'many conflagrations under Mount Vesuvius…which spewed forth fire over the fields'.[2] The geographer Strabo said the area was '…previously on fire…and was extinguished when the fuel failed…this is also the reason for the fruitfulness of the surrounding area. Just as at Catana [Catania in Sicily], the part covered up by the ash from Mt Etna made the country suited to vine growing'.[3] The historian Diodorus of Sicily wrote, 'Vesuvius formerly poured forth monstrous fire like Etna in Sicily…in previous times'.[4] The implication was that Vesuvius, in contrast to Etna, was no longer active.

Archaeology has confirmed there were several violent eruptions in the period before written records.[5] One of the most violent was the 'Avellino' eruption in about 1600 BC, which buried many settlements such as that at Poggiomarino, to the east of Vesuvius.[6] Subsequently there were smaller eruptions, and there was clearly volcanic activity in the area, as seen by the major eruption of the volcano on Ischia in about 680 BC, which devastated settlements such as Pithecoussae, the Greek trading port on the island.[7] After this there is no evidence for major eruptions until AD 79.

Could the Romans have known what was about to happen? In the decades before the eruption of AD 79 there were warning signs, which the inhabitants of the cities certainly noticed, but were unable to interpret. One of these was 'bradyseism', the interlinked rising and falling of the land mass and sea levels caused by activity in the magma (lava) chamber of Vesuvius.[8] In Herculaneum, buildings near the sea show clear evidence of damage, repair and sea erosion caused by bradyseism between about 100 BC and the AD 50s.[9] The lower parts of the walls of the Suburban Baths show clear signs of wave erosion and the lower portion of the windows were blocked to prevent ingress of sea water and spray. The 'tower' of the House of the Telephus Relief lost a storey to rising seawater as its lower arches were bricked in. At the time of the eruption the land was rising again and the sea retreating. If the Romans had been able to interpret these signs they would have understood that the magma chamber was filling, dangerously. But they could not. Vesuvius, as far as they could see, was at peace.

The first sign of real danger, as far as the Romans were concerned, came in the form of a massive earthquake on 5 February AD 62 or AD 63 (the two principal Roman sources disagree over the year). Romans date events either *Ab Urbe Condita* ('from the city's foundation'), that is counting back from the legendary founding of Rome in 753 BC, or by the names of the annually appointed Consuls, the highest Roman state officials. The historian Tacitus, writing thirty years after the earthquake, mentions the Consuls of AD 62, whereas the statesman and philosopher Seneca, a contemporary of the event, cites those of AD 63.

Seneca dedicated Chapter 6 of his book on natural phenomena[10] to earthquakes, and it is to Seneca we owe our picture of the destruction caused in AD 62/3: 'Pompeii that famous town of Campania has subsided...great devastation in Campania...part of the town of Herculaneum, too, fell down...Naples too lost many private buildings...' A marble relief from Pompeii (FIG. 357) shows the Temple of Jupiter in the Forum swaying wildly, perhaps recalling the earthquake.

Clearly the quake made many people fear for their safety and some undoubtedly left the area. Seneca criticizes those (who had the freedom and wealth to do so) '...who have renounced Campania, who have emigrated...and say that they will never go there

again...'.[11] He adds that 'the earthquake lasted several days...Campania shook continuously...there was great damage'.[12]

So what were the lasting effects of the earthquake? Some scholars[13] believe it was sufficiently deadly to have caused a visible drop in people in their mid-teens and mid-twenties at the time of the eruption (that is, those who would have been vulnerable children at at the time of the earthquake). Others think this and later earthquakes should have alerted the Romans to the possible risks of a volcanic eruption.[14] Did the Romans make that link? Seneca, writing at the very time of the AD 62/3 quake, did not. On the contrary, he shared the widely held belief that earthquakes were caused by massive movements of air.[15] If he did not see a link, then there is little reason to believe that the ordinary people of the cities did. If some people fled, it was because of the threat of earthquakes, not because of a perceived threat from Vesuvius.

The AD 62/3 earthquake was not the last. In AD 64 an earthquake rocked Naples, where the Emperor Nero was performing in the main theatre.[16] Tacitus, in his *Annals* (15,34), adds that '...as soon as the spectators left, the theatre collapsed without harming anyone'. Pliny the Younger, in his account of the eruption,[17] specifically states that the initial earthquakes accompanying the AD 79 eruption caused no great concern, '...because it is quite normal for Campania'.[18] From Naples comes an inscription recording repairs made to several public buildings by the Emperor Titus, in which the word earthquake is in the plural: *terrae motibus*.[19] Clearly Pompeii and Herculaneum were at or near the epicentre of at least two major earthquakes, perhaps more,[20] and damage in the cities would have been considerable, but can we find evidence of these earthquakes in the archaeology?

LIFE IN THE CITIES ON THE EVE OF THE ERUPTION

In response to the complex literary and archaeological evidence,[21] opinions are divided on what state the cities were in at the time of the eruption. Did the destruction, of Pompeii at least, start with the big earthquake of AD 62/3?[22] Were the cities (as suggested by Amedeo Maiuri, the legendary director of the sites for much of the mid-twentieth century) in crisis, decaying, abandoned by the rich,[23] racked by unrest and chaos, spilling over from the general instability following the assassination of the Emperor Nero in AD 68 and the civil wars of AD 69? What can the evidence tell us of civic and domestic life?

Looking first at civic life, the archaeology bears out Seneca's description of the damage caused in AD 62/3, and by subsequent earthquakes. There had clearly been considerable damage to public and private buildings.[24] But looking at public buildings and amenities it is also clear that a huge amount of rebuilding was under way or completed by AD 79.

Many buildings in the Forum of Pompeii, including the market (*macellum*) and the immense 'building of Eumachia', were complete and newly decorated[25] and there were clearly well-advanced programmes of rebuilding and repair in many others.[26] Paintings in the House of Julia Felix (P), believed to post-date the earthquake, show a thriving Forum with colonnades, statues and bustling civic life. In Herculaneum the so-called Augusteum, very possibly serving as a Forum for the city, was crammed with statuary, including newly erected images of the Emperor Titus and his family. His father, the Emperor Vespasian, had shown his concern through rebuilding projects after he came to the throne in AD 70, and the people of the cities showed their loyalty and gratitude in return.[27] In the nearby Basilica Noniana, dedications and marble citizen lists had been mounted on the walls and updated.

Temples were an essential part of the urban fabric and several had been restored. An inscription from Herculaneum[28] tells how in AD 75 the Emperor Vespasian restored the Temple of Magna Mater, the great mother goddess Cybele, which had collapsed in the earthquake: *terrae motu conlapsum*.[29] The Temple of Venus in the sacred precinct near the beach had also been restored, by a freedwoman called Vibidia Saturnina and her son.[30]

In Pompeii, an inscription found over the entrance to the Temple of Isis (FIG. 358)[31] says that it had collapsed in the earthquake, presumably that of AD 62/3, but had been completely rebuilt in the name of Numerius Popidius Celsinus, the six-year-old son of Numerius Popidius Ampliatus (see above p. 27).

Repairs were also taking place in many establishments that needed large supplies of water, and it seems likely that the aqueduct, which had been damaged during the earthquake, was about to be pressed into service again. Two of the great baths of Pompeii (the Suburban Baths and Stabian Baths) were nearly repaired and were being redecorated, while the baths near the Forum were open and being used. In Herculaneum, although the Suburban Baths were out of service with piles of building materials, such as flue tiles, heaped in the rooms,[32] the Central Baths seem to have been functioning. Dug-up pavements in both cities at the time of the eruption suggest repairs were being carried out on domestic supplies, too.

Clearly the city councils were functioning and there was still a solid citizen body to carry out public works. This civic organization would not have been necessary if urban life had declined to a low level – and public munificence in the Roman world was only worthwhile if there were peers and a public to be impressed by it. In the AD 70s the Emperor Vespasian sent a commissioner, Titus Suedius Clemens, to Pompeii to correct various abuses, including illegal occupation of land that had taken place during extensive and hurried rebuilding after the earthquake(s).[33] This intervention in Pompeii's political and social affairs shows a city in a period of change and needing regulation, but not necessarily a city in decline. And as for local politics, the electoral system, a particularly important area of Pompeian urban life, was clearly still in full swing, with the vast majority of the painted electoral 'posters' on the walls dating to the post-earthquake period.

The major earthquake of AD 62/3 and those that followed had, of course, caused serious damage to the cities. Some people left the area,[34] and there may have been a smaller population than there had been twenty years earlier.[35] Some of the urban fabric went unrepaired or was inferior to what had gone before. There was some breaking up of older, larger houses and some increase in the number of retail outlets. However, this in itself is hardly a sign of terminal decline, but rather a sign of change and, it could be argued, vitality.

Private and public buildings were being restored, and huge amounts of money were being spent by the city fathers and the emperor himself to ensure that important elements of city life – baths, temples and civic buildings – were usable once more. There were still enough people in the cities to warrant these changes, and they needed shops and apartments. Large areas of the cities may have been building sites, but this hardly made them ghost towns. It was not in the interests of the citizens, the city councillors, the tradesmen, nor of the emperor himself to let cities fail, and there is clear evidence that all levels of society were trying to pull things together. In these battered but recovering cities, people lived their lives as normally as they could until the catastrophic events of AD 79.

EVIDENCE FROM HOMES

Some have seen evidence of decline in the fact that fine, large houses were broken up into smaller units and apartments and, above all, in the invasion of small shopkeepers in the high streets, 'impinging' on noble houses.

However, it has also been argued that this was normal – and that the shops, far from suddenly encroaching on houses after AD 63, had always been there. In fact, there seems little evidence for a rash of 'new' shops after AD 63. Shops and other street-front businesses had always been perfectly acceptable ways to make money (see above pp. 51–2). The owner of a wealthy house may not have run such a business himself, but he may well have owned it and there was no stigma at all in having such premises as part of his urban property. On the contrary, it may have been a badge of pride – a display of the vitality of the household. If this were true in Rome, the capital of the empire, it was likely to be true for Pompeii and Herculaneum.[36] As for apartments being carved out of the large houses, this too was a long-established phenomenon. If anything, the rise in apartments (if there was one), and the thriving rental market suggested by advertisements for the properties of Julia Felix and Nigidius Maius (above pp. 31–2), might support the idea of growth, not decay, in the cities.[37]

The house interiors themselves offer interesting information. There are two main types of evidence for their condition prior to AD 79: their structure and decoration, and the artefacts they contained when excavated. One of the main criteria used to reconstruct the chronology of the latest period in the life of the cities is the use of the Fourth Style of wall painting (see pp. 210–12).[38] Appearing in the AD 50s, this style is most famous for its use in the palace, or 'Golden House', of Emperor Nero in Rome, dating from AD 64–8. This style is also the most popular and widespread in the cities,[39] appearing in many types of houses and commercial establishments.[40] Yet this style covers precisely the period, from

Fig. 358 Marble inscription commemorating the restoration of the Temple of Isis.

Temple of Isis, Pompeii
H. 49.5 cm, L. 2.35 cm
MANN 3765/CIL X 846

Fig. 359 Detail of unfinished fresco.

House of the Painters at Work, Pompeii

the 50s/60s onwards, that is supposed to have been most depressed. It would be impossible to telescope all the examples of the style found in the cities into a decade or so preceding AD 63 – yet this would necessarily be the case if the life of the cities had gone into suspended animation after AD 62/3.

Instead, many and varied Fourth Style schemes were commissioned and executed across the cities. Specialists have identified the work of separate workshops in Pompeii,[41] and very possibly a completely different group in Herculaneum with different colour schemes.[42] What is more, there was time and need for them to be replaced and repaired, overlaid and even partially destroyed by changing room use, by the erection of shelving, insertion of niches and so on.[43] In the House of the Painters at Work (P) there are rooms where the decorators were working right up to the moment of the eruption (FIG. 359).

In some cases we can hazard an approximate date for such changes and redecoration. In the House of the Old Hunt at Pompeii, a newly plastered section of the atrium was marked by the decorator (or perhaps a mischievous child) with impressions of a coin of Vespasian dating to AD 71,[44] so the redecoration took place no earlier than that year. Therefore, by no means all damage happened as a result of the 'big' quake of 62/3. Rather we must think of a series of quakes causing greater or lesser damage, with a subsequent wave of rebuilding, plastering and painting.

Apart from the decorative state of the rooms, there are other clues. The private supply of piped water, which had revolutionized the homes, or rather the gardens, of the wealthier citizens in the early first century AD, was severely disrupted. In the garden of the House of the Greek Epigrams (P) a sophisticated water distribution system and the garden's central fountain, having been repaired after a major event (perhaps the quake of 62/3), were abandoned and filled in after later disturbances.[45] Some gardens, even of the finer houses, were turned over to industrial use, as in the House of Marcus Fabius Rufus (P). Downgrading (or, more rarely, upgrading) of areas within a house might indicate a change of use or owner or both.[46] Sometimes the evidence of rebuilding is still there, such as the great lumps of gypsum, used for making plaster, in the garden of the House of the Lararium of Achilles (P) or the heap of plaster dust in the corner of the atrium of the House of Caius Julius Polybius (P), or the building materials, such as amphora fragments and sand (used to make *cocciopesto* flooring), in the House of the Painters at Work (P).[47]

There are several examples of houses in which objects such as sculptures and garden furniture, usually damaged or incomplete, have been discovered in rooms far from their original positions – perhaps having been moved while works were carried out.[48] These include the statue of Priapus in the House of the Vettii and the statue of Livia in the Villa of the Mysteries. Time and again, archaeologists find large numbers of artefacts that relate to daily life. These everyday items, more than any other features, tell us that life was going on. To give just one example, in kitchens throughout the cities people had frying pans, cooking pots and pickling jars, suggesting that the kitchens were functioning – a good sign that houses were inhabited in AD 79.[49] Very importantly, in that ultimate expression of vibrant urbanism, the excavations of the Cardo V drain in Herculaneum (pp. 265–9) show that the people in that city, at least, were generating masses of rubbish.

THE DATE OF THE ERUPTION

When exactly in AD 79 did Vesuvius erupt? When did the cities die? The two ancient writers who reported the events in any detail were Pliny the Younger, writing in about AD 100, and Cassius Dio, writing in about AD 200.

Pliny the Younger wrote two letters[50] in which he narrated the events as seen from his mother's house at the top of the Bay of Naples at Cape Misenum. His date for the eruption, as recorded in the oldest surviving manuscript, is *Nonum Kal. Septembres*, that is 24 August, but since the seventeenth century there have been arguments for pushing the date later, by between one and three months.[51]

There are numerous other texts giving no fewer than eleven different versions of the Roman date, ranging from 24 August to 24 October and early November.[52] Cassius Dio, writing in Greek, describes the period the eruption happened as *kat'auto to Phthinoporon*, 'in advanced autumn'[53] (for the Romans, autumn began in mid-August).

So the ancient writers do not agree – what can the archaeological evidence tell us? Sadly, the huge number of painted notices and advertisements still on the walls at Pompeii cannot really sharpen our knowledge of the date of the eruption. Although recent research has created a chronology of the years of election posters, the last office-holders, too, were in post by June, too early for any of our possible dates. 'Posters' for gladiator and other contests usually give an exact date, but do not usually carry the year, and some are clearly old, mentioning Nero as Emperor. Similarly, coins are unlikely to be able to pinpoint the time of year. There have been discoveries of coin types in Pompeii (albeit in very small quantities) that must post-date July AD 79, but again, this cannot indicate a particular month beyond that date. Recent research[54] seems to argue extremely convincingly that the coin of Titus from the House of the Golden Bracelet contains no imperial titles that need to be later than 24 August AD 79. This does not, of course, rule out the possibility they were buried in October.

Other evidence raises questions. The clothing worn by the people in the casts from Pompeii is interesting. Much of it is heavier than would be expected in Italy in August. Though this is understandable on people heading out into a volcanic blizzard, it is surprising on bodies found indoors. Equally surprising is the number of portable braziers discovered in the houses.[55] These portable stoves in bronze or iron could certainly have been used for cooking – but many had no pans or other utensils on them, although charcoal and ash still in them showed they had been used not long before the eruption. If they were being used for heating rather than cooking, their presence in August in the Bay of Naples is puzzling.

Moreover, there is evidence at several farms near Pompeii, such as Villa Regina near Boscoreale, for the vintage – the grape harvest.[56] In modern Italy this begins in late September to early October. Pliny the Elder gives similar dates for the harvest,

Fig. 360 Silver denarius of Titus, minted after 1 July AD 79.

House of the Golden Bracelet, Pompeii
MANN P14312/176

Fig. 361 Carbonized pomegranates from Oplontis.

24 September to 11 October.[57] Evidence of grapes and waste products from grape pressing has been found in several places.[58] Empty amphorae ready for filling, even in large quantities as in some houses in the cities or at Oplontis Villa B, are not by themselves an indication of the harvest, since new wine was put first into *dolia defossa* (buried storage jars). At Villa Regina there are many sealed dolia, so assuming they did not contain the previous year's produce, then, here at least, the vintage had taken place.

As well as grapes, other fruits and nuts have been found in the cities which ought to have been harvested later, sometimes considerably later, than August,[59] most notably pomegranates. These are usually harvested in late September, yet huge quantities (almost a ton) were found laid out on straw mats in Villa B at Oplontis and more were strewn over the floor of a room in the Villa of the Mysteries (P). Figs, usually harvested in September, are also common finds. Some were dried but the majority seem to be that year's harvest.[60] In addition, there are walnuts,[61] sweet chestnuts, carobs[62] and, very importantly, olives, all of which would normally be harvested in September/October.

We may never know for certain when the eruption happened, but it seems that the traditional date of 24 August cannot be viewed as definitive and that a later date – perhaps 24 October – is a distinct possibility.

AN EYEWITNESS ACCOUNT FROM A ROMAN WRITER

For the eruption of Vesuvius in AD 79, we possess an eyewitness account. A young man named Pliny (the Younger), later a famous writer, was staying in his family home near Cape Misenum at the north of the Bay of Naples, about 30 km (19 miles) to the west of Vesuvius. With him were his mother and her brother, also called Pliny (the Elder), author of an extensive encyclopaedia and Admiral of the fleet of the Bay of Naples.

They were all caught up, Pliny the Elder fatally so, in the events surrounding the eruption. In two letters, written thirty years later to his friend, the historian Tacitus, Pliny the Younger tells what happened and how it affected the area and his family. The two letters are reproduced in full in many other sources. In the following section we can see a précis of the major events, first as noted by Pliny, then as indicated by the archaeological evidence, in order to piece together the stages of the eruption, and their effects on the different sites.

THE BEGINNING OF THE ERUPTION

In his first letter,[63] Pliny the Younger tells Tacitus about how his uncle Pliny the Elder died and about the eruption that killed him. In the oldest surviving manuscript Pliny gives the traditional date 'on the 24th August'; his uncle had been bathing and sleeping when, at about the seventh hour (one in the afternoon) his mother pointed out a large, unusually-shaped cloud,[64] later confirmed as coming from Vesuvius. The cloud looked like an umbrella pine tree,[65] soaring up on a long trunk, then splitting off into different branches. He supposed the cloud had been thrown upwards by the rush of air and then, overcome by its own weight, had started to drift sideways and dissipate. It was sometimes white and sometimes black where he thought it had picked up earth and ash.

Pliny's uncle, Pliny the Elder, out of curiosity and a desire to rescue people, took his fleet to the cities along the densely populated bay. He made straight for the danger zone. Ash fell on the ships, hotter and denser as they got closer, then pumice and larger stones. Pumice (aerated magma) floats and so the whole shore and even the open sea were blocked with debris.

Pliny the Elder considered turning back but, after uttering the now famous phrase, 'Fortune favours the brave' (*Fortes Fortuna iuvat*)[66] he pressed on and moored at Stabiae, some 4 km (1¾ miles) down the coast from Pompeii, where his friend Pomponianus had a villa. He bathed, dined and then tried to reassure his friend. All that evening and night, sheets of fire and towering flames burned over Mt Vesuvius. Pliny the Elder tried again to calm his friends then tried to get some sleep. But the eruption carried on. The garden overlooked by his room filled with ash and pumice. If he had stayed any longer escape would have been impossible, so he went and joined the others. They had to decide whether to stay inside, among the violently shaking buildings, or go outside and face the rain of pumice. They went out, tying cushions on their heads with cloths to protect themselves from the hot pumice and ash.

By then it should have been dawn, but at Stabiae, as elsewhere on the bay, it was still dark, deep night. They tried escaping by sea but it was far too rough. Pliny lay down on a blanket and was drinking some water, when flames and sulphurous gases scattered the group. He stood up, supported by two servants, but collapsed, suffocated by the thick smoke. Later his body was found untouched, looking as though he were resting rather than dead.

Pliny the Younger's assumption that his uncle died because of the volcanic gases aggravating his respiratory system, known to be very weak, has led many to suggest that this was the fate of all those, particularly in Pompeii, who died at dawn on the second day. But there are other, perhaps more plausible, causes.

THE SECOND DAY

In Pliny the Younger's second letter,[67] he told of the events of the second day and what happened to him and his mother at Cape Misenum. After his uncle's departure Pliny had read, bathed, dined and gone to bed, but had slept badly because of the constant earth tremors. They had been happening for several days, which was not unusual for Campania, but that night they were so bad that everything seemed to be about to collapse.

In the early morning Pliny the Younger and his mother sat on a terrace overlooking the sea, watching the eruption. Pliny even read a book by Livy, the Roman historian who wrote in the first century BC, not budging when a friend of his uncle's shouted at them to leave. It was dawn but the light was dull and faint and violent tremors continued. Finally they and many other people decided to leave the town of Misenum. Only after they had left the buildings did they look back; they saw extraordinary and terrifying things. Carts moved crazily in all directions, even

though wedged with stones. The sea receded and the shore was left dry and littered with sea creatures.

Worst of all, a terrifying black cloud torn by jagged flames, larger than lightning, began to spread across the land. The great black cloud sank to earth, covering the sea and blotting out the Isle of Capri and even nearby Cape Misenum. Then the cloud, ever darker and more dense, began to advance towards them, and when Pliny looked over his shoulder he saw it was gaining on them. They came off the crowded road and had just taken shelter when the cloud reached them. It became as dark as night, he says: 'Not the darkness of a cloudy night or a night when there is no moon, but darkness as if the light has gone out in a room that is locked and sealed.'[68] In an emotional description Pliny conveys the terror and panic of the people around them. He describes women howling, children screaming and men shouting, with people crying out to their parents, their children or their partners, trying to find them in the darkness by their voices. Some people bewailed their own fate or that of their loved ones, and others just prayed for death. He tells how, as in every crisis, some prayed to their gods, but most thought the gods had abandoned them and that the world was being plunged into final and eternal night.

At last they saw light again – only to realize that it was in fact more fiery clouds. Darkness and falls of ash returned, the ash so clinging and heavy that people had to brush it off to avoid being covered and crushed. When the gloom lifted, and a pallid half-light finally returned, they saw to their horror that everything had changed. As far as the eye could see, everything was blanketed under a thick layer of ash.

People were still afraid and the earth still shook, but the eruption was over. Pliny the Younger and his mother were safe, but his uncle and thousands more were dead. The cities whose inhabitants he had set out to help, Herculaneum and Pompeii, the smaller settlements of Oplontis and Stabiae and countless farms and villages, were all gone.

FRIGHT AND FLIGHT

People in the cities met death in different ways and at different times, but they shared the basic instinct to take with them as they fled things that they believed were useful or that were simply dear to them. Carefully gathered together or grabbed quickly, these objects represent the choices made in those uncertain hours. Practical objects included lamps and lanterns (FIG. 362) – essential during any evening but also, in these exceptional circumstances, during the day. If the light was poor at Misenum, then the darkness in Herculaneum, and particularly Pompeii, overshadowed by the spreading volcanic cloud, must have been near-total. The lanterns they carried were fuelled by olive oil stored in the cylindrical reservoir at the base, and originally had shades made of thin sheets of animal horn. Some took the keys to their homes (FIG. 363) – eternal symbols of a hoped-for return – while others took objects to which they were attached sentimentally or which they hoped would bring them good fortune, such as the charm bracelet carried by one little girl in Herculaneum (below p. 291) or the amulets and 'lucky' jewellery carried by a girl who died outside the Porta Nola, Pompeii (below p. 300).

Many – understandably – took jewellery or coins, in varying quantities,

LEFT **Fig. 362 Bronze lantern, originally fitted with thin sheets of translucent horn.**

From Vesuvian area
H. 22.5 cm
The British Museum, 1856,1226.670

BELOW **Fig. 363 Bronze key.**

From Herculaneum, ancient shoreline, vault VII
L. 6 cm
SAP 78984

LEFT **Fig. 364 Wooden money box with silver inlaid decoration.**

From Terrace of M. Nonius Balbus, Herculaneum, next to skeleton no. 42
L. 13 cm, W. 6.5 cm
MANN 78574

BELOW **Fig. 365 Fused mass of coins, once contained in a wicker basket.**

From Herculaneum, ancient shoreline, vault 11
H. 10.5 cm, W. 23.5 cm
SAP 78675

as a safeguard against difficult times ahead. Someone on the beach at Herculaneum brought a wicker basket (FIG. 364) two-thirds full of bronze coins and a handful of silver *denarii*, perhaps a morning's takings from one of the city's shops or bars. Another person had a small wooden money box (FIG. 365), decorated with fine silver inlay, for just a few coins – a child's precious savings? A small wooden box from Torre Annunziata contained bronze coins, a small chain and other small items, and although the box has now largely decayed, the contents remain, fused into the shape of their container.

Coins and jewellery were not the only forms of wealth. One person on the beach at Herculaneum carried a small collection of silverware: two *paterae* (handled bowls), a jug and a ladle were stacked one inside the other. Compared to the great treasure of Boscoreale and the House of the Menander this little group does not seem to indicate a very wealthy person, but the vessels were found with valuable jewellery including gold rings, armlets and a massive gold chain necklace. These items symbolized their owner's hope of getting through this terrible night.

THE PHASES OF THE ERUPTION – THE ARCHAEOLOGICAL EVIDENCE

Analysis of deposits of pumice, ash, lapilli (small stones) and other volcanic material from numerous sites around the volcano have allowed archaeologists and vulcanologists to piece together the events of the eruption and compare these with Pliny the Younger's account. It is important to remember, though, that we cannot be absolutely sure of an exact hour-by-hour timetable of events.[69]

Pliny's mother saw the cloud at about one in the afternoon, but the eruption began some hours before. Several short, sharp explosions shook the mountain, the result of groundwater mixing with the magma chamber as the plug that had capped Vesuvius for so long disintegrated. A small volcanic cloud was created, dropping a minor quantity of ash and debris on sites to the east of Vesuvius. The cloud, as observed by Pliny the Younger and his family, was enormous – and had already grown to around 15 km (nearly 9 miles) high. As the cloud rose, the southerly winds began to spread it southwards.[70] To the north, the people of Herculaneum endured almost total darkness, violent tremors, noxious gases and unearthly noises coming from the mountain. To the south-east, Pompeii, Oplontis and Stabiae, which lay in the direction of the prevailing wind, endured the same terrible phenomena, with the addition of the rain of ash, lapilli and pumice and other debris dropped by the cloud. Whitish pumice fell relentlessly, accumulating by about 15 cm (6 in.) every hour, and continued to build during the afternoon. It fell not only on the streets, houses and open spaces of Pompeii and other towns, but also on the surrounding countryside. Fields, orchards, villas, small farms, huge estates, and even the sea and rivers were being slowly but surely covered and choked.[71]

By late afternoon, there was about 50 cm (20 in.) of pumice blanketing Pompeii and Oplontis, causing severe problems for the buildings and their inhabitants. Roofs and balconies came under increasing strain under the weight of the pumice and began to collapse, bringing structures down with them, creating even more panic among the terrified inhabitants. In addition to ash, lapilli and pumice, bigger pieces of debris, called lithics, between 15 and 30 cm (6 in. and 1 ft) across, hurtled to earth at 50 metres per second (about 112 mph) and caused damage, injury and even death. But pumice was the main threat. As the pumice built up, buildings became difficult to enter and, more worryingly (as Pliny the Elder discovered), to leave.

It was floating banks of pumice that caused such problems for Pliny the Elder as he tried to put in by ship, probably somewhere near Oplontis and Pompeii. By mid-to late afternoon, when he finally managed to make the harbour at Stabiae. The volcanic cloud was 20–25 km (12–16 miles) high and massive quantities of pumice were being deposited to the south. At about eight in the evening there was a change in the eruption. The white pumice was now some 140 cm (4½ ft) deep, but changes in the magma chamber below the volcano unleashed a hurricane of pumice that was grey and much denser and heavier.

This denser material was the last straw for many buildings in Pompeii and Oplontis, causing widespread collapses. In the House of the Chaste Lovers (P) ceilings collapsed but could not fall onto the floors of the rooms below because of the depth of pumice underneath. Furthermore, the heaviness of this new pumice had another major effect – it destabilized the great volcanic cloud and provoked the first appearance of the deadly pyroclastic surge, a fast-moving avalanche of superheated gas, ash and pumice. The first surge struck sites to the east of the volcano, such as the villa at Terzigno, though some believe (at this point) Herculaneum, too, was destroyed.[72] In effect, a series of these surges caused the destruction of the cities. What exactly were they and what caused them?

Eruptions of Vesuvius have taken two main forms: effusive and explosive.[73] The first occurs if the volcano erupts when there is no major plug of debris to block the magma chamber, and so much less of a build-up of energy. Lava flows, destructive but rarely deadly, are quite common in this type of eruption. The second, much more destructive and dangerous, is the 'Plinian' type of eruption of AD 79, named after Pliny the Younger's account. This type of eruption usually happens after a long period of inactivity, when the swollen magma chamber is blocked by a plug of solidified volcanic debris. It rarely produces lava, but instead the volcanic matter is rapidly pushed up as a cloud. Whatever buried Pompeii and Herculaneum, Oplontis and Stabiae, it was not lava. Plinian eruptions are characterized by explosive violence, by the enormous size of the volcanic cloud, and by the immense quantity of volcanic debris generated, along with the pyroclastic surges and flows which deposit this material on the ground.

The cloud rises ever higher, driven first by the sheer energy of the magma chamber and the low density of the initial material, and then by convection in the atmosphere, which adds 'pull' to the magma chamber's 'push'. When the eruption has been happening for some time the volcanic cloud reaches its greatest, densest extent, while the fuel remaining in the magma chamber decreases. When the energy supporting the cloud is outstripped by the cloud's enormous mass, the cloud falls down to earth, forming a pyroclastic surge: an avalanche of superheated gas and steam, with pulverized rock and ash. It was these surges that were responsible for the majority of the structural damage to the cities. The surges accompanying the eruption of AD 79 travelled at speeds of about 112 km/hour (70 mph) at a temperature between 250 and 400°C. Following the surge, only moments later, came the pyroclastic flow, less fast than the surge but denser and even hotter. When the magma chamber suddenly fired up again it was possible for the volcanic cloud to rise again, only to crash down in further surges. It is estimated that the eruption generated six of these surges, all of which brought destruction to different places at different times.

At some time around midnight it is estimated the cloud would have reached its maximum height of around 30 km (19 miles), with the magma chamber pouring out an estimated 200 tons of material every second.[74] But this cloud began to become unstable and, according to most experts, at about one o'clock in the morning of the second day it collapsed spectacularly. A massive pyroclastic surge cascaded down the western slopes of Vesuvius and headed straight for Herculaneum.

THE DESTRUCTION OF HERCULANEUM

In Herculaneum the first phases of the eruption – minor explosions, violent earthquakes and the rising up of the enormous 'umbrella pine'-shaped cloud – provoked disbelief, horror, and incomprehension at the sheer scale of what was happening, and the realization of its terrifying proximity. Herculaneum was only 7 km (4½ miles) away from the volcano – half the distance of Pompeii – and so everything was closer and more threatening.

Herculaneum was to the north-west of the volcano, so the pumice that fell on Pompeii from the first moments of the eruption, and the subsequent blocked roads and collapsing roofs, did not affect Herculaneum. Archaeological excavations in Herculaneum have revealed virtually no trace of pumice or other debris from the early phase of the eruption.[75] But if people in Herculaneum hoped the ordeal would finish quickly, then by mid-afternoon, when the violent tremors and roars of the volcano continued and even intensified, they realized it would not. Even without the build-up of heavy lapilli (pebble-sized pieces of solidified magma) as happened in Pompeii, structures in Herculaneum were collapsing because of the strength of the tremors. Some people undoubtedly made their escape by land, inevitably passing the volcano. Others stayed in their homes – though at Herculaneum fewer than thirty bodies have been found inside houses.

A sizable proportion of the population decided that the obvious route of escape was the sea, but there was no frantic, last-minute dash to the shore. The remains of the people who died on the beach show a wide variety of ages. They included many people

Fig. 366 Casts of skeletons discovered in the vaults on the beach of Herculaneum.

– the very young, the very old and the infirm – who could not have made the long and steep descent to the beach quickly or without help.[76]

Once on the beach, they waited for rescue from the sea. Herculaneum was a seaside city and vessels of all types, from small merchant boats to fishing smacks, put in at the small jetty on the beach and the port (as yet unlocated, but almost certainly south of the Suburban Baths). An idea of the boats serving the city is given by the carbonized remains of a boat discovered overturned in front of the Suburban Baths.[77] It was about 9 m (29½ ft) long and 2.25 m (7½ ft) at maximum width, was powered by three pairs of oars, and would have been similar in scale to a modern fishing vessel.[78] Remains of another, smaller boat and parts of several others just along the shore indicate activity connected with the sea. Some people may have escaped in boats like these in the early afternoon,[79] when the seas were still navigable. But, as Pliny's experience (above p. 280) shows, between swells and banks of lapilli, the seas will not have been navigable for long.

Others were either unable to get onto the boats or made a positive decision to stay. Many inhabitants of Herculaneum – over three hundred – were gathered on and around the beach. Some waited on the beach itself, while many took shelter inside the twelve so-called 'shipsheds', barrel-vaulted rooms forming the substructure of the terrace above the beach. The people gathered here had no idea of what was happening, nor when it would stop, and they certainly had no way of imagining what was coming.

At about one o'clock in the morning of the second day (some say earlier, see above p. 283), a pyroclastic surge, travelling at around 30 metres per second (about 68 mph) poured down the slopes of Vesuvius. When it struck the city it was not so destructive to structures as later surges would be, but its temperature was probably around 400–450°C.[80] This extreme heat had a dramatic effect on many of the artefacts and structures of the city. Organic items (that is, anything made of once-living, carbon-based materials, such as wood, leather and even foodstuffs) should have ignited and burnt to ash at this temperature, but instead they were immediately encased in ash, preventing further ignition. They were superheated and carbonized, reduced to carbon with all moisture and fat removed. Wood was carbonized in many areas of the city as the pyroclastic cloud enveloped public buildings, shops and homes, preserving doors, windows, staircases and even furniture.

Down at the seafront everyone heard the deafening roar but only those out on the beach would have seen the burning avalanche of gas and debris – and then only for a few moments. Those out on the beach seem to have been slammed to the ground by the surge, which instantly ignited their clothing and burnt their bodies, in some cases to the bone. Bones were broken through impact and blackened by extreme heat, which in some cases was so intense that the skull split open under the pressure of the brain expanding and boiling inside.[81] The effects on exposed bodies is shown by some skeletons with severe burning and cracking of bones on parts exposed but not on parts of the body that were in some way sheltered.[82]

Those who had taken refuge in the vaults did not die in quite the same way. The vaults provided a degree of protection, and skeletons inside the vaults show less intense blackening and damage. Nonetheless, temperatures were well over 300°C and death was instantaneous – if not from the direct blast, then through thermal shock. The limbs of many victims are contracted through extreme heat[83] and it is extremely unlikely that anyone would have survived long enough even to take a breath. The flow that followed moments later, denser and hotter than the surge, poured onto the beach and into the 'shipsheds', followed at about 2 am by the second surge and flow. The quantity of rubble and debris in the deposit of the second flow, ranging from wood, bricks and tiles to large chunks of masonry, shows that it was immensely destructive to the fabric of the city. Further surges and flows continued through the second morning until Herculaneum was buried by about 23 m (75 ft) of volcanic debris.[84] So much material had been expelled from Vesuvius – as much as 4 cubic kilometres (over 140 billion cubic ft)[85] – that at Herculaneum the sea shore was pushed out by almost 400 m (over 1,300 ft).

THE BODIES OF HERCULANEUM

Until the 1980s no-one knew about the tragedy on the beach. It was assumed there had been a proportionately lower mortality rate in Herculaneum than in Pompeii, where it has been possible to account for the remains of more than 1,150 victims, often poorly documented when discovered.[86] From 1982, excavations below the Suburban Baths in Herculaneum began to uncover the people on the beach.[87] In all, around 300 skeletons were uncovered, most huddled in the vaults. As the archaeologists uncovered these skeletons it became clear that a whole cross-section of the society of Herculaneum was present, with all their varied stories.

It is unusual for archaeologists to have the opportunity to examine a 'living' population rather than bodies from a cemetery.[88] Furthermore, the normal method of burial in this period was cremation, making the preservation of these bones even more special. This provides the rare chance to try to break down the population by age and sex (though both of these analyses are fraught with potential difficulties) and gain a fuller picture of the people of Herculaneum. Analysis in particular of the skull, teeth and pelvic area can be very valuable in asserting age and sex. We must be careful not to try to extract more information than is possible from these skeletons, or impose on them too much of our own imagination and ideas.[89] The very act of giving the bodies nicknames, such as 'the soldier', necessarily creates a character for the body that it possibly did not have. Nonetheless, with caution, these bodies can tell us a lot about the ordinary, and not-so-ordinary, people who were on the beach that night.

THE SOLDIER (HERCULANEUM SKELETON 26)

On 7 August 1982, in front of Vault 8, a man's body was discovered which stood out for his robust build and stature (about 175 cm or 5 ft 9 in. tall) and for the artefacts that he was carrying and wearing, which identified him in the mind of Sara Bisel, the first scholar to examine the bones, as a soldier.[90] Excavation photographs show the

ABOVE **Fig. 367 Skeleton of the 'soldier' on the ancient shore of Herculaneum.**

Fig. 368 Gold coin and a group of fused coins found with the skeleton of the 'soldier'.

Herculaneum, ancient shoreline, before vault VIII, skeleton no. 26
SAP 78393–4

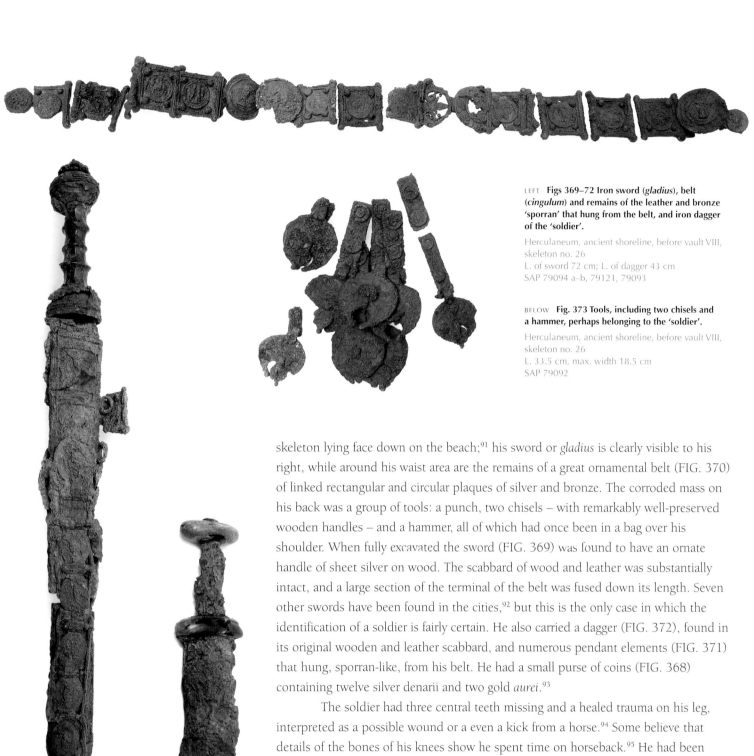

LEFT **Figs 369–72 Iron sword (*gladius*), belt (*cingulum*) and remains of the leather and bronze 'sporran' that hung from the belt, and iron dagger of the 'soldier'.**

Herculaneum, ancient shoreline, before vault VIII, skeleton no. 26
L. of sword 72 cm; L. of dagger 43 cm
SAP 79094 a–b, 79121, 79093

BELOW **Fig. 373 Tools, including two chisels and a hammer, perhaps belonging to the 'soldier'.**

Herculaneum, ancient shoreline, before vault VIII, skeleton no. 26
L. 33.5 cm, max. width 18.5 cm
SAP 79092

skeleton lying face down on the beach;[91] his sword or *gladius* is clearly visible to his right, while around his waist area are the remains of a great ornamental belt (FIG. 370) of linked rectangular and circular plaques of silver and bronze. The corroded mass on his back was a group of tools: a punch, two chisels – with remarkably well-preserved wooden handles – and a hammer, all of which had once been in a bag over his shoulder. When fully excavated the sword (FIG. 369) was found to have an ornate handle of sheet silver on wood. The scabbard of wood and leather was substantially intact, and a large section of the terminal of the belt was fused down its length. Seven other swords have been found in the cities,[92] but this is the only case in which the identification of a soldier is fairly certain. He also carried a dagger (FIG. 372), found in its original wooden and leather scabbard, and numerous pendant elements (FIG. 371) that hung, sporran-like, from his belt. He had a small purse of coins (FIG. 368) containing twelve silver denarii and two gold *aurei*.[93]

The soldier had three central teeth missing and a healed trauma on his leg, interpreted as a possible wound or a even a kick from a horse.[94] Some believe that details of the bones of his knees show he spent time on horseback.[95] He had been hurled down by the surge with such force that many of his bones had multiple fractures, and most of his skeleton was severely blackened,[96] including the surfaces of the fractures. His skull had partly erupted,[97] showing he was exposed to the full force and high temperature of the surge, but his death was instantaneous, as his body tissue vaporized down to the bone in seconds.

LEFT **Fig. 374 Gold ring with plain emerald bezel.**

Herculaneum, ancient shoreline, vault IX, skeleton 65
D. 2.3 cm
SAP 78354

BELOW **Fig. 375 Gold ring with garnet bezel showing a hen with three tiny chicks.**

Herculaneum, ancient shoreline, vault IX, skeleton 65
D. 2 cm
SAP 78355

BELOW **Fig. 376 Gold earrings, originally decorated with pearls.**

Herculaneum, ancient shoreline, vault IX, skeleton 65
W. 1.3 cm
SAP 78356-57

Fig. 377 Gold bracelets with snakehead terminals.

Herculaneum, ancient shoreline, vault IX, skeleton 65
D. 9.3 cm
SAP 078358-9

OPPOSITE **Fig. 378 Skeleton number 65 from Herclaneum, as pictured in *National Geographic Magazine*.**

THE NATIONAL GEOGRAPHIC LADY (HERCULANEUM SKELETON 65)

On 5 April 1983, on the beach outside Vault 9, Skeleton number 65 was found, a woman who was immortalized on the cover of the National Geographic magazine,[98] and who is in some ways iconic in our perceptions of the people on the beach.

Like the soldier, this lady was cut down by the force of the surge. She seems to have been in her mid-to-late forties, about 1.57 m (5 ft 2in.) tall, her beauty, according to Bisel, marred by her dental problems, including a strong overbite.[99] She had a small but beautiful collection of jewellery.[100] She wore two gold rings on her left hand; the one on her index finger (FIG. 375) had a garnet bezel engraved with a hen and three chicks. At her hip was a purse with a few coins and more jewellery, including a pair of earrings (FIG. 376) once decorated with pairs of dangling pearls. Sadly these were the more expensive sea, as opposed to river, pearls, which do not survive well in the conditions at Herculaneum. Also in the bag was a pair of golden 'snake' armlets, with bodies incised to resemble snakeskin and snake-head terminals with eyes of inlaid green glass (FIG. 377).

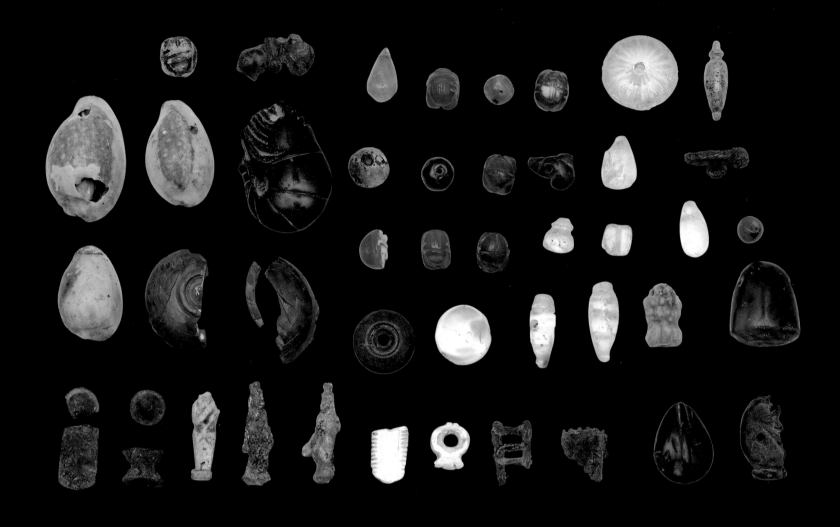
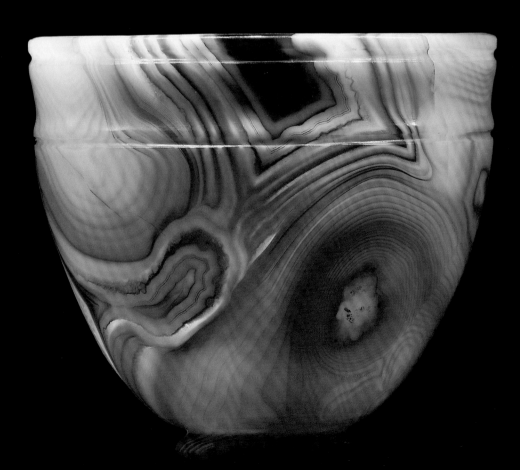

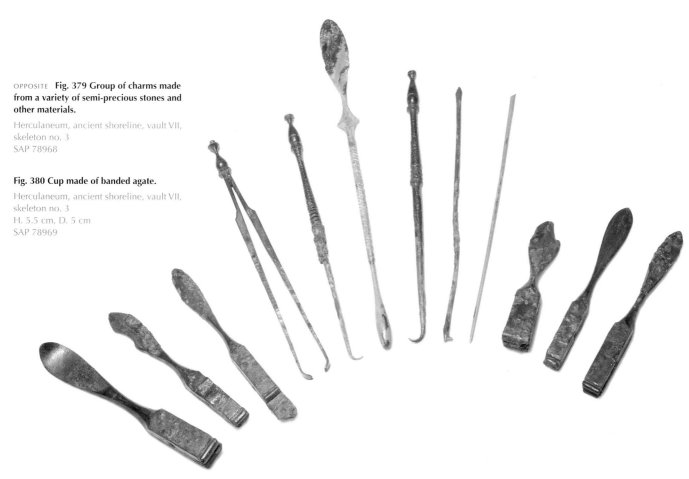

THE CHARM BRACELET GIRL (SKELETON VAULT 7 NO. 3)

In Vault 7, twelve bodies were discovered, the group christened by Sara Bisel, 'the household in flight'.[101] Bisel recognized three adult men, four women and five children. One of the children, identified by Bisel as a young girl, was associated with two items.[102] The first was a small, very fine cup made of a semi-precious banded stone called chalcedony, a rare and valuable object. The second was a charm bracelet, made of over forty charms in different materials from all over the empire and beyond. Alongside lead, glass and bronze was rock crystal, carnelian, amber from the Baltic and faience from Egypt. The bracelet may have been built up over some time and surely had sentimental value.

THE DOCTOR

In Vault 12, thirty-two people were found, of whom nine were children under twelve years old.[103] In one corner of the room, near a group of adults, was a set of medical instruments, comprising heavily corroded iron items and twelve bronze instruments. These included six bronze scalpels (one still retaining part of its iron blade), two hooks, a pair of forceps, a probe, with one extremity flat and leaf-shaped and the other rounded, and a needle. The instruments were found in the remains of the original medical carrying case, which included a space for a small slate tablet used, perhaps, to sharpen instruments or to mix salves and ointments, and bronze tubes for the instruments. Even assuming the case was brought to the beach by its medical owner, we can never know whether this was in order to safeguard the tools of his trade, or in a valiant attempt to help any wounded.

THE DESTRUCTION OF OPLONTIS

Surge 1, which snuffed out the people of Herculaneum, also brought death
to the settlement at Torre Annunziata, in effect almost a suburb of Pompeii some
3 km (2 miles) to the west. This was almost certainly Oplontis, a Roman town
on the Bay of Naples which is named only once, on an ancient scroll-like map
of the Roman Empire known as the *Tabula Peutingeriana*.[104]

Two substantial villa buildings have been investigated. 'Villa A',
first discovered in the eighteenth century and properly excavated between
1964 and 1984, is a palatial residence, with suites of beautifully
decorated rooms, marble sculptures, extensive gardens and an
Olympic-sized swimming pool. It has been suggested it may
have belonged to the family of the Empress Poppaea, second
wife of the Emperor Nero.[105]

Villa B, in contrast, was more functional, more
a farm or rural estate than a palatial residence. Found
during construction work in 1974[106] and not excavated
until the 1980s, the villa has at its centre a great
colonnaded two-storey courtyard, in and around which
was evidence for the villa's agricultural activity. Over
400 upside down wine amphorae were discovered in
the walkways around the courtyard. In one of the rooms
off the courtyard was a huge quantity of pomegranates,
banked up on straw mats, while in other rooms were
marble, lead and iron weights, used for weighing bulk
ingredients, or for distributing finished products. The
processing and bottling (if not the actual production) of
different types of food and drink were taking place in the villa. A
ring seal may even give us the occupant's name – Lucius Crassius Tertius.[107]

In Room 10 of the villa, a vaulted basement area, were discovered the remains
of seventy-four people, divided into two groups by separate moments of discovery,
and also by their social circumstances. The first group came to light in 1981 and was
immediately distinguished by the quantity of jewellery and coins the individuals had
about them. The second group, excavated in 1991, was remarkable for the lack of
possessions. It is tempting to see the two groups as very different elements of society;
those with the valuables were possibly the owners of the villa – or wealthier people who
had taken refuge inside its solid walls. Those without possessions were poorer people
who had taken refuge as well, or the slaves of the wealthier people. All of them, rich or
poor, died together at around one o'clock in the morning when surge 1 tore down the
western slopes of Vesuvius.

Although temperatures in the surge could well have reached 450°C,[108]
conditions in parts of Room 10 lessened the impact of the surge. Whereas some bodies
were burned down to the bone (such as Skeleton 27), others were only part scorched,
allowing casts to be taken (below, Skeleton 10).

ABOVE **Fig. 383 A selection of jewellery found with
a woman including earrings, an armlet, necklaces
and two body chains.**

Oplontis, Villa B, room 10, skeleton no. 27
MANN 73410; 73412a; 73409; 73401; 73412b–c;
73408; 73404; 73403

SKELETON 27

A woman, Skeleton 27, carried one of the greatest assemblages of wealth so far seen in the cities, comprising jewellery and two separate treasures of gold and silver coins (FIG. 379). Around her neck was a large necklace or 'body chain'. By her waist lay a bag that contained three gold finger rings, two pairs of earrings, a single earring, two short necklets, another 'body chain', an armlet and elements of a broken hemisphere armlet.

One ring was ornamented with the heads of *agathadaimones*, serpents of good fortune, holding a plate containing eggs, while another had a bezel incised with the image of a chariot and horses. The earrings in the group were examples of some of the most popular types in the cities, namely a pair of gold bar 'drop pearl' earrings – the *crotalia* or 'castanets' that Pliny the Elder had railed against (above p. 138) – and gold ball earrings of a type found as far afield as Egypt.[109] One single example of a simple wire hoop earring was found, damaged and unwearable.

One of the two necklets was made of simple gold links with a crescent pendant, the other of alternating ovoid gold beads and hexagonal prisms of roughly cut emerald. The two large necklaces were in effect body chains, one with a double chain, the other with a single, figure-of-eight link chain. These constitute rare examples of a type of jewellery very popular in the Hellenistic east but rarely found in Italy. The owner clearly had a degree of sophistication and refinement along with her obvious wealth. She must have been particularly attached to this piece of jewellery, as it is the only piece she was wearing,[110] as opposed to carrying.

One gold armlet was found, formed of a single gold sheet folded over, with a poorly shaped ovoid medallion showing Venus with her son Cupid. The goddess rests on a rudder, identifying her as *Venus Pompeiana*, the divine patron of the city. Her son Cupid dutifully holds up a round mirror so his mother can gaze on her beauty. Fragments of another armlet were found, comprising one golden hemisphere and twenty-two link elements. No other fragments of the armlet were found. The presence of the battered single earring and the scant remains of a 'hemisphere' armlet are interesting, as they suggest that what went into the bag was not her careful choice. Perhaps she had simply grabbed the pieces or tipped them into it, having taken them from a heavier, or more fixed, drawer or chest. This might explain the presence of broken 'odds and ends'.

Together with the jewellery were two large groups of coins. The first, of 15 gold aurei and 175 silver denarii, amounted to the considerable sum of over 2,200 sesterces, and was contained in a small wooden chest. This was dwarfed by second group, once contained in a bag or purse, comprising 37 denarii and a huge fortune of 86 gold aurei. This gave a joint value of almost 11, 000 sesterces, making this – together with the silverware and jewellery – one of the largest portable fortunes discovered in the cities.

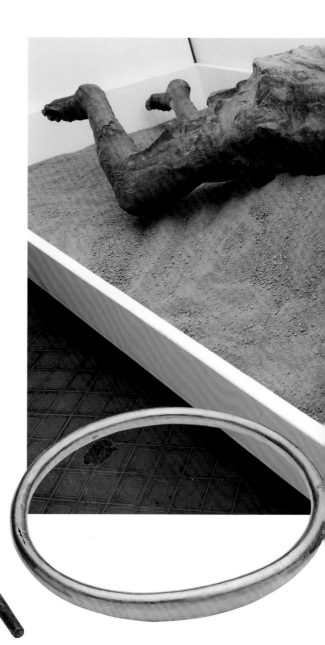

SKELETON 10: THE 'RESIN LADY'

Nearby was another woman, Skeleton 10 (FIG. 384), who was not carrying any expensive jewellery or coins, but instead wore a gold ring, a plain gold armlet (FIG. 386) and a silver hairpin (FIG. 385) decorated with a draped female figure, perhaps Aphrodite/Venus. But it is not the jewellery that Skeleton 10 wore that has made her famous, but rather the way in which she has been preserved and conserved.

For over a century plaster of Paris and other agents have been used to make the casts of the victims. But at Oplontis in 1984 a different technique was pioneered, and Skeleton 10 was selected for the trial. The void around the skeleton was injected with wax, which, when it hardened, was encased in a coating of plaster. This was then filled with liquid epoxy resin which replaced the wax – the 'lost wax' method used for casting bronze in the ancient world.[111] Resin is strong but inert and interacts far less than plaster with the bones inside. The resulting cast was more resistant to damage and decay, and was also transparent, revealing the jewellery and other objects that she was wearing and permitting examination of the skeleton by eye and by scientific techniques, notably X-ray. X-ray analysis in 1994 revealed that this cast was of a woman in her early 30s.[112]

This type of cast is preferable in many ways to the more traditional casts in plaster, cement or opaque resin, but factors such as cost and the tricky process mean that, for the moment, the 'Resin Lady' remains unique.

THE DESTRUCTION OF POMPEII

The cities and other settlements to the south of Vesuvius, such as Pompeii and Stabiae, endured a different ordeal. Pumice and ash fell like snow from the looming volcanic cloud and accumulated throughout the city at a rate of 15 cm (6 in.) every hour, creating severe difficulties. Pliny the Younger remarks that people tied pillows and cushions on their heads to keep the lapilli off – and the larger 'lithics' or volcanic bombs were potentially deadly. This debris, in effect stone, was very heavy. Accumulations outside houses blocked and submerged doors and even windows. In The House of the Chaste Lovers (P) it is possible to see thick layers of pumice and ash and the smaller, though much more lethal, bands marking pyroclastic flows and surges. Roofs and whole storeys caved in with the weight and fires broke out from lamps, hearths and firebrands from other burning structures.

In the early phases of the eruption people may have remained in their homes. Just under 400 of the 1,150 bodies so far discovered in Pompeii were found in houses,[113] lying in layers of lapilli, their deaths almost always the result of suffocation or structural collapse of the rooms in which they were sheltering.

People sought refuge in subterranean rooms, as in the House of the Cryptoporticus, or rooms on ground floors away from possible collapses, fire or debris, such as the rooms at the rear of the House of Caius Julius Polybius. People were still trying to save their possessions.[114] Goods were moved from more exposed gardens/courtyards and upstairs areas to 'safer' spaces deeper in the house. In the House of Caius Julius Polybius a very broad mix of bronze artefacts, from lampstands to serving vessels, some of them prized antiques, seem to have been gathered together in the centre of one of the rooms (EE), while in the House of the Menander and the Villa of the Silver Treasure at Boscoreale, valuable hoards of silverware were being safeguarded in unusual places – the cellar near the baths and a great storage jar.

By early morning, although the people of Pompeii did not know it, Herculaneum and Oplontis were gone, their populations wiped out. As dawn (such as it was) of the second day arrived there was still life in Pompeii. The volcanic cloud was producing considerably less material in the early morning, so people who had been cowering in their homes or other shelters may have believed that this lull was the end of the eruption. Many seem to have made it outside and to have been moving through the city when the final catastrophe struck.[115]

As the eruption reached its end the cloud would certainly have become less dense, but the lull was the calm before the final storm. From about 6 am the volcanic cloud became increasingly unstable as the magma chamber of the volcano began to collapse, emptied of fuel and slowly filling with debris and water. Four massive surges, 3–6, followed in the space of about an hour and a half. Between about 6 and 7 in the morning, surge 3 tumbled towards Pompeii but could not scale its walls. The city walls, built hundreds of years before and thought to be only a symbol of civic pride, had just saved the life of Pompeii – if only for an hour or so. At about 7–8 am surges 4 and 5, following in rapid succession, swirled around the walls of Pompeii, flowed over the earlier material and poured into the city.

Specialists argue over how hot these flows were and how the Pompeians died. Taking a lead from Pliny the Younger's account of the eruption, it is often assumed that the inhabitants killed in the last stages of the eruption died soley from suffocation or inhaling poisonous gases, as Pliny the Elder is supposed to have done. Certainly the surge engulfed people in fire, almost liquid ash, forcing it into nose and mouth. But recent research[116] suggests that many killed by surge 4 died instead of thermal shock.

The fact that clothing and hairstyles were preserved in the casts suggests that this surge cannot have been as hot as surge 1, which, at some 400–450°C, had snuffed out Herculaneum, killing and badly burning everyone in its path. The eruption had been continuing for almost twenty-four hours and was nearly at its end. But even so, it has been estimated that surge 4 was about 250–300°C, still hot enough to kill.[117] This estimate of temperature is based on the degree of discolouration of the bones, not nearly as blackened as the victims on the beach at Herculaneum, and also on the poses of the victims. Some victims display poses of 'cadaveric spasm' that seem life-like and suddenly suspended. Others exhibit the limb contraction of the so-called 'pugilist pose', when the tendons in the limbs contract with a characteristic clenching of hands and feet, which results from exposure of the body to lethal degrees of heat.

The heat of surge 4 was enough to kill all those it enveloped very quickly through radiant heat, but was not sufficiently hot to carbonize flesh and ignite clothing, allowing time for the ash to consolidate around the solid, in effect cooked, remains of the body. As the body rotted, it left an imprint in the ash from which casts could be made. These casts have come to play a very important role in understanding the people of Pompeii and have greatly increased public awareness of the site.

THE BODIES AND CASTS OF POMPEII

One of the features that set Pompeii apart from Herculaneum, from the very earliest excavations, was the frequent discovery of bodies. In Herculaneum, at least until the discovery of the bodies on the beach, it was believed that most people had escaped. In Pompeii, human remains had always been a source of fascination for excavators and visitors.[118] In 1772, during work on the suburban Villa of Diomedes, the remains of twenty bodies were found piled in the cellar. The ash around them preserved the imprint of clothing, faces and other parts of the body. One piece, preserving the imprint of the breast of a young woman, was taken to the Royal Museums at Portici and Naples and became a star attraction, even inspiring a novel, Theophile Gaultier's *Arria Marcella* of 1852.[119]

The bodies were about to become even more famous. In the mid-nineteenth century archaeologists working in Pompeii realized that plaster of Paris, poured into voids in the ash, created detailed impressions of long-vanished organic objects, such as doors and furniture.[120] In February 1863 Giuseppe Fiorelli, the director of the excavations at Pompeii, decided to use the same technique on voids left by people. He hoped that '…archaeology will be pursued not in marble or in bronzes, but over the very bodies of the ancients, carried off by death, after eighteen centuries of oblivion'.[121] The results were sensational. Here for the first time were the bodies of Roman people who had been walking and laughing the day before the eruption and who had died such

ABOVE **Fig. 388 Body cast of a man who died on a flight of stairs.**

House of Marcus Fabius Rufus, Pompeii

OPPOSITE **Fig. 389 Plaster cast of a dog.**

House of Orpheus, Pompeii (VI,14,20)H. 50 cm
SAP 25897

BELOW **Fig. 390 Plaster cast of the body of a man, the so-called 'muleteer'.**

Large Palaestra, Pompeii

a terrible death. On 17 February 1863 Luigi Settembrini, the writer and statesman, sent a long letter to the *Giornale di Napoli* in which he recounted the awe and emotion provoked by the casts and the huge achievement of Fiorelli:[122]

> *This is no work of art, no imitation, it is their bones, the remains of their flesh and their clothing mixed in with the plaster; it is the pain of death that once more takes over their bodies…So far they have rediscovered temples, houses and other artefacts that take the interest of educated people, artists and archaeologists; but you, oh my Fiorelli, have uncovered human suffering and whoever has an ounce of humanity will feel it.*

Now, in addition to the buildings and the artefacts, there were the casts of the people who had lived in them and used them. This created a wave of interest and endless speculation – often fuelled by the excavators themselves – about the people in the casts, their relationships and their lifestyles.[123] This fascination and ambivalence towards the casts is still alive today.[124] When we look at the casts, it is important to remember that very few are exactly as they were when they came out of the ground. Some – such as the 'muleteer' – were retouched, perhaps considerably,[125] to suit the aesthetics of the day. Nonetheless, the casts of the real people who had died in the eruption ensured that the public interest in Pompeii grew exponentially. Its momentum was unstoppable.

THE DOG

Oddly, the most famous cast of all is not of a person, but a dog. In November 1874 excavators uncovering the House of Orpheus (P) found in the entrance area a void which they filled with plaster and they discovered, to their surprise, the body of a dog, contorted in agony. The dog's presence near the entrance area and its collar certainly suggest it was a guard dog. It had been left to guard the house when the owners fled and as the area had gradually filled with ash it had climbed on top (as far as its chain would allow) until the fatal fourth surge overwhelmed it. By strange coincidence, in the room immediately to the right of the door was found the 'Watchdog' mosaic (above pp. 79–80).

THE 'MULETEER'

In the late 1930s excavations began to clear the grand *palaestra* or exercise ground in the east of the city. Several bodies were found there, but only two were cast. One of these was the so-called 'muleteer', named after the skeleton of a mule or donkey found nearby. The 'muleteer', presumed to be a man, was found pitched forward onto the bank of lapilli that had built up. FIG. 390 shows him leaning at an angle as he is correctly displayed at the Antiquarium of Boscoreale, not sitting on his haunches as he is often imagined. Amedeo Maiuri (1950, 83) who discovered the remains and made the cast, described him as:

> *…crouching on the ground next to the wall…like a beggar on the church steps… his head bent over till it touched his knees, the hem of his cloak pulled up to his mouth with both his hands, curled and huddled up like a worm, the better to hide himself in the bosom of the earth. A tragic figure from one of Dante's circles of hell.*

Across the city, in the extensive House of the Golden Bracelet on the western edges of Pompeii, a family desperately looked for refuge. They ran down the stairs that led towards the lowest level of the home. Here, looking out onto a garden terrace, were two rooms, the first completely covered with paintings of a beautiful garden (above pp. 171–7) and the other a dining room, covered with fine marble.

In the archway of the stairs they huddled and died together when they were overwhelmed by the heat and ash of the fourth surge. Two adults, a man and woman, were side by side, with a young child struggling up from the woman's lap. The child appears to be held up by the wall, with its mother now fallen backwards. The man, too, seems to be falling back; both he and the woman have their hands raised as if to protect themselves from the sudden heat and blast. In fact, their poses strongly suggest that they were killed by extreme heat rather than suffocation.[126] Their arms have assumed the so-called 'pugilist' (boxer) pose, caused by the contraction of tendons in extreme heat. This is seen in the woman and in the little child found near the three others, reasonably assumed to be part of the same family group. The little child, perhaps four or five years old, has remarkably well-preserved facial features and clothing, making this one of the most moving of all the casts found in Pompeii.

The family had huge wealth – and were very possibly the owners of the fine house in which they died. The woman was wearing an exceptional golden armlet weighing over 600 g (21 oz), with snake-head terminals holding a golden medallion of the goddess Selene/Luna (the moon) (FIG. 392). The goddess, often linked with Diana, goddess of the hunt and the moon, is shown with a crescent moon on her head, surrounded by seven stars, and holding her veil. Nearby were found two gold rings. One had a carnelian bezel engraved with the figure of a young man reining back a horse, below which is an inscription, *LIBER* (Liber Pater), an alternative name for Bacchus, god of wine. A cameo engraved with the figure of a woman dancing with veils (FIG. 391) was also found. In addition, the woman had a very valuable hoard of coins, comprising forty gold aurei and 173 silver denarii. Two of these denarii must post-date July AD 79 and so constitute the latest issues so far found in the cities. They do not, however, post-date the traditional date of the eruption in August AD 79 (see pp. 278–9).

ABOVE **Fig. 391 Agate/onyx gem incised with a nude female figure.**
House of the Golden Bracelet, Pompeii (VI,17,42)
1.2 cm x 0.99 cm
SAP 14311

BELOW **Fig. 392 Gold armlet with two snake heads holding a disc, found on the arm of the woman.**
House of the Golden Bracelet, Pompeii (VI,17,42)
D. 10.5 cm
SAP 14268

OPPOSITE **Fig. 393 Casts of a group of victims, two adults and two children, very probably a family.**
House of the Golden Bracelet, Pompeii

By early morning of the second day it seems many of the people of Pompeii had chosen not to remain in their hiding places any longer. One who tried to run from the city in the early hours of the second morning was a young woman who, with fourteen other people, reached the area outside the Nola gate in the east of the city. Here, amongst the tombs along the road, she and the others were cut down by surge 4. The 'Porta Nola' girl carried a group of objects (FIGS 394–400) which very poignantly underlined the extent to which the people of the cities believed themselves to be under the protection of the gods, even if also at their mercy.

The girl carried a silver statuette of the goddess Isis-Fortuna, seated on her throne, with her right hand gripping firmly the rudder that represents her control over man's destiny. The girl also carried two silver amulets with protective symbols, a phallus and a crescent moon on a small chain. She was wearing no fewer than four finger rings, three of which had a direct link with good fortune: an iron ring (itself believed to bring good luck) with a chalcedony bezel showing Fortuna with her cornucopia and rudder; a gold ring with scaled body and snake-head terminals; a silver ring with an incised palm branch or ear of corn, both considered to be lucky symbols; and a gold ring with a plain emerald bezel. This last ring, even though plain, could have held some personal importance for the girl. It is quite clear that, unless every item the girl possessed had a link with good luck and fortune, she may well have carefully selected the objects she took with her, ultimately, to her death.

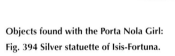

Not long after the Porta Nola girl, with all her 'lucky' jewellery, was struck down, the eruption ceased.

AFTERMATH

When the ash finally settled, this part of the Roman world had changed forever. Heavy pumice falls had reached as far as 75 km (47 miles) from Vesuvius, while fine ash, propelled by the wind, drifted as far as North Africa and Egypt.[127] Such was the huge quantity of material ejected from Vesuvius, perhaps as much as 4 cubic kilometres (over 140 billion cubic ft), that the coastline was pushed out some 400 m (over 1,300 ft) to the west, and Herculaneum lay buried 23 m (75 ft) underground. Pompeii was less deeply buried. Today the overburden on Pompeii also includes debris from later eruptions and agricultural soil. But immediately after the eruption, although in some places the ash and lapilli banked up to 5–6 m (16–19 ft) high, in most of the city the depth was 4–5 m (13–16 ft). The ruins of many buildings – in particular the baths, theatres and temples and even some of the grander houses – will have been protruding above the ash; and general contours, such as the line of the city walls, or the hollows of the Forum or amphitheatre, served as clear markers.

Outside the cities the complete agricultural and economic system of this part of southern Italy was in ruins.[128] Farms and estates with all their food stores were

Objects found with the Porta Nola Girl:

Fig. 394 Silver statuette of Isis-Fortuna.

H. 3.8 cm, W. 1.5 cm
SAP P15496

Fig. 395 Silver phallic amulet.

L. 1.5 cm, W. 0.6 cm
SAP P15501

Fig. 396 Silver ring with an incised palm branch.

D. 1.3 cm
SAP P15498

Fig. 397 Gold ring with plain rectangular emerald bezel.

D. 1.8 cm
SAP P23181

Fig. 398 Silver ring with serpent body and terminals.

D. 2.8 cm
SAP P15497

Fig. 399 Silver crescent pendant on small chain.

L. 3.5 cm, D. of pendant 1.5 cm
SAP P15499

Fig. 400 Iron ring with a sardonyx cameo
showing Fortuna.

W. 3.1 cm
SAP P15532

burned out or buried, with countless livestock dead, orchards blasted, fields and crops under metres of ash, and roads and ports buried or blocked.

The Emperor Titus intervened immediately,[129] appointing two commissioners for reconstructing Campania (*Curatores Campaniae restituendae*) who went down to the area (probably accompanied by the emperor himself) and began the process of assisting and compensating survivors. Those who had lost property or land were given a grant of money derived from the estates of those who had died in the disaster. There may have been a scheme to assess the feasibility of rebuilding the cities, but Herculaneum was simply too deeply buried, and the commissioners must rapidly have realized that Pompeii was not rescuable either.

At this point, or a little later, once the hot debris had cooled, people returned to Pompeii. They dug down with relative ease and began to salvage (or loot). We do not know who these people were, whether they were organized by the imperial government or were private individuals, but given the scale of what they achieved, central organization seems likely. They stripped the Forum, the baths, the theatres and the temples, taking away statues and precious marbles, even columns and the marble seating blocks of the theatres and amphitheatre.

Houses, too, were investigated; we cannot tell whether this was done by their original owners or by looters. Occasionally they left their mark – disturbed ash layers within a 'sealed' house, holes punched roughly though walls, looking like the Bourbon tunnels of Herculaneum but archaeologically dated to Roman times. This could be evidence for people trying to hack their way out of their homes as they found themselves trapped by rising debris – or it could be a sign of intrusion. On the exterior of a house in Pompeii is an odd Latin graffito (written in Greek letters), saying ΔΟΜΜΟΥС ΠΕΡΤΟΥСΛ ('house gone through').[130] If, as some believe, the graffito shows exploration of the house not long after the eruption then was it written by slaves of the original owners, or slaves of the commissioners?

What happened to the owners of that house and all the other people of the cities? Did everyone die? Almost certainly they did not. To date in Pompeii about 1,150 bodies have been accounted for, while in Herculaneum the figure stands at around 350, approximating to 10 per cent, perhaps a little less, of the populations of both cities. Where are the others? We should remember that about one-third of Pompeii and two-thirds of Herculaneum are still unexcavated. At Pompeii how many groups of people are lying in houses and public buildings and gardens? How many had run from the city and were taking their chances sheltering in fields, or near roads? At Herculaneum many people probably lie along the old shoreline and many hundreds more almost certainly wait to be found in the area of the as yet unexcavated port.

It seems probable, though, that a significant number of people, perhaps the majority, escaped. They had several hours during the first day to make their way to safety. Many from Herculaneum may have fled by land, or less likely, by boat, to the north of the Bay of Naples, mainly to Naples itself. Three centuries later there was still a 'Herculaneum' suburb in the town, perhaps a memory of refugees from the eruption.[131] Descendants of the people of Pompeii and Herculaneum may still be walking through the streets and houses of Naples today.

NOTES

INTRODUCTION

1 Statius, *Silvae*, IV,4,78–85.
2 Wallace-Hadrill 2011, 66–7.
3 Wallace-Hadrill 2011b, 145–6.
4 Wallace-Hadrill 2011b.
5 St Clair and Bautz 2012.
6 Beard 2009, 3–7.
7 Guidobaldi and Esposito 2012, 26.

I THE URBAN CONTEXT

1 Guzzo 2011, 13.
2 Dionysius of Halicarnassus, *Roman Antiquities*, I,44.
3 Isidore, *Etymologies*, XV,1,51.
4 Strabo, *Geography*, V,4,8.
5 Guidobaldi and Esposito 2012, 48.
6 Guzzo 2011, 12.
7 Coarelli and Pesando 2011, 37.
8 Coarelli and Pesando 2011, 40.
9 Coarelli and Pesando 2011, 42–3.
10 Guzzo 2011, 12; Coarelli and Pesando 2011, 38.
11 Guzzo 2011, 13.
12 Coarelli and Pesando 2011, 45.
13 Diodorus of Sicily, *The Historical Library*, XI,51,2.
14 Coarelli and Pesando 2011, 47.
15 Guzzo 2011, 15.
16 Coarelli and Pesando 2011, 48–50.
17 Livy, *The History of Rome*, X,45.
18 Orosius, *Histories*, V,18,22.
19 Berry 2007, 84.
20 Frontinus, *Stratagems*, I,5,21.
21 Cicero, *Letters to Atticus*, X,16,4.
22 Berry 2007, 122–30; Coarelli 2002.
23 Wallace-Hadrill 2011, 146–97.
24 Brennan 2011, 4.
25 Crawford et al. 2011, 628–30.
26 Van Andringa 2009, 9, fig. 15.
27 Cooley and Cooley 2004, 15–16.
28 Petersen 2006, 47–57.
29 Franklin 2007, 522.
30 CIL X 841.
31 Wallace-Hadrill 2011, 138.
32 Beard 2008, 194.
33 Jongman 2007, 512.
34 Beard 2008, 193–4.
35 Wallace-Hadrill 2011, 291–2.
36 CIL IV 3884.
37 Cooley and Cooley 2004, fig. 6.1.
38 Weeber 2011, 47–8.
39 CIL IV 1169.
40 CIL IV 705.
41 CIL IV 7164.
42 CIL IV 826.
43 CIL IV 6672.
44 CIL IV 7473.
45 CIL IV 743.
46 CIL IV 2184.
47 CIL IV 241.
48 Garcia y Garcia 2005, 52–4.
49 Weeber 2011, 66.
50 CIL IV 576.
51 CIL IV 443.
52 Berry 2007, 118; Bernstein 1988; Weeber 2011, 49–60.
53 Weeber 2011, 51.
54 CIL IV 7469.
55 CIL IV 7864.
56 Clarke 2003, 259–61.
57 CIL IV, 429.
58 Cooley and Cooley 2004, 48–54.
59 CIL IV 7990
60 Berry 2007, 140–9.
61 Cooley and Cooley 2004, 48–66.
62 Cooley and Cooley 2004, 51.
63 CIL IV 7989a, c.

64 CIL IV 9983a.
65 CIL IV 4299; CIL IV 9969.
66 CIL IV 10579.
67 Wallace-Hadrill 2011, 297.
68 Clarke 2003, 152–8.
69 CIL IV 138.
70 Pesando and Guidobaldi 2006, 172–6.
71 CIL IV 1136.
72 Cooley and Cooley 2004, 171.
73 CIL IV 8792.
74 CIL IV 64.
75 CIL IV 3864.
76 CIL IV 5112.
77 CIL IV 8657.
78 CIL IV 1904.
79 Wallace-Hadrill 2011, 174.
80 Wallace-Hadrill 2011, 38–9, 180–6; Wallace-Hadrill 2011a 141–57.
81 Wallace-Hadrill 2011, 186; Wallace-Hadrill 2011a 156.
82 Guidobaldi 2008, 259.
83 Guidobaldi 2008, 254–5; Wallace-Hadrill 2011, 186.
84 Guidobaldi 2008, 260; Wallace-Hadrill 2011, 134.
85 Guidobaldi et al. 2009, 91.
86 Gardner 1993, 8–11.
87 Gardner 1993, 18.
88 Camodeca 2008, 89–98; Wallace-Hadrill 2011, 139–42; de Ligt and Garnsey 2012, 70–2.
89 de Ligt and Garnsey 2012, 78–9.
90 Camodeca 2008, 90.
91 Wallace-Hadrill 2011, 194.
92 Camodeca 2008, 92; de Ligt and Garnsey 2012, 84.
93 de Ligt and Garnsey 2012, 83–5.
94 de Ligt and Garnsey 2012, 87.
95 Lazer 2009, 44–5.
96 Petrone et al. 2002, 70.
97 Guidobaldi 2008, 258.
98 Bernstein 2007, 530.
99 Berry 2007, 129.
100 CIL X 813.
101 Berry 2007, 115; Beard 2008, 300.
102 Franklin 2007, 523.
103 Bonfante 2003, 89–90.
104 Gardner 1993, 86–7.
105 Beard 2008, 215; Berry 2007, 118–19.
106 Gardner 1993, 90.
107 Mouritsen 1997, 81.
108 Mouritsen 1997, 69–70.

II LIVING ABOVE THE SHOP

1 Wallace-Hadrill 2011, 294–5.
2 Poehler 2006; Laurence 2007, 52–54; Beard 2008, 68–70.
3 Beard 2008, 79–80.
4 Beard 2008, 55–7.
5 Poehler 2012, 104–11.
6 Wallace-Hadrill 2011, 238; 291–292.
7 Laurence 2007, 45–51.
8 Keenan-Jones et al. 2011, 145.
9 Keenan-Jones et al. 2011, 145–6.
10 Allison 2004, 163; Hartnett 2008.
11 Beard 2008, 72–8.
12 Cooley and Cooley 2004, 180, H65.
13 Beard 2008, 62.
14 Wallace-Hadrill 1994, 78.
15 Wallace-Hadrill 1994, 140.
16 Wallace-Hadrill 1994, 123–4.
17 Coarelli and Pesando 2011, 52.
18 Cicero, *Letters to Atticus*, XIV,9,1.
19 Allison 2004, 174.
20 Holleran 2012, 157–8.
21 Beard 2012, 67–8.
22 Holleran 2012, 154–6.
23 Cicero, *Against Catiline*, IV,17.

24 Pirson 2007, 468.
25 Borgongino 2006, passim.
26 Guidobaldi 2006, 294.
27 CIL IV 8863.
28 Camodeca 2009, 21–5.
29 Roberts 1997.
30 De Felice 2007, 474.
31 Berry 2007, 216–17.
32 CIL IV 9850.
33 Stefani 2005, 115.
34 Stefani 2005, 115–28.
35 CIL IV 7863; 7864; De Felice 2007, 481–2.
36 De Felice 2007, 479.
37 Packer 1978, 7–9.
38 CIL IV 807.
39 Guzzo 2011.
40 De Felice 2007, 475.
41 Monteix 2007, 117.
42 Laurence 2007, 94–9.
43 Monteix 2007, 121–2.
44 Kastenmeier 2007, 93.
45 Suetonius, *Tiberius*, 34.
46 Suetonius, *Nero*, 16.
47 De Felice 2007, 479.
48 Pesando and Guidobaldi 2006, 115; Stefani 2006a, 160; De Felice 2007, 475.
49 d'Ambrosio 1996, 109–10; Beard 2008, 227.
50 Stefani 2006, 160.
51 Stefani 2005, 141–2.
52 d'Ambrosio 1996, 111–12.
53 Stefani 2005, 111–12.
54 Monteix 2007, 118–19.
55 Horace, *Epistles*, I,14,2.
56 Horace, *Satires*, II,4,62.
57 Cicero, *Against Piso*, VI,13.
58 CIL IV 3494.
59 Laurence 2007, 92–101; De Felice 2007, 479.
60 CIL IV 8442.
61 CIL IV 4259.
62 CIL IV 8248.
63 Beard 2008, 232.
64 Stefani 2005, 97.
65 Laurence 2007, 67–9.
66 Wallace-Hadrill 2011, 276.
67 Stefani 2005, 139.
68 Laurence 2007, 67.
69 Pirson 2007, 462; Stefani 2005, 98.
70 CIL IV 538.
71 Lazer 2009, 170–1.
72 Borgongino 2006, 49; 140–3.
73 Guzzo and Ussani 2011.
74 Varone 2000, 328.
75 Stefani 2006, 159–60.
76 Stefani 2006, 158.
77 Stefani 2006, 164.
78 Allison 2004, 110.
79 Borgongino and Stefani 2002, 178.
80 Borgongino 2006, 57.
81 Stefani 2006, 157.
82 Stefani 2005, 101.
83 Stefani 2006, 160; Berry 2007, 216–17.
84 Stefani 2006, 164.
85 CIL IV 9313.
86 Stefani 2006b, 168.
87 CIL IV 1679.
88 Stefani 2005, 99; Wallace-Hadrill 2011, 291.
89 Wallace-Hadrill 2011, 233.
90 CIL IV 3948.
91 Grocock and Grainger 2006, 373–87.
92 Pliny the Elder, *Natural History*, XXXI,97.
93 Pliny the Elder, *Natural History*, XIII,102.
94 Pliny the Elder, *Natural History*, XXXI,94.
95 Curtis 1988, 32.
96 CIL IV 10150.
97 Curtis 1988, 31–4.

98 Stefani 2005, 99; Curtis 1988, 29.
99 Curtis 1979, 10.
100 Laurence 2007, 71–7; Pirson 2007, 466–7.
101 Ciarallo et al. 1999, 174, no. 196; Pirson 2007, 467.
102 Ciarallo et al. 1999, 164, no. 178.
103 Guidobaldi 2006, 335.
104 Cooley and Cooley 2004, 174–5.
105 Wallace-Hadrill 2011, 275–80.
106 Wallace-Hadrill 2011, 284.
107 CIL IV 8505.
108 Laurence 2007, 71–5.
109 Pirson 2007, 463–6.
110 Guidobaldi 2006, 335.
111 Croom 2011, 95–102

III ATRIUM

1 Prayon 2009, 60; Bergman 2007, 226.
2 Coarelli and Pesando 2011, 51.
3 De Carolis 2007, 16.
4 De Carolis 2007, 17.
5 De Carolis 2007, 11; Wallace-Hadrill 1994.
6 Vitruvius, *On Architecture*, VI,5,2.
7 Wallace-Hadrill 1994, 86.
8 Juvenal, *Satires*, I,109–16
9 Hales 2003, 136.
10 Allison 2004, 69.
11 De Carolis 2007, 132–40.
12 Allison 2004, 165.
13 Croom 2011, 56–60.
14 Allison 2004, 164.
15 Wallace-Hadrill 1994, 8–9; Allison 2004, 156–7.
16 Cornelius Nepos, *Lives of Eminent Commanders*, 6–8.
17 Allison 2004, 165.
18 Bisel and Bisel 2002, 453–4.
19 CIL IV 8565.
20 Beard 2008, 76–7.
21 Dixon 1992, 116–19.
22 Gardner 1993, 19.
23 Wallace-Hadrill 1994, 116.
24 Wallace-Hadrill 1994, 117.
25 Wallace-Hadrill, 1994, 84.
26 De Carolis 2007, 16.
27 Coarelli and Pesando 2011, 52.
28 Garcia y Garcia 2006, 150–2.
29 De Carolis 2007, 143.
30 Van Andringa 2009, 228.
31 d'Ambrosio et al. 2004, 158–60.
32 d'Ambrosio et al. 2004, 172–3.
33 Livy, *The History of Rome*, V,47,4.
34 Varro, *On the Latin Language*, V,125.
35 De Carolis 2007, 109.
36 Livy, *The History of Rome*, XXXIX,6,7.
37 De Carolis 2007, 108.
38 Stefani 2006a.
39 Stefani 2006b.
40 Mastroroberto 2006.
41 Giove 2006.
42 De Carolis 2006.
43 Hales 2003, 47–8.
44 Comodeca 2009, 18.
45 Petersen 2006, 176.
46 Seneca, *Natural Questions*, VI,1,2.
47 Welch 2007, 567.
48 Petersen 2006, 178.
49 La Rocca et al. 2009, 302.
50 Van Andringa 2009, 217.
51 Van Andringa 2009, 240–2.
52 d'Ambrosio and Borriello 2001.
53 De Carolis 2007, 140; Mols 1999, 188–200.
54 Wallace-Hadrill 2011a, 218–9.
55 Van Andringa 2009, 244; 249.
56 Robinson 2002, 95.
57 Robinson pers. comm.
58 Van Andringa 2009, 259–65.
59 Moormann 2011, 171.

60 CIL IV 8010.
61 CIL IV 4976.
62 Bragantini and Sampaolo 2009, 417.
63 Wallace-Hadrill 2011, 313–15.
64 Clarke 2003, 252–3; Hales 2003, 126.
65 Charles-Laforge 2007.
66 Hales 2003, 126.
67 Pliny the Elder, *Natural History*, XXXVI,6.
68 De Simone 2011, 289–94.
69 Clarke 2003, 78–81.
70 Curtis 1988.
71 Grocock and Grainger 2006, 64.
72 Schnurr 1957, 28.
73 Esposito 2006, 507–42.
74 Curtis 1988, 26–28.
75 De Carolis 2007, 52.
76 Hales 2003, 107.
77 Vitruvius, *On Architecture*, VI,5,2.
78 Wallace-Hadrill 1994, 11.
79 Hales 2003, 107–8.
80 Pliny the Elder, *Natural History*, XXXV,2,7.
81 Allison 2004, 134.
82 Allison 2004, 168.
83 Sider 2005.
84 Sider 2005, 62.
85 Allison 2004, 121.
86 Camodeca 2009, 27–9.
87 Camodeca 2009, 29.
88 Sider 2005, 26–33.
89 Camodeca 2008, 99.
90 Suetonius, *Nero*, 17.
91 Clarke 2003, 261–7.
92 La Rocca et al. 2009, 303.
93 La Rocca et al. 2009, 303.
94 Bragantini and Sampaolo 2009, 517, no. 296.
95 Castren 2008, 27.
96 Del Mastro 2003.
97 Sider 2005.
98 Sider 2005, 47–51.
99 Sider 2005, 53.
100 Jongman 2007, 507; Beard 2008, 177; Camodeca 2009, 18.
101 Jongman 1991, 216.
102 CIL IV 8863.
103 Jongman 2007, 508.
104 Jongman 1991, 222.
105 Wallace-Hadrill 2011, 144–5; Camodeca 2009, 34.
106 Camodeca 2009, 30–2.
107 Camodeca 2009, 30–2.
108 Wallace-Hadrill 2011, 237–8; Camodeca 2009, 32–4.
109 Wallace-Hadrill 1994, 179–81; Camodeca 2008, 99–102.
110 Camodeca 2008, 99, no. 2 (THerc. 5).
111 Gardner 1993, 18.
112 Camodeca 2008, 99, no. 3.
113 Camodeca 2008, 99, no. 1 (THerc. 89).
114 Gardner 1993, 18.
115 Horace, *Epistles*, II,1,156–7.
116 Cooley and Cooley 2004, 220–1.
117 Garcia y Garcia 2005, 142.
118 Wallace-Hadrill 2011, 297–8.
119 Beard 2008, 184.
120 Garcia y Garcia 2005, 148.
121 CIL IV 4078.

IV CUBICULUM

1 Riggsby 1997, 37.
2 Riggsby 1997, 40.
3 Varro, *On the Latin Language*, V,162.
4 Pliny the Elder, *Natural History*, XXX,52.
5 Riggsby 1997, 41.
6 Riggsby 1997, 37–9.
7 Allison 2004, 71.
8 Martial, *Epigrams*, XXII,104,5–8.
9 Martial, *Epigrams*, XIV,39.
10 Varro, *On the Latin Language*, VIII,32.
11 De Carolis 2007, 86–91.
12 De Carolis 2007, 157–60.

13 Wallace-Hadrill 1994, 113.
14 Pliny the Elder, *Natural History*, XXXIV,14.
15 Laurence 2007, 82–92.
16 Riggsby 1997,45–6.
17 Riggsby 1997, 44–5.
18 George 2007, 539–40.
19 CIL IV 1863.
20 Levin-Richardson 2011, 322; Varone 2002.
21 CIL IV 6842.
22 CIL IV 1410.
23 CIL IV 1824.
24 Bisel and Bisel 2002, 453–4.
25 Dioscorides, *On Medical Substances*, II,210.
26 Dioscorides, *On Medical Substances*, I,77.
27 Hobson 2009, 134.
28 Hobson 2009, 136.
29 Petronius, *Satyricon*, XXVII.
30 CIL IV 4957.
31 Hobson 2009, 137.
32 Wilson 2011A, 95.
33 Allison 2004, 54
34 Stefani 2006b, 223, nos 386–7.
35 Seneca, *Natural Questions*, I,17.
36 Ovid, *The Art of Loving*, III,135–6.
37 Seneca, *Natural Questions*, I,17.
38 d'Ambrosio 2001, 8.
39 Martial, *Epigrams*, I,87.
40 Martial, *Epigrams*, III,74.
41 Pliny the Elder, *Natural History*, XXVIII, 255–6.
42 Garcia y Garcia 2007, 44–6.
43 Garcia y Garcia 2007, 37–8; Stefani 2006, 157.
44 Pliny the Elder, *Natural History*, XVIII,117; Martial, *Epigrams*, III,13.
45 CIL IV 2597; CIL IV 10282.
46 Ovid, *The Art of Loving*, III,209–10.
47 Ovid, *Cosmetics for the Female Face*, LIII,65.
48 Ovid, *Cosmetics for the Female Face*, LIII–LV.
49 Pliny the Elder, *Natural History*, XXX,30.
50 Pliny the Elder, *Natural History*, XXX,30.
51 Ovid, *The Art of Loving*, III,200–4.
52 Baraldi et al. 2004, 113–14.
53 Baraldi et al. 2004, 114.
54 Garcia y Garcia 2007, 9–10.
55 Pliny the Elder, *Natural History*, XIII,20.
56 Martial, *Epigrams*, XIII,126.
57 Garcia y Garcia 2007, 7.
58 Garcia y Garcia 2007, 7.
59 Pliny the Elder, *Natural History*, XIII,14–15.
60 Garcia y Garcia 2007, 30.
61 Garcia y Garcia 2007, 19–20.
62 Pliny the Elder, *Natural History*, XIII,26.
63 Pliny the Elder, *Natural History*, XVIII, 111.
64 Pliny the Elder, *Natural History*, XIII,1.
65 Pliny the Elder, *Natural History*, XIII,3.
66 Pliny the Elder, *Natural History*, XXI,125,133.
67 CIL IV 609; Garcia y Garcia 2007, 25–6.
68 Pliny the Elder, *Natural History*, XIII,5.
69 Columella, *On Country Life*, XII,45.
70 Garcia y Garcia 2007, 19–20.
71 Pliny the Elder, *Natural History*, XIII,19.
72 Pliny the Elder, *Natural History*, XXXII,23.
73 Pliny the Elder, *Natural History*, XXVIII,19.
74 Pliny the Elder, *Natural History*, XXXVII,50.
75 Ovid, *The Loves*, I,14.
76 Pliny the Elder, *Natural History*, XXVIII,166.
77 Martial, *Epigrams*, II,26.
78 Martial, *Epigrams*, XIV,24.
79 d'Ambrosio 2001, 19.
80 Ciarallo and De Carolis 1999, 177, no. 202.

81 Martial, *Epigrams*, III,43,1–4.
82 CIL IV 7345.
83 Seneca, *Epistles*, 56,1–2.
84 CIL IV 6890.
85 Garcia y Garcia 2007, 88–9.
86 Horace, *Satires*, I,1,94.
87 Garcia y Garcia 2007, 82–9.
88 Clarke 1998, 295, n. 82.
89 Juvenal, *Satires*, III,186.
90 Plutarch, *Lives*, I,2.
91 Pliny the Elder, *Natural History*, XXIX,114.
92 d'Ambrosio 2001, 48.
93 d'Ambrosio 2001, 30–1.
94 Tacitus, *Annals*, III,53.
95 Pliny the Elder, *Natural History*, XII,84.
96 d'Ambrosio 2001, 31.
97 Pliny the Elder, *Natural History*, IX,117.
98 d'Ambrosio 2001, 32.
99 Juvenal, *Satires*, VI,27.
100 Pliny the Elder, *Natural History*, XXXIII,12.
101 Pliny the Elder, *Natural History*, XXXVII,30–1.
102 *Rediscovering Pompeii* 1992, 153.
103 d'Ambrosio 2001, 39–40.
104 Walker and Bierbrier 1997, 41–4; 162–3.
105 Pliny the Elder, *Natural History*, IX,112.
106 Pliny the Elder, *Natural History*, IX,114.
107 Juvenal, *Satires*, VI,457–9.
108 Petronius, *Satyricon*, LXVII.
109 d'Ambrosio 2001, 41–2.
110 d'Ambrosio 2001, 42.
111 Pliny the Elder, *Natural History*, XXXVII,16.
112 Pliny the Elder, *Natural History*, XXXIII,4.
113 Mols 1999, 63; 217–18, cat. 41.
114 Cato, *On Agriculture*, XCVIII.1.
115 Pliny the Elder, *Natural History*, XI,76.
116 Horace, *Satires*, I,II.
117 Bonifacio 2004, 14.
118 Juvenal, *Satires*, III,172; 177–8.
119 Bonfante 2003, 48–9.
120 Bonfante 2003, 92–3.
121 Plautus, *The Little Carthaginian*, 210.

V GARDEN

1 Ciarallo 2007, 169.
2 Wallace-Hadrill 1994, 86.
3 Jashemski 2007, 489–90.
4 Garcia y Garcia 2007, 34–7.
5 Macaulay-Lewis 2006, 210.
6 Jashemski and Meyer 2002, 23.
7 Jashemski and Meyer 2002, 16.
8 Petersen 2006, 136
9 Jashemski and Meyer 2002, 16.
10 Martial, *Epigrams*, II,18.
11 Wallace-Hadrill 1994, 22.
12 Allison 2004, 173.
13 Hales 2003, 158.
14 Petersen 2006, 153–6.
15 Jansen 2011b, 71–3.
16 Pliny the Elder, *Natural History*, XXXI,21.
17 Croom 2011, 18
18 Ciarallo et al. 1999, 312, no. 395.
19 Hardy et al. 1994, 224.
20 Varone 2000, 319.
21 Jashemski and Meyer 2002; Robinson 2008.
22 Varone 2000, 328.
23 Varone 2000, 327.
24 Robinson 2008, 155.
25 Macaulay-Lewis 2006, 208–14; Ciarallo 2007, 173.
26 Pliny the Elder, *Natural History*, XII,16.
27 Macaulay-Lewis 2006, 209.
28 Carroll 2003, 25.
29 Robinson 2008, 157.
30 Ciarallo 2007, 167.
31 Robinson 2008, 158.
32 Jashemski and Meyer 2002, 20.
33 Jashemski and Meyer 2002, 21; Ciarallo

2007, 166.
34 Pliny the Elder, *Natural History*, XXI,14–69.
35 Robinson 2002, 97.
36 Jashemski and Meyer 2002, 104–5.
37 Jashemski and Meyer 2002, 143.
38 Jashemski and Meyer 2002, 16.
39 Beretta and Di Pasquale 2004, 109–19.
40 Pliny the Elder, *Natural History*, XIX,64.
41 Columella, *On Country Life*, II,3,52.
42 De Carolis 2007, 39.
43 Petersen, 2006, 134
44 Pliny the Elder, *Natural History*, XIX,50.
45 Kuivalainen 2008, 137.
46 Suetonius, *Tiberius*, 43.
47 Beard 2012, 68.
48 Beard 2012, 61–4.
49 Levin-Richardson 2011, 329.
50 Jashemski and Meyer 2002, 22.
51 Van Andringa 2009, 244.
52 *Rediscovering Pompeii*, 153; Varone 2011.
53 CIL IV 2069.
54 Petersen 2006, 144–5.
55 *Rediscovering Pompeii*, 234–8.
56 Nava et al. 2007, 59.
57 Pliny the Elder, *Natural History*, XXI,184.
58 *Rediscovering Pompeii* 235–7.
59 Petersen 2006, 161.

VI LIVING ROOMS AND INTERIOR DESIGN

1 De Carolis 2007, 42.
2 Vitruvius, *On Architecture*, VI,3,3–10.
3 Pliny the Elder, *Natural History*, XXXVI,184.
4 Allison 2004, 170.
5 Vitruvius, *On Architecture*, VII,9,2.
6 Melini 2008, 36–7.
7 Pliny the Elder, *Natural History*, XXXV,165; Dunbabin 1999, 53–4.
8 Dunbabin 1999, 18–37.
9 Wallace-Hadrill 1994, 158; De Carolis 2007, 51.
10 De Carolis 2007, 52.
11 De Carolis 2007, 50–2.
12 De Carolis 2007, 52–3.
13 Dunbabin 1999, 300–3; Ling 1991, 217–20.
14 Esposito 2009, 38–9.
15 Dunbabin 1999, 45–7.
16 Darmon and Manière-Lévêque 2003, 87–99.
17 Esposito 2009, 34.
18 Beard 2008, 254–5.
19 Pliny the Elder, *Natural History* XXXV,110.
20 Esposito 2009, 34.
21 Maiuri 1927, 45–46.
22 Wallace-Hadrill 2011, 299; 302.
23 Esposito 2009, 43.
24 Wallace-Hadrill 1994, 168; Esposito 2009, 47.
25 Vitruvius, *On Architecture*, VII,9,3.
26 Ling 1991, 207–9.
27 Pliny the Elder, *Natural History*, XXXV,30.
28 Baraldi et al. 2006, 52.
29 Ling 1991, 207.
30 Pliny the Elder, *Natural History*, XXXV,31–48.
31 Ling, 219–220; De Carolis 2007, 42.
32 Pliny the Elder, *Natural History*, XXXV,112; Ling 1991, 213–14.
33 Esposito 2009, 37–9.
34 Pesando and Guidobaldi 2006, 140.
35 Ling 1991, 214–17.
36 Esposito 2009, 33.
37 Ling 1991, 213.
38 Esposito 2009, 35–36.
39 Berry (ed.) 1998, 61–2.
40 Esposito 2009, 47; Beard 2008, 121–4.
41 Varone 2000, 325.
42 Esposito 2009, 47.
43 Varone 2000, 326.
44 Esposito 2009, 42; Ling 1991, 218.
45 Esposito 2009, 42.
46 Ling 1991, 206–7.
47 Vitruvius, *On Architecture*, II,8,9.

48 Pliny the Elder, *Natural History*, XXXV,113.
49 Esposito 2009, 40.
50 Esposito 2009, 34; Ling 1991, 204.
51 *Vivere a Pompei* 2010, 98
52 Guidobaldi et al., 2009, 158–60.
53 Guidobaldi 2010, 80–97; Guidobaldi and Esposito 2012, 163–4.
54 Vitruvius, *On Architecture*, VII,5.
55 Mau 1882.
56 Hales 2003, 136.
57 De Carolis 2007, 49.
58 Hales 2003, 130.
59 De Carolis 2007, 49; Hales 2003, 136.
60 Wallace-Hadrill 1994, 143.
61 Berry 2007, 170–71; Beard 2008, 135–7.
62 Vitruvius, *On Architecture*, VII,5,1.
63 La Rocca et al. 2009, 265; Coarelli and Pesando 2011, 51; 57, colour fig. B.
64 Vitruvius, *On Architecture*, VII,5,2.
65 De Carolis 2001, 60–1; Maulucci Vivolo 1993, 76–110.
66 Pappalardo 2009, 49–63; Ling 1991, 101–4; Beard 2008, 131–4.
67 Bergmann 2007, 239–50.
68 Hales 2003, 130; Petersen 2006, 138–41.
69 Vitruvius, *On Architecture*, VII,5,3.
70 Vitruvius, *On Architecture*, VII,5,4.
71 Hales 2003, 147–8.
72 Provenzale 2008, 144–6.
73 Petersen 2006, 138.
74 Wallace-Hadrill 2011, 303.
75 Esposito 2009,41; Wallace-Hadrill 2011, 303.
76 Esposito 2009, 32; 42.
77 Esposito 2009, 41.
78 Esposito 2009, 47.
79 Wallace-Hadrill 1994, 168.
80 Wallace-Hadrill 2011, 251–2.
81 Guidobaldi and Esposito 2012, 206–7.
82 Jenkins 1996, 41–3.
83 Amery and Curran 2002, 177–81.
84 d'Hancarville 1766–7; Gell and Gandy 1817–19; Gell 1832.
85 Mattusch 2008, 286–8.
86 Piggott 2004, 98–102; Zimmermann 2008, 124–6.
87 Esposito 2009, 34.
88 Pliny the Elder, *Natural History*, XXXVI,189.
89 Wallace-Hadrill 2011, 211.
90 Esposito 2009, 43; Wallace-Hadrill 2011, 302.
91 Wallace-Hadrill 2011, 241.
92 Guidobaldi and Esposito 2012, 309–11.
93 Guidobaldi and Esposito 2012, 308.
94 Guidobaldi and Esposito 2012, 151–5.
95 Guidobaldi and Guzzo 2010.
96 Guidobaldi 2010, 254–5; De Simone 2011, 309.
97 De Simone 2011.
98 Guidobaldi et al. 2009, 89–91.
99 Guidobaldi and Guzzo 2010.
100 Wallace-Hadrill 2011, 302.
101 Cicero, *Letters to Atticus*, I,10,3.
102 Wallace-Hadrill 2011, 303.
103 Camardo et al. 2010; Camardo et al. 2010a.
104 Guidobaldi and Esposito 2012, 303–11.

VII DINING

1 De Carolis 2007, 20.
2 Beard 2008, 221.
3 Roller 2006, 176.
4 Suetonius, *Augustus*, 64,3.
5 Clarke 2003, 292.
6 Martial, *Epigrams*, X,387–8.
7 Melini 2008, 45; Martial, *Epigrams*,IX.77.
8 Cooley & Cooley 2004, 73–4; CIL IV 7698a–c.
9 Grocock and Grainger 2006, 64.

10 Pliny the Elder, *Natural History*, VIII,223.
11 Grocock and Grainger 2006.
12 Horace, *Satires*, 1,3,6.
13 Apicius, *On Cookery*, IX,8,3.
14 Apicius, *On Cookery*, III,9,6.
15 Apicius, *On Cookery*, III,1.
16 Apicius, *On Cookery*, VIII,9.
17 Kastenmeier 2007, 70.
18 Apicius, *On Cookery*, VII,9,1.
19 Apicius, *On Cookery*, II,3,1.
20 Apicius, *On Cookery*, VI,6,1.
21 Apicius, *On Cookery*, IV,2,12.
22 Cooley and Cooley 2004, 163; Beard 2008, 223–5; CIL IV 5380.
23 Robinson and Rowan 2012.
24 Seneca, *Dialogues*, XII,10,3.
25 Faas 2003, 74–5.
26 Pliny the Elder, *Natural History*, XXXIII,26.
27 Stefani 2005, 69.
28 Guzzo 2006, 87.
29 Roller 2006, 181–8.
30 Horace, *Odes*, I,6,115.
31 Horace, *Satires*, II,4,61.
32 Pliny the Elder, *Natural History*, XXI,131.
33 Sider 2005, 91–3.
34 Harden et al. 1987, 74–8.
35 *Pompeianarum Antiquitatum Historia* II.

VIII KITCHENS, TOILETS AND BATHS

1 Kastenmeier 2007, 82.
2 Allison 2004, 99–103.
3 Grocock and Grainger 2006, 73.
4 Seneca, *Epistles*, CIV,6.
5 Kastenmeier 2007, 80; Grocock and Grainger 2006, 75.
6 Hobson 2009, 93.
7 Allison 2004, 192–6.
8 Grocock and Grainger 2006, 63.
9 Cicero, *Against Piso*, 67.
10 Cicero, *On Duties*, I,150.
11 Grocock and Grainger 2006, 65.
12 Juvenal, *Satires*, XI,136.
13 Kastenmeier 2007, 78.
14 Kastenmeier 2007, 70–71.
15 Cubberley et al., 1988.
16 Grocock and Grainger 2006, 80, figs 7–8.
17 Stefani 2006, 165.
18 Borgongino 2006, 79, cat. 88.
19 Pliny the Elder, *Natural History*, XIX,140; Columella, *On Country Life*, XII,10,1.
20 Apicius, *On Cookery*, IV,2,14.
21 Varro, *On Agriculture*, III,15.
22 Borgongino 2006, 148–9.
23 Borgongino 2006, 66–9.
24 Borgongino 2006, 121.
25 Kastenmeier 2007, 74.
26 Koloski-Ostrow 2011, 52.
27 Hobson 2009, 51.
28 Hobson 2009, 119.
29 Hobson 2009, 122.
30 Hobson 2009, 122.
31 Hobson 2009, 74.
32 Hobson 2009, 75.
33 Hobson 2009, 48.
34 Camardo and Notomista, forthcoming.
35 Hobson 2009, 123–6.
36 Hobson 2009, 82.
37 Hobson 2009, 169–70.
38 Hobson 2009, 169.
39 Hobson 2009, 45; Jansen 2011, 76.
40 Jansen 2011, 77.
41 Hobson 2009, 141; Wilson 2011, 147.
42 CIL IV 10606, 100. Hobson 2009, 99; Wilson 2011, 147.
43 Jansen 2011a, 173.
44 CIL IV 10619; Hobson 2009, 144.
45 CIL IV 5244.
46 Moormann 2011a, 61–3.
47 Hobson 2009, 169–70.
48 Jansen 2011a, 167; Hobson 2009, 111; 124.

49 Varone and Stefani 2009, 276.
50 CIL IV 6641.
51 Hobson 2009, 106–7.
52 Jansen 2011, 76.
53 Wilson 2011, 157.
54 Jackson 1988, 51; Wilson 2011, 103.
55 Martial, *Epigrams*, XII,48.
56 Seneca, *Epistles*, LXX,20.
57 Hobson 2009, 148.
58 Hobson 2009, 148.
59 Celsus, *On Medicine*, II,8,30–1.
60 Hobson 2009, 150.
61 Celsus, *On Medicine*, IV,24.
62 Camardo 2011, 90–1.
63 Hobson 2009, 89–93.
64 Croom 2011, 135.
65 Robinson and Rowan, forthcoming.
66 Camardo and Siano, forthcoming.
67 Garzia, forthcoming.
68 Wallace-Hadrill 2011, 276–8.

IX THE DEATH OF THE CITIES

1 Cooley and Cooley 2004, 29–31.
2 Vitruvius, *On Architecture*, II,6,2.
3 Strabo, *Geography*, V,4,8.
4 Diodorus of Sicily, *The Historical Library*, IV,21,5.
5 De Carolis and Patricelli 2003, 25–7.
6 Sigurdsson 2007, 44–6.
7 Meller and Dickmann 2011, 67–72.
8 Cinque et al. 2009, 267–74.
9 Wallace-Hadrill 2011, 22–5.
10 Seneca, *Natural Questions*, VI,1,2.
11 Seneca, *Natural Questions*, VI,1,10.
12 Seneca, *Natural Questions*, VI,31,1.
13 Petrone et al. 2002, 70–71.
14 Allison 2004, 19.
15 Seneca, *Natural Questions*, VI,31,2.
16 Suetonius, *Nero*, 20.
17 Pliny the Younger, *Letters*, VI,20.
18 Pliny the Younger, *Letters*, VI,20,3.
19 CIL X 1481.
20 Allison 2004, 179.
21 Allison 2004, 20–1, 197; Berry 2007, 242–3.
22 Wallace-Hadrill 1994, 98.
23 Wallace-Hadrill 1994, 117.
24 Berry 2007, 238.
25 Pesando 2009, 379.
26 Berry 2007, 237–9.
27 Pesando 2009, 382.
28 CIL X 1406.
29 Pesando 2011, 16–17.
30 Pesando 2009, 382.
31 De Caro 1992, 67–68, cat 2.1.
32 Wallace-Hadrill 2011, 36–7.
33 Berry 2007, 242–3.
34 Seneca, *Natural Questions*, VI,1,10.
35 Allison 2004,197.
36 Wallace-Hadrill 1994, 126–30.
37 Wallace-Hadrill 1994, 123.
38 Esposito 2009, passim.
39 Wallace-Hadrill 1994, 164–6.
40 Esposito 2009, 36–41.
41 Esposito 2009, 36.
42 Esposito 2009, 41–2.
43 Esposito 2009, 44; Allison 2004, 190–2.
44 Allison 2004, 191; Pesando and Guidobaldi 2006, 219–20.
45 Staub Gierow 2008, 98.
46 Allison 2004, 179.
47 Varone 2000, 319.
48 Allison 2004, 184–5.
49 Allison 2004, 192.
50 Pliny the Younger, *Letters*, VI,16; 20.
51 Borgongino and Stefani 2002, 177–83.
52 Borgongino and Stefani 2002, 178.
53 Cassius Dio, *Roman History*, XLVI,21.
54 Abdy 2013.
55 Borgongino and Stefani 2002, 190–2.
56 Borgongino and Stefani 2002, 193–4.

57 Pliny the Elder, *Natural History*, XVIII,319.
58 Borgongino 2006, 40.
59 Borgongino and Stefani 2002, 205.
60 Borgongino 2006, 23.
61 Borgongino 2006, 23, 36.
62 Borgongino 2006, 35.
63 Pliny the Younger, *Letters*, VI,16.
64 Pliny the Younger, *Letters*, VI,16,5.
65 Pliny the Younger, *Letters*, VI,16,5.
66 Pliny the Younger, *Letters*, VI,11.
67 Pliny the Younger, *Letters*, VI,20.
68 Pliny the Younger, *Letters*, VI,20,14.
69 Lazer 2009, 82–4.
70 Sigurdsson 2007, 52.
71 De Carolis and Patricelli 2003, 85–7.
72 Gurioli et al. 2002, 949.
73 Mastrolorenzo 2002, 29.
74 Mastrolorenzo 2002, 32.
75 Capasso 2001, 21.
76 Capasso 2001, 27.
77 Wallace-Hadrill 2011, 126–7.
78 http://sbanap.campaniabeniculturali.it/eventi-della-soprintendenza/il-padiglione-della-barca-di-ercolano.
79 Capasso 2001, 25.
80 Mastrolorenzo 2002, 35.
81 Petrone 2002, 41.
82 Capasso 2001, 30.
83 Petrone 2002, 42–3.
84 Capasso 2001, 33.
85 Wallace-Hadrill 2011, 36.
86 Lazer 2009, 76–8.
87 De Carolis 2004; Pagano 2004.
88 Bisel and Bisel 2002, 451.
89 Lazer 2009, 38–32; Wallace-Hadrill 2011, 130.
90 National Geographic Magazine, Vol. 165, no. 5, May 1984, 572–3; Bisel and Bisel 2002, 468; Capasso 2001, 249–58.
91 Capasso 2001, 32.
92 De Carolis 2004, 138.
93 Pagano 2004, 124.
94 Capasso 2001, 257.
95 Bisel and Bisel 2002, 468.
96 Capasso 2001, 43.
97 Capasso 2001, 30.
98 National Geographic Magazine, Vol. 165, no. 5, May 1984.
99 Bisel and Bisel 2002, 461–3.
100 De Carolis 2004, 147–8.
101 National Geographic Magazine May 1984, 595.
102 De Carolis 2004, 140.
103 Pagano 2004, 134.
104 Fergola 2004a, 152.
105 Fergola 2004a, 152–3.
106 Fergola 2004a, 154.
107 Fergola 2004a, 156.
108 Mastrolorenzo et al. 2010.
109 Walker and Bierbrier 1997, 41–4; 162–3.
110 d'Ambrosio and De Carolis 1997, 65.
111 Fergola 2004b, 165.
112 Lazer 2009, 261–3.
113 Mastrolorenzo et al. 2010.
114 Allison 2004, 192.
115 De Carolis and Patricelli 2003, 118–20.
116 Mastrolorenzo et al. 2010.
117 Mastrolorenzo et al. 2010; Cioni et al.2004.
118 Jacobelli 2008, 11.
119 De Carolis and Patricelli 2003, 121–3.
120 Dwyer 2010, 37.
121 Dwyer 2010, frontispiece.
122 Dwyer 2010, 48–52.
123 Lazer 2009, 251–3.
124 Dwyer 2010; Lazer 2009; Deem 2005.
125 Lazer 2009, 254–5.
126 Mastrolorenzo 2010.
127 Cassius Dio, *Roman History*, LXVI,23,4.
128 Pesando 2009, 378
129 Cassius Dio, *Roman History*, LXVI,24,1.
130 CIL IV 2311.
131 Pesando 2009, 384.

BIBLIOGRAPHY

Abdy, R.A. (2013) 'The last coin in Pompeii: a re-appraisal', *Numismatic Chronicle*, 172

Allison, P. (2004) *Pompeian Households: An Analysis of the Material Culture*, Los Angeles: Cotsen Institute of Archaeology at University of California, Los Angeles

Allison, P. (2006) *The Insula of the Menander at Pompeii. Volume III: The Finds, a Contextual Study*, Oxford: Clarendon Press

Amery, C. and Curran, B. (Jr) (2002) *The Lost World of Pompeii*, London: Frances Lincoln

Aßkamp, R., Brouwer, M., Christiansen, J. and Kenzler, H. (eds) (2007) *Luxus und Dekadenz. Römisches Leben am Golf von Neapel*, Mainz: Verlag Philipp von Zabern

Baraldi, P., Baraldi, C., Fagnano, C., Ferioli, V. and Gamberini, M.C. (2004) 'Ricerche sui contenuti dei balsamari di Oplontis', *Rivista di Studi Pompeiani* XV, 109–25

Baraldi, P., Fagnano C., Loschi Gittoni, A., Tassi, L. and Zannini, P. (2006) 'Vibrational spectra of some pigments from Pompeii', *Automata* 1, 49–64

Beard, M. (2008) *Pompeii: The Life of a Roman Town*, London: Profile Books

Beard, M. (2009) 'Pompeii: the art of reconstruction', *Annals of the Architectural Association School of Architecture* 58, 3–7

Beard, M. (2013) 'Dirty little secrets: changing displays of Pompeian "erotica"', in Gardner Coates, V.C., Lapatin, K. and Seydl, J.L., *The Last Days of Pompeii. Decadence, Apocalypse, Resurrection*, Los Angeles: J. Paul Getty Museum, 60–9

Beretta, M. and Di Pasquale, G. (2004) *Vitrum: Il vetro fra arte e scienza nel mondo romano*, Florence–Milan: Giunti

Bergmann, B. (2007) 'Seeing women in the Villa of the Mysteries', in Gardner Coates, V.C. and Seydl, J.L., *Antiquity Recovered*, Los Angeles: J. Paul Getty Museum, 231–69

Bernstein, F. (1988) 'Pompeian women and the programmata', in Curtis, R.I. (ed.), *Studia Pompeiana & Classica in Honor of Wilhelmina F. Jashemski*, New York: Orpheus, 1–18 SEE CURTIS 1988

Bernstein, F. (2007) 'Pompeian women', in Dobbins, J.J. and Foss, P.W., *The World of Pompeii*, New York: Routledge, 526–37

Berry, J. (2007) *The Complete Pompeii*, London: Thames & Hudson

Berry, J. (ed.) (1998) *Unpeeling Pompeii*, Milan: Electa

Bisel, S.C. and Bisel, J.F. (2002) 'Health and nutrition at Herculaneum: an examination of human skeletal remains', in Jashemski, W.F. and Meyer, F.G. (eds), *The Natural History of Pompeii*, Cambridge: CUP, 451–75

Bonfante, L. (2003) *Etruscan Dress*, Baltimore: Johns Hopkins University Press

Bonifacio, G. (2004) 'L'abbigliamento', in Stefani, G. (ed.), *Moda, costume e bellezza a Pompei e dintorni*, Herculaneum: Buona Stampa, 5–24

Borgongino, M. (2006) 'Archeobotanica: Reperti vegetali da Pompei e dal territorio vesuviano', *Studi della Soprintendenza Archeologica di Pompei* 16, Rome: L'Erma di Bretschneider

Borgongino, M. and Stefani, G. (2002) 'Intorno all data dell'eruzione del 79 d.C. *Rivista di Studi Pompeiani* XII–XIII, 177–215

Borriello, M., d'Ambrosio, A., De Caro, S. and Guzzo, P.G. (eds) (1996) *Pompei: Abitare sotto il Vesuvio*, Ferrara: Ferrara Arte

Bragantini, I. and Sampaolo, V. (2009) *La Pittura Pompeiana*, Naples: Electa

Brennan, B. (2011) *Herculaneum: A Sourcebook*, Sydney: Ancient History Seminars

Camardo, D. (2011) 'Case study: Ercolano: La eicostruzione dei sistemi Fognari', in Koloski-Ostrow, A.O., Jansen, G.C.M. and Moormann, E.M. (eds), *Roman Toilets: Their Archaeology and Cultural History*, BABesch Supplement 19, Leiden: Peeters, 90–3

Camardo, D. and Notomista, M. (forthcoming) *Le latrine di Ercolano*

Camardo, D. and Siano, S. (forthcoming) *La 'fogna' del Cardo V, Ercolano. Studio dei materiali*, Herculaneum Conservation Project

Camardo, D., Esposito, D., Imperatore, C., Notomista, M., Court, S. and Wallace-Hadrill, A. (2010) 'Archaeological results from the Herculaneum Conservation Project in 2009', *Papers of the British School at Rome* 78, 318–22

Camardo, D., Notomista, M. and Court, S. (2010) 'Raising the roof', *Current World Archaeology* 42, 43–5

Camodeca, G. (2008) 'La popolazione degli ultimo decennia di Ercolano', in Guidobaldi, M.P. (ed.), *Ercolano: Tre Secoli di Scoperte*, exhibition catalogue, Naples: Electa, 87–103

Camodeca, G. (2009) 'Gli archive private di tabulae ceratae e di papyri documentary a Pompei ed Ercolano: case ambient e modalità di conservazione', *Vesuviana* 1, 17–42

Capasso, L. (2001) *I Fuggiaschi di Ercolano*, Rome: L'Erma di Bretschneider

Carroll, M. (2003) *Earthly Paradises: Ancient Gardens in History and Archaeology*, Los Angeles: Getty Publications

Cassani, S. (ed.) (2001) *Pompeii. Images from the Buried Cities*, Naples: Electa

Castrén, P. (2008) 'Notizie su Marco Lucrezio', in Castrén, P. (ed.), *Domus Pompeiana. Una Casa a Pompei*, Helsinki: Otava, 26–8

Charles-Laforge, M.-O. (2007) 'Imagines Maiorum et portraits d'ancêtres à Pompéi', *Contributi di Archeologia Vesuviana* III, Rome: L'Erma di Bretschneider, 158–69

Ciarallo, A. (2012) *Gli spazi Verdi dell'antica Pompei*, Rome: Aracne

Ciarallo, A. (2007) 'A Roma e in provincia: i giardini dell'impero', in Di Pasquale, G. and Paolucci, F., *Il giardino antico da Babilonia a Roma*, Livorno: Sillabe, 166–77

Ciarallo, A., De Carolis, E. and Di Pasquale, G. (eds) (1999) *Homo Faber. Natura, scienza e tecnica nell'antica Pompei*, Milan: Electa

Cinque, A., Irollo, G. and Camardo, D. (2009) 'Antiche attivita estrattive e cicli bradisismici sulla costa dell'antica Herculaneum: Percorsi, esisti e prospettive di una ricerca geoarcheologica', in Corallini, A. (ed.), *Vesuviana. Archeologia e Confronto. Atti del Convegno Internazionale. Bologna 14–16 Gennaio, 2008*, Bologna: Ante Quem, 261–76

Cioni, R., Gurioli, L., Lanza, R. and Zanella, E. (2004) 'Temperatures of the AD 79 pyroclastic density current deposits (Vesuvius, Italy), *Journal of Geophysical Research* 109

Clarke, J.R. (2003) *Art in the Lives of Ordinary Romans*, London: University of California Press

Clarke, J.R. (2008) *Looking at Lovemaking*, California: University of California Press

Coarelli, F. (ed.) (2002) *Pompeii*. Translated by Patricia A. Cockram, New York: Riverside Book Company

Coarelli, F. and Pesando, F. (2011) 'The urban development of north-west Pompeii: the archaic period to the 3rd century BC', in Ellis, S.J.R. (ed.), *The Making of Pompeii*, JRA Supplement Series 85, 37–58

Cooley, A. and Cooley, M., (2004) *Pompeii. A Sourcebook*, London: Routledge

Crawford, M.H. *et al.* (eds) (2011) *Imagines Italicae*, London Institute of Classical Studies, University of London

Croom, A. (2011) *Running the Roman Home*, Stroud: The History Press Ltd

Cubberley, A.L., Lloyd, J.A., Roberts, P.C. (9188) 'Testa and clibani: the baking covers of classical Italy', *Papers of the British School at Rome* 61, 98–119

Curtis, R.I. (1979) 'The Garum Shop of Pompeii (I.12.8)', *Cronache Pompeiane* V, 5–23

Curtis, R.I. (1988) 'A. Umbricius Scaurus of Pompeii', in Curtis, R.I. (ed.), *Studia Pompeiana et Classica in Honour of Wilhelmina F. Jashemski*, New Rochelle, NY, 19–50

d'Ambrosio, A. (2001) *La Bellezza Femminile a Pompei*, Rome: L'Erma di Bretschneider

d'Ambrosio, A. (1996) 'Thermopolio e casa di L. Vetuzio Placido', in *Pompei: Abitare sotto il Vesuvio*, exhibition catalogue, Ferrara: Ferrara Arte, 108–13

d'Ambrosio, A. and Borriello, M. (2001) *Arule e bruciaprofumi fittili da Pompei*, Naples: Electa

d'Ambrosio, A. and De Carolis, E. (1997) *I monili dall'area Vesuviana*, Rome: L'Erma di Bretschneider

d'Ambrosio, A., Guzzo, P.G. and Mastroroberto, M. (2004) *Storie da un'eruzione: Pompei, Ercolano, Oplontis*, Milan: Electa

Darmon, J.-P. and Manière-Lévêque, A.-M. (2003), 'La mosaïque de la pièce 13', 87–99, in Abadie-Reynal, C. and Darmon, J.-P, 'La maison e la mosaïque des Synaristôsai', 79–99, *Zeugma: Interim Reports*, JRA Supplement 51

De Caro, S. (1992) *Alla ricerca di iside*, Rome: Arti

De Carolis, E. (2007) *Il mobile a Pompei ed Ercolano*, Rome: L'Erma di Bretschneider

De Carolis, E. (2001) 'The house of the Cryptoporticus', in Cassani, S. (ed.), *Pompeii. Images from the Buried Cities*, Naples: Electa, 59–62

De Carolis, E. (2004) 'La Marina di Ercolano e lo scavo dei fornici 7 & 8', *Storie da un'Eruzione*, exhibition catalogue, Milan: Electa, 137–49

De Carolis, E. (2006) 'Casa dei quadretti teatrali (I,6,11)', in Guzzo, P.G. (ed.), *Argenti a Pompei*, exhibition catalogue, Milan: Electa, 191–223

De Carolis, E. and Patricelli, G. (2003) *Vesuvio 79 d.C. La distruzione di Pompei ed Ercolano*, Roma: L'Erma di Bretschneider

Deem, J.M. (2005) *Bodies from the Ash*, Boston: Houghton Mifflin Company

De Felice, J. (2007) 'Inns and taverns', in Dobbins, J.J. and Foss, P.W., *The World of Pompeii*, New York: Routledge, 474–82

de Ligt, L. and Garnsey, P. (2012) 'The album of Herculaneum and a model of the town's demography', *Journal of Roman Archaeology* 25, 69–94

Del Mastro, G. (2003) 'I papiri trovati a Pompeii', *Studii Pompeiani* XIV, 374–8

De Simone, G.F. (2011) 'Con Dioniso fra I vigneti del vaporifero Vesuvio', in *Cronache Ercolanesi* 41, 289–310

d'Hancarville, P. (1766–7) *Antiquités etrusques, grecques et romaines: Tirées du cabinet du M. William Hamilton, envoyé extraordinaire de. S.M. Britanique en cour de Naples*, 4 vols, Naples

Dixon, S. (1992) *The Roman Family*, Maryland: John Hopkins University

Dunbabin, K.M. (1999) *Mosaics of the Greek and Roman World*, Cambridge: CUP

Dwyer, E. (2010) *Pompeii's Living Statues*, Ann Arbor: University of Michigan Press

Esposito, D. (2009) *Le officine pittoriche di IV stile a Pompeii*, Rome: L'Erma di Bretschneider

Esposito, D. (2006) 'Casa di Umbricius Scaurus'I and II', in Aoyagi, M. and Pappalardo, U., *Pompei (Regiones VI–VII) Insula Occidentalis* Vol.1, Naples: Valtrend Editore, 505–42

Faas, P. (2003) *Around the Roman Table*, New York: Palgrave Macmillan

Fergola, L. (2004a) 'Oplontis', in *Storie da un'Eruzione*, exhibition catalogue, Milan: Electa, 152–7

Fergola, L. (2004b) 'Le Vittime', in *Storie da un'Eruzione*, exhibition catalogue, Milan: Electa, 164–71

Franklin, J.L. (2007) 'Epigraphy and society', in Dobbins, J.J. and Foss, P.W., *The World of Pompeii*, New York: Routledge, 518–25

Garcia y Garcia, L. (2005) *Pupils, Teachers and Schools in Pompeii*, Rome: Bardi Editore

Garcia y Garcia, L. (2006) *Donni di guerra a Pompeii*, Rome: L'Erma di Bretschneider

Garcia y Garcia, L. (ed.) (2007) *Perfumes, Unguents and Hairstyles in Pompeii*, Rome: Bardi Editore

Gardner, J. (1993) *Being a Roman Citizen*, London: Routledge

Garzia, D. (forthcoming) 'Le monete rinvenute nel deposito organico della fogna dell'Insula Orientalis II', in Camardo, D. and Siano, S., *La 'fogna' del Cardo V, Ercolano. Studio dei materiali*

Gell, W. (1832) *Pompeiana. The Topography of Edifices and Ornaments of Pompeii*, London: Jennings and Chaplin

Gell, W. and Gandy, J.P. (1817–18) *Pompeiana. The Topography of Edifices and Ornaments of Pompeii*, 2 vols, London: Rodwell and Martin

Gentili, G. (ed.) (2008) *Giulio Cesare: l'uomo, le imprese, il mito*, Milan: Silvana Editoriale

George, M. (2007) 'The lives of slaves', in Dobbins, J.J. and Foss, P.W., *The World of Pompeii*, London: Routledge, 538–49

Giove, T. (2006) 'Casa dell'argenteria (VI,7,20–22)', in Guzzo, P.G. (ed.), *Argenti a Pompei*, Milan: Electa, 114–12

Grocock, C. and Grainger, S. (2006) *Apicius*, London: Prospect

Guidobaldi, M.P. (2006) *Ercolano: guida agli scavi*, Naples: Electa

Guidobaldi, M.P. (ed.) (2008) *Ercolano: Tre Secoli di Scoperte*, exhibition catalogue, Naples: Electa

Guidobaldi, M.P. (2010) 'Arredi di lusso in legno e avorio da Ercolano', *LANX* 6, 63–99

Guidobaldi, M.P. and Esposito, D. (2012) *Ercolano. Colori da una citta sepolta*, Verona: Arsenale Editrice

Guidobaldi, M.P. and Guzzo, P.G. (2010) 'Un rilievo neoattico da Ercolano', *Cronache Ercolanesi* 40, 251–60

Guidobaldi, M.P., Esposito, D. and Formisano, E. (2009) 'L'Insula 1, l'insula nord- occidentale e la Villa dei Papiri di Ercolano: una sintesi delle conoscenze alla luce delle recenti indagini archeologiche, con una premessa da Pietro Giovanni Guzzo', *Vesuviana* 1, 43–180

Gurioli, L., Cionti, R., Sbrana, A. and Zanella, E. (2002) 'Transport and deposition of pyroclastic density currents over an inhabited area: the deposits of the AD 79 eruption of Vesuvius at Herculaneum, Italy', *Sedimentology* 49, 929–53

Guzzo, P.G. (ed.) (2006) *Argenti a Pompei*, Milan: Electa

Guzzo, P.G. (2011) 'The origins and development of Pompeii: the state of our understanding and some working hypotheses', in Ellis, S.J.R. (ed.), *The Making of Pompeii*, JRA Supplement Series 85, 11–18

Guzzo, P.G. and Guidobaldi, M.P. (2008) *Nuove ricerche archeologiche nell'area Vesuviana (scavi 2003–2006)*, Rome: L'Erma di Bretschneider

Guzzo, P.G. and Ussani, V.S. (2011) 'Casti Amanti? Pistrina, triclinia, halicariae a Pompei' *Vesuviana* 3, 53–66

Hales, S. (2003) *The Roman House and Social Identity*, Cambridge: CUP

Harden, D.B., Hellenkemper, H., Painter, K. and Whitehouse, D. (1987) *Glass of the Caesars*, Milan: Olivetti

Hardy, C., Vigne, J.-D., Cesañe, D., Dennebouy, N., Mounolou, J.-C. and Monnerot, M. (1994) 'Origin of European rabbit (oryctolagus cuniculus) in a Mediterranean island', *Journal of Evolutionary Biology* 7, 217–26

Hartnett, J. (2008) '*Si quis hic sederit*: streetside benches and urban society in Pompeii', *American Journal of Archaeology* 112.1, 91–119

Hobson, B. (2009) *Latrinae et Fornicae: Toilets in the Roman World*, London: Duckworth

Holleran, C. (2012) *Shopping in Ancient Rome*, Oxford: OUP

Jacobelli, L. (2008) 'Pompeii tra mito e turismo', in Jacobelli, L. (ed.), *Pompei La Costruzione di un Mito*, Rome: Bardi Editore, 9–20

Jansen, G.C.M. (2011) 'Waste disposal for toilets', in Koloski-Ostrow, A.O., Jansen, G.C.M. and Moormann, E.M. (eds), *Roman Toilets: Their Archaeology and Cultural History*, BABesch Supplement 19, Leiden: Peeters, 76–8

Jansen, G.C.M. (2011a) 'Interpreting images and epigraphic testimony', in Koloski-Ostrow, A.O., Jansen, G.C.M., and Moormann, E.M. (eds), *Roman Toilets: Their Archaeology and Cultural History*, BABesch Supplement 19, Leiden: Peeters, 165–81

Jansen, G.C.M. (2011b) 'Water supply into the city and to the toilets in the town and houses', in Koloski-Ostrow, A.O., Jansen, G.C.M., and Moormann, E.M. (eds), *Roman Toilets: Their Archaeology and Cultural History*, BABesch Supplement 19, Leiden: Peeters, 71–3

Jashemski, W.F. (2007) 'Gardens', in Dobbins, J.J. and Foss, P.W., *The World of Pompeii*, New York: Routledge 487–98

Jashemski, W.F. and Meyer, F.G. (2002) *The Natural History of Pompeii*, Cambridge: CUP

Jenkins, I. (1996) 'Contemporary minds: Sir William Hamilton's affair with antiquity', in Jenkins, I. and Sloan, K., *Vases and Volcanoes*, London: British Museum Press, 40–64

Jongman, W. (1991) *The Economy and Society of Pompeii*, Amsterdam: J.C. Gieben

Jongman, W. (2007) 'Pompeian economy and society between past and present', in Dobbins, J.J. and Foss, P.W. (2007) *The World of Pompeii*, New York: Routledge, 499–517

Kastenmeier, P. (2007) *I luoghi del lavoro domestic nella casa pompeiana*, Rome: L'Erma di Bretschneider

Keenan-Jones, D., Hellstron, J. and Drysdale, R. (2011) 'Lead contamination in the drinking water of Pompeii', in Poehler, E., Flohr, M. and Cole, K., *Pompeii: Art, Industry and Infrastructure*, Oxford: Oxbow, 131–48

Koloski-Ostrow, A.O. (2011) 'Design and architecture of toilets', in Koloski-Ostrow, A.O., Jansen, G.C.M., and Moormann, E.M. (eds), *Roman Toilets: Their Archaeology and Cultural History*, BABesch Supplement 19, Leiden: Peeters, 51–5

Kuivalainen, I. (2008) 'Le sculture del giardino', in Castrén, P. (ed.), *Domus Pompeiana. Una Casa a Pompei*, Helsinki: Otava, 127–37

La Rocca, E., de Vos, M. and de Vos, A. (1976) *Guida Archeologica di Pompei*, Verona: Arnoldo Mondadori Editore

La Rocca, E., Ensoli, S., Totorella, S., Papini, M. (eds) (2009) *Roma: la pittura di un impero*, Rome: Skira

Laurence, R. (2007) *Roman Pompeii: Space and Society*, London: Routledge

Lazer, E. (2009) *Resurrecting Pompeii*, London: Routledge

Le Collezioni del Museo Nazionale di Napoli I, 1 (1986), Rome: De Luca Editore

Le Collezioni del Museo Nazionale di Napoli I, 2 (1989), Rome: De Luca Edizioni d'Arte

Levin-Richardson, S. (2011) 'Modern tourists, ancient sexualities', in Hales, S. and Paul, J., *Pompeii in the Public Imagination from its Rediscovery to Today*, Oxford: OUP, 316–30

Ling, R. (1991) *Roman Painting*, Cambridge: CUP

Lo Sardo, E. (2005) *Eureka! Il genio degli antichi*, Naples: Electa

Macaulay-Lewis, E. (2006) 'The role of Ollae Perforatae in understanding horticulture, planting techniques, garden design and plant trade in the Roman world', in Morel, J.P., Juan, J.T. and Matamala, J.C. (eds) *The Archaeology of Crop Fields and Gardens*, Bari: Edipuglia, 207–19

Maiuri, A. (1927) 'Pompei. Relazione sui lavori di scavo dal marzo 1924 al marzo 1926', *Notizie degli Scavi di Antichità*, 52, 3–117

Mastrolorenzo, G. (2002) 'Effettivulcanici e conseguenze sull'ambiente', in Petrone, P.P. and Fedele, F. (eds), *Vesuvio 79 A.D. Vita e morte ad Ercolano*, Naples: Fridericiana Editrice Universitaria, 29–34

Mastrolorenzo, G., Petrone, P.P., Pappalardo, L. and Guarino, F.M. (2010) 'Lethal thermal impact at periphery of pyroclastic surges: evidences at Pompeii', *PLOS ONE*, online journal

Mastroroberto, M. (2006) 'Il tesoro di Moregine', in Guzzo, P.G. (ed.), *Argenti a Pompei*, Milan: Electa, 224–37

Mattusch, C.C. (2008) *Pompeii and the Roman Villa*, exhibition catalogue, Washington: National Gallery of Art, 286–8

Mau, A. (1882) *Geschichte der dekorativen Wandmalerei in Pompeji*, Berlin: G. Reimer

Maulucci Vivolo, F.P. (1993) *Pompei. I graffiti figurati*, Foggia: Bastoggi

Melini, R. (2008) *Suoni sotto le ceneri: la musica nell'antica area Vesuviana*, Pompeii: Flavius

Meller, H. and Dickmann, J.-A. (eds) (2011) *Pompeji – Nola – Herculaneum: Katastrophen am Vesuv*, exhibition catalogue, Munich: Hirmer

Mols, S.T.A.M. (1999) *Wooden Furniture in Herculaneum. Form, Technique and Function*, Amsterdam: J.C. Gieben

Monteix, N. (2007) '*Cauponae, popinae* et "*thermopolia*", de la norme littéraire et historiographique à la réalité pompéienne', in *Contributi di Archeologia Vesuviana III*, Rome: L'Erma di Bretshneider, 117–28

Moormann, E.M. (2011) 'Christians and Jews at Pompeii in late nineteenth-century fiction', in Hales, S., *Pompeii in the Public Imagination from its Rediscovery to Today*, Oxford: OUP, 171–84

Moorman, E.M. (2011a) 'Decorations on Roman toilets', in Koloski-Ostrow, A.O., Jansen, G.C.M., and Moormann, E.M. (eds), *Roman Toilets: Their Archaeology and Cultural History*, BABesch Supplement 19, Leiden: Peeters, 55–63

Mouritsen, H. (1997) 'Mobility and social change in Italian towns during the Principate', in Parkins, H., *Roman Urbanism: Beyond the Consumer City*, London: Routledge, 59–82

Nava, M.L., Paris, R. and Friggeri, R. (eds) (2007) *Rosso Pompeiano: La decorazione pittorica nelle collezioni del Museo di Napoli e a Pompei*, exhibition catalogue, Milan: Electa

Nitti, P., De Caro, S., Sampaolo, V. and Varone, A. (eds) (2011) *Pompéi. Un art de vivre*, Paris: Editions Gallimard

Packer, J. (1978) 'Inns at Pompeii: a short survey', *Cronache Pompeiane* IV, 5–

Pagano, M. (2004) 'Gli scheletri dei fuggiaschi: L'indagine archeologica dale prime scoperte alle indagini interdisciplinary sui fornaci 4 e 12', *Storie da un'Eruzione*, exhibition catalogue, Milan: Electa, 124–36

Pagano, M. and Prisciandaro, R. (2006) *Studio sulle provenienze degli oggetti rinvenuti negli scavi borbonici del regno di Napoli*, 2 vols, Naples: Nicola Longobardi Editore

Pappalardo, U. (2009) *The Splendor of Roman Wall Painting*, Los Angeles: J. Paul Getty Museum

Pesando, F. (2009) 'Prima della catastrofe: Vespasiano e le città vesuviane', in Coarelli, F. (ed), *Divus Vespasianus*, exhibition catalogue, Milan: Electa, 378–85

Pesando, F. (2011) 'Ruinae et Parietinae Pompeianae. Distruzioni e abbandoni a Pompei all'epoca dell'eruzione', *Vesuviana* 3, 9–30

Pesando, F. and Guidobaldi, M.-P. (2006) *Pompei, Oplontis, Ercolano, Stabiae*, Rome: Laterza

Petersen, L.H. (2006) *The Freedman in Roman Art and Art History*, Cambridge: CUP

Petrone, P.P. (2002) 'Le vittime dell'eruzione', in Petrone, P.P. and Fedele, F. (eds) *Vesuvio 79 A.D. Vita e morte ad Ercolano*, Naples: Fridericiana Editrice Universitaria, 35–45

Petrone, P.P., Coppa, A. and Fattore, L. (2002) 'La popolazione di Ercolano', in Petrone, P.P. and Fedele, F. (eds), *Vesuvio 79 A.D. Vita e morte ad Ercolano*, Naples: Fridericiana Editrice Universitaria, 67–73

Piggott J. (2004), *Palace of the People: the Crystal Palace at Sydenham 1854–1936*, Wisconsin: University of Wisconsin Press

Pirson, F. (2007) 'Shops and industries', in Dobbins, J.J. and Foss, P.W., *The World of Pompeii*, New York: Routledge, 457–73

Poehler, E. (2006) 'The circulation of traffic in Pompeii's Regio VI', *Journal of Roman Archaeology* 19, 53–74

Poehler, E. (2012) 'The drainage system at Pompeii: mechanisms, operation and design', *Journal of Roman Archaeology* 25, 95–120

Prayon, E. (2009) 'The atrium as Italo-Etruscan architectural concept and as societal form', in Swaddling, J. and Perkins, P. (eds), *Etruscan by Definition: The Cultural, Regional and Personal Identity of the Etruscans*, London, British Museum, 60–3

Provenzale, V. (2008) *Echi di propaganda imperiale in scene di coppia a Pompeii*, Rome: Quasar

Rediscovering Pompeii (1992), Ministero per I Beni Culturali e Ambientali & Soprintendenza Archeologica di Pompei, Rome: L'Erma di Bretschneider

Riggsby, A. (1997) '"Public" and "private" in Roman culture: the case of the cubiculum', *Journal of Roman Archaeology* 10, 36–56

Roberts, P.C. (1997) 'Mass-production of Roman finewares', in Freestone, I. and Gainster, D., *Pottery in the Making*, London: British Museum Press, 188–93

Robinson, M. (2002) 'Domestic burnt offerings and sacrifices at roman and pre Roman Pompeii, Italy', *Vegetation History and Archaeobotany* 11, 93–9

Robinson, M. (2008) 'Evidence for garden cultivation and the use of bedding-out plants in the peristyle garden of the House of the Greek Epigrams (V 1, 18i) at Pompeii', *Opuscula Romana* 31–32 (2006–2007), 155–9

Robinson, M. and Rowan, E. (forthcoming) 'Roman food remains in archaeology and the contents of a Roman sewer at Herculaneum', in Wilkins, J. and Nadeau, R. (eds), *A Companion to Food in the Ancient World*, Wiley-Blackwell

Roller, M.B. (2006) *Dining Posture in Ancient Rome*, Princeton: Princeton University Press

St Clair, W. and Bautz, A. (2012) 'Imperial decadence: the making of myths in Edward Bulwer-Lytton's *The Last Days of Pompeii*', *Victorian Literature and Culture* 40, 359–96

Schnurr, H. (1957) 'The age of Petronius Arbiter', PhD Thesis, University of New York

Sider, D. (2005) *The Library of the Villa Dei Papiri at Herculaneum*, Los Angeles: Getty Publications

Sigurdsson, H. (2007) 'The environmental and geomorphological context', in Dobbins, J.J. and Foss, P.W., *The World of Pompeii*, New York: Routledge, 43–62

Staub Gierow, M. (2008) 'Casa degli epigrammi Greci V,1,18,11–12', in Guzzo, P.G. and Guidobaldi, M.P., *Nuove ricerche archeologiche nell'area Vesuviana (scavi 2003–2006)*, Rome: L'Erma di Bretschneider, 93–102

Stefani, G. (2006) 'I contenitori di alimenti di origine vegetale', in Borgongino, M., 'Archeobotanica: Reperti vegetali da Pompei e dal territorio vesuviano', *Studi della Soprintendenza archeologica di Pompei* 16, Rome: L'Erma di Bretschneider, 157–69

Stefani (2006a) 'La villa del tesoro delle argentarie di Boscoreale', in Guzzo, P.G. (ed.), *Argenti a Pompei*, Milan: Electa, 180–90

Stefani, G. (2006b) 'Casa del Menandro (I,10)', in Guzzo, P.G. (ed.), *Argenti a Pompei*, Milan: Electa, 191–223

Stefani, G. (ed.) (2002) *Uomo e ambiente nel territorio vesuviano. Guida all'Antiquarium di Boscoreale*, Ercolano: Marius

Stefani, G. (ed.) (2005) *Cibi e sapori a Pompei e dintorni*, Pompeii: Flavius

Van Andringa, W. (2009) *Quotidien des dieux et des hommes: la vie religieuse dans les cités du Vésuve à l'époque romaine*, Rome: École Française de Rome

Varone, A. (2000) *Pompei, i misteri di una città sepolta*, Rome: Newton Compton

Varone, A. (2002) *Erotica Pompeiana*, Rome: L'Erma di Bretschneider

Varone, A. and Stefani, G. (2009) 'Titulorum Pictorum Pompeianorum', in *Studi della Soprintendenza archeologica di Pompei* 29, Rome: L'Erma di Bretschneider

Walker, S. (1991) *Roman Art*, London: British Museum Press

Walker, S. and Bierbrier, M. (1997) *Ancient Faces: Mummy Portraits from Ancient Egypt*, London: British Museum Press

Wallace-Hadrill, A. (1994) *Houses and Society in Pompeii and Herculaneum*, Princeton: Princeton University Press

Wallace-Hadrill, A. (2011) *Herculaneum: Past and Future*, London: Francis Lincoln Limited

Wallace-Hadrill, A. (2011a) 'The monumental centre of Herculaneum: in search of the identities of the public buildings', *Journal of Roman Archaeology* 24, 121–60

Wallace-Hadrill, A (2011b) 'Ruins and forgetfulness: the case of Herculaneum', in Hales, S. and Paul, J., *Pompeii in the Public Imagination*, Oxford: OUP, 367–79

Ward-Perkins, J. and Claridge, A. (1976) *Pompeii AD 79*, Bristol: Imperial Tobacco Limited

Weeber, K.-W. (2011) *Fièvre électorale à Pompéi*, Paris: Les Belles Lettres

Welch, K.E. (2007) 'Pompeian men and women in portrait sculpture', in Dobbins, J.J. and Foss, P.W., *The World of Pompeii*, New York: Routledge, 550–84

Wilson, A. (2011) 'The economy of ordure', in Koloski-Ostrow, A.O., Jansen, G.C.M., and Moormann, E.M. (eds), *Roman Toilets: Their Archaeology and Cultural History*, BABesch Supplement 19, Leiden: Peeters, 147–56

Wilson, A. (2011A) 'Urination and defecation Roman style', in Jansen, G.C.M., Kolowski-Ostrow A.O. and Moormann, E.M., *Roman Toilets: Their Archaeology and History*, BaBesch Supplement 19, Leiden: Peeters, 95–7

Zimmermann, V. (2008) *Excavating Victorians*, Albany: State University of New York Press

ABBREVIATIONS

CIL = *Corpus Inscriptionum Latinarum*
PAH = *Pompeianorum Antiquitatum Historia*

ANCIENT AUTHORS

Apicius, *On Cookery*
Cassius Dio, *Roman History*
Cato, *On Agriculture*
Celsus, *On Medicine*
Cicero, *Against Catiline*
Cicero, *Against Piso*
Cicero, *Letters to Atticus*
Cicero, *On Duties*
Columella, *On Country Life*
Cornelius Nepos, *Lives of Eminent Commanders*
Diodorus of Sicily, *The Historical Library*
Dionysius of Halicarnassus, *Roman Antiquities*
Dioscorides, *On Medical Substances*
Frontinus, *Stratagems*
Horace, *Epistles*
Horace, *Odes*
Horace, *Satires*
Isidore, *Etymologies*
Juvenal, *Satires*
Livy, *The History of Rome*
Martial, *Epigrams*
Orosius, *Histories*
Ovid, *Cosmetics for the Female Face*
Ovid, *The Art of Loving*
Ovid, *The Loves*
Petronius, *Satyricon*
Plautus, *The Little Carthaginian*
Pliny the Elder, *Natural History*
Pliny the Younger, *Letters*
Plutarch, *Lives*
Seneca, *Dialogues*
Seneca, *Epistles*
Seneca, *Natural Questions*
Statius, *Silvae*
Strabo, *Geography*
Suetonius, *The Twelve Caesars*
Tacitus, *Annals*
Varro, *On Agriculture*
Varro, *On the Latin Language*
Vitruvius, *On Architecture*

LIST OF EXHIBITS

The following objects feature in the exhibition *Life and death in Pompeii and Herculaneum*. Details correct at the time of going to press. 'FIG.' at the end of each entry denotes objects illustrated in this book.

Note on the dating of objects
The majority of the objects in the exhibition were produced during the 1st century AD. In some cases objects, such as statues and frescoes, can be dated more closely. Some, such as foodstuffs, liquids and their containers and are dated individually.

Bronze statue of Lucius Mammius Maximus
AD 41–54
H. 227 cm, W. 105 cm
Herculaneum, Theatre
Naples, MANN 5591
Selected literature: Ward-Perkins and Claridge (1976), no. 46; Guidobaldi (2008), p. 259, no. 40
FIG. 19

Fresco of lovers drinking
AD 50–79
H. 66 cm, W. 66 cm
Herculaneum
Naples, MANN 9024
Selected literature: *Le Collezioni del Museo Nazionale di Napoli* I,1 (1986), p. 170, no. 340; Nava et al. (2007), p. 140
FIG. 266

Carbonized wooden table
H. 60 cm
Herculaneum, House of the Mosaic Atrium (IV,1-2)
Herculaneum, SAP 81601
Selected literature: Mols (1999), no. 14
FIG. 265

Plaster cast of a dog
Modern
H. 50 cm
Pompeii, House of Orpheus (VI,14,20)
Pompeii, SAP
Selected literature: Ward-Perkins and Claridge (1976), no. 21; Stefani (ed.) (2002), p. 47
FIG. 389

Bronze statue of the Empress Livia
AD 41–54
H. 214 cm, W. 100 cm
Herculaneum, Theatre
Naples, MANN 5589
Selected literature: *Le Collezioni del Museo Nazionale di Napoli* I,2 (1989), p. 120, no. 119; Guidobaldi (2008), p. 258, no. 37
FIG. 22

Marble statue of the priestess Eumachia
c. AD 2
H. 194 cm
Pompeii, Building of Eumachia
Naples, MANN 6232
Selected literature: *Le Collezioni del Museo Nazionale di Napoli* I,2 (1989), p. 120, no. 116; Meller and Dickmann (2011), pp. 149–50
FIG. 23

Marble inscription written in Oscan
200–150 BC
H. 31 cm, W. 45 cm
Pompeii, Porta Nola
The British Museum, 1867,0508.76
Selected literature: Ward-Perkins and Claridge (1976) no. 2; Crawford et al. (2011), pp. 62830
FIG. 11

Bronze inscription for the statue of Lucius Mammius Maximus
AD 41–54
L(ucio) MAMMIO MAXIMO AUGUSTALI MUNICIPES ET INCOLAE AERE CONLATO
H. 74 cm, W. 50 cm
Herculaneum, Theatre
Naples, MANN 3748
Selected literature: CIL X, 1452; Ward-Perkins and Claridge (1976), no. 47; Guidobaldi (2008), p. 259, no. 41
FIG. 20

Fragment of a marble panel with citizen lists
c. AD 60–79
H. 41 cm, W. 72 cm
Herculaneum, Decumanus Maximus
Herculaneum, SAP 79062
Selected literature: CIL X, 14031; Guidobaldi (2008), pp. 96–7
FIG. 21

Painted electoral notice
June AD 79
H. 70 cm, W. 103 cm
Pompeii, Villa of Cicero
Naples, MANN 4714
Selected literature: Varone and Stefani (2009), p. 515
FIG. 15

Marble plaque marking property boundaries
H. 15 cm, L. 33 cm, W. 2 cm
Herculaneum, Cardo IV superiore
Herculaneum, SAP 3465/78762
Selected literature: Wallace-Hadrill (2011), pp. 215–17
FIG. 24

Bronze wind-chime (*tintinnabulum*) with a hanging lamp
H. 21 cm, W. 18 cm
Pompeii, workshop of Verus (I,6,3)
Pompeii, SAP 1260
Selected literature: La Rocca et al. (1976), p. 205
FIG. 41

Fresco showing tavern life
c. AD 50–79
H. 50 cm, W. 205 cm
Pompeii, Caupona of Salvius (VI,14,35–36)
Naples, MANN 111482
Selected literature: CIL IV 3494; Ward-Perkins and Claridge (1976), no. 227; d'Ambrosio et al. (2004), pp. 27–23
FIGS 57–8

Bronze wine jug
H. 26 cm, W. 25 cm
Vesuvian area
Naples, MANN 68927
FIG. 65

Terracotta amphora with painted inscription (*dipinto*)
I SEXT
H. 64 cm, W. 27 cm
Vesuvian area
Pompeii, SAP 31824
FIG. 66

Fragment of a terracotta amphora with painted inscription (*dipinto*)
POMPEII ALBUCIAE TYCHE
H. 18 cm, W. 25 cm
Pompeii, shop near the Vesuvius Gate
Pompeii, SAP 13915
FIG. 67

Fragment of the rim and neck of a terracotta amphora with painted inscription (*dipinto*)
35 BC
FAL L VER
H. 17 cm
Pompeii (VIII,2,30)
Pompeii, SAP 5139

Painted tavern sign showing a phoenix
c. AD 5079
H. 123 cm, W. 124 cm
Pompeii, Bar of Euxinus (I,11,11)
Pompeii, SAP 41671
Selected literature: Cassani (2001) no. 32, p.89
FIG. 53

Terracotta fish sauce (*garum*) bottle with painted inscription (*dipinto*)
GAR CAST
H. 46 cm
Pozzuoli
The British Museum, 1856,1226.337
FIG. 68

Small terracotta fish sauce (*garum*) bottle with painted inscription (*dipinto*)
H. 24 cm
Vesuvian area
Pompeii, SAP 81744

Carbonized foodstuffs: oak galls, grain, dates, millet, beans
Herculaneum, Decumanus Maximus
Herculaneum, SAP 77614, 77616, 77609, 77623, 77625

Hexagonal glass bottle
H. 36 cm, W. 17 cm
Pompeii
Naples, MANN 13181
Selected literature: Ward-Perkins and Claridge (1976), no.240
FIG. 44

Pottery container with two glass bottles
H. 15 cm (max)
Pompeii, Villa of Cicero
Naples, MANN 12845
Selected literature: Ward-Perkins and Claridge (1976), no.244; Beretta and Di Pasquale (2004), p. 337, no. 4.76
FIG. 43

Bronze weight in the form of a sow
H. 22 cm
Pompeii, shop (VI,4,20)
Naples, MANN 74390
Selected literature: CIL X 8067, 88; Pagano and Prisciandaro II (2006), 71

Bronze grain measure (*modius*) with inscription
DDPP HERC
c. AD 50–79
H. 18 cm, D. 20 cm
Herculaneum
Naples, MANN 6331
Selected literature: Pagano and Prisciandaro II(2006), pp. 288, 367, no. 310
FIG. 48

Bronze weighing scales with decorated pans
H. 40 cm, W. 48 cm
Vesuvian area
Naples, MANN 74157
FIG. 45

Bronze funnel
H. 33 cm, D. 32 cm
Vesuvian area
Naples, MANN 73839
FIG. 46

Pottery cup from southern France (South Gaulish) with marbled finish
Stamp: VIDI (?)
c. AD 50–79
H. 5.5 cm, D. 12 cm
Pompeii
Naples, MANN 109640
Selected literature: *Le Collezioni del Museo Nazionale di Napoli* I,1 (1986) p. 194, no. 151
FIG. 50

Pottery cup from Syria (Eastern Sigillata A)
c. AD 50–79
H. 6 cm, D. 11 cm
Vesuvian area
Naples, MANN 211957
FIG. 50

Pottery cup from central Italy (Italian Red Slip Ware)
Stamp on interior: SMF (?)
c. AD 50–79
Vesuvian area
H. 7 cm, D. 13 cm
Naples, MANN 16482
FIG. 50

Pottery amphora from Tunisia (African Red Slip Ware)
c. AD 70–79
H. 22 cm, D. 13 cm
Pompeii
Naples, MANN 110388
Selected literature: *Le Collezioni del Museo Nazionale di Napoli* I,1 (1986), p. 194, no. 154
FIG. 49

Pottery lamp with a cupid holding baskets
H. 4.8 cm, W. 4 cm, L. 10.1 cm
Pompeii (1,20,3)
Pompeii, SAP 12383 B
FIG. 71

Plaster lamp mould
H. 5.5 cm, W. 11.5 cm, L. 16 cm
Pompeii (1,20,3)
Pompeii, SAP 12398 A
FIG. 70

Marble and bronze *herm* of Lucius Caecilius Iucundus
Inscription: GENIO L(uci) NOSTRI FELIX
L(ibertus)
c. AD 1–15
H. 173 cm, W. 35 cm
Pompeii, House of Lucius Caecilius Iucundus
(V,1,26)
Naples, MANN 110663
Selected literature: CIL X 860; *Le Collezioni del Museo Nazionale di Napoli* I,2 (1989),
p. 122, no. 129; Meller and Dickmann
(2011), pp. 178–9
FIGS 90–91

Foldable bronze seat (*sella curulis*)
H. 53 cm, W. 66 cm
Pompeii
Naples, MANN 73152.
Selected literature: Gentili (ed.) (2008), p.139,
no. 11

Mosaic of a dog
AD 50–79
H. 80 cm, W. 80 cm
Pompeii, House of Orpheus (VI,14,20)
Naples, MANN 110666
Selected literature: *Le Collezioni del Museo Nazionale di Napoli* I,1 (1986), p. 120, no. 35
FIG. 80

Fresco showing the distribution of bread
AD 50–79
H. 69 cm, W. 60 cm
Pompeii (VII,3,30)
Naples. MANN 9071
Selected literature: *Le Collezioni del Museo Nazionale di Napoli* I,1 (1986), p. 168, no. 329
FIG. 16

Mosaic of a fish sauce (*garum*) bottle with an inscription
G(ari) F(los) SCOM(bri) SCAURI EX
OFFICINA SCAURI
AD 50–79
H. 74 cm, W. 31 cm
Pompeii, House of Aulus Umbricius Scaurus
(VII,16,15)
Pompeii, SAP 15190
Selected literature: Borriello et al. (1996),
p.198; Berry (2007), pp. 226–7
FIG. 107

Mosaic portrait of a woman
30–1 BC
H. 34 cm, W. 29 cm
Pompeii (VI,15,14)
Naples, MANN 124666
Selected literature: Ward-Perkins and Claridge
(1976), no. 72; La Rocca et al. (2009), p. 302
FIG. 92

Bronze strong box
50 BC–AD 79
H. 101 cm, W. 92 cm, D. 58 cm
Pompeii
Naples, MANN 73021
Selected literature: *Le Collezioni del Museo Nazionale di Napoli* I,1 (1986), p. 184, no. 80;
Nitti et al. (eds) (2011), p. 71, no. 23

Marble display table
H. 89 cm; 43 x 63 cm (table top)
Pompeii (V,4c)
Pompeii, SAP 54947
FIG. 87

Silver jug
50 BC–AD 79
H. 22.5 cm
Pompeii, House of Inachus and Io (VI,7,19)
Naples, MANN 25691
Selected literature: Guzzo (ed) (2006), p. 176,
no. 231

Silver plate
50 BC–AD 79
D. 22 cm
Pompeii, House of Inachus and Io (VI,7,19)
Naples, MANN 25296
Selected literature: Guzzo (ed) (2006), p. 177,
no. 240

Silver ladle (*simpulum*)
50 BC–AD 79
H. 10.5 cm
Pompeii, House of Inachus and Io (VI,7,19)
Naples, MANN 25714
Selected literature: Guzzo (ed) (2006), p. 174,
no. 223
FIG. 89

Small silver dish/bowl
50 BC–AD 79
H. 3 cm, D. 14.2 cm
Pompeii, House of Inachus and Io (VI,7,19)
Naples, MANN 25318
Selected literature: Guzzo (ed) (2006), p. 178,
nos 256–9
FIG. 278

One-handled silver cup (*calathus*)
50 BC–AD 79
H. 9.5 cm, D. 13 cm
Pompeii, House of the Silver Treasure (VI,7,20-22)
Naples, MANN 25368
Selected literature: Guzzo (ed) (2006), p. 84,
no. 20; Pagano and Prisciandaro II (2006),
p. 62
FIG. 89

Silver cup stands (*mensulae*)
50 BC–AD 79
H. 3.4 cm, D. 7.8 cm (max)
Pompeii, House of Inachus and Io (VI,7,19)
Naples, MANN 25548, 25549, 25550, 25551
Selected literature: Guzzo (ed) (2006), p. 176,
no. 239
FIG. 286

Marble relief showing Pompeii during an earthquake
AD 62/63–AD 79
H. 13.5, L. 87.5
Pompeii, House of Lucius Caecilius Iucundus
(V,1,26)
Naples, MANN 20470
Selected literature: Ward-Perkins and Claridge
(1976), no. 16
FIG. 357

Fresco of Bacchus
AD 50–79
H. 130 cm, W. 90 cm
Pompeii, House of the Centenary (IX,8,3-6)
Naples, MANN 112286
Selected literature: *Le Collezioni del Museo Nazionale di Napoli* I,1 (1986), p. 168, no.
321; Bragantini and Sampaolo (2009), p. 426,
no. 221
FIG. 106

Wooden statuette, possibly representing a female ancestor
c. 20 BC–AD 20
H. 30.4 cm, D. 12.5 cm
Herculaneum, House of the Wattlework
(III,13-15)
Herculaneum, SAP 75598
Selected literature: Guidobaldi (2008), p. 281,
no. 122; Guidobaldi and Esposito (2012),
p. 64, 70
FIG. 101

Wooden statuette of a male ancestor on a block base
c. 20 BC–AD 20
H. 28 cm, W. 9.5 cm
Herculaneum, House of the Mosaic Atrium
(IV,1-2)
Herculaneum, SAP 79404
FIG. 104

Terracotta statuette of a man wearing the toga
AD 50–79
H. 25 cm
Moregine, Building B
Pompeii, SAP 85201
Selected literature: d'Ambrosio et al. (2004),
p. 467
FIG. 160

Bronze statuette of Jupiter
H. 12.5 cm, W. 7 cm
Pompeii, House of King Joseph II (VIII,2,39)
Pompeii, SAP 5050
Selected literature: Pagano and Prisciandaro II
(2006), p. 24
FIG. 98

Bronze statuettes of household gods (*Lares*)
H. 21.5 cm, W. 10.5 cm
Pompeii, House of the Red Walls (VIII,5,37)
Naples, MANN 113261–113262
Selected literature: Nitti et al. (eds) (2011),
pp. 778, no. 3031
FIG. 97

Small marble altar with bronze attachments
H. 20 cm, W. 20 cm
Pompeii (I,7,1)
Pompeii, SAP 3217
FIG. 100

Terracotta incense burner containing ash
H. 13.5 cm, D. 25 cm
Pompeii (II,8,5)
Pompeii, SAP 10697
FIG. 99

Carbonized wooden storage cupboard
H. 56 cm, W. 48 cm
Herculaneum
Herculaneum, SAP 78448
Selected literature: Mols (1999), no. 40;
Guidobaldi and Esposito (2012), pp. 163–4
FIG. 77

Fresco of a woman spinning wool
AD 50–79
H. 19 cm, W. 11.8 cm
Vesuvian area
Naples, MANN 9523
FIG. 78

Fresco of the baker Terentius Neo and his wife
AD 50–79
H. 60 cm, W. 70 cm
Pompeii, House of T. Terentius Neo (VII,2,6)
Naples, MANN 9058
Selected literature: Ward-Perkins and Claridge
(1976), no. 23; *Le Collezioni del Museo Nazionale di Napoli* I,1 (1986), p. 156, no. 236
FIG. 112

Bronze curtain holder in the shape of a ship's prow
H. 15.5 cm, W. 14.9 cm
Herculaneum, House of Apollo the Lyre Player
(V,11)
Herculaneum, SAP 77231
FIG. 108

Carbonized wooden tablet from the archive of Lucius Caecilius Iucundus
22 January AD 55
H. 13.5 cm, W. 12 cm
Pompeii, House of Lucius Caecilius Iucundus
(V,1,26)
Naples, MANN 8A/155868
Selected literature: CIL IV, 3340,X; Aßkamp et al.
(eds) (2007), p. 216, no. 2.6
FIG. 115

Bronze seal ring
C POPPAEI I D R I
W. 5.5 cm
Pompeii (I,11)
Pompeii, SAP 10788

Bronze seal ring
M FAB(ius) R(u)F(us)
W. 5.5 cm
Pompeii, House of Marcus Fabius Rufus
(VII,16,17-22)
Pompeii, SAP 14250
FIG. 27

Fresco of writing materials
AD 50–79
H. 20 cm, W. 31.4 cm
Pompeii, House of Marcus Lucretius (IX,3,5)
Naples, MANN 9818
Selected literature: *Le Collezioni del Museo Nazionale di Napoli* I,1 (1986), no. 284;
Bragantini and Sampaolo (2009), p. 384, no. 183
FIG. 113

Graffito with quotation from Vergil's Eclogues
H. 16 cm, W. 22 cm
Pompeii, House of the Ship Europa (I,15,3)
Pompeii, SAP 20566
Selected literature: CIL IV, 8625

Fresco of a young man with a scroll labelled 'Homer'
AD 50–79
H. 44.4 cm, W. 44.8 cm
Pompeii, House of the Apartment (V,2,h)
Naples, MANN 120620a
Selected literature: Bragantini and Sampaolo
(2009), p. 523, no. 303a; Stefani and Varone
(2009) p. 302
FIG. 121

Fresco of a young man with a scroll labelled
'Plato'
AD 50–79
H. 44.8 cm, W. 44.7 cm
Pompeii, House of the Apartment (V,2,h)
Naples, MANN 12062b
Selected literature: Bragantini and Sampaolo
(2009), p. 523, no. 303b; Stefani and Varone
(2009) p. 302
FIG. 122

Bronze and silver statuette
H. 65 cm, W. 35 cm
Pompeii (VI,10)
Naples, MANN 5014
Selected literature: Pagano and Prisciandaro II
(2006), p. 24
FIG. 119

Fresco of lovers on a bed
AD 50–79
H. 51.7 cm, W. 44 cm
Pompeii, House of Lucius Caecilius Iucundus
(V,1,26)
Naples, MANN 110569
Selected literature: *Le Collezioni del Museo
Nazionale di Napoli* I,1 (1986), p. 170, no. 345
FIG. 131

Fresco of Venus and Cupid
AD 50–79
H. 48.5 cm, W. 46.5 cm
Pompeii, House of Meleager (VI,9,2)
The British Museum, 1857,0415.3

Fresco of a satyr and a maenad
30 BC–AD 50
H. 51 cm, W. 52.7 cm
Pompeii, House of Lucius Caecilius Iucundus
(V,1,26)
Naples, MANN 110590
Selected literature: *Le Collezioni del Museo
Nazionale di Napoli* I,1 (1986), p. 134, no. 86
FIG. 134

Fresco of a snake, with a graffito warning
a lover
30 BC–AD 79
H. 54.7 cm, W. 41.1 cm
Pompeii (VI,7,6)
Naples, MANN 4694
Selected literature: CIL IV, 1410
FIG. 132

Carbonized wooden cradle
H. 49 cm, L. 81 cm, W. 50 cm
Herculaneum, House of Marcus Pilius
Primigenius Granianus (OI,1a)
Herculaneum, SAP 78444
Selected literature: Mols (1999), no. 11
FIG. 128

Bronze bed fixtures and fittings
H. 17 cm, L. 25 cm
Vesuvian area
The British Museum, 1784,0131.4
FIG. 129

Alabaster perfume bottle (*alabastron*)
H. 13.5 cm, D. 6 cm
Pompeii (I,14,9)
Pompeii, SAP 12043
FIG. 143

Bone lidded vessel (*pyxis*) with pink pigment
(cosmetics?)
H. 2.3 cm, D. 2.8 cm
Pompeii (I,20,4)
Pompeii, SAP 12412C
FIG. 142

Bronze lidded vessel (*pyxis*) with scale
decoration
H. 10 cm, D. 8.5 cm
Herculaneum, Decumanus Maximus, Shop 4
Herculaneum, SAP 78274
FIG. 144

Bronze toiletry casket with compartments
containing residue
L. 11.2 cm, W. 6.5 cm
Pompeii, Praedia of Julia Felix (II,4,10)
Pompeii, SAP 9042
FIG. 142

Bronze tweezers
L. 7.5 cm
Pompeii (I,12,7)
Pompeii, SAP 12938A
FIG. 142

Pumice stone and bronze holder
H. 4.5 cm, D. 5.7 cm
Vesuvian area
Pompeii, SAP 7150
FIG. 142

Bronze razor with a bone handle
H. 9.3 cm, W. 11.5 cm
Pompeii (1,13,7)
Pompeii, SAP 11148
FIG. 142

Bone hair pin decorated with a woman's
head
L. 11 cm
Pompeii (1,14,3)
Pompeii, SAP 12244
FIG. 148

Carbonized wooden stool with an inlaid seat
H. 45 cm, W. 45 cm
Herculaneum, House of the Two Atria (VI,28-
29)
Herculaneum, SAP 78445
Selected literature: Mols (1999), no. 23
FIG. 141

Fresco of a seated woman with a mirror
AD 50–79
H. 50 cm, W. 33 cm
Stabiae, Villa Arianna
Naples, MANN 9088
Selected literature: *Le Collezioni del Museo
Nazionale di Napoli* I,1 (1986), p. 144, no. 154
FIG. 139

Silver-handled mirror
50 BC–AD 79
H. 30.5 cm, D. of face 18 cm
Pompeii, House of Inachus and Io (VI,7,19)
Naples, MANN 25718
Selected literature: Guzzo (ed) (2006), no. 230
FIG. 140

Bronze washing bowl
H. 11.7 cm, D. 41 cm
Pompeii, I,14,9
Pompeii, SAP 12097
FIG. 138

Bronze scoop in the form of a shell
H. 8.9 cm, W. 22.8 cm
Pompeii
The British Museum, 1856,1226.929
FIG. 137

Bronze furniture ornament in the shape
of a female head
AD 1–50
H. 14 cm, W. 6.5 cm
Herculaneum, Decumanus Maximus
Herculaneum, SAP 77838
Selected literature: Nitti et al. (eds) (2011),
p. 167, no. 136
FIG. 147

Gold cloth
L. 29 cm
Herculaneum, ancient shoreline, vault V
Herculaneum, SAP 78548

Pair of gold earrings with emerald clusters
AD 50–79
D. 2.2 cm
Vesuvian area
The British Museum, 1856,1226.1405
Selected literature: Ward-Perkins and Claridge
(1976), no. 53
FIG. 151

Gold bracelet/armlet of paired hemispheres
L. 24 cm
Vesuvian area
The British Museum, 1946,0702.1
FIG. 153

Gold bracelet in the form of a snake
D. 7.6 cm
Pompeii
The British Museum, 1946,0702.2
FIG. 153

Gold necklace with crescent pendant
L. 33 cm
Herculaneum, ancient shoreline, vault VII,
skeleton 8
Herculaneum, SAP 78958
Selected literature: d'Ambrosio et al.(2004),
p. 140
FIG. 152

Gold ring with incised carnelian bezel
D. 2 cm
Herculaneum, ancient shoreline, vault VII,
skeleton 8
Herculaneum, 78959
Selected literature: d'Ambrosio et al.(2004),
p. 140
FIG. 149

Bronze armlet with incised figure of
Aphrodite
D. 9 cm
Pompeii, House of Gratus (IX,6,5)
Naples, MANN 115603
Selected literature: d'Ambrosio et al.(2004),
p. 280
FIG. 154

Bronze necklace of hemispheres with glass
pendant
L. 11.5 cm
Pompeii, House of Gratus (IX,6,5)
Naples, MANN 118270
Selected literature: d'Ambrosio et al.(2004),
p. 281
FIG. 155

Bronze armlet with silver medallion of Sol,
god of the Sun
D. 9.5 cm
Vesuvian area
Naples, MAN, no inv. (446)
FIG. 156

Gold ring with green gem and tightened hoop
D. 2.4 cm
Pompeii, Caupona of Salvius (VI,14,3536)
Naples, MANN 110910
Selected literature: d'Ambrosio et al. (2004),
p. 271
FIG. 157

Carbonized wooden linen chest
H. 45 cm, W. 103 cm, D. 63 cm
Herculaneum, Decumanus Maximus, north-east
side
Herculaneum, SAP 77619
Selected literature: Mols (1999), no. 41
FIG. 158

Bronze lampstand (*candelabrum*)
H. 136.3 cm (when assembled)
Herculaneum, House of Neptune and Amphitrite
(V,67)
Herculaneum, SAP 76214
FIG. 126

Terracotta oil lamp in the form of a satyr with
an enormous phallus
H. 22.3 cm, W. 11.5 cm
Pompeii
Naples, MANN 11661
FIG. 127

Terracotta chamber pot
H. 19 cm
Vesuvian area
Pompeii, SAP 31699
Fig. 136

Bronze toilet vase with lid
H. 15.60
Vesuvian area
The British Museum, 1814,0704.1576A/B
FIG. 135

Bronze heating brazier
H. 28.5 cm, D. 45 cm
Pompeii (III,4,3)
Pompeii, SAP 2664

Fresco of Flora, goddess of flowers and spring
30 BC–AD 50
H. 39.5 cm, W. 32.5 cm
Stabiae, Villa of Arianna
Naples, MANN 8834
Selected literature: *Le Collezioni del Museo
Nazionale di Napoli* I,1 (1986), p. 138, no. 111
FIG. 162

Frescoed walls of a room showing garden
scenes
AD 30–50
North wall: H. 400 cm, W. 370 cm; east wall
with lunette: H. 503 cm, W. 288 cm; south wall:
H. 400 cm, W. 370 cm; west (entrance) wall:
H. 213 cm, W. 288 cm
Pompeii, House of the Golden Bracelet
(VI,17,42)
Pompeii, SAP 40690–40693
Selected literature: *Rediscovering Pompeii* (1992)
pp. 226–36, no. 163; Nava et al. (2007),
p. 50–9
FIGS 202–9

Marble fountain with a fluted square basin
H. 76.5 cm, W. 57.5 cm
Pompeii
Naples, MANN 126203
Selected literature: Mattusch (2008) p. 171,
no. 64; Nitti et al. (eds) (2011), p. 204,
no. 189
FIG. 174

Bronze fountain spout in the form of a
rabbit
H. 13 cm, W. 12 cm
Vesuvian area
Naples, MANN 124912
FIG. 179

Bronze fountain spout in the form of a
peacock
H. 30cm, W. 11.5 cm
Pompeii, House of Camillus (VII,12,2224)
Naples, MANN 69784
Selected literature: Lo Sardo(2005), p. 136
FIG. 178

Bronze fountain spout in the form of a
pinecone
Height 53.5
Pompeii
The British Museum, 1856,1226.1007
FIG. 177

Faience fountain spout in the form of a
crocodile
H. 9 cm, L. 39 cm, W. 13 cm
Pompeii, House of the Silver Wedding (V,2,1)
Naples, MANN 121324
Selected literature: *Le Collezioni del Museo
Nazionale di Napoli* I,1 (1986), p. 202, no. 6;
Lo Sardo(2005), p. 142
FIG. 176

Faience fountain spout in the form of a frog
H. 17.5 cm, W. 23 cm
Naples, MANN 121322
FIG. 175

Bronze statue of a woman fastening her
dress (so-called *danzatrice*)
20 BC–AD 20
H. *c.*150 cm
Herculaneum, Villa of the Papyri
Naples, MANN 5619
Selected literature: Mattusch (2008), pp.
22830; Guidobaldi (2008), p. 271, no. 83
FIGS 180–1

Marble statue of a little boy
AD 1–50
Height 40.5 cm
Pompeii, House of the Painters at Work
(IX,12,9)
Pompeii, SAP 41462
Selected literature: Nitti et al. (2011), p. 194,
no. 175

Marble statue of Pan and a goat
AD 1–20
H. 44 cm, base 49 x 47 cm
Herculaneum, Villa of the Papyri
Naples, MANN 27709
Selected literature: *Le Collezioni del Museo
Nazionale di Napoli* I,2 (1989), p. 126, no. 154;
Guidobaldi (2008), p. 264, no. 57
FIG. 196

Marble statue of the drunken Hercules
H. 55.4 cm, W. 31.5 cm
Herculaneum, House of the Stags (IV,21)
Herculaneum, SAP 75802
Selected literature: *Rediscovering Pompeii*
(1992), pp. 268–9, no. 190
FIG. 184

Marble statue of a satyr pouring wine
H. 75.2 cm, W. 43.2 cm
Herculaneum, House of the Stags (IV,21)
Herculaneum, SAP 75797
Selected literature: *Rediscovering Pompeii*
(1992), pp. 268–71, no. 191; Guidobaldi and
Esposito (2012), p. 64

Marble statue of a stag and hounds
H. 63.7 cm, W. 62.7 cm
Herculaneum, House of the Stags (IV,21)
Herculaneum, SAP 75796
Selected literature: *Rediscovering Pompeii*
(1992), pp. 270–3, no. 192; Guidobaldi and
Esposito (2012), p. 64
FIG. 183

Marble statue of a stag and hounds
H. 67.5 cm, W. 62.7 cm
Herculaneum, House of the Stags (IV,21)
Herculaneum, SAP 75801
Selected literature: *Rediscovering Pompeii*
(1992), pp. 270–3, no. 193; Guidobaldi and
Esposito (2012), p. 64

Marble sundial
H. 26 cm, W. 25.5 cm
Pompeii, House of Julius Polybius (IX,13,13)
Pompeii, SAP 24544
Selected literature: Borriello et al. (1996),
p. 230, no. 223
FIG. 185

Carbonized wooden bench
H. 40 cm, W. 41 cm, L. 104 cm
Herculaneum, Decumanus Maximus
Herculaneum, SAP 3153/78450
Selected literature: Mols (1999), no. 26
FIG. 186

Bronze wind-chime (*tintinnabulum*)
H. 13.6 cm
Pompeii
The British Museum, 1856,1226.1086
Selected literature: Ward-Perkins and Claridge
(1976), no. 216
FIG. 187

Marble decorative disc (*oscillum*)
D. 30.5 cm
Pompeii
The British Museum, 1856,1226.1671
FIG. 188

Glass window pane
AD 50–79
H. 54 cm, W. 31 cm
Herculaneum
The British Museum, 1772,0317.21
FIG. 192

Mica window pane
AD 50–79
H. 29cm, W. 11cm
Pompeii
Naples, MANN 313338

Fresco fragment with numerous graffiti
H. 20 cm, W. 63 cm
Pompeii, House of Marcus Fabius Rufus
(VII,16,1722)
Pompeii, SAP 20564
Selected literature: *Rediscovering Pompeii*
(1992), p. 150, no. 13; Nitti et al. (eds)
(2011), p. 182, no. 161
FIG. 200

Graffito on fragment of a column
H. 17 cm, W. 23 cm
Boscoreale, Villa of Agrippa Postumus
Pompeii, SAP 20518
FIG. 197

Graffito of gladiators
H. 31.4, W. 37.8
Pompeii (IX,1,12)
Pompeii, SAP 20562
FIG. 18

Graffito giving a date in 6 BC
6 BC
H. 16 cm, W. 42 cm
Pompeii, House of Amarantus (I,9,12)
Pompeii, SAP 20514
FIG. 199

Marble well-head (*puteal*)
H. 55 cm, D. 45 cm
Pompeii (I,13,8)
Pompeii, SAP 44908
FIG. 167

Carbonized wooden winch (windlass) used
for drawing water
H. 60 cm, W. 70 cm
Herculaneum, House of the Two Atria
(VI,2829)
Herculaneum, SAP 77283
FIG. 169

Bronze tap
AD 1–60
H. 15 cm
Oplontis
The British Museum, 1856,1226.864
FIG. 173

Lead water tank with two pipes
H. 17 cm
AD 1–60
Vesuvian area
Pompeii, SAP 56309
FIG. 172

Pottery plant pot with drainage holes
H. 16.5 cm, D. 15 cm
Pompeii, House of the Ship Europa
(I,15,23,4,6)
Pompeii, SAP 14583
FIG. 189

Pottery plant pot with drainage holes
H. 13 cm, D. 11.5 cm
Pompeii, House of the ship Europa
(I,15,23,4,6)
Pompeii, SAP 14574
FIG. 190

Iron mattock
H. 5.5 cm, W. 11.5 cm, L. 22.5 cm
Pompeii (I,14,15)
Pompeii, SAP 40372
FIG. 191

First Style fresco fragment
150–90 BC
H. 50 cm, W. 53 cm
Pompeii, House of the Fleet (VI,10,11)
Pompeii, SAP 87283
Selected literature: Guzzo and Guidobaldi (eds)
(2008), p. 166
FIG. 235

Second Style fresco fragment featuring
graffiti of animals
90–30 BC
H. 205 cm, W. 273 cm
Pompeii, House of the Cryptoporticus (I,6,2)
Pompeii, SAP 59469B
Selected literature: d'Ambrosio et al. (2004),
pp. 329–30
FIG. 236

Third Style fresco fragment
30 BC–AD 50
H. 94 cm, W. 165 cm
Pompeii, House of the Golden Bracelet
(VI,17,42)
Pompeii, SAP 86076
Selected literature: d'Ambrosio et al. (2004),
p. 405, no. IV. 534

Stamped pigment in a pottery bowl
ATTIORU(M)
H. 9 cm
Pompeii, Taberna Attiorum (IX,2,11)
Naples, MANN 112228
Selected literature: *Le Collezioni del Museo
Nazionale di Napoli* I,1 (1986) p.200, no.197;
Pagano and Prisciandaro II (2006), p. 85
FIG. 229

Fresco of a woman's face
30 BC–AD 50
H. 19.7 cm, W. 15.4 cm
Herculaneum
Naples, MANN 9094
Selected literature: *Le Collezioni del Museo
Nazionale di Napoli* I,1 (1986), p. 132, no. 65;
Nava et al. (2007), p. 116; Guidobaldi and
Esposito (2012), pp. 136–7
FIG. 243

Fresco of Theseus and the Minotaur
AD 50–79
H. 97 cm, W. 88 cm
Pompeii, House of Gavius Rufus (VII,2,16)
Naples, MANN 9043
Selected literature: Ward-Perkins and Claridge
(1976), no. 150; *Le Collezioni del Museo
Nazionale di Napoli* I,1 (1986), p.146, no.173
FIG. 242

Fresco of the Three Graces
30 BC–AD 50
H. 57 cm, W. 53 cm
Pompeii, House of Titus Dentatius Panthera
(IX,2,16)
Naples, MANN 9236
Selected literature: *Le Collezioni del Museo
Nazionale di Napoli* I,1 (1986), p.136, no. 100;
Ward-Perkins and Claridge (1976), no. 158

Fresco of a flying maenad
AD 50–79
H. 68.5 cm, W. 49 cm
Herculaneum
Naples, MANN 8835
Selected literature: Aßkamp et al. (eds) (2007),
p. 234, no. 5.6

Fresco of a maritime landscape
AD 50–79
H. 32 cm, W. 61 cm
Boscoreale
The British Museum, 1899,0215.2
Selected literature: Walker (1991), 53
FIG. 246

Fresco of a couple in a roundel
AD 50–79
D. 17.5 cm
Pompeii
The British Museum, 1856,1226.1621
Selected literature: Walker (1991), 1

Fresco of a parrot eating cherries
AD 5079
H. 11.5 cm, W. 24 cm
Pompeii
The British Museum, 1867,0508.1359

Mosaic of sea creatures
150–90 BC
H. 103 cm, W. 103 cm
Pompeii (VIII,2,16)
Naples, MANN 120177
Selected literature: Ward-Perkins and Claridge
(1976), no. 253; Mattusch (2008), p. 34
FIG. 219

Mosaic of a theatrical mask
90–30 BC
H. 15 cm, W. 15 cm
Vesuvian area
The British Museum, 1856,1226.1643

Mosaic of a theatrical mask
90–30 BC
H. 14.5 cm, W. 14 cm
Vesuvian area
The British Museum, 1856,1226.1644
FIG. 218

Mosaic of a skeleton holding two wine jugs
(askoi)
AD 50–79
H. 91 cm, W. 70 cm
Pompeii (VI,Ins.Occ.,1926)
Naples, MANN 9978
Selected literature: Ward-Perkins and Claridge
(1976), no. 18; Le Collezioni del Museo
Nazionale di Napoli I,1 (1986), p. 120, no.38;
FIG. 294

Fresco panel in a wooden frame
H. 96 cm, W. 89 cm
Herculaneum (V, 17)
Herculaneum, SAP 77872
FIG. 232

Ivory panel from a tripod showing Silenus
and Dionysus
H. 16 cm, W. 10 cm
Herculaneum, Villa of the Papyri, pavilion
Herculaneum, Herc R4
Selected literature: Guidobaldi and Esposito
(2012), pp. 163–4

Ivory panel from a tripod showing Bacchus
H. 14 cm, W. 7.5 cm
Herculaneum, Villa of the Papyri, pavilion
Herculaneum, Herc O4
Selected literature: Guidobaldi and Esposito
(2012), pp. 163–4
FIG. 233

Ivory panels on part of a wooden tripod
Herculaneum, Villa of the Papyri, pavilion
Herculaneum, Herc R4
Selected literature: Guidobaldi and Esposito
(2012), pp. 163–4

Ivory foot from a tripod in the form of a
lion's paw
H. 5 cm, W. 10 cm
Herculaneum, Villa of the Papyri, pavilion
Herculaneum, Herc R
Selected literature: Guidobaldi and Esposito
(2012), pp. 163–4

Marble relief showing a ceremony in honour
of Bacchus
20 BC–AD 20
H. 56 cm, W. 109.5 cm
Herculaneum, House of the Dionysiac Reliefs
Herculaneum, SAP 88091
Selected literature: Guidobaldi and Esposito
(2012), pp. 151–5
FIG. 256

Marble relief showing a satyr and a maenad
20 BC–AD 20
H. 39.5 cm, W. 97 cm
Herculaneum, House of the Dionysiac Reliefs
Herculaneum, SAP 79613
Selected literature: Guidobaldi and Esposito
(2012), pp. 151–5
FIG. 257

Wooden panel from a ceiling
L. 87 cm, W. 50 cm
Herculaneum, ancient shoreline, originally
from the House of the Telephus Relief (oI,2-3)
Herculaneum

Fresco of a dinner party with a singing guest
AD 50–79
FACITIS.VOBIS.SVAVITER.EGO.CANTO
EST.ITA.VALEAS
H. 60 cm, W. 64 cm
Pompeii (V,2,4)
Naples, MANN 120031
Selected literature: Ward-Perkins and Claridge
(1976), no. 260
FIG. 267

Fresco of a dinner party
AD 50–79
H. 68 cm, W. 66 cm
Pompeii (V,2,4)
Naples, MANN 120029
Selected literature: Ward-Perkins and Claridge
(1976), no. 259; Le Collezioni del Museo
Nazionale di Napoli I,1 (1986), p. 170, no. 342;
FIG. 263

Fresco of a music lesson
AD 50–79
H. 58 cm, W. 80 cm
Pompeii
The British Museum, 1867,0508.1353
FIG. 213

Bronze stool
H. 35.5 cm, W 38 cm
Oplontis
The British Museum, 1856,1226.667

Bronze and silver lampstand (candelabrum)
with four hanging lamps
H. 121 cm, W. 58 cm, D. 66 cm
Pompeii, House of Pansa (VI,6,1)
Naples, MANN 4563
Selected literature: Mattusch (2008), p.140
FIGS 268–9

Bronze food heater
H. 96 cm, W. 44 cm
Pompeii, House of the Four Styles (I,8,11)
Pompeii, SAP 6798
Selected literature: Rediscovering Pompeii
(1992), p. 173, no. 59; Nitti et al. (2011),
p. 164, no. 132
FIG. 271

Bronze water heater (samovar)
H. 41 cm, D. 27 cm
Pompeii
Naples, MANN 111048
Selected literature: Le Collezioni del Museo
Nazionale di Napoli I,1 (1986), p. 182, no. 72;
Lo Sardo (2005), p.140
FIG. 273

Bronze vessel for mixing wine (crater)
decorated with mythological figures
20 BC–AD 20
H. 60 cm, W. 35 cm
Pompeii, House of Julius Polybius (IX,13,13)
Pompeii, SAP 45180
Selected literature: d'Ambrosio et al.(2004),
p. 425; Nitti et al. (2011), p. 163, no. 131
FIG. 118

Bronze vessel for mixing wine (situla)
H. 41.5 cm, W. 33 cm
Vesuvian area
Naples, MANN 68866
Selected literature: Aßkamp et al. (eds) (2007),
p. 158, fig. 9
FIG. 292

Bronze wine jug (askos) with a lizard handle
H. 14 cm
Pompeii, House of the Greek Epigrams (V,1,18)
Naples, MANN 111563
FIG. 295

Bronze and silver statuette of a vendor with
a huge phallus
H. 26 cm
Pompeii, House of the Ephebe (I,7,11)
Naples, MANN 143761
Selected literature: Ward-Perkins and Claridge
(1976), no. 104; Nitti et al. (2011), p. 155,
no. 121
FIG. 272

Cameo glass jug 'the Auldjo jug'
25 BC–AD 15
H. 22.8 cm, D. 14.3 cm
Pompeii
The British Museum, 1859,0216.1
Selected literature: Harden et al. (1987),
p. 79, no. 34
FIG. 296

Cameo glass plaque
25 BC–AD 15
H. 25.5 cm, L. 39.5 cm
Pompeii, House of Fabius Rufus (VII,16,22)
Naples, MANN 153651
Selected literature: Le Collezioni del Museo Nazionale
di Napoli I,1 (1986), p. 226, no. 51; Harden et al.
(1987), pp. 7033, no. 32B
FIG. 297

Silver bowl with fluted edges
50 BC–AD 79
H. 5.5 cm, D. 12 cm
Pompeii, House of Inachus and Io (VI,7,19)
Naples, MANN 25554
Selected literature: Guzzo (ed) (2006), p. 175,
no. 226229
FIG. 275

Silver plate
50 BC–AD 79
H. 2.5 cm, D. 20.5cm
Pompeii, House of Inachus and Io (VI,7,19)
Naples, MANN 25302
Selected literature: Guzzo (ed) (2006), p. 177,
no. 244247
FIG. 277

Rectangular silver tray with incised scale pattern
50 BC–AD 79
H. 4.5 cm, W. 20 cm, L. 16 cm
Pompeii
Naples, MANN 25362
Selected literature: Guzzo (ed) (2006), p. 90,
no. 226229
FIG. 274

Silver shell-shaped dish
50 BC–AD 79
H. 6.5 cm, D. 23 cm
Pompeii, House of Inachus and Io (VI,7,19)
Naples, MANN 110863
Selected literature: Guzzo (ed) (2006), p. 128,
no. 126

Silver spoon with deep oval bowl (ligula)
50 BC–AD 79
L. 18 cm, W. 4.5 cm
Vesuvian area
Naples, MANN 25413
Selected literature: Guzzo (ed) (2006), p.96
FIG. 279

Silver spoon with shallow round bowl
50 BC–AD 79
L. 15.5 cm, W. 2.9 cm
Pompeii, House of Inachus and Io (VI,7,19)
Naples, MANN 25431
Selected literature: Guzzo (ed) (2006), p. 176;
Pagano and Prisciandaro II (2006), p.63

Two-handled silver drinking cup (cantharus)
with centaurs and cupids
50 BC–AD 79
H. 14 cm, W. across handles 17 cm
Pompeii, House of the Silver Treasure (VI,7,20-22)
Naples, MANN 25376
Selected literature: Guzzo (ed) (2006), p. 118,
no. 106

Silver jug
50 BC–AD 79
H. 11.3 cm, D. 7.5 cm
Pompeii, House of the Silver Treasure (VI,7,20-22)
Naples, MANN 25372
Selected literature: Guzzo (ed) (2006), p. 122,
no. 110

Silver ladle (*simpulum*)
50 BC–AD 79
H. 10.2 cm, D. 6.5 cm
Herculaneum
Naples, MANN 25707
Selected literature: Guzzo (ed) (2006), p. 82,
no. 10

Silver handled bowl (*patera*)
50 BC–AD 79
H. 5.8 cm, L. 20.3 cm
Pompeii, House of Inachus and Io (VI,7,19)
Naples, MANN 25344
Selected literature: Ward-Perkins and Claridge
(1976), no. 330; Guzzo (ed) (2006), p.174,
no. 221

Small silver dish/bowl
50 BC–AD 79
H. 2.7 cm, D. 10.5 cm
Pompeii, House of Inachus and Io (VI,7,19)
Naples, MANN 25321
Selected literature: Guzzo (ed) (2006), p. 179,
no. 264267
FIG. 276

Silver cup on three feet
50 BC–AD 79
H. 7 cm, D. 10.3 cm
Herculaneum
Naples, MANN 25601
Selected literature: Guzzo (ed) (2006), p. 89,
no. 39; Pagano and Prisciandaro II (2006),
p. 63

Fresco of a man with a drinking horn
(*rhyton*)
AD 50–79
H. 14.5 cm, W. 21.5 cm
Pompeii
The British Museum, 1856,1226.1623
FIG. 281

Glass drinking horn (*rhyton*)
AD 50–79
L. 21.2 cm, D. 5 cm
Pompeii (I,16,5)
Pompeii, SAP 12493
Selected literature: Beretta and Di Pasquale
(2004), p. 306, no. 4.3
FIG. 280

Glass dish in the form of a boat
AD 25–50
H. 7.6cm, L. 22.5 cm
Pompeii
The British Museum, 1868,0501.153
Selected literature: Harden et al. (1987), p. 48,
no. 24; Mattusch (2008), p. 144, no. 49
FIG. 291

Blue glass lidded vessel (*pyxis*) (lid missing)
H. 6.7 cm, D. 13 cm
Pompeii (II,1,3)
Pompeii, SAP 10232

Amber glass bowl
H. 14.7cm, D. 23 cm
Pompeii, SAP 59872

Glass beaker with indentations
H. 14 cm, D. 7 cm
Pompeii (II,3,2)
Pompeii, SAP 6861
Selected literature: Beretta and Di Pasquale
(2004), p. 216, no. 1.48;

Burnt pottery bowl from southern France
(South Gaulish) with moulded design
Stamp: []ANDVILM
AD 50–79
H. 8.5 cm, D. 17.5 cm
Pompeii (VIII,5,9)
Naples, MANN 112926

Pottery bowl from southern France (South
Gaulish) with motto
BIBE AMICE DE MEO
AD 50–79
H. 12 cm, D. 26 cm
Vesuvian area
Naples, MANN 203894
FIG. 289

Pottery cup with bone toothpicks
Height 5 cm
Pompeii (I,9,9)
Pompeii, SAP 9498a-b
FIG. 287

Pottery cup decorated with a face
H. 9.2 cm, D. 13.5 cm
Herculaneum, House of the Gem (o.I,1)
Herculaneum, SAP 76550
FIG. 288

Painted shrine (*lararium*) from a kitchen
wall
H. 223 cm, W. 286.5 cm
Terzigno, villa 6
Pompeii, SAP 86755
Selected literature: Nitti et al. (2011), p. 75,
no. 27
FIG. 302

Fresco showing a loaf of bread and two figs
AD 50–79
H. 23 cm, W. 23 cm
Herculaneum, House of the Stags
Naples, MANN 8625
Selected literature: Ward Perkins and Claridge
(1976), no. 254; Pagano and Prisciandaro II
(2006), p. 32

Carbonized loaf of bread with name stamp
CELERIS Q GRANI VERI SER(vus)
D. 21 cm
Herculaneum, House of the Stags (IV,21)
Naples, MANN 84596
Selected literature: Meller and Dickmann
(2011), p. 93, fig. 8
FIG. 62

Cylindrical glass bottle with rancid olive oil
H. 27.8 cm, D. 10.3 cm
Pompeii
Naples, MANN 313337
Selected literature: Beretta and Di Pasquale
(2004), p. 327, no. 4.51
FIG. 314

Carbonized foodstuffs: peas, figs, chickpeas,
walnuts, almonds and onions.
Herculaneum, Decumanus Maximus
Herculaneum, SAP 77613, 77615, 77610,
77622, 77611, 77621

Carbonized woven basket
H. 4.5 cm, D. 14.5 cm
Herculaneum, House of the Beautiful
Courtyard (V,8)
Herculaneum, SAP 77190
FIG. 318

Carbonized woven basket with lid
H. 6.5 cm, D. 13 cm
Herculaneum
Herculaneum, SAP 79127
FIG. 319

Still-life frescoes of food
AD 50–79
H. 41 cm, W. 129 cm
Herculaneum, House of the Stags (IV,21)
Naples, MANN 8644
Selected literature: Ward-Perkins and Claridge
(1976), no.257; Bragantini and Sampaolo
(2009), p. 375, no. 174
FIG. 270

Pottery jar for rearing dormice (*glirarium*)
H. 38.3 cm, D. 33.5 cm
Pompeii (II,2,2)
Pompeii, SAP 10744
FIG. 313

Domed pottery cooking vessel with a lid
(*clibanus*)
H. 10 cm, D. 46 cm
Herculaneum
Naples, MANN, no inv.
Selected literature: Pagano and Prisciandaro II
(2006), pp. 288, 366, no. 299
FIG. 305

Stone pestle and mortar
Mortar D. 30 cm; pestle L. 6.6 cm
Pompeii (I,11,17)
Pompeii, SAP 12790
Selected literature: Beretta and Di Pasquale
(2004), p. 318, no. 4.30
FIG. 312

Bronze colander with pierced inscription
Inscription under rim: EVODUS PERTVDIE
EXOFFICINIA M[arci] BADI HERMAES
Inscription on sector of rim: VERN(a) M.H.P.
H. 9.3 cm, D. 26 cm
Pompeii, House of the Menander (I,10,4)
Pompeii, SAP 5020
Selected literature: Allison (2006), p. 138

Bonze mould in the form of a hare
L. 65 cm, W. 16 cm
Pompeii, Bakery of Donatus (VII,12,1)
Naples, MANN 76355
Selected literature: Pagano and Prisciandaro II
(2006), p. 72
FIG. 311

Bronze pan with handle
L. 47 cm
Vesuvian area
The British Museum, 1856,1226.1008

Bronze pan with six compartments
L. 35 cm
Vesuvian area
The British Museum, 1856,1226.699
FIG. 309

Bronze square dish
H. 4.5 cm, L. 18 cm
Vesuvian area
Naples, MANN 76555

Bronze cooking pot (*caccabus*)
H. 27 cm, D. 53 cm
Vesuvian area
Naples, MANN 73120
FIG. 307

Bronze jar with lid
H. 20 cm, D. 29 cm
Vesuvian area
Naples, MANN 6478
FIG. 306

Bronze kettle with lid
H. 20 cm, D. 29 cm
Vesuvian area
Naples, MANN 74806

Pottery cooking pot (*caccabus*) with iron
tripod
H. (with tripod) 41.5 cm, D. (across handles)
30 cm
Pompeii, House of the Tragic Poet (VI,8,3)
Naples, MANN 23322
Selected literature: Borriello et al. (1996),
p. 242, no. 3412
FIG. 308

Portable pottery brazier
H. 43 cm, D. 46 cm
Moregine, building B
Pompeii, SAP 85204
Selected literature: Nitti et al. (eds) (2011),
p. 110, no. 70
FIG. 300

Fresco of the goddess Isis Fortuna
CACATOR CAVE MALUM
AD 50–79
H. 68.7 cm, W. 80.3 cm
Pompeii (IX,7,22)
Naples, MANN 112285
Selected literature: *Le Collezioni del Museo
Nazionale di Napoli* I,1 (1986), p. 168, no. 324
FIG. 327

Objects from the Cardo V drain
Red Slip Ware pottery; pottery oil lamps;
cooking pots, jars and coarse ware; glass
vessels; glass bottles; bone die and glass
gaming counters; loomweight and bone
spindle whorl; bone pins and scoops; shell
with red pigment; bone comb; marble
building materials; roof tile and terracotta roof
ornament; gold ring with carnelian gem; four
incised carnelian gems; terracotta statuette;
pottery burner; pottery amphora; bone hinges;
2 bronze coins.
Herculaneum, Cardo V drain
Herculaneum Conservation Project nos (red
slip ware) 6, 11, 13, 16, 17; (oil lamps) 18,
19, 79, 81, 91; (cooking pots, jars and coarse
ware) 27, 30, 402, 36, 37, 54, 55, 59, 76;
(glass vessels) 611, 84, 86, 87, 113; (glass
bottles) 6670; (die and counters) 101, 103,
11418; (loomweight and whorl) 48, 99; (pins
and scoops) 4951, 198; (shell) 105; (comb)
241; (tile and roof ornament) 89, 106; (marble
fragments) 109112; (ring and gems) 958, 102;
(statuette) 92; (burner) 43; (amphora) 82;
(hinges) 236,253; (coins) EF21, EF22.
Selected literature: Camardo and Siano
(forthcoming)
FIGS 145, 146, 214, 315, 316, 329, 330–55

Iron key
L. 6 cm
Herculaneum, ancient shoreline, vault VII
Herculaneum, SAP 78984
FIG. 363

Bronze lantern
H. 22.5 cm
Oplontis
The British Museum, 1856,1226.670
FIG. 362

Partly carbonized wooden money box
L. 13 cm, W. 6.5 cm
Herculaneum, Terrace of M. Nonius Balbus,
next to skeleton no. 42
Herculaneum, SAP 78574
Selected literature: *Rediscovering Pompeii*
(1992), p.168–9, no. 55
FIG. 364

**Fused silver and bronze coins in remains of
a wicker basket**
AD 50–79
H. 10.5 cm, W. 23.5 cm
Herculaneum, ancient shoreline, vault XI, next
to skeleton 21
Herculaneum, SAP 78675
Selected literature: d'Ambrosio et al. (2004),
p. 132, no. 1.71
FIG. 365

Fused contents of a box
W. 10 cm
Oplontis
The British Museum, 1856,1226.692

Stack of silver vessels
50 BC–AD 79
H. 17 cm
Herculaneum, ancient shoreline, vault VIII,
between skeletons 11 and 12
Herculaneum, SAP 78986
Selected literature: d'Ambrosio et al.(2004),
p. 144, no. I.11516

Gold ring with emerald bezel
D. 2.3 cm
Herculaneum, ancient shoreline, vault IX,
skeleton 65
Herculaneum, SAP 78354
Selected literature: d'Ambrosio et al.(2004),
p. 148, no. I.129
FIG. 374

**Gold ring with an incised garnet gem
showing a bird**
D. 2 cm
Herculaneum, ancient shoreline, vault IX,
skeleton 65
Herculaneum, SAP 78355
Selected literature: d'Ambrosio et al.(2004),
p. 147, no. I.128
FIG. 375

**Gold bar earrings with drop pearls (now
missing)**
AD 50–79
W. 1.3 cm
Herculaneum, ancient shoreline, vault IX,
skeleton 65
Herculaneum, SAP 78356-57
Selected literature: d'Ambrosio et al.(2004),
p. 147, no. I.1245
FIG. 376

**Gold bracelets in the form of snakes with
glass paste eyes (one surviving)**
D. 9.3 cm
Herculaneum, ancient shoreline, vault IX,
skeleton 65
Herculaneum, SAP 783589
Selected literature: d'Ambrosio et al.(2004),
p. 147, no. I.1267; Guidobaldi and Esposito
(2012), p. 13
FIG. 377

Bronze and iron medical instruments
12 pieces
Herculaneum, ancient shoreline, vault XII
Herculaneum, SAP 78999
Selected literature: d'Ambrosio et al. (2004),
p. 135, no. I.823; Guidobaldi and Esposito
(2012), p. 14

**Bronze and iron medical instrument case
with slate mixing tablet**
L. 15.2 cm, W. 16.1 cm
Herculaneum, ancient shoreline, vault XII
Herculaneum, inv. 79000
Selected literature: d'Ambrosio et al. (2004),
p. 135, no. I.823; Guidobaldi and Esposito
(2012), p. 14
FIG. 382

**Iron sword with a belt and hanging elements
of iron, silver and wood**
L. 72 cm
Herculaneum, ancient shoreline, before vault
VIII, skeleton no. 26
Herculaneum, SAP 79094a (sword); 79094b,
79121 (belt)
Selected literature: d'Ambrosio et al. (2004),
p. 148, no. I.130 + 132; Guidobaldi and
Esposito (2012), p. 16
FIGS 369–371

Iron dagger with sheath
L. 43 cm
Herculaneum, ancient shoreline, before vault
VIII, skeleton no. 26
Herculaneum, SAP 79093
Selected literature: d'Ambrosio et al.(2004),
p. 148, no. I.131; Guidobaldi and Esposito
(2012), p. 16
FIG. 372

Iron, wood and bronze tools
L. 33.5 cm, max. W. 18.5 cm
Herculaneum, ancient shoreline, before vault
VIII, skeleton no. 26
Herculaneum, SAP 79092
Selected literature: d'Ambrosio et al. (2004),
p. 148-9, no. I.134
FIG. 373

Group of coins
Single gold coin: D. 1.5cm; group of fused
coins: L. 7cm
Herculaneum, ancient shoreline, before vault
VIII, skeleton no. 26
Herculaneum, SAP 78393 (group); 78394
(single coin)
FIG. 368

Banded agate cup
H. 5.5 cm, D. 5 cm
Herculaneum, ancient shoreline, vault VII,
skeleton no. 3
Herculaneum, 78969
Selected literature: d'Ambrosio et al. (2004),
p. 140, no. I.93
FIG. 380

Charms from a bracelet
Amber/cornelian/onyx/chalcedony agate/lead/
bronze/glass/bone/chalcedony/mother-of-pearl/
rock crystal/shell
Herculaneum, ancient shoreline, vault VII,
skeleton no. 3
Herculaneum, SAP 78968
Selected literature: d'Ambrosio et al. (2004),
p. 140, no. I.94
FIG. 379

**Body of a woman preserved in transparent
resin**
Oplontis, Villa B, room 10, skeleton no. 10
Boscoreale, SAP
Selected literature: *Rediscovering Pompeii*
(1992), p. 1323, no. 2; d'Ambrosio et
al.(2004), p. 166, no. II.31
FIG. 384

Gold armlet
D. 8 cm
Oplontis, Villa B, room 10, skeleton no. 10
Naples, MANN 73308
Selected literature: d'Ambrosio et al. (2004),
p. 166, no. II.32
FIG. 386

Silver hairpin decorated with a female figure
L. 6.6 cm
Oplontis, Villa B, room 10, skeleton no. 10
Naples, MANN 74625
Selected literature: d'Ambrosio et al. (2004),
p. 166, no. II.33
FIG. 385

**Gold ring with incised chalcedony gem
showing Mercury**
D. (max) 2.2 cm
Oplontis, Villa B, room 10, skeleton no. 10
Naples, MANN 73309
Selected literature: d'Ambrosio et al. (2004),
p. 166, no. II.31
FIG. 387

Gold body chain with disc terminals
Oplontis, Villa B, room 10, skeleton no. 27
Naples, MANN 73411
Selected literature: d'Ambrosio et al. (2004),
p. 167, no. II.41
FIG. 383

**Gold fine-mesh body chain with disc
terminals**
L. 67.5 cm
Oplontis, Villa B, room 10, skeleton no. 27
Naples, MANN 73410
Selected literature: d'Ambrosio et al.(2004),
p. 167, no. II.40
FIG. 383

Emerald and gold beaded necklace
L. 52.7 cm
Oplontis, Villa B, room 10, skeleton no. 27
Naples, MANN 73412a
Selected literature: d'Ambrosio et al. (2004),
p. 167, no. II.42
FIG. 383

Gold necklace with crescent pendant
L. 37.6 cm
Oplontis, Villa B, room 10, skeleton no. 27
Naples, MANN 73409
Selected literature: d'Ambrosio et al. (2004),
p. 167, no. II.39
FIG. 383

**Gold armlet with relief decoration of Venus
and cupid**
D. 7.7 cm
Oplontis, Villa B, room 10, skeleton no. 27
Naples, MANN 73401
Selected literature: d'Ambrosio et al. (2004),
p. 167, no. II.37
FIG. 383

Gold elements of an armlet
Small pieces: 1.1 x 1 mm; main element:
3 x 1.7 mm
Oplontis, Villa B, room 10, skeleton no. 27
Naples, MANN 73412b-c
Selected literature: d'Ambrosio et al. (2004),
p. 167, no. II.38
FIG. 383

Gold earring, damaged
D. (max) 1.2 cm
Oplontis, Villa B, room 10, skeleton no. 27
Naples, MANN 73405
Selected literature: d'Ambrosio et al. (2004),
p. 170, no. II.44
FIG. 383

Gold ball earrings
D. (max) 2.4 cm
Oplontis, Villa B, room 10, skeleton no. 27
Naples, MANN 73408
Selected literature: d'Ambrosio et al. (2004),
p. 170, no. II.43
FIG. 383

Gold bar earrings with drop pearls
AD 50–79
L. (max) 3.4 cm, W. (max) 5 cm
Oplontis, Villa B, room 10, skeleton no. 27
Naples, MANN 73407
Selected literature: d'Ambrosio et al.(2004),
p. 170, no. II.45
FIG. 383

Gold ring with incised image (chariot?)
D. 2 cm
Oplontis, Villa B, room 10, skeleton no. 27
Naples, MANN 73404
Selected literature: d'Ambrosio et al. (2004),
p. 166, no. II.35
FIG. 383

Gold ring
D. 1.8 cm
Oplontis, Villa B, room 10, skeleton no. 27
Naples, MANN 73402
Selected literature: d'Ambrosio et al.(2004),
pp. 1667, no. II.36
FIG. 383

Gold ring with snake heads
D. 2.4 cm
Oplontis, Villa B, room 10, skeleton no. 27
Naples, MANN 73403
Selected literature: d'Ambrosio et al. (2004),
p. 166, no. II.34
FIG. 383

**Coins from hoard found with skeleton no.
27 from Oplontis**
86 gold coins (*aurei*), 37 silver coins (*denarii*)
Oplontis, Villa B, room 10, skeleton no. 27
Naples, MANN 73437

Silver ring with incised palm branch
D. 1.3 cm
Pompeii, young girl outside Porta Nola
Pompeii, SAP 15498
Selected literature: d'Ambrosio et al. (2004),
p. 314, no. IV.263
FIG. 396

Iron ring with incised chalcedony sardonyx
gem showing the goddess Fortuna
W. 3.1 cm
Pompeii, young girl outside Porta Nola
Pompeii, SAP 15532
Selected literature: d'Ambrosio et al. (2004),
p. 314, no. IV.265
FIG. 400

Silver ring with two snake heads holding
a disc
D. 2.8 cm
Pompeii, young girl outside Porta Nola
Pompeii, SAP 15497
Selected literature: d'Ambrosio et al. (2004),
p. 314, no. IV.262
FIG. 398

Gold ring with emerald bezel
D. 1.8 cm
Pompeii, young girl outside Porta Nola
Pompeii, SAP 23181
Selected literature: d'Ambrosio et al. (2004),
p. 314, no. IV.264
FIG. 397

Silver crescent pendant on a chain
L. 3.5 cm, D. of pendant 1.5 cm
Pompeii, young girl outside Porta Nola
Pompeii, SAP 15499
Selected literature: d'Ambrosio et al. (2004),
p. 315, no. IV.267
FIG. 399

Silver pendant in the form of a phallus
L. 1.5 cm, W. 0.6 cm
Pompeii, young girl outside Porta Nola
Pompeii, SAP 15501
Selected literature: d'Ambrosio et al. (2004),
p. 315, no. IV.266
FIG. 395

Silver statuette of the goddess Fortuna
seated
H. 3.8 cm, W. 1.5 cm
Pompeii, young girl outside Porta Nola
Pompeii, SAP 15496
Selected literature: d'Ambrosio et al.(2004),
p. 315, no. IV.268
FIG. 394

Replica cast of the body of a man
Modern
Pompeii, Large Palaestra
SAP
FIG. 390

Replica casts of the bodies of a family
Modern
Pompeii, House of the Gold Bracelet (VI,17,42)
SAP
FIG. 393

Gold armlet with two snake heads holding
a disc
D. 10.5 cm
Pompeii, House of the Golden Bracelet
(VI,17,42)
Pompeii, SAP 14268
Selected literature: d'Ambrosio et al. (2004),
p. 407, no. IV.537
FIG. 392

Gold ring
D. 2 cm
Pompeii, House of the Golden Bracelet
(VI,17,42)
Pompeii, SAP 14269
Selected literature: d'Ambrosio et al. (2004),
p. 407, no. IV.538

Gold ring with carnelian gem
D. 2.2 cm
Pompeii, House of the Golden Bracelet
(VI,17,42)
Pompeii, SAP 14311
Selected literature: d'Ambrosio et al. (2004),
p. 407, no. IV.539

Agate and onyx gem incised with a nude
female figure
1.2 x 0.99 cm
Pompeii, House of the Golden Bracelet
(VI,17,42)
Pompeii, SAP 14311
Selected literature: d'Ambrosio et al. (2004),
p. 407, no. IV.539
FIG. 391

Marble head of a woman (Terentia)
H. 50 cm, W. 19.5 cm
Herculaneum
Naples, MANN 6247
Selected literature: Le Collezioni del Museo
Nazionale di Napoli I,2 (1989), p. 122,
no. 133; Guidobaldi (2008), p. 235, 279
no. 113
FIG. 94

Bronze bust of a man
H. 37.5 cm, W. 23.5 cm
Pompeii, House of the Citharist (I,4,5)
Naples, MANN 4989
Selected literature: Le Collezioni del Museo
Nazionale di Napoli I,2 (1989), p. 122, no.
130; Mattusch (2008) p. 109
FIG. 93

ILLUSTRATION ACKNOWLEDGEMENTS

Except for the illustrations listed below, all images are © Soprintendenza Speciale per i Beni Archeologici di Napoli e Pompei.

© The Trustees of the British Museum, courtesy of the Department of Photography and Imaging: Figs 1, 11, 68, 129, 135, 137, 151, 153, 173, 177, 187, 188, 192, 196, 213, 218, 246, 281, 291, 296, 309, 310, 362. Further information about objects in the collection of the British Museum can be found on the Museum's website at britishmuseum.org.

© The Trustees of the British Museum (artwork by Kate Morton): Figs 5, 6, 7, 9

Paul Roberts, courtesy of Soprintendenza Speciale per i Beni Archeologici di Napoli e Pompei: Figs 10, 12, 13, 28, 29, 30, 37, 64, 70, 71, 72, 73, 83, 96, 125, 133, 163, 182, 198, 211, 223, 313, 366

© Sosandra/Herculaneum Conservation Project: Figs 233, 260

Other sources:

Fig. 3 © Stefano Bianchetti/CORBIS
Fig. 4 © Bettmann/CORBIS
Figs 8 and 17 Museo Archeologico Nazionale, Naples, Italy/The Bridgeman Art Library
Fig. 53 © Giraudon/The Bridgeman Art Library
Figs 57 and 58 © 2012. Photo Scala, Florence – courtesy of the Ministero Beni e Att. Culturali
Fig. 225 © Superstock
Fig. 243 © Museo Archeologico Nazionale, Naples, Italy/Alinari/The Bridgeman Art Library
Fig. 251 © National Trust Images/Bill Batten
Fig. 252 © Private Collection/The Stapleton Collection/The Bridgeman Art Library
Fig. 271 Photo courtesy of Pio Foglia
Fig. 367 © Jonathan Blair/National Geographic Stock
Fig. 378 © Jonathan Blair/Corbis

INDEX

Note: page numbers in **bold** refer to information contained in captions. Entries followed by a (P) refer to locations within Pompeii, entries followed be an (H) refer to locations within Herculaneum.

Acte, Livia (freedwoman) 112–13, **112**
Adam, Robert and James 213–15, **213**
aedicula (domestic shrine) 95–8, **95**, 100
aedile (junior magistrate) 26, 27, 28, 29, 51
agriculture 278–9, 300
Alexander the Great
   bronze statuette 114–15, **114**
   'The Alexander' mosaic 115, 190–2, **192**
Alexandria 110, 183
Alleius Nigidius Maius, Gnaeus2, 9, 31–2, 40
altars 95, **97**, 98, 100
amphitheatre (P) 15, 22, **22**, 29, **30**, 31, 36, 51, 59, 67
Amphitrite, mosaic of 215–16, **216**
amphorae (pottery transport vessels) 55–6, **55**, 59, **69**, 256
   for cosmetics 134
   for fish sauce 69
   transport **264**, 268
   for wine 67, 68, 70, 292
ancestor worship 100
Anubis 99
Apicius, Marcus Gavius, cookery books of 102, 231–3, 234, 252, 254
aqueducts 48, 153, 275
arca (strongbox) 83–6, **83**
Ariadne 104, 172, 202, **244**
aristocracy 35, 37, 89, 102
armlets/bracelets 137, 140–2, 282, **292**, 293–4
   bronze
      gilded bronze hemispheres and glass paste 140, **142**
      incised with Venus 140, 142
      with silver medallion of Sol 140–2, **142**
   gold 294, **295**
      with double band of joined hemispheres 140, **140**
      snake 140, **140**
      with snake heads holding a disc 298, **298**
      with snakehead terminals 288, **288**
Arrius Pollius insula (P) 31–2
Asellina 28, 59
ash, volcanic 12, 14, 15, 272, 278, 280–5, 295–6, 300
askos (wine jug) 241, 243, **243**
atrium 73–115, **74**, **83**, 277
   Corinthian 80, **81**
   furniture for 77, **77**
   layout 79–80
   purpose and importance 74–9
   as statement of ancestry/pedigree 83, 88–95
   as statement of power/status 83, 88
   as statement of religious observance 83, 95–100
   as statement of wealth 83–8

tablinum 77, 102, 103–13
   testudinate 80
   tetrastyle 80, **81**
   Tuscan 80
auctions 110
Augustales (guild/society) 34, 39
Augusteum (H) 33, 220, 274
Augustus, Emperor 32, 33, 34, 48, 135, 153, 206, 217, 241
   cult of 37
Auldjo, family 244
Auldjo Jug 243–4, **244**

baby's cradle, carbonized 121, **123**
Bacchus 61, 66, 70, 80, 86, 104, 121, 126, 153, 154, 162, 172, 298
   bronze statuette riding a panther 230, **231**
   cameo glasswork of **244**
   on drinking vessels 239, **239**
   as god of the garden 168
   on household shrines 52, **52**, 100, **100**
   marble wall relief of 217–20, **217**
   on tripod leg 199, **199**
   wall paintings of 201, 202
bakeries 63–6, **64–5**, 70
Balbus, Marcus Nonius 24
balconies 49, **49**
   painted 199
banking 88–9
bars 51, **51**, 59–63, **60–2**, 67, 68, 70
   all-night (*popina*) 61, 63
   Bar of Asellina 28, 59
   Bar of Athictus 63
   Bar of Euxinus 59, **59**
   Bar of Lucius Vetutius Placidus 52, **52**, **60–2**, 61–3, 154, **154**, 227
   Bar of Salvius 63, **63**, 142
Basilica Noniana (H) 35–6, **36**, 112–13, 275
basilica (P) 32
basins, washing 129–30, **129**
baskets 257, 2 2557, 281–2, **282**
baths 24, 248,8–61, **258**, **261**
   see also public baths
Bay of Naples 12, 23, **23**, 24, 30
beards 136
beauty routines 131–3, 145
bedrooms 118–21, **118**, 125
   wall paintings 200, 210, **210**
   washing in 258
beds 118, 120–1, **121**
   niches for 118, **120**
belts, ornamental 287, **287**
benches
   carbonized wooden 162, **162**
   fixed masonry 49, 50, 228, **228**
benefaction 32, 33, 95
biclinium (two couch dining area) 166, 226
bodies 281–2, 284–91, **284**, 286–300, **286**, **288**, **295**, 297–8
   Herculaneum's mortality rate 301
   mummified 15, **15**
   plaster casts of 15, 294, 296–300, **297–8**
   Pompeian mortality rate 137, 286, 301
   preserved in resin 294, **295**
   'pugilist pose' 296, 298
   skeletons **284**, 285, 286–94, **286–8**

vaporization 285, 287, 296
body chains **292**, 293–4
bombing raid on Pompeii 1943 16, 59, 80
Boscoreale
   Villa B 67
   Villa Regina 67, **67**, 165, 278
   Villa of the Silver Treasure 86, 88, **88**, 235, 295
bottles
   alabaster perfume **133**, 134
   for fish sauce **69**
   glass storage **55**, 56
   terracotta **69**
Bourbon Kings of Naples 15, 33
bowls
   pottery **240**
   silver 235, **235**
bracelets
   charm 281, 291, **291**
   see also armlets/bracelets
bradyseism (changing sea levels) 273
braziers 248, 249, 278
   terracotta **248**, 249
bread 63–6
   carbonized 65, **65**
   public giving of 29, **29**, 65
brothel (lupanar) 125, 254
Buckingham Palace, London, 'Pompeian Room' 215, **215**
building materials 269, **269**
Bulwer-Lytton, Sir Edward 15, 215
busts 32, 100, 113
   of Lucius Calpurnius Piso Pontifex 109, **114**
   of a *materfamilias* 89, 95
   of Pyrrhys, king of Epirus 114, **114**
   see also herms

caccabus (cooking pot) 252, **253**, 254
Caecilius Felix, Lucius 109
Caecilius lucundus, Lucius 78, 105, 109–10
   herm 88–9, **89**, 95
   House of (P) 88–9, 109–10, 125
Caesar, Julius 170
caldarium (hot room) 185, 258–61, **258**
calendars 170
Calpurnius Piso Pontifex, Lucius 109
   bust of 109, **114**
cameo glasswork **244**
Campania 22, 23, 31, 133, 273–4, 280, 301
cantharus (drinking cup) 239, **239**
Cape Misenum 279, 280, 281
Capua 23, 133
carbonization 285
Cardo V drain, Herculaneum 57, 59, 70, 71, 98, 128, 180, 233, 240, 264, 265–9, 278
cartibulum (display tables) 86, **86**, 238
cat, mosaic of 185, **189**
caupona (bars) 60–2
   Caupona of Lucius Vetutius Placidus (P) 52, **52**, **60–2**, 61–3, 154, **154**, 227
   Caupona of Salvius (P) 63, **63**, 142
ceilings 222–3, **222**
   wooden panels 222 3, **222**
Celer, Aemilius (slave named on bread stamp) 26–7, 65, **65**

centaurs, fresco frieze of 212, **212**
Central Baths (H) 275
cesspits 261, 262
chamber pots 128–9, **128**
Charles, Prince of Capua 244
Charm Bracelet Girl, The (skeleton fornice 7 no. 3) (H) 281, 291, **291**
chests, wooden clothing 142, 142–3, **143**
children 37
   beds 121
   bodies of 291, 298, **298**
   dining 227, **227**
   in the home 78
   washing 258
China 137, 143
Christianity 99–100
Cicero 24, 52, 55, 63, 220, 250
cisterns 79, 153-4
City wall (P) **24**, 295
Clan (*familia*) 26
Claudius, Emperor 33, 36, 220
clibanus (domed pottery cooking vessel) 252, **252**
clothing 33, 142–5, 278
   dyes 143
   togas 144, **144**
   tunics 144
   sandals and shoes 144, 145
coastline, the effect of the eruption of Vesuvius on 286, 300
codex 107
coins 62–3, 86, 140, 268, 277, 278, **278**, 281–2, **282**, **286**, 287
   gold **286**, 287, 293, 294, 298
   silver 293, 294, 298
combs 135
Cominius Primus, Lucius 105, 112
commercial premises 50–71
   see also bars; shops
compluvium (roof opening in Atrium) 79
Consuls 273
cooking 55, **55**, 252–5
   external 248, **248**, 249
   see also foodstuffs
cooking jars, bronze **253**
cooking platforms 248, 252, **252**, 261–2
cooking pots 248, 252–4, **253**
cooking vessels 268
cooks 249–50
cosmetics 132–3, **132**
cosmetics containers **132–4**, 133–5, 268
cotton 143
couches 226–8
   fixed masonry garden 166–7, **166**
councillors (*Decuriones*) 25
councils 25–6, 27, 275
counters (gaming) 182, **182**, 268
cradle, carbonized 121, **123**
crustae 183, 185
Crystal Palace, London, Exhibition Hall 215
cubiculum 117–45, **118**, **120**
   cosmetics containers from 133–5
   dressing in 142–5
   flooring 185
   furniture 120–1
   jewellery 137–42
   lighting 120–1
   painted with a garden scene 171, **171**

perfumes 133–5
　as place for beauty routines 131–3
　as place for hair care 135–6
　as place for male grooming 136–7
　sexual activity in 120, 125–8
　toilets in 118, 128–9
　washing in 129–30, 258
culina (kitchen) 248–9, 256
Cumae 23, 30
　naval battle of 23
cupboards, carbonized wooden 77, **77**
Cupid 107, 294
　fresco of 126, **126**
cupids 210
　fresco of 199, **199**
　gemstone showing 268, **268**
cups
　amber glass handled **240**
　banded agate **291**
　pottery 58, **58**, 240, **240**
　Red Slip Ware 58, **58**
curtain holders, bronze **109**
Cybele 275

daggers 287, **287**
'dancers' (bronze statues) 109, 159, **159**
date
　of the eruption 278–9
　see also calendars

days of the week 57
Decumanus Maximus (H) **44**, 57, 59, 68, 112
Decuriones (councillors) 25
dental hygiene 131
desserts 233
Diana 128, 298
dice 182, **182**
dining 166, 225–45
　in gardens 166, 226, **226**
dining rooms 201, **201**, 226–8, **226**, **228**
dinner parties 227, **227**, 228–30
Dioskourides of Samos, mosaics by 189, **190**
disease 265
discs, decorative 162, **162**
display table (*cartibulum*) 86, **86**, 238
'Doctor', The (skeleton, H) 291, **291**
documents 105–10, **110**
dogs
　mosaics of 80, 183
　on strongbox (Molossian hound) 83–6
　The Dog (P) 297, **297**
dolia (storage jars) 60, 61, 63, 67, **67**, 256, 279
dominus (master of the house) 77, 78
donkeys 66, **66**
dormouse 231, 232, 252
　fattening jars 255, **255**
drainage 48
　see also Cardo V drain, Herculaneum
drinking 61, 241–3
　see also wine
drinking cups, silver 239, **239**
drinking horns 238–9, **238**
drinking parties (*symposium*) 241
drinking vessels 238–40, **238–9**
duumvir (senior magistrate) 26, 27, 28, 31, 39, 56, 102
dyeing workshops 70, 71
dyes
　clothing 143
　hair 135, 136

earrings 137, 138, **292**, 293
　gold
　　with emeralds 138, **138**
　　originally with pearls 288, **288**
earthquakes 12, 16, 66, 89, 211, 269, **272**
　AD 62/3 24, 36, 51, 71, 107, 110, 273–7
　AD 64 274
　rebuilding following 274–7
eating and drinking establishments 59–63
　see also bars
Egypt 34, 63, 107, 110, 133, 134, 138, 143, 167, 190, 240, 293, 300
Egyptian gods 99, 167
elections/electioneering 27–31, **27**, 65, 275
　electoral notices/posters 44–6, 275, 278
emblemata (mosaic panels) 185–9, **185**, **189**, 195, 196, 199, 226, 241
emerald 137, 138–40, **138**, 288, **288**, 300, **300**
Epidius Rufus, Marcus, House of (P) 80, **81**, 95, **95**
Etna, Mount 272
Etruscans 22, 23, 24, 74
　atria 80
　clothing 144
　cuisine 227
　inscriptions 25
　women 40
Eumachia 36, 95
　building of Eumachia (P) 39–40, **39**, 110, 274
　marble statue of, building of Eumachia (P) 39–40, **39**
Europa 62
exedra (living room) 180–2, **181**

Fabius Rufus, Marcus, bronze seal ring of 46, **46**
familila (clan, family unit) 18, 78–9, 89
farms 278–9, 300
Felix (freedman) 88–9
Felix, Julia 32, 51, 59, 276
　Praedia of Julia Felix (P) **50**, 51, 61, **111**, 228, **228**
Fiorelli, Giuseppe 15, 296–7
　city numbering system of 46
fish sauce (*garum*) 63, 69, **69**, 102, **102**
flooring 183–93
　mosaic 102, **102**, 183–93, **183**, **189**–90, **192**, 195, 226–7, 241, **243**, 258, **258**
　opus sectile 185, **189**, 193, **195**, 196
　signinum 183, **183**, 185, 249
Flora, goddess of flowers and spring, fresco of **148**, 150
flowers 164–5
'fly-tipping' 266
folk art 199
food heaters 234, 234–5, **234**
food moulds 254, **254**
foodstuffs 16, 61, 63–6, 69, 231–40, 254, 279, **279**
　beef 232–3
　courses 234
　eggs 257, **257**
　figs 57, 98, 279
　fish sauce (*garum*) 63, 69, **69**, 102, **102**
　meal times 232
　meat 232–3

olives 279
pomegranates 279, 292
sea urchin 232
still life of **232**
storage 256–7, **256–7**
waste 266, 268
walnuts 98, 279
　see also cooking
Fortuna 264, 269, 300, **300**
Forum (P) 15, 32, 102, 274, 300–1
　Capitoline temple 89
　frescoes of 29, **29**, 44, 50–1, **51**
　school of 78
　vendors of 254
　and weights and measures 56
fountain spouts
　bronze 154, **155–7**
　pottery 154
fountains
　garden 79, 151, **151**, 153–4, 277
　mosaic decorations of 215, **216**
　public 48, **48**, 153
freedmen 18, 25, 26–7, 34–7, 78, 83, 102, 109
　Acte, Livia (freedwoman) 112–13, **112**
　banking 88–9
　dedications to former owners 88–9, 95
　guild of 34
　Julia, neighbour of M. Nonius Dama 41
　Venidius Ennychus, Lucius 36, 107, 112–13, **112**
　and wall paintings 211
frescoes *see* wall paintings
friezes 201, 212, **212**
fullers' workshops 70, 71
　fullonica of Stephanus (P) 71, **71**

games (boardgames) 182, **182**, 268
garden rooms 171–3, **171–2**
gardens 147–73, **150–1**, **155**, 170, **170**, 180
　dining in 166, 226, **226**
　erotica/exotica 167–9
　furnishings 159–62
　graffiti 170–1
　produce 148, 164–5
　sculpture 159–62
　transformation of 148–52
　water supply 153–4
gates
　Herculaneum Gate (P) 102
　Nola Gate (P) 25, **25**, 44
　Salt Gate (Herculaneum Gate) (P) 44
　Stabiae Gate (P) 44
　Vesuvius Gate (P) 86, 264
geese, sacred 83–6, **83**
Gell, Sir William 215
gem stones 137–40, 268, **268**, 298
　emeralds 137, 138–40, **138**, 288, **288**, 300, **300**
gem-cutters 70
Gladiators' Barracks (P) 15, 30–1
gladiatorial combat 29–30, 29–31, **30**, 264
　graffito showing **31**, 278
gladius (sword) 286–7, **287**
glass 240
　-handled cups **240**
　cameo glasswork **244**
　dishes **240**
　mosaics 215
　paste gems 140, **142**
　storage bottles **55**, 56

storage vessels 256, **256**
unguentarium 134, **134**, 268
gods/goddesses 281
　of desire 126–8
　Egyptian 99, 167
　of the garden 167–9
　piety to the 83, 95–100
　wall paintings of 207
　see also specific gods
government, local 25–6
　see also councils
graffiti 25, **31**, 57, 59, 65, 68, 70, 301
　cesspit emptier's 262
　children's 78, **79**
　dining room 201
　garden 170–1, **170**
　and Greek culture 114
　latrine 262
　poetic 114
　regarding Jewish communities 99
　sexual 63, 125, 126, **126**
grain
　grinding 252
　measure 56, **57**
grape harvest 278–9
Greeks 22, 23, 24, 113–15
　art 159, 183, 200
　cuisine 226, 227, 231, 249
　culture 113–15, 207
　inscriptions 25
　literature 113–14
　scrolls 109

hair care 135–6
hair removal 131–2
hairpins 135, 268
　silver 294, **295**
Hamilton, Sir William 213, 215
Harpocrates 99
Herculaneum 12, **12**, 36, 37–9
　aftermath 300–1
　atria 77, **77**, 80, 95–8, **98–9**, 100, 102–5, **103**, 109, 111–14
　bodies of 281–2, 284–91, 296
　　bodies on the beach 16, 284–91, **286–8**, **291**, 296
　　National Geographic Lady (skeleton 65) 288, **288**
　　The Charm Bracelet Girl (skeleton fornice 7 no. 3) 281, 291, **291**
　　The Doctor 291, **291**
　　The Soldier (skeleton 26) 286–7, **286–7**
　body count 137, 301
　commercial premises 55–7, 59, 61, 65, 68, 70, 71
　cubicula 120–1, 128–9, 131, 134–8, 142–3
　depth of burial 300, 301
　dining 226, 228, 233–4, 240
　documents of 111–13
　drainage 48
　early excavations 12, 14–16
　earthquakes 273, 274–6
　eating and drinking establishments 59–63
　elections/electioneering 27
　and the eruption 272–3, 281–2, 284–91, 296
　escape from 301
　eve of the eruption 274–8
　fabric of society 36
　facilities 17–18

freedmen 35–6, **36**
future excavations 16–17
gardens 151, **151**, 153, 159, 162, 164, 166, 168–9
gladiatorial combat 30–1
golden age 24
and Greek culture 114
housing 44–6
    see also specific houses
kitchens 252, 257
living rooms and interior decor 180, 182–3, **183**, **185**, 195, 199–200, **200**, 210–13, 215–17, **216–17**, 220, 222–3
name 22
past (history and myth) 22
plan of **17**
political system 25–6
population 17
property ownership 40–1, **41**
reconstruction 16
Roman occupation 24
size 17
streets 44, **44**, 46–50, **49**
toilets 261–4
twentieth century excavations 16
urban context 22
    see also Cardo V drain
Herculaneum Conservation Project 265
Hercules 22, 166
    drunken, marble statue of 159–62, **159**
herms 88–9, 100, 201, **201**
    Lucius Caecilius Iucundus 88–9, **89**, 95
Hogg, Dr 244
Holconius Rufus, Marcus 26–7, **26**
    House of 171
Homer 113, 115
homosexuality 125
Horace 63, 113, 136, 232, 241
hot room (*caldarium*) 185, 258–61, **258**
House of Actius Anicetus (P) 31
House of the Alcove (H) **50**, 105
House of the Apartment (P) 115
House of Apollo (P) 212
House of Aulus Umbricius Scaurus (P) 102, **102**
House of the Baker (P) 28–9, **29**
House of the Beautiful Courtyard (H) 183
House of the Bicentenary (H) 51, 100, 111
House of the Black Living Room (H) 51, 112, 182, 210–11, 262
House of the Ceii (P) 49, 50, 77, 80, **81**, 151–2, **152**
House of the Centenary (P) 100, **100**, 118, **120**, 125
House of the Chaste Lovers (P) 52, **53**, 60, **64–6**, 65–6, 78, 107, 166, 241, 283, 295
House of the Cryptoporticus (P) 78, **79**, 201, 295
House of Decimus Octavius Quartio (P) 46, 154, 166, **166**, 196, 212
House of the Dionysiac Reliefs (H) 217–20, **217**
House of the Dioscuri (P) 151, 216, 262, **262**
House of the Ephebe (P) 166, 193, **248**
House of Fabius Rufus (P) 138, 166, 170–1, 185, 197, 216, 249, 262, 277, **297**
House of the Fabric (H) 143
House of the Faun (P) **15**, 51, 67, 115, 190–2, 200, 243–4

House of the Fleet (P) 200
House of the Four Styles (P) 153, 200, 234
House of the Gardens of Hercules (P) 80, 133, 148, 166, **226**, 248
House of the Gem (H) 262
House of the Gilded Cupids 99, 131, 167, 183, 212
House of the Golden Bracelet (P) 142, 164, 171–3, **172–3**, 197, 278, 298
    Family of the 171, 298, **298**
House of the Grand Duke Michael (P) 51
House of the Grand Portal (H) 211
House of Gratus (P) 140
House of the Greek Epigrams (P) 98, 164, 277
House of Inachus and Io (P) 235
House of Julia Felix (P) 274
House of Julius Polybius (P) **98**, 99, 142, 148, 151, 162, 222, **222**, 249, 277, 295
House of the Lararium of Achilles (P) 121, 277
House of the Lararium of the River Sarnus (P) 100, **100**
House of Lucius Caecilius Iucundus (P) 88–9, 109–10, 125
House of Lucretius Fronto (P) 104, **104**, 152
House of Marcus Epidius Rufus (P) 80, 81, 95, **95**
House of Marcus Holconius Rufus 171
House of Marcus Lucretius (P) 108, 168
House of Marcus Terentius Eudoxus (P) 70
House of the Menander (P) 51, 136, 182, 282, 295
    atrium of the **74**, 95, **95**, **99**, 100
    baths 185, 241, 258–61, **258**, **261**
    dining area 226
    flooring 185, 226, 241
    lararium of the 95, **95**, **99**, 100
    treasure 86, 235
    wall painting 212, **212**
House of the Moralist (P) 230–1
House of the Mosaic *Atrium* (H) 166
House of Neptune and Amphitrite (H) 46, 55, **55**, **151**, 215–16, **216**
House of Obellius Firmus (P) 83, **83**, 180, **181**, 249
House of the Old Hunt (P) 277
House of the Orchard (P) 171, **171**, 197
House of Orpheus (P) 79, **80**, 297
House of the Painters at Work (P) 162, 164, 170, 196–7, **196**, 199, 277
House of Pansa 32
House of the Piglet (P) 199, 249, 250
House of the Prince of Naples (P) 46, 86, **86**, 210, **211**
House of the Relief of Telephus (H) 212, 216–17, 222–3, 226, 273
House of the Ship Europa (P) 67, 114, 148, 200
House of the Silver Treasure (P) 239
House of the Silver Wedding (P) 46, 67, 154
House of the Skeleton (H) 151, 182
House of the Small Fountain (P) 79, 151, **151**, 215, **216**
House of the Stags (H) 65, 159, 182, 261
House of Terentius Neo (P) 107
House of the Theatrical Paintings 88
House of the Tragic Poet (P) 15, 46, 79, 80, 162, 215
House of the Triclinium 230, 234
House of the Two Atria (H) 111, 252

House of Venus in the Shell (P) 167, **167**
House of the Vettii (P) **150**, 154, 277
House of the Wattlework (H) **49**
House of the Wooden Partition (H) 24, 46, 49, **49**, 50, 80, 109, **109**
House of the Wooden Shrine (H) 95–8, 111
House of the Workman 131
House of the Wounded Bear (P) 183, **185**
houses **15**, 18, 24–5, 276–8, 301
    living above the shop 43–71
    ownership 40–1, **41**, 44–6
    plan of **18**
    see also specific domestic spaces; specific houses
Hygiea 264
hygiene 264–5

impluvium (pool) in Atrium 79, 80, 153
imports 57–8
incense burners 267, 268
    terracotta 95, **97**
India 137, 234
inscriptions 25, **25**, **26**
    electoral 27–8, **27**
    of freedmen 35–6, **36**
    strong box (Greek) 83, **83**
    workshop 70
interior design 179–223
Isis 99, 167, **262**, 264, 269, 300, **300**
Iulius Polybius, Caius 29, 65
Iusta, Petronia 107, 111
ivory 199

Jason and the Argonauts 241
jewellery 86, 108, 137–42, **137–8**, **140**, **142**, 268, 281–2, 288, **288**, 292–4, **292**, **295**, 298, **298**, 300, **300**
Jewish communities 99
jugs **69**
    Auldjo Jug 243–4, **244**
    bronze wine 241, **243**
Junian Latins 112–13
Juno 128
Juno Moneta, sacred geese of 83–6, **83**
Jupiter 57, 99
    bronze statuette of **96**
Juvenal 64, 77, 129, 138, 144, 227

kitchens 248–57, **248**, 277–8
    lararium 99, 199, 250–2, **250**
    painted 199
kosher products 69, 99

'La Cività' ('the city' - Pompeii) 14
lamp-making 70, **70**
lamps 120, **120–1**, 281
    oil 249
        mould-made **267**, 268
        in the shape of a satyr (pottery) 120, **121**
lampstands
    bronze 120, **120**
    bronze and silver 228–9, **228**
lanterns 281
    bronze **281**
lararium (shrine to household gods) 52, 60, 61, 83, **83**, 89, 95–100, **98–100**
    depicting earthquakes **272**
    garden 162
    of the House of the Menander (P) 95, **95**, **99**, 100

kitchen 99, 199, 250–2, **250**
    painted 199
Lares (domestic guardian spirits) 52, **52**, 99, 100, 250
    bronze statuettes of 95, **96**, 140
latrina see toilets
laundries 71
lead
    in cosmetics 133
    piping 48, 153–4, **154**
    poisoning 48
Lesbos 189–90
libraries, domestic 104
lighting 120–1, 228–30, 249
    street 47
    see also lamps
linen 143
literature, Greek 113–14
lithics (volcanic debris) 283, 295
Livia 33, 39, 135
    bronze statue of, theatre (H) **36**, 37–8
    statue of 277
living rooms 179–223, **181**
    ceilings 222–3, **222**
    floor decoration 183–93
    marble wall reliefs 217–20, **217**
    marble wall veneering 216–17, **217**
    painted marble panels 220, **220**
    wall mosaics 215–16
    wall paintings 195–215
Livy 86, 280
local government 25–6
    see also councils
looters 301
Lucretius, Marcus 108, 168
Luna (the moon) 57, 298

maenads 66, 80, 126–8, 162, 163, 168, 172, 210, 217, **244**
magistrates 26, 27–9, 35, 48, 69, 77, 144, **144**
    aedile (junior) 26, 27, 28, 29, 51
    duumvir (senior) 26, 27, 28, 31, 39, 56, 102
    Meddix Tuticus (the people's magistrate) 25
    praetors (senior) 112–13
    quinquennalis (highest form) 26
Maiuri, Amedeo 16, 51, 55, 274, 297
male grooming 136–7
Mammius Maximus, Lucius 33–4, **33**, 37, 220
manumission 35
market place (*macellum*) (H) 33
market place (*macellum*) (P) 274
Mars 57, 104, 167
    wall paintings of 207–9
Martial 69, 133–6, 142, 230, 232, 264
masseurs 136
master of the house (*dominus*) 77, 78
materfamilias (female head of household), bust of 89, 95
Mau, August 199–200, 210
meal times 232
Meddix Tuticus (the people's magistrate) 25
medical instrument case, bronze **291**
medical instruments, bronze/iron **291**
megalography 201
Menander (plays shown on mosaics) 189–90
Mercury 57, 99, 140
    fresco of, young boy as 210, **210**
    gem stone carved with 268, **268**
    gold ring with incised gem showing **295**

shop sign depicting 52, **53**
shrine depicting 52, **52**
metalworkers 83
millstones, lava 64–6, **65**, 252, **253**
mirrors 131, **131**, 140
Miseunum 153
money boxes, wooden, with silver inlay 282, **282**
monopodium (display table) 86, **86**
Moregine (Murecine) 57, 69, 88
mortar and pestle, stone 255, **255**
mosaics 98
artists 189–92
for *atria* 79, **80**, 89, **89**
floors 102, **102**, 182, 183–93, **183**, **189–90**, **192**, **195**, 226–7, 241, **243**, 258, **258**
subjects of 189–92
wall 215–16
Mozart, Wolfgang Amadeus 15
mules 66
'Muleteer, The' (P) 297, **297**
music 182, 230
Mytilene, Lesbos 189–90

names
Greek 36
Roman 26–7
Naples 15, 18, 133, 182, 274
suburb of Herculaneum 301
Narcissus 166, **166**, 197
National Geographic Lady (skeleton 65) (H) 288, **288**
Neapolis (Naples) 57
see also Naples
necklaces 137, 138–40, **292**, 293–4
gold chain 282
gold linked circles **138**, 140
Neo, Terentius and wife, fresco of 65, 107–8, **107**
'neo-Attic' style of sculpture 217
Neptune, mosaic of 215–16, **216**
Nero, Emperor 29, 31, 61, 107, 132, 135, 213, 274, 276, 278, 292
North Africa 34, 69, 300
Nuceria 31, 57, 110

oecus (living room) 180, **181**, 182, 196, **196**, 210, **211**
oils, perfumed for lamps 228
Oplontis 12, 140, 281, 282–3
destruction of 292–4
skeleton 10 the 'Resin Lady' 294, **295**
skeleton 27 292–4
Villa A 257, 283, 292
Villa B 83–6, **83**, 279, 292
opus sectile flooring 185, **189**, 193, **195**, 196
opus vermiculatum 185, **185**
Ordo (city Council) 25–6, 27
organic materials, preservation 12, 14, 285
Oscan language 24, 25, **25**, 44
Oscans 22, 23
Ovid 129, 131–2, 135

paint/pigment 195, **195**, 196–7
painted ceilings 222–3, **222**
painted marble panels 220, **220**
painted notices 278
bar signs 59, **59**
electoral inscriptions 27–8, **27**
property notices 31–2
painted walls *see* wall paintings

painters 196–9
imaginarius 196
parietarius 196
Pan 162, 168–9
Pan and the Goat 109, 168–9, **168**
terracotta copy **169**, 169
papyrus 14, 107–9, 111
paradeisos (wildlife park) 152
parasites, intestinal 265
pearls 137, 138, 288, **288**
pedestrianization 47, **47**
pendants, silver crescent 300, **301**
perfume bottles
alabaster **133**, 134
unguentarium 134, **134**, 268
perfumes 133–5, 165
peristyle (colonnaded courtyard) 148, 151, 159
bath suite 261, **261**
two-sided **151**
Petronius 102, 138
phallic imagery 52, **52–3**, 258
lucky **64**, 65
phallus wind-chime 162, **162**
pottery oil lamp 120, **121**
silver amulet **300**
'piglet', bronze statue of 109, 159, **159**
pinacotheca (public picture galleries) 206
pinakes 201, **201**
pine cones
carbonized 98
plaster casts, of eruption victims 15, 294, 296–300, **297–8**
Plautus 60, 145
Pliny the Elder 69, 83, 100, 103, 118, 132, 133, 137, 138–40, 164–7, 172, 180, 195, 199, 215, 216, 234, 241, 278, 279–80, 281, 283, 285, 293, 295
Pliny the Younger 274, 278, 279–81, 282, 295, 296, 301
poetry 113–14
'Pompeian Parlour', Hinxton Hall, South Cambridgeshire 215
'Pompeian Room', Garden Pavilion, Buckingham Palace, London 215, **215**
Pompeii
aftermath 300–1
atria 74, **74**, 77–80, **79–81**, 83, **83**, 86, 88–9, 95, **95**, **98–100**, 99–100, 102, 104–5, 107–10, 114–15
baths 258, **258**
bodies 286, 295–300
'Porta Nola' girl 140, 281, 300, **300–1**
The Dog 297, **297**
The Family of the House of the Golden Bracelet 171, 298, **298**
The 'Muleteer' 297, **297**
body count 137, 286, 301
bombing raid 1943 16, 59, 80
civitas foederata (allied city) of Rome 24
commercial premises 50–71
cubicula 118, 120–1, **120**, 125–9, 131–8, 140, 142
depth of burial 300
dining 226–8, **226**, **228**, 230, 233–5, 239, 243–4
documents of 109–13
drainage 48
early excavations 15–16
earthquakes 273, 274–6
eating and drinking establishments 59–63

elections/electioneering 27–8
and the eruption 272, 278, 281, 282–4, 295–300
escape from 301
eve of the eruption 274–7
fabric of society 36–7
facilities 17–18
future excavations 16–17
gardens 148, **150–2**, 151–4, **154**, 162, 164–7, **166–7**, 170–1, **171–2**
gladiatorial combat 29–31
golden age 24
and Greek culture 114
housing 44–6
see also specific houses
kitchens 248–9, **248**, 250, 252, 254–7
living rooms and interior design 180, 189–92, **181**, 182–3, 185, **185**, 195–7, 199–201, **201**, **206**, 209–13, **211**, 215–16, **216**, 222–3, **222**
name 22
past (history and myth) 22–5
plan of **17**
political system 25–6
population 17, 37
reconstruction 16
riot of AD 59 **30**, 31
roads 22–3
Roman invasion 24
size 17
statues 39–40, **39**
streets 44, 46–50, **47**, **48**
Sullan siege, 80 BC **24**
toilets 261–5, **261–2**
trade networks 24
twentieth century excavations 16
urban context 22–5
water supply 48, **48**
Popidii clan 25
Popidius Ampliatus, Numerius 27, 275
Popidius Celsinus, Numerius 27, 275
popina (all-night bar) 61, 63
Poppaea, Empress 132, 135, 292
'Porta Nola' girl (P) 140, 281, 300, **300–1**
portraiture 32, 88–95
posters
electoral 44–6, 275, 278
for gladiatorial games 29–30
pottery
Attic Greek 23
bowls **240**
bucchero 23
cooking vessels 252–5, **252–3**
cups 58, **58**, 240, **240**
fountain spouts 154
jars 255, **255**
lamps 120, **121**
planting pots 164, **164**
rubbish 266, 268
storage vessels 256–7, **256–7**
thin-walled wares **266**, 268
water spouts 154
workshops 70, **70**
see also Red Slip Ware
Pozzuoli (Puteoli) 52, 57, 69, 182
Praedia of Julia Felix (P) **50**, 51, 61, 111, 228, **228**
praetors (senior magistrates) 112–13
prayer 98
priestesses 39–40, 95
privacy 145
property notices 31–2
property ownership 32, 40–1, **41**, 44–6

prostitution 63
see also brothel
Psyche, lover of Cupid 107
fresco of 126, **126**
public baths 129, 258, 275
public benefit, acts of 29, **29**, 65
pumice 280, 282–3, 284, 295, 300
cosmetic uses 131, **132**
puteal (well head) 79, 153
marble 153, **153**
terracotta 152, 153
Puteoli (Pozzuoli) 52, 57, 69, 182
pygmies 167, 226
pyroclastic surges 12, 16, 283–6, **287**, 292, 295–301
pyxis
bone **132**, 134
bronze **133**, 134
glass 240

quinquennalis (highest magistrate) 26

rainwater collection 153
razors, folding **132**, 136
Red Slip Ware 57–8, 240, **265**, 268
amphora **57**
cups 58, **58**
rings 137
gold 282, 293, 298
with emerald bezel 288, **288**, 300, **300**
with garnet bezel 288, **288**
with gem 268, **268**
with incised chalcedony gem showing Mercury **295**
taken in at the back of the hoop 142, **142**
iron, with sardonyx cameo of Fortuna 300, **301**
silver
incised with palm branch 300, **300**
with serpent body and terminals 300, **300**
see also seal rings
riot of AD 59, Pompeii **30**, 31
roads 22–3
Roman Senate 31, 36, 231
Rome 18, 24, 34, 41, 57, 86, 111, 137, 209, 216, 262
rubbish 266–9, 278

sacrifices, domestic 98, 100, 250–2
salutatio (morning meeting) 77, 80
Samnite House (H) 24, 25
atrium 77, **77**
entrance way **200**
flooring 183, **183**
wall painting 200
Samnite period 25, 27, 44, 56
Samnites 22, 23, 24
samovars 234–5, **235**, 258
Sarnus, River 69, 100
satyr 126–8, **126**, 162, 168, 172, 199, 202, 217, **244**, 268, **268**
schools 78
Scott, Sir Walter 244
scrolls 14, 107–9
sea creatures, mosaic of 185, **185**
seal rings 95, 107, 137–8, 292
bronze 46, **46**, 59
gold, with carnelian stone **137**
secret cabinet (*oggetti riservati*) 169
sella curulis (ornate folding stool) 77

Semo Sancus 68
Senate 31, 36, 231
Seneca 129, 131, 136, 249, 264, 273–4
septic tanks 265 9
Serapis 99
Settembrini, Luigi 297
sewers 262
sexual activity 120, 125–8, 166
sexual imagery (erotica) 125–8, 167–9
sexual morality 63
shaving 136–7
shipsheds (H) 285–6, 288, 291
shops 50–2, **51**, 55–8, 59, 70, 276
shrines, household *see lararium*
signinum (waterproof substance) 153
    flooring 183, **183**, 185, 249
Silenus 202
silk 143
silverware, 86–8, **88**, 227, 235–9, **235**,
    238–9, 282, 295
    mensulae (three-legged stand) 239,
        239
    modiolus (mug-shaped vessel) 239
    plates **235**
    serving trays 235, **235**
spoons 235, **235**
sinopia 196, 197
skeletons
    mosaic 241, **241**
    of Herculaneum 284, 285, 286–91,
        286–8
    of Oplontis 292–4
skin care 132
slaves 18, 34–6, 37, 89, 109, 145, 301
    Celer, Aemilius (slave named on bread
        stamp) 26–7, 65, **65**
    cleaning 257
    cooking 248, 250
    dining 227–8, 230, 233–4, 241, 245
    gardening 164
    graffiti of 170, **170**, 171
    for hair care (*ornatrix*) 135
    names 26–7
    place in the home 78–9
    selling of 110
    and sex 125
    sleeping arrangements 118
    toga management 144
    and toilet areas 262
    verna (born in household) 78
soap 132
social change 25, 40–41
society, fabric of 36–7
Sol 57, 140
Soldier, The (skeleton 26) (H) 286–7,
    286–7
Spain 34, 69
Spartacus 24
Stabiae (Castellammare di Stabia) 12, 14,
    131, 190, 197, 280–3, 295
    Villa Arianna 150, **150**
Stabian Baths (P) 275
stag and hounds, marble statue of 159,
    159
statues 14–15, 18, 79
    garden 159
    public images 32–3
statuettes
    ancestors **98–9**
    garden animals 156
    gods 95, **96**, 98, 99, 140
    'mother nursing baby' (terracotta)
        269, **269**

man in a toga' (terracotta) **144**
stools
    ornate folding (*sella curulis*) 77
    wooden 131, **131**
storage jars (*dolia*) **60**, 61, 63, 67, **67**,
    256, 279
Strabo 22, 272
street lighting 47
streets 44, **44**, 46–50, **47–9**
strongboxes (*arca*) 83–6, **83**
stylus (writing instrument) 107, 109
Suburban Baths (H) 273, 275, 286
Suburban Baths (P) 275
sundial 162, **162**
sword (*gladius*) 286–7, **287**
symposium (drinking party) 241

tables
    carbonized wooden dining 228, **228**
    display (*cartibulum*) 86, **86**, 238
    fixed masonry 228, **228**
tablets 16
    marble 113
    wooden 105–13, **110**, **112**
tablinum 77, 102, 103–13, **103–4**
Tacitus 31, 36, 137, 273, 274, 279
taps **155**
Temple of Apollo (P) 23
Temple of Isis (P) 15, 25, 27, 275, **276**
Temple of Magna Mater (H) 275
Temple of Mars (P) (not yet identified) 108
Temple of Venus (H) 275
Temple of Venus (P) 164
Terentius Eudoxus, Marcus, House of (P)
    70
Terzigno, nr Pompeii 250–2, 283
tesserae 183, **183**, **185**, 215, 216
textile-makers 71
theatres
    Herculaneum 14, 33, 37
    Pompeii 15, 24, 26, **26**, 32
theatrical masks 83, **83**
Themis, Calatoria 105–7, 111
thermal shock 286, 296, 298
Theseus and the Minotaur 197
    fresco of 207, **207**
'Three Graces', fresco of 207, **209**
Tiberius, Emperor 61, 140, 168
tintinnabulum (wind chimes) **53**, 162, **162**
Titus, Emperor 262, 274–5, 278, 301
toiletry casket, bronze **132**, **134**, 135
toilets 118, 128–9, **128**, 248, 261–5
    decoration 262–4, **262**, **264**
    hygiene 264–5
    location within cooking areas 249,
        261–2, **261**, 264–5
    two-seater 262, **262**
    typical **262**
tombs 40, 102
    Gaius Vestorius Priscus 86, **86**
    jewellery for 137
Torre Annunziata (Oplontis) 292
traffic 46–7
Trajan, Emperor 112
treasure
    family 86–8
    see also silverware, family
trees 148, 165
triclinium (dining area) 166–7, 171, 215,
    226–8, **226**, 231, 243, 248, 262
tripods 199, **199**
triptych (three-tablet document) 108
Tunnelling, Herculaneum 14–15, 33

Turkey 34, 58, 63, 86
tweezers 131
    bronze **132**

Umbricius Scaurus, Aulus 69, 102, **102**
Umbricius Scaurus, Aulus (son of Aulus
    Umbricius Scaurus) 102
unguentarium (glass perfume bottle) 134,
    134, 268

Varro 86, 118, 120, 121, 255
veneering, marble 216–17, **217**
Venidius Ennychus, Lucius (freedman) 36,
    107, 112–13, **112**
Venus 39, 57, 99, 104, 126, 140, 294
    as goddess of the garden 167, **167**
    as patroness of Pompeii 209, 294
    wall paintings of 207–9
Vergil 113, 114
Vespasian, Emperor 275, 277
Vestorius Priscus, Gaius, tomb of 86, **86**,
    238
Vesuvius, Mount **12**
    aftermath of the eruption 300–1
    bradyseism 273
    crater of 24
    eruption 12, 272–4, 278–300
        'Avellino' 272
        date of the 278
        effusive 283
        explosive 283–4
        eyewitness account of the 279–82
        phases of the 282–4
        Plinian 283–4
    fresco of 100, **100**
Vetutius Placidus, Lucius, bar of (P) 52,
    52, **60–2**, 61–3, 154, **154**, 227
Via Consolare (P) 59
Via dell'Abbondanza (P) **14**, **27**, 32, 44,
    47, 51, **51**, 59, 59–60, 61, 66, 264
Via Mercurio (P) 23
Villa A, Oplontis, nr Pompeii 257, 283,
    292
Villa of Agrippa Postumus, nr Pompeii 136
Villa Arianna, Stabiae 150, **150**
Villa B, Boscoreale 67
Villa B, Oplontis, nr Pompeii 83–6, **83**,
    279, 292
Villa of Cicero (P) 189
Villa della Pisanella 67, 68
Villa of Diomedes, nr Pompeii 296
Villa of the Mysteries (P) 67, 118, **118**,
    142, **181**, 195, 201–2, 226–7, 250,
    277, 279
Villa of Papyri (H) 14, 104, 109, 114, 159,
    168, 199
Villa Regina, Boscoreale 67, **67**, 165, 278
Villa of the Silver Treasure, Boscoreale 86,
    88, **88**, 235, 295
Villa of Terzigno, nr Pompeii 199
vineyards 67, 278–9
viridarium (small garden) 151–2
Vitruvius 74–6, 103, 180, 195, 197,
    199–201, 206, 210, 272

wall paintings 14–15, 18, 195
    Four 'Pompeian' styles 199–215
    First 'Pompeian' Style 200, **200**, 206,
        209, 210
    Second 'Pompeian' Style 197, 200,
        201–2, **201–2**, 206, 209, 210
    Third 'Pompeian' Style 200, 206–10,
        206–7, **209–10**, 222

Fourth 'Pompeian' style 107, 113, 197,
    199–200, 207–15, 216, 220, 222,
    276–7
a secco technique 196
alfresco 195
bar 63, **63**, 67, 182
cartibulum, Tomb of Vestorius Priscus
    86
dining 135–6, 227–8, **227–8**, **230**,
    241, **243**
garden **148**, 151–2, **152**, 166–7,
    166–7
garden room 171–3, **171–3**
Greek influences on 115, **115**
for living rooms 181–2, 182, 196, **196**,
    199–202, **199**, **201–2**, 207, **207**,
    209, 212–15, **212–13**, **215**
political 28–9, **29**
for toilet areas 262, 264
writing materials shown **105**, 107,
    107, 108, **108**, 111
wall treatments
    marble reliefs 217–20, **217**
    marble veneering 216–17, **217**
    mosaics 215–16
    painted marble panels 220, **220**
    see also wall paintings
wardrobes 118, **118**, 142–3
washing 129–30, **129**, 258–61
    see also baths
washing up 257
waste water 154, **154**
water supplies 48, 153–4, 248
    disruption to 129
    piped 79, 153–4, 249, 277
    rainwater 79
    well-heads 79
    wells 153
water towers 48, **48**
water-boiling vessels, bronze-lidded 258,
    258
weaving 70, 77
weights and measures 56, **57**
well-heads *see* puteal
wells 153
wheel ruts 46, **47**
windlass 153
    carbonized wooden 153, **153**
window shutters 180, **181**
windows 49–50, **50**
    glass pane 165, **165**
    muscovite mica 165–6
wine 61, 63, 66–8, 70, 100
    preparation 241
wineries 66–7, 278–9
women **105**, 107–9, **107**, 159, **159**
    bar workers 28, 59
    beauty routines 131–3, 145
    clothing 144–5
    commemorations of 37–40
    dining 227, **227**
    domestic portraiture 89, **89**, 131, **131**
    electioneering 28
    hair care 135–6
    in the home 77–8
    names 26
    property ownership 32, 41, **41**
    social realities of 37, 40–1
Women's Baths (H) **185**
wool 71, **78**, 143
workshops 70–1
    painting 196–9